MICROSOFT
PowerPoint 97
Complete Concepts and Techniques

MICROSOFT
PowerPoint 97
Complete Concepts and Techniques

Gary B. Shelly
Thomas J. Cashman
Sherry L. Green
Marvin M. Boetcher
Susan L. Sebok

COURSE TECHNOLOGY
ONE MAIN STREET
CAMBRIDGE MA 02142

an International Thomson Publishing company I(T)P*

CAMBRIDGE • ALBANY • BONN • CINCINNATI • LONDON • MADRID • MELBOURNE

MEXICO CITY • NEW YORK • PARIS • SAN FRANCISCO • TOKYO • TORONTO • WASHINGTON

© 1998 Course Technology
One Main Street
Cambridge, Massachusetts 02142

I(T)P® International Thomson Publishing
The ITP logo is a registered trademark
of International Thomson Publishing.

Printed in the United States of America

For more information, contact Course Technology:

Course Technology
One Main Street
Cambridge, Massachusetts 02142, USA

International Thomson Publishing Europe
Berkshire House
168-173 High Holborn
London, WC1V 7AA, United Kingdom

Thomas Nelson Australia
102 Dodds Street
South Melbourne
Victoria 3205 Australia

Nelson Canada
1120 Birchmont Road
Scarborough, Ontario
Canada M1K 5G4

International Thomson Editores
Campos Eliseos 385, Piso 7
Colonia Polanco
11560 Mexico D.F. Mexico

International Thomson Publishing GmbH
Konigswinterer Strasse 418
53227 Bonn, Germany

International Thomson Publishing Asia
Block 211, Henderson Road #08-03
Henderson Industrial Park
Singapore 0315

International Thomson Publishing Japan
Hirakawa-cho Kyowa Building, 3F
2-2-1 Hirakawa-cho, Chiyoda-ku
Tokyo 102, Japan

ISBN 0-7895-1347-1

PHOTO CREDITS: *Project 1, pages PP 1.4-5,* Man, money bag, and movie camera, Courtesy of Corel Professional Photos CD-ROM Image usage; food collage, © Metatools, created by PhotoSpin; *Project 2, pages PP 2.2-3,* Iceberg, Courtesy of Corel Professional Photos CD-ROM Image usage; Titanic provided by Brown Brothers; Molly Brown provided by Colorado Historical Society; Euro-poster provided by PhotoDisc, Inc. © 1996; *Project 3, pages PP 3.4-5,* Oil pump and charts, Courtesy of Corel Professional Photos CD-ROM Image usage; *Project 4, pages PP 4.2-3,* Magnifying glass, outline of body, overhead transparency, projector, gavel, judge, and globe, Courtesy of Corel Professional Photos CD-ROM Image usage.

5 6 7 8 9 10   BC   2 1 0 9 8

MICROSOFT
PowerPoint 97
Complete Concepts and Techniques

CONTENTS

Microsoft PowerPoint 97

Preface

The Shelly Cashman Series® offers the finest textbooks in computer education. The Microsoft Office 97 books continue with the innovation, quality, and reliability that you have come to expect from this series. We are proud that both our Office 95 and Office 4.3 books are best-sellers, and we are confident that our Office 97 books will join their predecessors.

With Office 97, Microsoft has raised the stakes by adding a number of new features, especially the power of the Internet. The Shelly Cashman Series team has responded with Office 97 books that present the core application concepts required in any introductory application software course, as well as new features such as the Office 97 Internet tools.

In our Office 97 books, you will find an educationally sound and easy-to-follow pedagogy that combines a step-by-step approach with corresponding screens. Every project and exercise in the books are new and designed to take full advantage of the Office 97 features. The popular Other Ways and More About features have been amended to offer in-depth knowledge of Office 97. The all-new project openers provide a fascinating perspective on the subject covered in the project. The Shelly Cashman Series Office 97 books will make your computer application software class an exciting and dynamic one that your students will remember as one of their better educational experiences.

Objectives of This Textbook

Microsoft PowerPoint 97: Complete Concepts and Techniques is intended for a two-unit course that presents Microsoft PowerPoint 97. No experience with a computer is assumed, and no mathematics beyond the high school freshman level is required. The objectives of this book are:

- ▶ To teach the fundamentals of Microsoft PowerPoint 97
- ▶ To help students demonstrate their proficiency in Microsoft PowerPoint 97 and prepare them to pass the Expert level Microsoft Office User Specialist Exam for Microsoft PowerPoint 97
- ▶ To foster an appreciation of presentations as a useful tool in the workplace
- ▶ To give students an in-depth understanding of designing and creating quality presentations
- ▶ To expose students to examples of the computer as a useful tool
- ▶ To develop an exercise-oriented approach that allows students to learn by example
- ▶ To encourage independent study and help those who are working on their own in a distance education environment

Approved by Microsoft as Courseware for the Microsoft Office User Specialist Program — Expert Level

This book has been approved by Microsoft as courseware for the Microsoft Office User Specialist program. After completing the projects and exercises in this book, the student will be prepared to take the Expert level Microsoft Office User Specialist Exam for Microsoft PowerPoint 97. By passing the certification exam for a Microsoft software program, students demonstrate their proficiency in that program to employers. This exam is offered at participating test centers, participating corporations, and participating employment agencies. For more information about certification, please visit Microsoft's World Wide Web site at http://microsoft.com/office/train_cert/.

The Shelly Cashman Approach

Features of the Shelly Cashman Series Office 97 books include:

▶ Project Orientation: Each project in the book uses the unique Shelly Cashman Series screen-by-screen, step-by-step approach.

▶ Screen-by-Screen, Step-by-Step Instructions: Each of the tasks required to complete a project is identified throughout the development of the project. Then, steps to accomplish the task are specified. The steps are accompanied by screens. Hence, students learn from this book the same as if they were using a computer.

▶ Thoroughly Tested Projects: The computer screens in the Shelly Cashman Series Office 97 books are captured from the author's computer. The screen is captured immediately after the author performs the step specified in the text. Therefore, every screen in the book is correct because it is produced only after performing a step, resulting in unprecedented quality in a computer textbook.

▶ Multiple Ways to Use the Book: This book can be used in a variety of ways, including: (a) Lecture and textbook approach — The instructor lectures on the material in the book. Students read and study the material and then apply the knowledge to an application on the computer; (b) Tutorial approach — Students perform each specified step on a computer. At the end of the project, students have solved the problem and are ready to solve comparable student assignments; (c) Other approaches — Many instructors lecture on the material and then require their students to perform each step in the project, reinforcing the material lectured. Students then complete one or more of the In the Lab exercises at the end of the project; and (d) Reference — Each task in a project is clearly identified. Therefore, the material serves as a complete reference.

▶ Other Ways Boxes for Reference: Microsoft PowerPoint 97 provides a wide variety of ways to carry out a given task. The Other Ways boxes included at the end of most of the step-by-step sequences specify the other ways to execute the task completed in the steps. Together, the steps and the Other Ways box make a comprehensive and convenient reference unit; you no longer have to reference tables at the end of a project or at the end of a book.

▶ **Other Ways**
1. Click Hide Slide button on Slide Sorter toolbar
2. On Slide Show menu click Hide Slide
3. Press ALT+D, press H

More *About* **Delivering Presentations**

A presentation is most effective when all audience members can see your slides easily. The maximum viewing distance is eight times the width of the slide. For example, if your slide is five feet wide when it projects on a screen, the farthest distance anyone should sit is 40 feet.

▶ **More About Feature:** The More About features in the margins provide background information that complements the topics covered, adding interest and depth to the learning process.

Organization of This Textbook

Microsoft PowerPoint 97: Complete Concepts and Techniques provides detailed instruction on how to use PowerPoint 97. The material is divided into four projects and two integration features as follows:

Project 1 – Using a Design Template and Style Checker to Create a Presentation In Project 1, students are introduced to PowerPoint terminology, the PowerPoint window, and the basics of creating a multi-level bulleted list presentation. Topics include selecting a design template; changing font style; decreasing font size; saving a presentation; displaying slides in an electronic slide show; checking a presentation for spelling errors; identifying design inconsistencies using Style Checker; printing copies of the slides to make overhead transparencies; and using PowerPoint Help.

Project 2 – Using Outline View and Clip Art to Create an Electronic Slide Show In Project 2, students create a presentation in outline view, insert clip art, and add animation effects. Topics include creating a slide presentation by promoting and demoting text in outline view; changing slide layouts; inserting clip art; adding slide transition effects; adding text animation effects; animating clip art; running an animated slide show, and printing audience handouts from an outline.

Integration Feature – Importing Clip Art from the Microsoft Clip Gallery Live Web Site In this section, students are introduced to importing clip art from a source on the World Wide Web into a presentation. Topics include downloading clip art to the Microsoft Clip Gallery 3.0; importing clip art to a presentation; and applying an animation effect.

Project 3 – Using Embedded Visuals to Enhance a Slide Show In Project 3, students create a presentation from a Microsoft Word outline and then enhance it with embedded visuals. Topics include creating a slide background using a picture; embedding a Microsoft Excel chart; creating and embedding an organization chart; embedding a picture; adding a border to a picture; scaling an object; ungrouping clip art; resizing objects; and applying slide transition and text preset animation effects.

Project 4 – Creating a Presentation Containing Interactive OLE Documents In Project 4, students customize the presentation created in Project 3 by inserting a company logo, changing the Design Template, and then modifying the color scheme. Topics include drawing a company logo; creating a graphic image from text using Microsoft WordArt; grouping the logo and graphic image into a logo object; embedding an object on the Slide Master; changing organization chart formatting; using object linking and embedding to create a slide containing interactive documents; using guides to position and size objects; ending a presentation with a black slide; hiding a slide; animating an object; and running a slide show to display a hidden slide in an active interactive document.

Integration Feature – Creating Web Pages from a PowerPoint Presentation In this section, students convert a PowerPoint slide show to HTML format and view it using their Web browser. Topics include selecting page styles; choosing graphic style types; selecting monitor resolution; picking custom colors and buttons for the Web page; choosing a layout style; and running the presentation using a Web browser.

End-of-Project Student Activities

A notable strength of the Shelly Cashman Series Office 97 books is the extensive student activities at the end of each project. Well-structured student activities can make the difference between students merely participating in a class and students retaining the information they learn. The activities in the Office 97 books include:

▶ **What You Should Know** A listing of the tasks completed within a project together with the pages where the step-by-step, screen-by-screen explanations appear. This section provides a perfect study review for students.

▶ **Test Your Knowledge** Four pencil-and-paper activities designed to determine students' understanding of the material in the project. Included are true/false questions, multiple-choice questions, and two short-answer activities.

▶ **Use Help** Any user of PowerPoint 97 must know how to use Help, including the Office Assistant. Therefore, this book contains two Use Help exercises per project. These exercises alone distinguish the Shelly Cashman Series from any other set of Office 97 instructional materials.

▶ **Apply Your Knowledge** This exercise requires students to open and manipulate a file on the Data Disk that accompanies the Office 97 books.

▶ **In the Lab** Three in-depth assignments per project require students to apply the knowledge gained in the project to solve problems on a computer.

▶ **Cases and Places** Seven unique case studies require students to apply their knowledge to real-world situations.

Instructor's Resource Kit

A comprehensive Instructor's Resource Kit (IRK) accompanies this textbook in the form of a CD-ROM. The CD-ROM includes an electronic Instructor's Manual (called ElecMan) and teaching and testing aids. The CD-ROM (ISBN 0-7895-1334-X) is available through your Course Technology representative or by calling one of the following telephone numbers: Colleges and Universities, 1-800-648-7450; High Schools, 1-800-824-5179; and Career Colleges, 1-800-477-3692. The contents of the CD-ROM are listed below.

▶ ElecMan (*Electronic Instructor's Manual*) ElecMan is made up of Microsoft Word files. The files include lecture notes, solutions to laboratory assignments, and a large test bank. The files allow you to modify the lecture notes or generate quizzes and exams from the test bank using your own word processor. Where appropriate, solutions to laboratory assignments are embedded as icons in the files. When an icon appears, double-click it; the application will start and the solution will display on the screen. ElecMan includes the following for each project: project objectives; project overview; detailed lesson plans with page number references; teacher notes and activities; answers to the end-of-project exercises; test bank of 110 questions for every project (50 true/false, 25 multiple choice, and 35 fill-in-the-blank) with page number references; and transparency references. The transparencies are available through the Figures on CD-ROM described below.

▶ **Figures on CD-ROM** Illustrations for every screen in the textbook are available. Use this ancillary to create a slide show from the illustrations for lecture or to print transparencies for use in lecture with an overhead projector.

▶ **Course Test Manager** This cutting-edge Windows-based testing software helps instructors design and administer tests and pretests. The full-featured online program permits students to take tests at the computer where their grades are computed immediately. Automatic statistics collection, student guides customized to the student's performance, and printed tests are only a few of the features.

▶ **Lecture Success System** Lecture Success System files are designed for use with the application software package, a personal computer, and a projection device. The files allow you to explain and illustrate the step-by-step, screen-by-screen development of a project in the textbook without entering large amounts of data.

▶ **Instructor's Lab Solutions** Solutions and required files for all the In the Lab assignments at the end of each project are available.

▶ **Lab Tests/Test Outs** Tests that parallel the In the Lab assignments are supplied for the purpose of testing students in the laboratory on the material covered in the project or testing students out of the course.

▶ **Student Files** All the files that are required by students to complete the Apply Your Knowledge and a few of the In the Lab exercises are included.

▶ **Interactive Labs** Eighteen hands-on interactive labs that take students from ten to fifteen minutes each to step through help solidify and reinforce mouse and keyboard usage and computer concepts.

Shelly Cashman Online

Shelly Cashman Online is a World Wide Web service available to instructors and students of computer education. Visit Shelly Cashman Online at www.scseries.com. Shelly Cashman Online is divided into four areas:

▶ **Series Information** Information on the Shelly Cashman Series products.

▶ **The Community** Opportunities to discuss your course and your ideas with instructors in your field and with the Shelly Cashman Series team.

▶ **Teaching Resources** Designed for instructors teaching from and using Shelly Cashman Series textbooks and software. This area includes password-protected instructor materials that can be downloaded, course outlines, teaching tips, and much more.

▶ **Student Center** Dedicated to students learning about computers with Shelly Cashman Series textbooks and software. This area includes cool links, data from Data Disks that can be downloaded, and much more.

Acknowledgments

The Shelly Cashman Series would not be the leading computer education series without the contributions of outstanding publishing professionals. First, and foremost, among them is Becky Herrington, director of production and designer. She is the heart and soul of the Shelly Cashman Series, and it is only through her leadership, dedication, and tireless efforts that superior products are made possible. Becky created and produced the award-winning Windows 95 series of books.

Under Becky's direction, the following individuals made significant contributions to these books: Peter Schiller, production manager; Ginny Harvey, series specialist and developmental editor; Ken Russo, Mike Bodnar, Stephanie Nance, Greg Herrington, and Dave Bonnewitz, graphic artists; Jeanne Black, Quark expert; Patti Koosed, editorial assistant; Nancy Lamm, Lyn Markowicz, Cherilyn King, Marilyn Martin, and Steve Marconi, proofreaders; Cristina Haley, indexer; Sarah Evertson of Image Quest, photo researcher; and Peggy Wyman and Jerry Orton, Susan Sebok, and Nancy Lamm, contributing writers.

Special thanks go to Jim Quasney, our dedicated series editor; Lisa Strite, senior product manager; Lora Wade, associate product manager; Scott MacDonald and Tonia Grafakos, editorial assistants; and Sarah McLean, product marketing manager. Special mention must go to Suzanne Biron, Becky Herrington, and Michael Gregson for the outstanding book design; Becky Herrington for the cover design; and Ken Russo for the cover illustrations.

Gary B. Shelly
Thomas J. Cashman
Sherry L. Green
Marvin M. Boetcher
Susan L. Sebok

Shelly Cashman Series – Traditionally Bound Textbooks

The Shelly Cashman Series presents the following computer subjects in a variety of traditionally bound textbooks as shown in the table below. For more information, see your Course Technology representative or call one of the following telephone numbers: Colleges and Universities, 1-800-648-7450; High Schools, 1-800-824-5179; and Career Colleges, 1-800-477-3692.

COMPUTERS	
Computers	Discovering Computers: A Link to the Future, World Wide Web Enhanced
	Discovering Computers: A Link to the Future, World Wide Web Enhanced Brief Edition
	Using Computers: A Gateway to Information, World Wide Web Edition
	Using Computers: A Gateway to Information, World Wide Web Brief Edition
	Exploring Computers: A Record of Discovery 2e with CD-ROM
	A Record of Discovery for Exploring Computers 2e
	Study Guide for Discovering Computers: A Link to the Future, World Wide Web Enhanced
	Study Guide for Using Computers: A Gateway to Information, World Wide Web Edition
	Brief Introduction to Computers 2e (32-page)

WINDOWS APPLICATIONS	
Integrated Packages	Microsoft Office 97: Introductory Concepts and Techniques, Brief Edition (6 projects)
	Microsoft Office 97: Introductory Concepts and Techniques, Essentials Edition (10 projects)
	Microsoft Office 97: Introductory Concepts and Techniques (15 projects)
	Microsoft Office 97: Advanced Concepts and Techniques
	Microsoft Office 95: Introductory Concepts and Techniques (15 projects)
	Microsoft Office 95: Advanced Concepts and Techniques
	Microsoft Office 4.3 running under Windows 95: Introductory Concepts and Techniques
	Microsoft Office for Windows 3.1 Introductory Concepts and Techniques Enhanced Edition
	Microsoft Office: Advanced Concepts and Techniques
	Microsoft Works 4* • Microsoft Works 3.0*
Windows	Introduction to Microsoft Windows NT Workstation 4
	Microsoft Windows 95: Introductory Concepts and Techniques (96-page)
	Introduction to Microsoft Windows 95 (224-page)
	Microsoft Windows 95: Complete Concepts and Techniques
	Microsoft Windows 3.1 Introductory Concepts and Techniques
	Microsoft Windows 3.1 Complete Concepts and Techniques
Word Processing	Microsoft Word 97* • Microsoft Word 7* • Microsoft Word 6* • Microsoft Word 2.0
	Corel WordPerfect 8 • Corel WordPerfect 7 • WordPerfect 6.1* • WordPerfect 6* • WordPerfect 5.2
Spreadsheets	Microsoft Excel 97* • Microsoft Excel 7* • Microsoft Excel 5* • Microsoft Excel 4
	Lotus 1-2-3 97* • Lotus 1-2-3 Release 5* • Lotus 1-2-3 Release 4* • Quattro Pro 6
Database Management	Microsoft Access 97* • Microsoft Access 7* • Microsoft Access 2
	Paradox 5 • Paradox 4.5 • Paradox 1.0 • Visual dBASE 5/5.5
Presentation Graphics	Microsoft PowerPoint 97* • Microsoft PowerPoint 7* • Microsoft PowerPoint 4*

DOS APPLICATIONS	
Operating Systems	DOS 6 Introductory Concepts and Techniques
	DOS 6 and Microsoft Windows 3.1 Introductory Concepts and Techniques
Word Processing	WordPerfect 6.1 • WordPerfect 6.0 • WordPerfect 5.1
Spreadsheets	Lotus 1-2-3 Release 4 • Lotus 1-2-3 Release 2.4 • Lotus 1-2-3 Release 2.3
Database Management	dBASE 5 • dBASE IV Version 1.1 • dBASE III PLUS • Paradox 4.5

PROGRAMMING AND NETWORKING	
Programming	Microsoft Visual Basic 5
	Microsoft Visual Basic 4 for Windows 95* (available with Student version software)
	Microsoft Visual Basic 3.0 for Windows*
	QBasic • QBasic: An Introduction to Programming • Microsoft BASIC
	Structured COBOL Programming (Micro Focus COBOL also available)
Networking	Novell NetWare for Users
	Business Data Communications: Introductory Concepts and Techniques
Internet	The Internet: Introductory Concepts and Techniques (UNIX)
	Netscape Navigator 4: An Introduction
	Netscape Navigator 3: An Introduction • Netscape Navigator 2 running under Windows 3.1
	Netscape Navigator: An Introduction (Version 1.1)
	Netscape Composer
	Microsoft Internet Explorer 3: An Introduction

SYSTEMS ANALYSIS	
Systems Analysis	Systems Analysis and Design, Second Edition

*Also available as a Double Diamond Edition, which is a shortened version of the complete book

Shelly Cashman Series – **Custom Edition**® Program

If you do not find a Shelly Cashman Series traditionally bound textbook to fit your needs, the Shelly Cashman Series unique **Custom Edition** program allows you to choose from a number of options and create a textbook perfectly suited to your course. Features of the **Custom Edition** program are:

▶ Textbooks that match the content of your course

▶ Windows- and DOS-based materials for the latest versions of personal computer applications software

▶ Shelly Cashman Series quality, with the same full-color materials and Shelly Cashman Series pedagogy found in the traditionally bound books

▶ Affordable pricing so your students receive the **Custom Edition** at a cost similar to that of traditionally bound books

The table on the right summarizes the available materials.

For more information, see your Course Technology representative or call one of the following telephone numbers: Colleges and Universities, 1-800-648-7450; High Schools, 1-800-824-5179; and Career Colleges, 1-800-477-3692.

For Shelly Cashman Series information, visit Shelly Cashman Online at **www.scseries.com**

COMPUTERS	
Computers	Discovering Computers: A Link to the Future, World Wide Web Enhanced
	Discovering Computers: A Link to the Future, World Wide Web Enhanced Brief Edition
	Using Computers: A Gateway to Information, World Wide Web Edition
	Using Computers: A Gateway to Information, World Wide Web Brief Edition
	A Record of Discovery for Exploring Computers 2e (available with CD-ROM)
	Study Guide for Discovering Computers: A Link to the Future, World Wide Web Enhanced
	Study Guide for Using Computers: A Gateway to Information, World Wide Web Edition
	Introduction to Computers (32-page)

OPERATING SYSTEMS	
Windows	Microsoft Windows 95: Introductory Concepts and Techniques (96-page)
	Introduction to Microsoft Windows NT Workstation 4
	Introduction to Microsoft Windows 95 (224-page)
	Microsoft Windows 95: Complete Concepts and Techniques
	Microsoft Windows 3.1 Introductory Concepts and Techniques
	Microsoft Windows 3.1 Complete Concepts and Techniques
DOS	Introduction to DOS 6 (using DOS prompt)
	Introduction to DOS 5.0 or earlier (using DOS prompt)

WINDOWS APPLICATIONS	
Integrated Packages	Microsoft Works 4*
	Microsoft Works 3.0*
Microsoft Office	Using Microsoft Office 97 (16-page)
	Using Microsoft Office 95 (16-page)
	Microsoft Office 97:Introductory Concepts and Techniques, Brief Edition (396-page)
	Microsoft Office 97: Introductory Concepts and Techniques, Essentials Edition (672-page)
	Object Linking and Embedding (OLE) (32-page)
	Microsoft Outlook 97 • Microsoft Schedule+ 7
	Introduction to Integrating Office 97 Applications (48-page)
	Introduction to Integrating Office 95 Applications (80-page)
Word Processing	Microsoft Word 97* • Microsoft Word 7* • Microsoft Word 6* • Microsoft Word 2.0
	Corel WordPerfect 8 • Corel WordPerfect 7 • WordPerfect 6.1* • WordPerfect 6* • WordPerfect 5.2
Spreadsheets	Microsoft Excel 97* • Microsoft Excel 7* • Microsoft Excel 5* • Microsoft Excel 4
	Lotus 1-2-3 97* • Lotus 1-2-3 Release 5* • Lotus 1-2-3 Release 4* • Quattro Pro 6
Database Management	Microsoft Access 97* • Microsoft Access 7* • Microsoft Access 2* • Paradox 5 • Paradox 4.5 • Paradox 1.0 • Visual dBASE 5/5.5
Presentation Graphics	Microsoft PowerPoint 97* • Microsoft PowerPoint 7* • Microsoft PowerPoint 4*

DOS APPLICATIONS	
Word Processing	WordPerfect 6.1 • WordPerfect 6.0 • WordPerfect 5.1
Spreadsheets	Lotus 1-2-3 Release 4 • Lotus 1-2-3 Release 2.4 • Lotus 1-2-3 Release 2.3 • Quattro Pro 3.0 • Quattro with 1-2-3 Menus
Database Management	dBASE 5 • dBASE IV Version 1.1 • dBASE III PLUS • Paradox 4.5 • Paradox 3.5

PROGRAMMING AND NETWORKING	
Programming	Microsoft Visual Basic 5 • Microsoft Visual Basic 4 for Windows 95* (available with Student version software) • Microsoft Visual Basic 3.0 for Windows*
	Microsoft BASIC • QBasic
Networking	Novell NetWare for Users
Internet	The Internet: Introductory Concepts and Techniques (UNIX)
	Netscape Navigator 4: An Introduction
	Netscape Navigator 3: An Introduction
	Netscape Navigator 2 running under Windows 3.1
	Netscape Navigator: An Introduction (Version 1.1)
	Netscape Composer
	Microsoft Internet Explorer 3: An Introduction

*Also available as a mini-module

Microsoft
PowerPoint 97

Using a Design Template and Style Checker to Create a Presentation

Objectives:

You will have mastered the material in this project when you can:

▶ Start a new PowerPoint document
▶ Describe the PowerPoint window
▶ Select a design template
▶ Create a title slide
▶ Change the font size of selected text
▶ Italicize selected text
▶ Save a presentation
▶ Add a new slide
▶ Demote a bulleted paragraph
▶ Promote a bulleted paragraph
▶ View a presentation in slide show view
▶ Quit PowerPoint
▶ Open a presentation
▶ Use Style Checker to identify spelling, visual clarity, case, and end punctuation inconsistencies
▶ Edit a presentation
▶ Change line spacing on the slide master
▶ Display a presentation in black and white
▶ Print a presentation in black and white
▶ Use online Help

A THoUsaNd aND OnE WaYs tO MaKE a HiT

What if your very life depended on your ability to make a captivating presentation? This was the predicament faced by Princess Scheherazade, the fabled storyteller to whom we owe the tales of the *Arabian Nights*. Married to King Schahriar, who beheaded each new bride after the wedding night, she beguiled him with a continuing story so fabulous and intriguing, that each night he spared her life, so she might relate the next installment. Thus, she successfully staved off the king's sword for a thousand and one nights, when at last, he granted her a permanent stay of execution, a tribute to her powers of presentation.

Fortunately, in today's world, the stakes usually are not that high. Yet, the skill to present an argument or a concept in the most dynamic and pleasing way possible may spell the difference between huge success or severe failure. Salespeople the world over know the truth in this, as do politicians seeking election, scientists pursuing funding for a project, or any of countless situations where the ability to persuade is the key to victory.

In some ways, modern requirements are more demanding than in Scheherazade's time. Today, mere words are not enough. Because audiences have developed a taste for multimedia, they demand both aural and graphical ingredients in presentations. This means that appearance is just as important as the words — you not only have to "talk the talk," you have to "walk the walk." The presentation of food in commercials is an excellent example. Food stylists, who are a special breed of presenters, prepare food especially for displays, photographs, or films, *styling* the product to fit the message. And for many people, the presentation of food in restaurants — from the chef's artistic arrangement of food on a plate to the waiter's proud delivery to the table — is just as important as the cuisine.

Conversely, the wrong image can confuse or distort one's message. Many familiar instances exist in literature and movies: *The Hunchback of Notre Dame,* Yoda in *Star Wars, Rain Man, Powder, Mask, Forrest Gump,* and *The Elephant Man,* where appearances obscure the understanding of true worth.

Now, Microsoft's PowerPoint 97 makes it easier than ever to deliver your presentation with panache while ensuring your audience understands the true value of your message. Whether you are a new user or just in a hurry, templates give you ready-made patterns, and the AutoLayout feature provides shortcuts for maintaining your design. With PowerPoints's Style Checker, you analyze visual clarity and consistency, and then you can make your presentation sizzle with clip art and multimedia effects.

So, before you plunge into that next persuasive effort, take a cue from the Princess Scheherazade. Leave them thirsting for more — with help from PowerPoint.

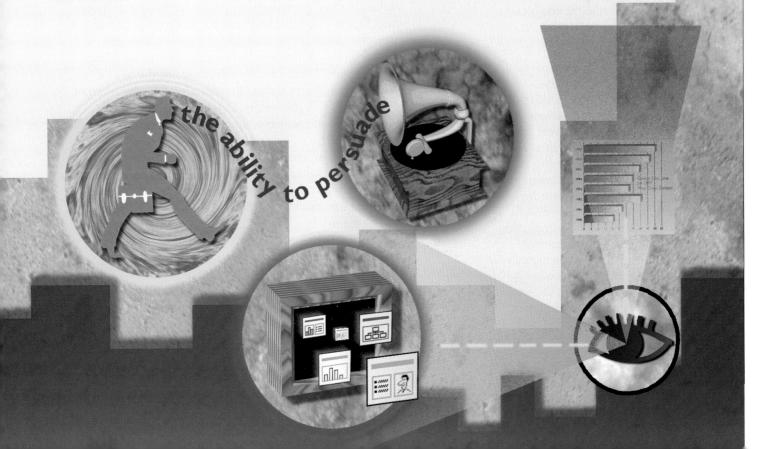

Project 1

Microsoft
PowerPoint 97

Using a Design Template and Style Checker to Create a Presentation

Case Perspective

Everyday, more and more people are connecting to the Internet via the World Wide Web. The World Wide Web, often called the Web, is a collection of hypertext links that creates an interconnected network of links within the Internet. The most popular method of accessing the World Wide Web is a graphical software program called a browser. A person having a browser, and the proper hardware and communications requirements, easily can explore a wealth of information on the Internet. But what exactly are those requirements?

Elizabeth McGiver is a World Wide Web expert. She has prepared a short presentation to explain the requirements for connecting to the World Wide Web. Her presentation identifies the minimum hardware and software requirements for connecting to the World Wide Web as well as options for Internet service providers. Ms. McGiver selected a design template to create a consistent look throughout the presentation. To make the presentation more appealing, she adjusted paragraph spacing. In the event that the location in which she speaks does not have the equipment necessary to conduct an electronic presentation, she prepared a copy of the presentation on transparency film to use with an overhead projector.

What Is PowerPoint?

Microsoft PowerPoint is a complete presentation graphics program that allows you to produce professional-looking presentations. PowerPoint gives you the flexibility to make informal presentations using overhead transparencies (Figure 1-1a), make electronic presentations using a projection device attached to a personal computer (Figure 1-1b), make formal presentations using 35mm slides (Figure 1-1c), or take advantage of the World Wide Web and run virtual presentations on the Internet (Figure 1-1d). Additionally, PowerPoint can create paper printouts, outlines, speaker notes, and audience handouts.

PowerPoint contains several features to simplify creating a presentation. For example, you can instruct PowerPoint to create a predesigned presentation, and then you can modify the presentation to fulfill your requirements. You quickly can format a presentation using one of the professionally designed presentation design templates. To make your presentation more impressive, you can add tables, graphs, pictures, video, sound, and, animation effects. You can be certain your presentation meets specific design criteria by using Style Checker to locate inconsistencies in spelling, visual clarity, uppercase and lowercase usage, and end punctuation.

(a) Overhead Transparencies

(b) Projection Device Connected to a Personal Computer

(c) PowerPoint Presentation Over the World Wide Web

(d) 35mm Slides

FIGURE 1-1

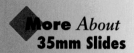

More *About*
Electronic
Presentations

Use an electronic presentation for any size audience. The choice of projection device depends on the number of people in the audience. Be certain you test the system before you deliver the presentation.

More *About*
35mm Slides

35mm slides are best for formal presentations made to any size audience and are highly recommended when audience size exceeds 50 people. 35mm slide presentations are best-suited for a non-interactive presentation because the room is dark.

For example, you can instruct PowerPoint to restrict the number of bulleted items on a slide or limit the number of words in each paragraph. Additional PowerPoint features include the following:

▶ **Word processing** — allows you to create bulleted lists, combine words and images, find and replace text, and use multiple fonts and type sizes. Using its IntelliSense features, PowerPoint can perform tasks such as checking spelling and formatting text – *all while you are typing.*

▶ **Outlining** — allows you quickly to create your presentation using an outline format. You also can import outlines from Microsoft Word or other word processing programs.

▶ **Graphing** — allows you to create and insert charts into your presentations. Graph formats include two-dimensional (2-D) graphs: area, bar, column, combination, line, pie, xy (scatter); and three-dimensional (3-D) graphs: area, bar, column, line, and pie.

▶ **Drawing** — allows you to create diagrams using shapes such as arcs, arrows, cubes, rectangles, stars, and triangles. Drawing also allows you to modify shapes without redrawing.

▶ **Clip art** — allows you to insert artwork into your presentation without creating it yourself. You can find hundreds of graphic images in the Microsoft Clip Gallery, or you can import art from other applications. With the **AutoClipArt feature**, PowerPoint can suggest a clip art image appropriate for your presentation.

▶ **Multimedia effects** — adds interest and keeps your audience attentive by adding effects, such as sound and video, to your presentations. PowerPoint 97 allows you to create interactive multimedia presentations that can be placed on the World Wide Web.

▶ **Wizards** — a tutorial approach for quickly and efficiently creating a presentation. PowerPoint wizards make it easy to create quality presentations by prompting you for specific content criteria. For example, the **AutoContent Wizard** prompts you for what are you going to talk about and the type of presentation you are going to give, such as recommending a strategy or selling a product. When giving a presentation away from the computer, on which it was created, it is important you take all the necessary files. The **Pack and Go Wizard** helps you bundle everything you need, including any objects associated with that presentation. If you cannot confirm that the computer on which you are presenting has PowerPoint, you also can pack **PowerPoint Viewer**, a program that allows you to run, but not edit, a PowerPoint presentation.

Project One – Unlocking the Internet

This book presents a series of projects using PowerPoint to produce slides similar to those you would develop in an academic or business environment. Project 1 uses PowerPoint to create the presentation shown in Figure 1-2. The objective is to produce a presentation, called Unlocking the Internet, to be presented using an overhead projector. As an introduction to PowerPoint, this project steps you through the most common type of presentation, a bulleted list. A **bulleted list** is a list of paragraphs, each preceded by a bullet. A **bullet** is a symbol (usually a heavy dot (•)) that precedes text when the text warrants special emphasis. The first of the four slides is called the title slide. The **title slide** introduces the presentation to the audience.

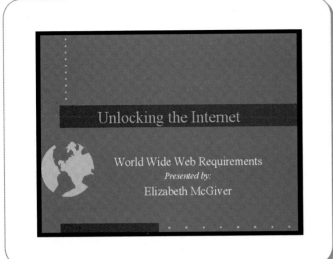

(a)

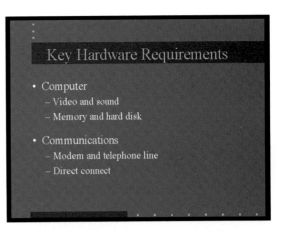

(b)

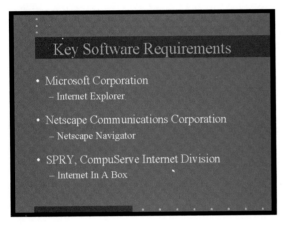

(c)

(d)

FIGURE 1-2

Mouse Usage

In this book, the mouse is used as the primary way to communicate with PowerPoint. You can perform seven operations with a standard mouse: point, click, right-click, double-click, triple-click, drag, and right-drag. If you have a **Microsoft IntelliMouse**, then you also have a wheel between the left and right buttons. This wheel can be used to perform three additional operations: rotate wheel, click wheel, or drag wheel.

Point means you move the mouse across a flat surface until the mouse pointer rests on the item of choice on the screen. As you move the mouse, the mouse pointer moves across the screen in the same direction. **Click** means you press and release the left mouse button. The terminology used in this book to direct you to point to a particular item and then click is, Click the particular item. For example, Click the Bold button means point to the Bold button and click.

Right-click means you press and release the right mouse button. As with the left mouse button, you normally will point to an item on the screen prior to right-clicking.

More *About* **Presentation Graphics**

Presentation graphics help people *see* what they *hear*. People remember:
- 10% of what they *read*
- 20% of what they *hear*
- 30% of what they *see*
- 70% of what they *see* and *hear*

◆**More** *About*
Presentation Design

Identify the purpose of the presentation. Is it to sell an idea or product, report results of a study, or educate the audience? Whatever the purpose, your goal is to capture the attention of the audience and to explain the data or concept in a manner that is easy to understand.

Double-click means you quickly press and release the left mouse button twice without moving the mouse. In most cases, you must point to an item before double-clicking. In this book, **triple-clicking** in a text object selects the entire paragraph. **Drag** means you point to an item, hold down the left mouse button, move the item to the desired location on the screen, and then release the left mouse button. **Right-drag** means you point to an item, hold down the right mouse button, move the item to the desired location, and then release the right mouse button.

If you have a Microsoft IntelliMouse, then you can use **rotate wheel** to view parts of the presentation that are not visible. The wheel also can serve as a third button. When the wheel is used as a button, it is referred to as the **wheel button**. For example, dragging the wheel button causes some applications to scroll in the direction you drag.

The use of the mouse is an important skill when working with Microsoft PowerPoint 97.

Slide Preparation Steps

The preparation steps summarize how the slide presentation shown in Figure 1-2 on the previous page will be developed in Project 1. The following tasks will be completed in this project.

1. Start a new Office document.
2. Select a design template.
3. Create a title slide.
4. Save the presentation on a floppy disk.
5. Create three multi-level bulleted lists.
6. Save the presentation again.
7. Quit PowerPoint.
8. Open the presentation as a Microsoft Office document.
9. Style check the presentation.
10. Edit the presentation.
11. Print the presentation.
12. Quit PowerPoint.

The following pages contain a detailed explanation of these tasks.

Starting a Presentation as a New Office Document

◆**More** *About*
Design Templates

When deciding on a design template, choose one designed to display light colored text on a medium to dark background. Light text on a dark background provides a stronger contrast than light text on a light background.

A PowerPoint document is called a **presentation**. The quickest way to begin a new presentation is to use the **Start button** on the **taskbar** at the bottom of your screen. When you click the Start button, the **Start menu** displays several commands for simplifying tasks in Windows 95. When Microsoft Office 97 is installed, the Start menu displays two commands: New Office Document and Open Office Document. You use the **New Office Document** command to designate the type of Office document you are creating. Then, you specify the design template or wizard on which you wish to base your document. A **design template** provides consistency in design and color throughout the entire presentation. The design template determines the color scheme, font and font size, and layout of your presentation. Then PowerPoint starts and the specified template or wizard displays. The Open Office Document command is discussed later in this project. Perform the steps on the following pages to start a new presentation, or ask your instructor how to start PowerPoint on your system.

Steps To Start a New Presentation

1 **Point to the Start button on the taskbar at the lower-left corner of the desktop.**

When you position the mouse pointer on the Start button, it displays as a left pointing block arrow and a ScreenTip displays, Click here to begin (Figure 1-3). Your computer system displays the time on the clock at the right end of the taskbar.

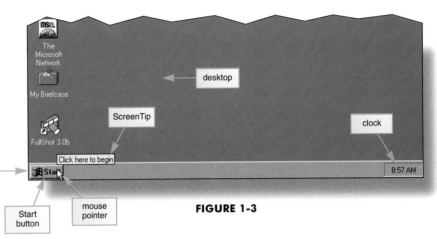

FIGURE 1-3

2 **Click the Start button. When the Windows 95 Start menu displays, point to New Office Document.**

The Windows 95 Start menu displays the names of several programs. The mouse pointer points to New Office Document (Figure 1-4). When the mouse pointer points to a name on the menu, the name is highlighted.

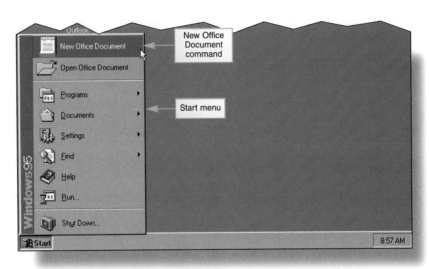

FIGURE 1-4

3 **Click New Office Document. When the New Office Document dialog box displays, point to the Presentatio . . . tab.**

The New Office Document dialog box automatically displays the General sheet and the mouse pointer points to the Presentatio . . . (Presentation Designs) tab (Figure 1-5). Depending on your installation, your computer may display a Presentation Designs tab or a Designs tab.

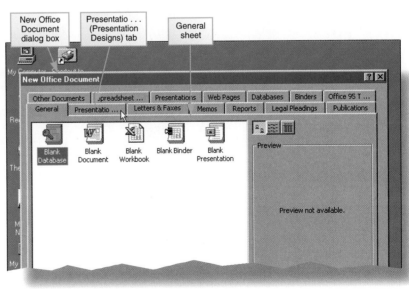

FIGURE 1-5

4 **Click the Presentatio . . . tab. When the Presentatio . . . sheet displays, point to Contempo. . . (Contemporary).**

The Presentatio . . . sheet displays the names and icons for several design templates (Figure 1-6). The Preview box displays a message about how to see a preview of a presentation design template. The OK button currently is dimmed, which means it is not available because a design template icon has not been selected. The Cancel button is available, however, as indicated by the black text on the button. The Cancel button is used to close the New Office Document dialog box and return to the desktop or return to the window from which you started.

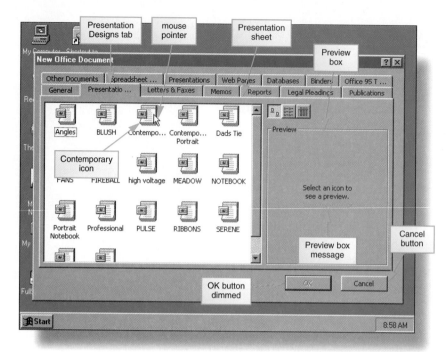

FIGURE 1-6

5 **Click Contempo. . ..**

The Contempo. . . design template icon is highlighted and a thumbnail view of the design template displays in the Preview box (Figure 1-7). The OK button now is available as indicated by the black text on the button.

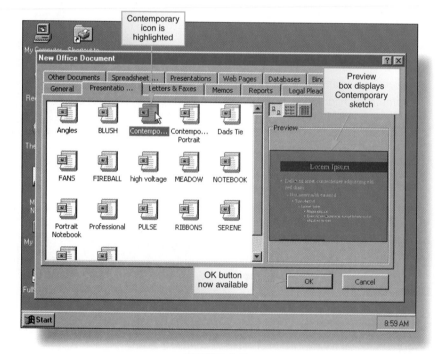

FIGURE 1-7

6 **Double-click Contempo. . .. When the Office Assistant displays, point to the Close button on the Office Assistant.**

Double-clicking the Contemporary design template icon indicates that you are applying a PowerPoint design template. As a result, PowerPoint starts and displays the New Slide dialog box, the Common Tasks toolbar, and the Office Assistant (Figure 1-8). The Office Assistant displays if it was active during the last computer session or when Microsoft Office 97 starts for the first time. You learn how to use the Office Assistant later in this project. Microsoft PowerPoint displays as a button on the taskbar at the bottom of the screen.

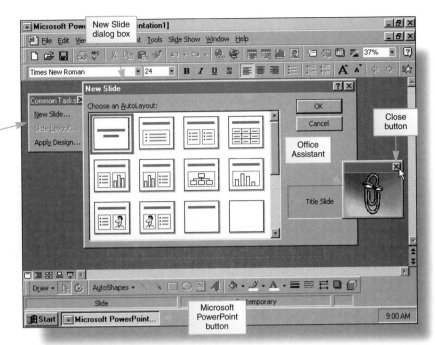

FIGURE 1-8

7 **Click the Close button and then point to the OK button in the New Slide dialog box.**

The Office Assistant closes. A frame displays around the Title Slide AutoLayout to indicate it is selected (Figure 1-9). The name of the selected AutoLayout displays on the lower-right corner of the New Slide dialog box.

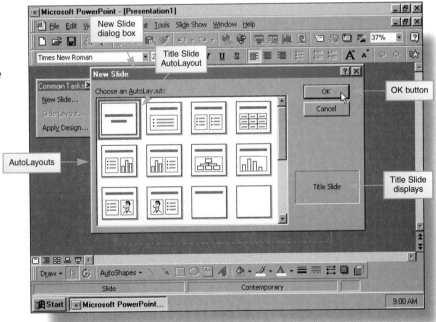

FIGURE 1-9

8 **Click the OK button.**

PowerPoint displays the Title Slide AutoLayout and the Contemporary design template on Slide 1 (Figure 1-10). The title bar identifies this as a Microsoft PowerPoint presentation currently titled Presentation1. The status bar displays information about the current slide, such as the slide number and the current design template.

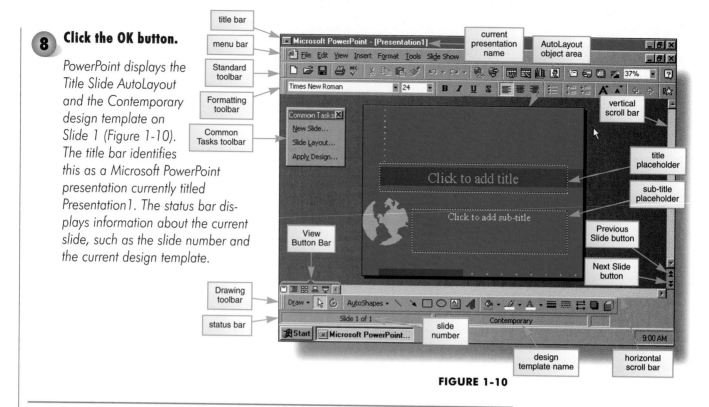

FIGURE 1-10

As an alternative to double-clicking the Contemporary design template in Step 6, you can click the OK button to apply the selected design template. The Office Assistant, closed in Step 7, is discussed later in this project.

The PowerPoint Window

The basic unit of a PowerPoint presentation is a **slide. Objects** are the building blocks for a PowerPoint slide. A slide contains one or many objects, such as a title, text, graphics, tables, charts, and drawings. In PowerPoint, you have the option of using the PowerPoint default settings or establishing your own. A **default setting** is a particular value for a variable that is assigned initially by PowerPoint and remains in effect unless canceled or overridden by the user. These settings control the placement of objects, the color scheme, the transition between slides, and other slide attributes. **Attributes** are the properties or characteristics of an object. For example, if you underline the title of a slide, the title is the object and the underline is the attribute. When you start PowerPoint, the default **slide layout** is **landscape orientation**, in which the slide width is greater than its height. In landscape orientation, the slide size is preset to 10 inches wide and 7.5 inches high. The slide layout can be changed to **portrait orientation,** so that the slide height is greater than its width, by clicking Page Setup on the File menu. In portrait orientation, the slide height is 10 inches and its width is 7.5 inches.

PowerPoint Views

PowerPoint has five views: slide view, outline view, slide sorter view, notes page view, and slide show view. A **view** is the mode in which the presentation displays on the screen. You may use any or all views when creating your presentation, but you can use only one at a time. Change views by clicking one of the view buttons found on the **View Button Bar** at the bottom of the PowerPoint screen (Figure 1-10). The PowerPoint window display is dependent on the view. Some views are graphical while others are textual.

Table 1-1 identifies the view buttons and provides an explanation of each view.

Table 1-1

BUTTON	BUTTON NAME	FUNCTION
	Slide View	Displays a single slide as it appears in your presentation. Use slide view to create or edit a presentation. Slide view also is used to incorporate text and graphic objects and to create line-by-line progressive disclosure, called build effects.
	Outline View	Displays a presentation in an outline format showing slide titles and text. It is best used for organizing and developing the content of your presentation.
	Slide Sorter View	Displays miniature versions of all slides in your presentation. You then can copy, cut, paste, or otherwise change slide position to modify your presentation. Slide sorter view also is used to add slide transitions.
	Notes Page View	Displays the current notes page. Notes page view allows you to create speaker's notes to use when you give your presentation. Each notes page corresponds to a slide and includes a reduced slide image.
	Slide Show View	Displays your slides as an electronic presentation on the full screen of your computer's monitor. Looking much like a slide projector display, you can see the effect of transitions, build effects, and slide timings.

PowerPoint Window in Slide View

The PowerPoint window in slide view contains: the title bar; the menu bar; the status bar; the toolbars: Standard, Formatting, Drawing, and Common Tasks; the AutoLayout object area; the mouse pointer; the scroll bars; and the View Button Bar.

TITLE BAR The **title bar** (Figure 1-10) displays the name of the current PowerPoint document. Until you save your presentation, PowerPoint assigns the default name Presentation1.

MENU BAR The **menu bar** (Figure 1-10) displays the PowerPoint menu names. Each menu name represents a list of commands that allows you to retrieve, store, print, and change objects in your presentation. To display a menu, such as the File menu, click File (the name) on the menu bar.

STATUS BAR Located at the bottom of the PowerPoint window, the **status bar** consists of a message area and a presentation design template identifier (Figure 1-10). Most of the time, the current slide number and the total number of slides in the presentation display in the message area. For example, in Figure 1-10, the message area displays Slide 1 of 1. Slide 1 is the current slide, and of 1 indicates there is only one slide in the presentation.

SCROLL BARS The **vertical scroll bar** (Figure 1-10), located on the right side of the PowerPoint window, allows you to move forward or backward through your presentation. Clicking the **Next Slide button** (Figure 1-10), located on the vertical scroll bar, advances to the next slide in the presentation. Clicking the **Previous Slide button** (Figure 1-10), located on the vertical scroll bar, backs up to the slide preceding the current slide.

The **horizontal scroll bar** (Figure 1-10 on page PP 1.14), located on the bottom of the PowerPoint window, allows you to display a portion of the window when the entire window does not fit on the screen.

It should be noted that in slide view, both the vertical and horizontal scroll bar actions are dependent on the **Zoom** settings. You control how large or small a document displays on the PowerPoint window by zooming in or out. If you are in slide view and Zoom is set such that the entire slide is not visible in the Slide window, clicking the up arrow on the vertical scroll bar displays the next portion of your slide, not the previous slide. Recall that to go to the previous slide, click the Previous Slide button. To go to the next slide, click the Next Slide button.

AUTOLAYOUT OBJECT AREA The **AutoLayout object area** (Figure 1-10) is a collection of placeholders for the title, text, clip art, graphs, tables, and media clips (video and sound). These placeholders display when you create a new slide. You can change the AutoLayout any time during the creation of your presentation by clicking the Slide Layout button on the Common Tasks toolbar and then selecting a different slide layout.

PLACEHOLDERS Surrounded by a dashed line, **placeholders** are the empty objects on a new slide. Depending on the AutoLayout selected, placeholders will display for the title, text, graphs, tables, organization charts, media clips, and clip art. Once you place contents in a placeholder, the placeholder becomes an object. For example, text typed in a placeholder becomes a text object.

TITLE PLACEHOLDER Surrounded by a dashed line, the **title placeholder** is the empty title object on a new slide (Figure 1-10). Text typed in the title placeholder becomes the **title object**.

SUB-TITLE PLACEHOLDER Surrounded by a dashed line, the **sub-title placeholder** is the empty sub-title object that displays below the title placeholder on a title slide (Figure 1-10).

MOUSE POINTER The **mouse pointer** can become one of several different shapes depending on the task you are performing in PowerPoint and the pointer's location on the screen. The different shapes are discussed when they display in subsequent projects. The mouse pointer in Figure 1-10 has the shape of a left-pointing block arrow.

TOOLBARS PowerPoint **toolbars** consist of buttons that allow you to perform tasks more quickly than when using the menu bar. For example, to save a presentation, click the Save button on the Standard toolbar. Each button face has a graphical representation that helps you remember its function. Figures 1-11 through 1-14 illustrate the buttons on each of the four toolbars that display when you start PowerPoint and display a slide in slide view. They are the Standard toolbar, the Formatting toolbar, the Drawing toolbar, and the Common Tasks toolbar. Each button is explained in detail when it is used.

PowerPoint has several additional toolbars you can display by clicking View on the menu bar. You also can display a toolbar by pointing to a toolbar and right-clicking to display a shortcut menu, which lists the available toolbars. A **shortcut menu** contains a list of commands or items that relate to the item to which you are pointing when you right-click.

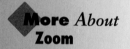

More *About*
Zoom

Increase the Zoom setting when working with small objects to better see details, such as when modifying a graphic. Decrease the Zoom setting to work with large objects.

More *About*
Toolbars

Hiding a toolbar that you no longer need increases the Zoom setting and displays a larger PowerPoint view. To hide a toolbar, right-click any toolbar and then click the check mark next to the name of the toolbar you wish to hide.

PowerPoint allows you to customize all toolbars and to add the toolbar buttons you use most often. In the same manner, you can remove those toolbar buttons you do not use. To customize a toolbar, click Tools on the menu bar, and then click Customize to modify the toolbar to meet your requirements. Another way to customize a toolbar is to click View on the menu bar, click Toolbars, click Customize, and then make changes in the Customize dialog box to fulfill your requirements.

STANDARD TOOLBAR The **Standard toolbar** (Figure 1-11) contains the tools to execute the more common commands found on the menu bar, such as Open, Print, Save, Copy, Cut, Paste, and many more. The Standard toolbar contains a button for setting Zoom. Recall that you control how large or small a document displays in the PowerPoint window with the Zoom list.

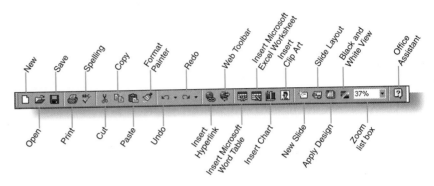

FIGURE 1-11

FORMATTING TOOLBAR The **Formatting toolbar** (Figure 1-12) contains the tools for changing text attributes. The Formatting toolbar allows you to quickly change font, font size, and alignment. It also contains tools to bold, italicize, underline, shadow, color, and bullet text. The five **attribute buttons**, **Bold**, **Italic**, **Underline**, **Shadow**, and **Bullets**, are on/off switches, or toggles. Click the button once to turn the attribute on; then click it again to turn the attribute off.

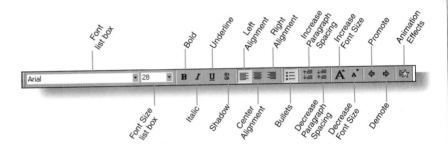

FIGURE 1-12

DRAWING TOOLBAR The **Drawing toolbar** (Figure 1-13) is a collection of tools for drawing objects such as lines, circles, and boxes. The Drawing toolbar also contains tools to edit the objects once you have drawn them. For example, you can change the color of an object with the **Fill Color button**, or rotate an object by clicking the **Free Rotate** button.

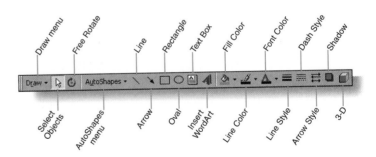

FIGURE 1-13

COMMON TASKS TOOLBAR The **Common Tasks toolbar** (Figure 1-14) contains the three more frequently used commands; **New Slide button**, **Slide Layout button**, and the **Apply Design button**.

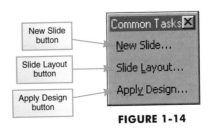

FIGURE 1-14

Creating a Title Slide

The purpose of a title slide is to introduce the presentation to the audience.
PowerPoint assumes the first slide in a new presentation is the title slide. With the
exception of a blank slide, PowerPoint also assumes every new slide has a title. To
make creating your presentation easier, any text you type after a new slide displays becomes the title object. In other words, you do not have to first select the
title placeholder before typing the title text. The AutoLayout for the title slide has
a title placeholder near the middle of the window and a sub-title placeholder
directly below the title placeholder (Figure 1-15).

Entering the Presentation Title

The presentation title for Project 1 is Unlocking the Internet. Type the presentation title in the title placeholder on the title slide. Perform the following step to
create the title slide for this project.

Steps **To Enter the Presentation Title**

1 **Type** Unlocking the
Internet **in the title
placeholder. Do not
press the ENTER key.**

*The title text, Unlocking the Internet,
displays in the title text box (Figure
1-15). The recessed Center Alignment button indicates the title text is
center-aligned in the title text box.
When you type the first character,
the selection rectangle, a slashed
outline, displays around the title
box. A blinking vertical line (|),
called the **insertion point**, indicates
where the next character will display.*

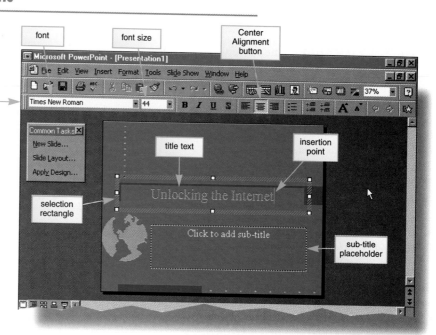

FIGURE 1-15

Notice that you do not press the ENTER key after the word Internet. If you
press the ENTER key after typing the title, PowerPoint creates a new paragraph. A
paragraph is a segment of text with the same format that begins when you press
the ENTER key and ends when you press the ENTER key again. Pressing the ENTER
key creates a new line in a new paragraph. Therefore, do not press the ENTER key
unless you want to create a two-paragraph title. Additionally, PowerPoint **line
wraps** text that exceeds the width of the placeholder. For example, if the slide title
was, Experiencing the World Wide Web, it would exceed the width of the title
placeholder and display on two lines.

The title is centered in the window because the Contemporary design template
alignment attribute is centered. The Center Alignment button is recessed on the
Formatting toolbar in Figure 1-15.

Correcting a Mistake When Typing

If you type the wrong letter and notice the error before pressing the ENTER key, press the BACKSPACE key to erase all the characters back to and including the one that is incorrect. If you mistakenly press the ENTER key after entering the title and the insertion point is on the new line, simply press the BACKSPACE key to return the insertion point to the right of the letter t in the word Internet.

When you first install PowerPoint, the default setting allows you to reverse up to the last 20 changes by clicking the **Undo button** on the Standard toolbar. The ScreenTip that displays when you point to the Undo button changes to indicate the type of change just made. For example, if you type text in the title placeholder and then point to the Undo button, the ScreenTip that displays is Undo Typing. For clarity, when referencing the Undo button in this project, the name displaying in the ScreenTip is referenced. Another way to reverse changes is to click the Undo command on the Edit menu. Like the Undo button, the Undo command name reflects the last type of change made to the presentation.

You can reapply a change that you reversed with the Undo button by clicking the Redo button on the Standard toolbar. Clicking the **Redo button** reverses the last undo action. The ScreenTip name reflects the type of reversal last preformed.

Entering the Presentation Subtitle

The next step in creating the title slide is to enter the subtitle text into the sub-title placeholder. Complete the steps below to enter the presentation subtitle.

Steps **To Enter the Presentation Subtitle**

1 **Click the label, Click to add sub-title, located inside the sub-title placeholder.**

The insertion point is in the sub-title text box (Figure 1-16). The mouse pointer changes to an I-beam. The I-beam mouse pointer indicates the mouse is in a text placeholder. The selection rectangle indicates the sub-title placeholder is selected.

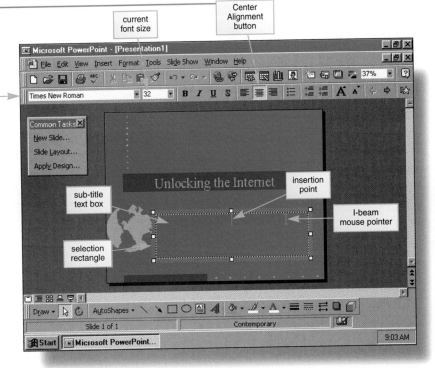

FIGURE 1-16

<blockquote>
More *About*
Undo

The number of times you can click the Undo button to reverse changes can be modified. To increase or decrease the number of undos, click Tools on the menu bar, click Options, and then click the Edit tab. Use the up and down arrows in the Maximum number of undos box to change the number of undos. The maximum number of undos is 150; the minimum number is 3.
</blockquote>

2 **Type** World Wide Web Requirements **and press the ENTER key. Type** Presented by: **and press the ENTER key. Type** Elizabeth McGiver **but do not press the ENTER key.**

The text displays in the sub-title object as shown in Figure 1-17. The insertion point displays after the letter r in McGiver.

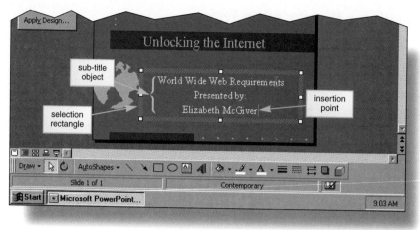

FIGURE 1-17

The previous section created a title slide using an AutoLayout for the title slide. PowerPoint displayed the title slide layout because you created a new presentation. You entered text in the title placeholder without selecting the title placeholder because PowerPoint assumes every slide has a title. You could, however, click the title placeholder to select it and then type your title. In general, to type text in any text placeholder, click the text placeholder and begin typing. You also added a subtitle that identifies the presenter. While this is not required, it often is useful information for the audience.

Text Attributes

This presentation is using the Contemporary design template that you selected from the Presentation sheet. Each design template has its own text attributes. A **text attribute** is a characteristic of the text, such as font, font size, font style, or text color. You can adjust text attributes any time before, during, or after you type the text. Recall that a design template determines the color scheme, font and font size, and layout of your presentation. Most of the time, you use the design template's text attributes and color scheme. There are times when you wish to change the way your presentation looks, however, and still keep a particular design template. PowerPoint gives you that flexibility. You can use the design template you wish and change the text color, text font size, text font, and text font style. Table 1-2 explains the different text attributes available in PowerPoint.

The next two sections explain how to change the font size and text font style attributes.

Table 1-2

ATTRIBUTE	DESCRIPTION
Font	Defines the appearance and shape of letters, numbers, and special characters.
Text color	Defines the color of text. Displaying text in color requires a color monitor. Printing text in color requires a color printer or plotter.
Font size	Specifies the size of characters on the screen. Character size is gauged by a measurement system called points. A single point is about 1/72 of an inch in height. Thus, a character with a point size of eighteen is about 18/72 (or 1/4) of an inch in height.
Text font style	Defines text characteristics. Text font styles include plain, italic, bold, shadowed, and underlined. Text may have one or more font styles at a time.
Subscript	Defines the placement of a character in relationship to another. A subscript character displays or prints slightly below and immediately to one side of another character.
Superscript	Defines the placement of a character in relationship to another. A superscript character displays or prints above and immediately to one side of another character.

Changing the Font Size

The Contemporary design template default font size is 32 points for body text and 44 points for title text. A point is 1/72 of an inch in height. Thus, a character with a point size of 44 is about 44/72 (or 11/18) of an inch in height. Slide 1 requires you to decrease the font size for the paragraph, Presented by:. Perform the following steps to decrease font size.

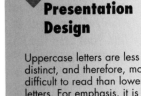

 Steps **To Decrease Font Size**

1 Triple-click the paragraph, Presented by:, in the sub-title object.

The paragraph, Presented by:, is highlighted (Figure 1-18).

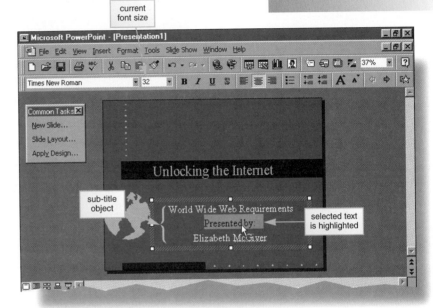

FIGURE 1-18

2 With Presented by: highlighted, point to the Decrease Font Size button on the Formatting toolbar.

When you point to a button on a toolbar, PowerPoint displays a ScreenTip. A **ScreenTip** *contains the name of the tool to which you are pointing. When pointing to the* **Decrease Font Size button,** *the ScreenTip displays the words, Decrease Font Size (Figure 1-19).*

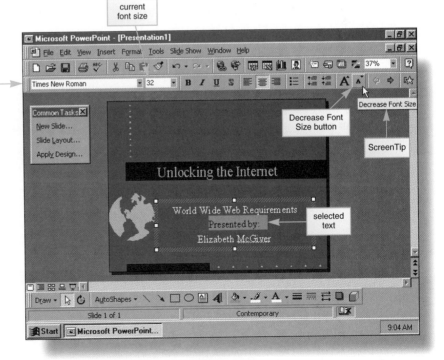

FIGURE 1-19

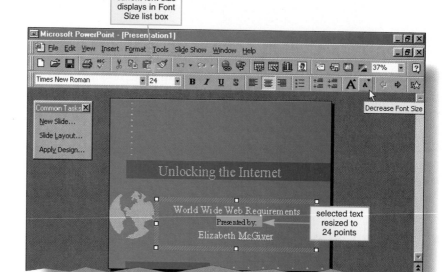

current font size
displays in Font
Size list box

3 **Click the Decrease Font Size button twice so that 24 displays in the Font Size list box on the Formatting toolbar.**

The paragraph, Presented by:, reduces to 24 points (Figure 1-20). The Font Size list box displays the new font size as 24.

selected text
resized to
24 points

FIGURE 1-20

If you need to increase the font size, click the **Increase Font Size button,** located immediately to the left of the Decrease Font Size button on the Formatting toolbar.

Changing the Style of Text to Italic

Text font styles include plain, italic, bold, shadowed, and underlined. PowerPoint allows you to use one or more text font styles in your presentation. Perform the following steps to add emphasis to the title slide by changing plain text to italic text.

Steps **To Change the Text Font Style to Italic**

1 **With the paragraph, Presented by:, highlighted, click the Italic button on the Formatting toolbar.**

The text is italicized and the Italic button is recessed (Figure 1-21).

Formatting
toolbar

Italic

Italic button
recessed

selected text
with italic
attribute

FIGURE 1-21

To remove italics from text, select the italicized text and then click the Italic button. As a result, the Italic button is not recessed and the text does not have the italic font style.

Saving a Presentation to a Floppy Disk

While you are building your presentation, the computer stores it in main memory. It is important to save your presentation frequently because, if the computer is turned off or you lose electrical power, the presentation is lost. Another reason to save your work is that if you run out of lab time before completing your project, you may finish the project later without having to start over. You must, therefore, save any presentation you will use later. Before you continue with Project 1, save the work completed thus far. Perform the following steps to save a presentation to a floppy disk using the Save button on the Standard toolbar.

Steps To Save a Presentation to a Floppy Disk

1 **Insert a formatted floppy disk in drive A. Then click the Save button on the Standard toolbar.**

The Save dialog displays (Figure 1-22). The insertion point displays in the File name list box. The default folder, My Documents, displays in the Save in list box. Presentation displays in the Save as type list box. The Save button is dimmed (not available) because you have not yet entered a name in the File name list box. The Cancel button is available, as indicated by the black text on the button. Clicking the Cancel button closes the Save dialog box and returns to the PowerPoint window.

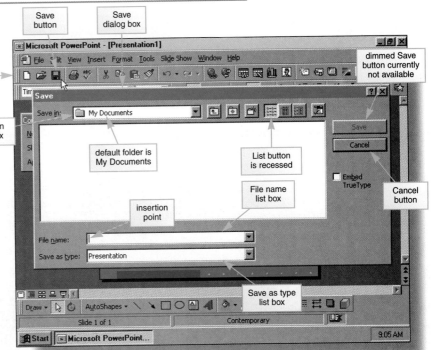

FIGURE 1-22

More *About*
Saving

Before you make extreme changes to your presentation, save a copy of it with a different file name using the Save As command on the File menu. This way, if you decide you do not like the new version, you still will have a copy of the original presentation.

2 **Type** Unlocking the Internet **in the File name list box. Do not press the ENTER key after typing the file name.**

The name, Unlocking the Internet, displays in the File name list box (Figure 1-23). The black text on the Save button indicates it is available.

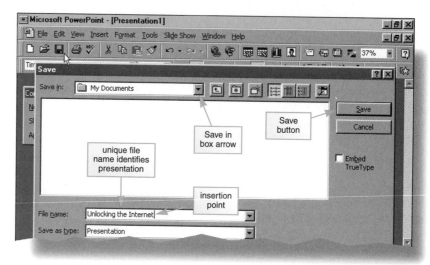

FIGURE 1-23

3 **Click the Save in box arrow. Point to 3½ Floppy (A:) in the Save in list.**

The Save in list displays a list of locations to which you can save your presentation (Figure 1-24). Your list may look different depending on the configuration of your system. 3½ Floppy (A:) is highlighted.

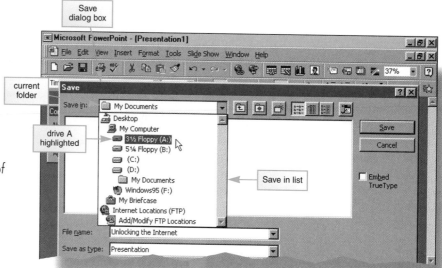

FIGURE 1-24

4 **Click 3½ Floppy (A:). Then point to the Save button.**

Drive A becomes the current drive (Figure 1-25).

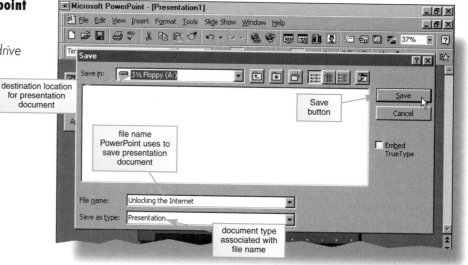

FIGURE 1-25

⑤ **Click the Save button.**

PowerPoint saves the presentation to your floppy disk in drive A. Slide 1 displays in slide view. The title bar displays the file name used to save the presentation, Unlocking the Internet (Figure 1-26).

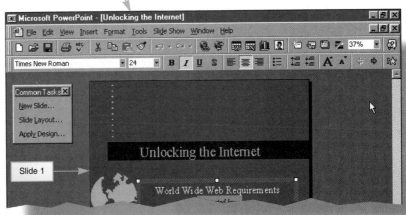

file name displays in title bar

Slide 1

FIGURE 1-26

Other Ways
1. On File menu click Save
2. Press CTRL+S or press SHIFT+F12

PowerPoint automatically appends to the file name, Unlocking the Internet, the extension **.ppt**, which stands for **P**ower**P**oint. Although the presentation, Unlocking the Internet, is saved on a floppy disk, it also remains in main memory and displays on the screen.

It is a good practice to save periodically while you are working on a project. By doing so, you protect yourself from losing all the work you have done since the last time you saved.

Adding a New Slide to a Presentation

The title slide for your presentation is created. The next step is to add the first bulleted list slide in Project 1. Clicking the New Slide button on the Common Tasks toolbar adds a slide into the presentation immediately after the current slide. Usually when you create your presentation, you are adding slides with text, graphics, or charts. When you add a new slide, PowerPoint displays a dialog box for you to choose one of the Auto-Layouts. These AutoLayouts have placeholders for various objects, such as a title, text, graphics, graphs, and charts. Some placeholders provide access to other PowerPoint objects by allowing you to double-click the placeholder. Figure 1-27 displays the 24 different AutoLayouts available in PowerPoint. More information about using AutoLayout placeholders to add graphics follows in subsequent projects. Perform the steps on the next page to add a new slide using the Bulleted List AutoLayout.

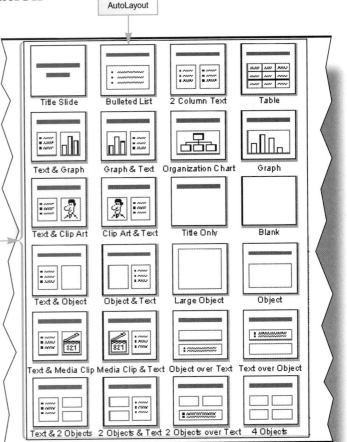

Bulleted List AutoLayout

24 different AutoLayouts

FIGURE 1-27

Steps **To Add a New Slide Using the Bulleted List AutoLayout**

1 Point to the New Slide button on the Common Tasks toolbar (Figure 1-28).

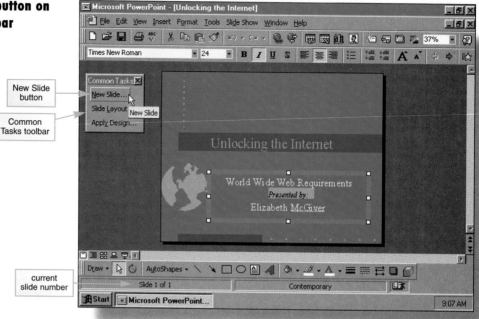

FIGURE 1-28

2 Click the New Slide button. When the New Slide dialog box displays, point to the OK button.

The New Slide dialog box displays (Figure 1-29). The Bulleted List AutoLayout is selected and the AutoLayout title, Bulleted List, displays at the bottom-right corner of the New Slide dialog box.

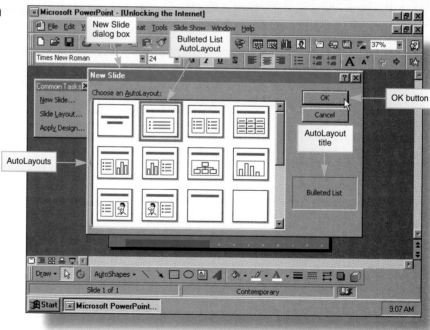

FIGURE 1-29

3 **Click the OK button.**

Slide 2 displays, keeping the attributes of the Contemporary design template (Figure 1-30). Slide 2 of 2 displays on the status bar.

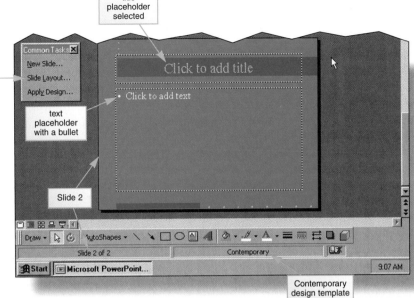

FIGURE 1-30

Because you selected the Bulleted List AutoLayout, PowerPoint displays Slide 2 with a title placeholder and a text placeholder with a bullet. You can change the layout for a slide at any time during the creation of your presentation by clicking the Slide Layout button on the Common Tasks toolbar and then double-clicking the AutoLayout of your choice.

▶ *Other***Ways**

1. Click New Slide button on Standard toolbar
2. On Insert menu click New Slide
3. Press CTRL+M

Creating a Bulleted List Slide

The bulleted list slides in Figure 1-2 on page PP 1.9, contain more than one level of bulleted text. A slide with more than one level of bulleted text is called a **multi-level bulleted list slide**. A **level** is a position within a structure, such as an outline, that indicates a magnitude of importance. PowerPoint allows for five paragraph levels. Each paragraph level has an associated bullet. The bullet font is dependent on the design template. Figure 1-31 identifies the five paragraph levels and the bullet fonts for the Contemporary design template. Beginning with the Second level, each paragraph indents to the right of the preceding level.

An indented paragraph is said to be **demoted**, or pushed down to a lower level. For example, if you demote a First level paragraph, it becomes a Second level paragraph. This lower-level paragraph is a subset of the higher-level paragraph. It usually contains information that supports the topic in the paragraph immediately above it. You demote a paragraph by clicking the **Demote button** on the Formatting toolbar.

◆ **More** *About*
Bulleted Lists

Short lines of text are easier to read than long lines.

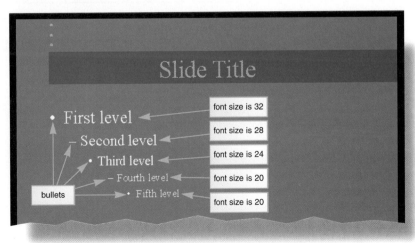

FIGURE 1-31

When you want to raise a paragraph from a lower level to a higher level, you **promote** the paragraph by clicking the **Promote button** on the Formatting toolbar.

Creating a multi-level bulleted list slide requires several steps. Initially, you enter a slide title. Next, you select a text placeholder. Then you type the text for the multi-level bulleted list, demoting and promoting paragraphs as needed. The next several sections explain how to add a multi-level bulleted list slide.

Entering a Slide Title

PowerPoint assumes every new slide has a title. Any text you type after a new slide displays becomes the title object. The title for Slide 2 is Key Hardware Requirements. Perform the following step to enter this title.

 Steps To Enter a Slide Title

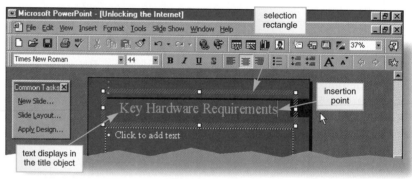

1 **Type** Key Hardware Requirements **in the title placeholder. Do not press the ENTER key.**

The title, Key Hardware Requirements, displays in the title object (Figure 1-32). The insertion point displays after the s in Requirements.

FIGURE 1-32

Selecting a Text Placeholder

Before you can type text into the text placeholder, you first must select it. Perform the following step to select the text placeholder on Slide 2.

 Steps To Select a Text Placeholder

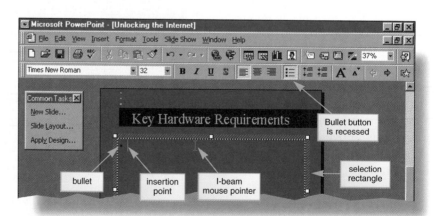

1 **Click the bulleted paragraph labeled, Click to add text.**

The insertion point displays immediately after the bullet on Slide 2 (Figure 1-33). The Bullets button is recessed.

FIGURE 1-33

OtherWays
1. Press CTRL+ENTER

Typing a Multi-level Bulleted List

Recall that a bulleted list is a list of paragraphs, each of which is preceded by a bullet. Also recall that a paragraph is a segment of text ended by pressing the ENTER key. The next step is to type the multi-level bulleted list, which consists of the six entries shown in Figure 1-2 on page PP 1.9. Perform the following steps to type a multi-level bulleted list.

Steps To Type a Multi-level Bulleted List

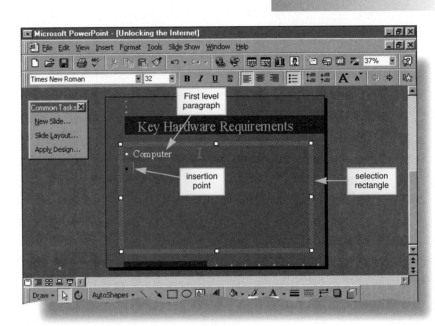

1 **Type** Computer **and press the ENTER key.**

The paragraph, Computer, displays. The font size is 32. The insertion point displays after the second bullet (Figure 1-34). When you press the ENTER key, the word processing feature of PowerPoint marks the end of one paragraph and begins a new paragraph. Because you are using the Bulleted List AutoLayout, PowerPoint places a bullet in front of the new paragraph.

FIGURE 1-34

2 **Point to the Demote button on the Formatting toolbar (Figure 1-35).**

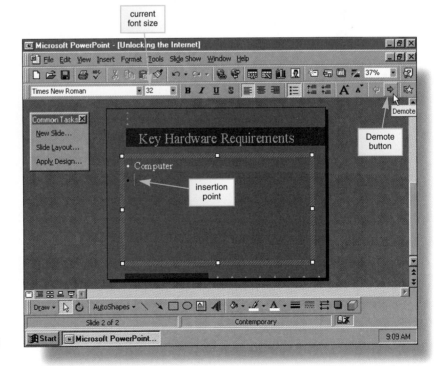

FIGURE 1-35

3 **Click the Demote button.**

The second paragraph indents under the first and becomes a Second level paragraph (Figure 1-36). Notice the bullet in front of the second paragraph changes from a dot to a dash and the font size for the demoted paragraph is now 28. The insertion point displays after the dash.

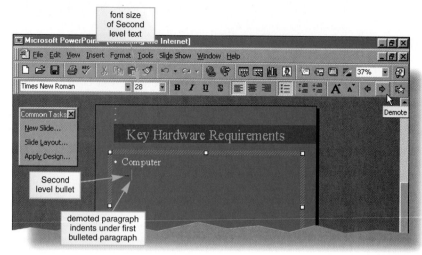

FIGURE 1-36

4 **Type** Video and sound **and press the ENTER key. Type** Memory and hard disk **and then press the ENTER key.**

Two new Second level paragraphs display with dash bullets (Figure 1-37). When you press the ENTER key, PowerPoint adds a new paragraph at the same level as the previous paragraph.

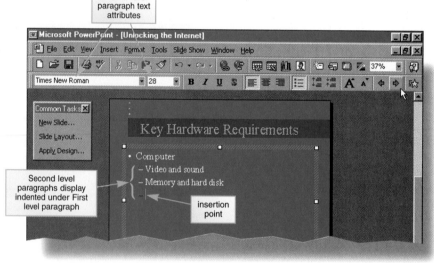

FIGURE 1-37

5 **Point to the Promote button on the Formatting toolbar (Figure 1-38).**

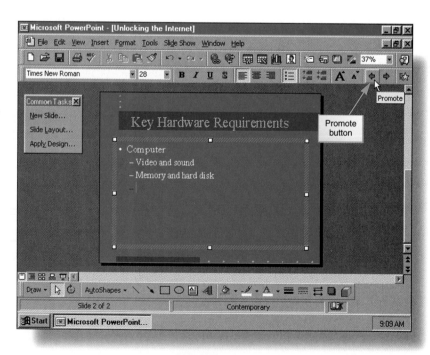

FIGURE 1-38

6 **Click the Promote button.**

The Second level paragraph becomes a First level paragraph (Figure 1-39). Notice the bullet in front of the new paragraph changes from a dash to a dot and the font size for the promoted paragraph is 32. The insertion point displays after the dot bullet.

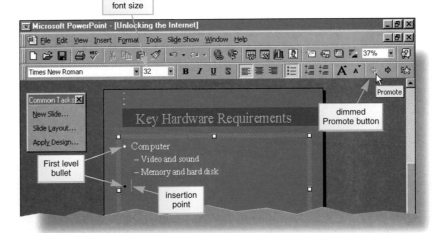

FIGURE 1-39

Perform the following steps to complete the text for Slide 2.

TO TYPE THE REMAINING TEXT FOR SLIDE 2

Step 1: Type Communications and press the ENTER key.
Step 2: Click the Demote button.
Step 3: Type Modem and telephone line and press the ENTER key.
Step 4: Type Direct connect and do not press the ENTER key.

The insertion point displays after the t in connect (Figure 1-40).

Notice that you did not press the ENTER key after typing the last paragraph in Step 4. If you press the ENTER key, a new bullet displays after the last entry on this slide. To remove an extra bullet, press the BACKSPACE key.

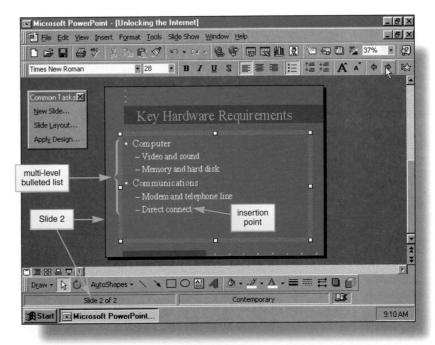

FIGURE 1-40

Adding a New Slide with the Same AutoLayout

When you add a new slide to a presentation and want to keep the same Auto-Layout used on the previous slide, PowerPoint gives you a shortcut. Instead of clicking the New Slide button and clicking an AutoLayout in the New Slide dialog box, you can press and hold down the SHIFT key and click the New Slide button. Perform the step on the next page to add a new slide (Slide 3) and keep the Bulleted List AutoLayout used on the previous slide.

More *About*
Presentation Design

Two acronyms pertain directly to presentation design:
— KIS (Keep It Simple)
— CCC (Clutter Creates Confusion)

Steps **To Add a New Slide with the Same AutoLayout**

① **Press and hold down the SHIFT key. Click the New Slide button on the Common Tasks toolbar. Then release the SHIFT key.**

Slide 3 displays the Bulleted List AutoLayout (Figure 1-41). Slide 3 of 3 displays on the status bar.

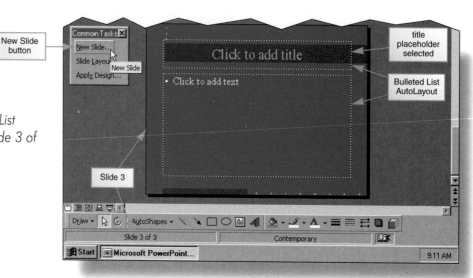

FIGURE 1-41

▶**Other**Ways

1. Press SHIFT+CTRL+M

Slide 3 is added to the presentation. Perform the following steps to add text to Slide 3 and create a multi-level bulleted list.

TO CREATE SLIDE 3

Step 1: Type Key Software Requirements in the title placeholder.
Step 2: Click the text placeholder.

Step 3: Type Microsoft Corporation and press the ENTER key.
Step 4: Click the Demote button. Type Internet Explorer and press the ENTER key.
Step 5: Click the Promote button. Type Netscape Communications Corporation and press the ENTER key.
Step 6: Click the Demote button. Type Netscape Navigator and press the ENTER key.
Step 7: Click the Promote button. Type SPRY, CompuServe Internet Division and press the ENTER key.
Step 8: Click the Demote button. Type Internet In A Box but do not press the ENTER key.

Slide 3 displays as shown in Figure 1-42.

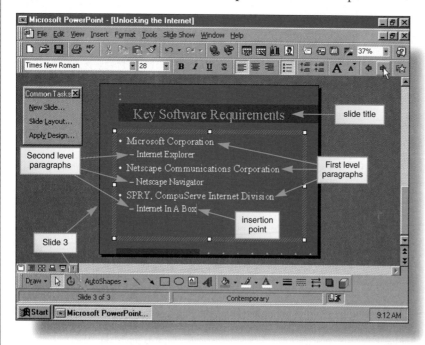

FIGURE 1-42

Slide 4 is the last slide in this presentation. It, too, is a multi-level bulleted list. Perform the following steps to create Slide 4.

TO CREATE SLIDE 4

Step 1: Press and hold down the SHIFT key and click the New Slide button on the Common Tasks toolbar. Release the SHIFT key.
Step 2: Type Key Internet Providers in the title placeholder.
Step 3: Click the text placeholder.
Step 4: Type Online services and press the ENTER key.
Step 5: Click the Demote button. Type The Microsoft Network and press the ENTER key.
Step 6: Type America Online and press the ENTER key.
Step 7: Type CompuServe and press the ENTER key.
Step 8: Type Prodigy and press the ENTER key.
Step 9: Click the Promote button. Type Local services but do not press the ENTER key.

The slide title and text object display as shown in Figure 1-43.

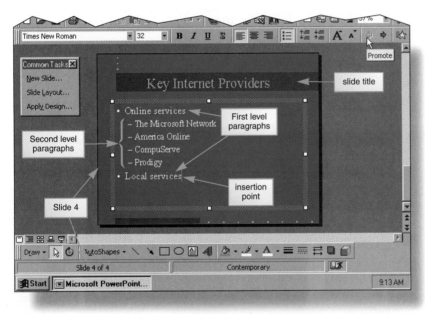

FIGURE 1-43

All slides for the Unlocking the Internet presentation are created. This presentation consists of a title slide and three multi-level bulleted list slides.

Saving a Presentation with the Same File Name

Saving frequently never can be overemphasized. When you first saved the presentation, you clicked the Save button on the Standard toolbar and the Save dialog box displayed. When you want to save the changes made to the presentation after your last save, you again click the Save button. This time, however, the Save dialog box does not display because PowerPoint updates the document called Unlocking the Internet.ppt on your floppy disk. Perform the steps on the next page to save the presentation again.

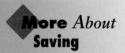

More *About* **Saving**

Protect yourself by making a second copy of a presentation prior to making several edits. On the File menu, click Save As, then save the presentation with a new name. Make your changes to the original file. When satisfied you no longer need the second file, delete it.

TO SAVE A PRESENTATION WITH THE SAME FILE NAME

Step 1: Be sure your floppy disk is in drive A.

Step 2: Click the Save button on the Standard toolbar.

PowerPoint overwrites the old Unlocking the Internet.ppt document on the floppy disk in drive A with the revised presentation document, Unlocking the Internet.ppt. Slide 4 displays in the PowerPoint window.

Moving to Another Slide in Slide View

When creating or editing a presentation in slide view, you often want to display a slide other than the current one. Dragging the vertical scroll bar box up or down moves you through your presentation. The box on the vertical scroll bar is called the **scroll box** and is shown in Figure 1-44. When you drag the scroll box, the **slide indicator** displays the number and the title of the slide you are about to display. Releasing the mouse button displays the slide.

Using the Vertical Scroll Bar to Move to Another Slide

Before continuing with Project 1, you want to display the title slide. Perform the following steps to move from Slide 4 to the Slide 1 using the vertical scroll bar.

Steps To Use the Vertical Scroll Bar to Move to Another Slide

1 **Position the mouse pointer on the scroll box. Press and hold down the left mouse button.**

Slide: 4 of 4 Key Internet Providers, displays in the slide indicator (Figure 1-44).

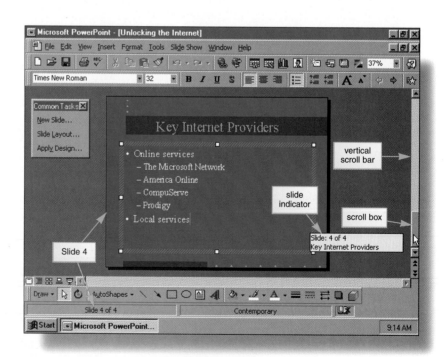

FIGURE 1-44

2 **Drag the scroll box up the vertical scroll bar until Slide: 1 of 4 Unlocking the Internet displays in the slide indicator.**

Slide: 1 of 4 Unlocking the Internet, displays in the slide indicator. Slide 4 still displays in the PowerPoint window (Figure 1-45).

3 **Release the left mouse button.**

Slide 1, titled Unlocking the Internet, displays in the PowerPoint window.

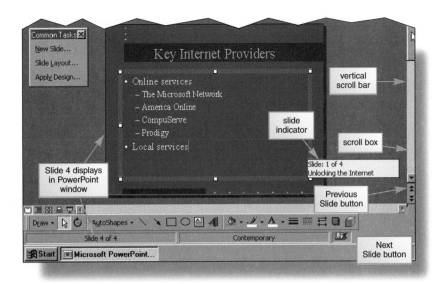

FIGURE 1-45

OtherWays

1. Click Next Slide button on vertical scroll bar to move forward one slide, or click Previous Slide button on vertical scroll bar to move back one slide

2. Press PAGE DOWN to move forward one slide, or press PAGE UP to move back one slide

Viewing the Presentation Using Slide Show

The **Slide Show button,** located at the bottom left of the PowerPoint window, allows you to display your presentation electronically using a computer. The computer acts like a slide projector, displaying each slide on a full screen. The full screen slide hides the toolbars, menus, and other PowerPoint window elements.

Starting Slide Show View

Slide show view begins when you click the Slide Show button. PowerPoint then displays the current slide on the full screen without any of the PowerPoint window objects, such as the menu bar or toolbars. Perform the following steps to start slide show view.

Steps To Start Slide Show View

1 **Point to the Slide Show button on the View Button Bar.**

The Slide View button is recessed because you are still in slide view (Figure 1-46).

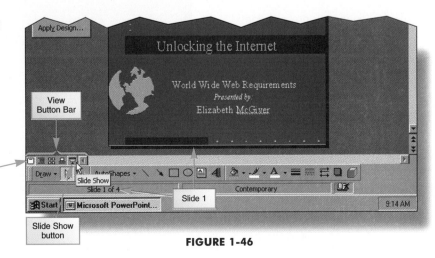

FIGURE 1-46

2 **Click the Slide Show button.**

The title slide fills the screen (Figure 1-47). The PowerPoint window is hidden.

title slide in slide show view

Unlocking the Internet

World Wide Web Requirements
Presented by:
Elizabeth McGiver

FIGURE 1-47

Advancing through a Slide Show Manually

After you begin slide show view, you can move forward or backward through your slides. PowerPoint allows you to advance through your slides manually or automatically. Automatic advancing is discussed in a later project. Perform the step below to manually move through your slides.

Steps To Manually Move Through Slides in a Slide Show

1 **Click each slide until the last slide of the presentation, Slide 4, Key Internet Providers, displays.**

Each slide in your presentation displays on the screen, one slide at a time. Each time you click the mouse button, the next slide displays (Figure 1-48).

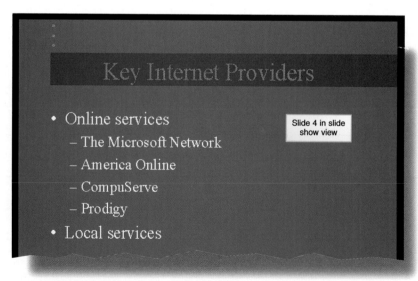

Key Internet Providers

• Online services
  – The Microsoft Network
  – America Online
  – CompuServe
  – Prodigy
• Local services

Slide 4 in slide show view

FIGURE 1-48

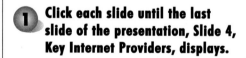

Displaying the Popup Menu in Slide Show View

Slide show view has a shortcut menu, called **Popup Menu**, that displays when you right-click a slide in slide show view. The Popup Menu contains commands to assist you during a slide show. For example, clicking the **Next command** moves you to the next slide. Clicking the **Previous command** moves you to the previous slide. You can jump to any slide in your presentation by clicking the **Go command** and then clicking Slide Navigator. The **Slide Navigator dialog box** contains a list of the slides in your presentation. Jump to the requested slide by double-clicking the name of that slide.

Additional Popup Menu commands allow you to create a list of action items during a slide show, change the mouse pointer from an arrow to a pen, blacken the screen, and end the slide show. Popup Menu commands are discussed in subsequent projects. Perform the following step to display the Slide Show View Popup Menu.

 Steps To Display the Slide Show View Popup Menu

1 **With Slide 4 displaying in slide show view, right-click the slide.**

The Popup Menu displays on Slide 4 (Figure 1-49). Your screen may look different because the Popup Menu displays near the location of the mouse pointer at the time you right-click.

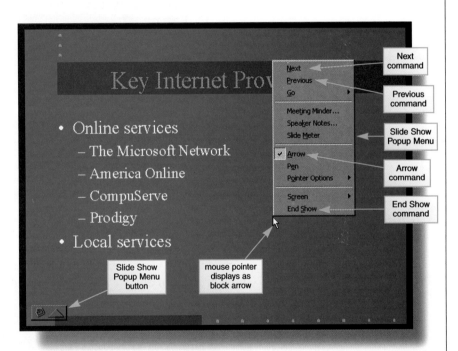

FIGURE 1-49

Some presenters prefer to right-click to move backward through a slide show. Because PowerPoint allows you to display the Slide Show View Popup Menu by clicking the Slide Show View Popup Menu button, you can turn off the option setting that displays the Popup menu when you right-click. To turn off the Popup menu on right mouse click option on the Tools menu, click Options, click the View tab to display the View sheet, click Popup menu on right mouse click to remove the check, and then click the OK button. After turning off the Popup menu on right mouse click option setting, you can right-click to move backward, one slide at a time, in slide show view.

Using the Popup Menu to End a Slide Show

The **End Show command** on the Popup Menu exits slide show view and returns to the view you were in when you clicked the Slide Show button. Perform the following step to end slide show view.

Steps To Use the Popup Menu to End a Slide Show

1 **Click End Show on the Popup Menu.**

PowerPoint exits slide show view and displays the slide last displayed in slide show view, which in this instance, is Slide 4 (Figure 1-50).

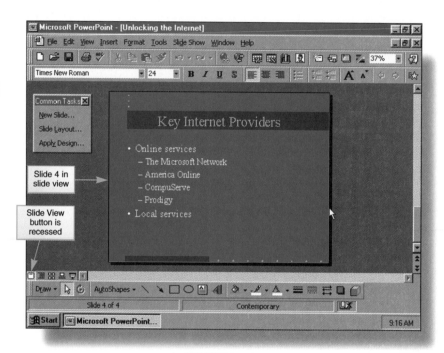

FIGURE 1-50

OtherWays

1. Click last slide in presentation to return to slide at which you began slide show view
2. Press ESC to display slide last viewed in slide show view

Slide show view is excellent for rehearsing a presentation. You can start slide show view from any view: slide view, outline view, slide sorter view, or notes page view.

Quitting PowerPoint

The Unlocking the Internet presentation now is complete. When you quit PowerPoint, PowerPoint prompts you to save any changes made to the presentation since the last save, closes all PowerPoint windows, and then quits PowerPoint. Closing PowerPoint returns control to the desktop. Perform the following steps to quit PowerPoint.

More *About*
Quitting
PowerPoint

If you notice your computer system is performing more slowly than normal, close all unnecessary applications. This releases memory held by those open applications and should improve your system's performance.

Steps **To Quit PowerPoint**

1 **Point to the Close button on the title bar (Figure 1-51).**

2 **Click the Close button.**

PowerPoint closes and the Windows 95 desktop displays. If you made changes to the presentation since your last save, a Microsoft PowerPoint dialog box displays the question, Do you wish to save the changes you made to Unlocking the Internet?. Click the Yes button to save the changes to the presentation before closing PowerPoint. Click the No button to quit PowerPoint without saving the changes. Click the Cancel button to terminate the Close command and return to the presentation.

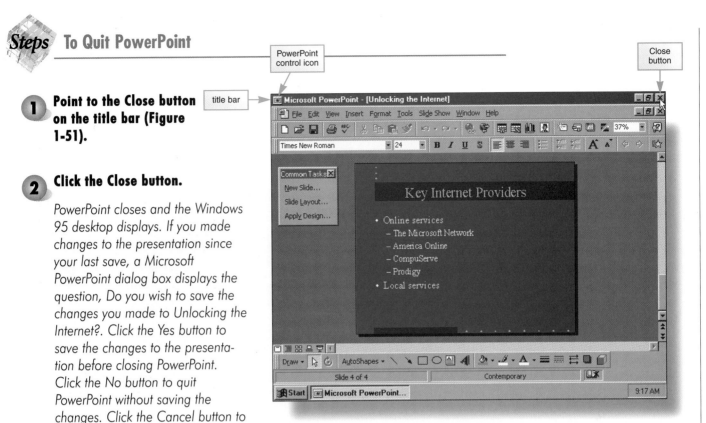

FIGURE 1-51

Opening a Presentation

Earlier, you saved the presentation on a floppy disk using the file name, Unlocking the Internet.ppt. Once you create and save a presentation, you may need to retrieve it from the floppy disk to make changes. For example, you may want to replace the design template or modify some text. Recall that a presentation is a PowerPoint document. Use the **Open Office Document command** to open an existing presentation.

Opening an Existing Presentation

Ensure that the floppy disk used to save Unlocking the Internet.ppt is in drive A. Then perform the steps on the next page to open the Unlocking the Internet presentation using the Open Office Document command on the Start menu.

Other**Ways**

1. On title bar double-click PowerPoint control icon; or on title bar, click PowerPoint control icon, click Close
2. On File menu click Exit
3. Press CTRL+Q or press ALT+F4

More *About*
Opening
Presentations

PowerPoint allows you to open more than one presentation at a time. To display another open presentation, click Window on the menu bar and then click the desired presentation.

Steps To Open an Existing Presentation

1 **Click the Start button on the taskbar and point to Open Office Document.**

The Windows 95 Start menu displays (Figure 1-52). Open Office Document is highlighted.

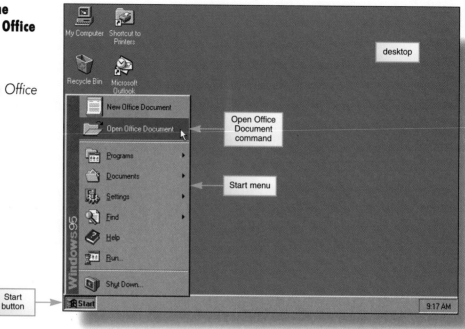

FIGURE 1-52

2 **Click Open Office Document. When the Open Office Document dialog box displays, click the Look in box arrow and then click 3½ Floppy (A:) (see Figures 1-23 and 1-24 on page PP 1.24 to review this process).**

The Open Office Document dialog box displays (Figure 1-53). A list of existing files on drive A displays because your floppy disk is in drive A. Notice that Office Files displays in the Files of type list box. The file, Unlocking the Internet, is high-lighted. Your list of existing files may be different depending on the files saved on your floppy disk.

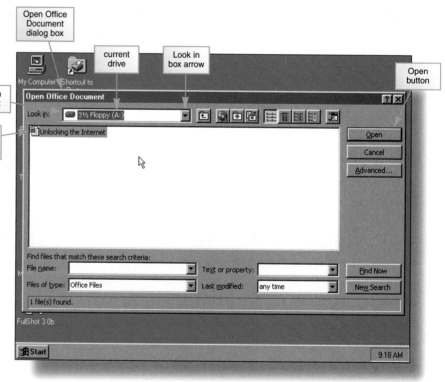

FIGURE 1-53

3 **Double-click Unlocking the Internet.**

PowerPoint starts and opens Unlocking the Internet.ppt from drive A into main memory and displays the first slide on the screen (Figure 1-54). The presentation displays in slide view because PowerPoint opens presentations in the same view in which they were saved.

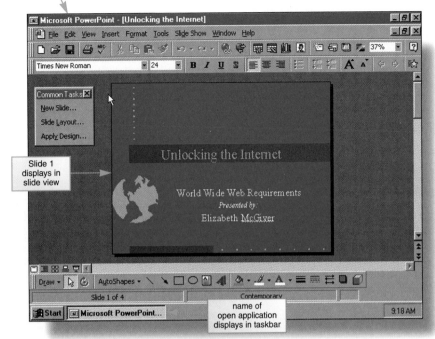

FIGURE 1-54

Other Ways

1. Click Open a Document button on Microsoft Office Shortcut Bar, click folder or drive name in Look in list, double-click document name

2. On Start menu click Documents, click document name

When an application is open, its name displays on a button on the taskbar. The **active application** is the one displaying in the foreground of the desktop. That application's corresponding button on the taskbar displays recessed.

When more than one application is open, you can switch between applications by clicking the button labeled with the name of the application to which you want to switch.

Checking a Presentation for Visual Clarity, Consistency, and Style

After you create a presentation, you should proofread it for errors. Typical errors include spelling errors, punctuation errors, and design errors. PowerPoint has a tool, called **Style Checker**, that helps you identify errors in your presentation. When you start Style Checker, the Style Checker dialog box displays three check boxes: Spelling, Visual clarity, and Case and end punctuation. A check mark in a check box instructs Style Checker to look for that particular type of inconsistency. For example, a check mark in the Spelling check box causes Style Checker to check the presentation for spelling errors. Table 1-3 identifies the purpose of each check box in the Style Checker dialog box.

Table 1-3	
CHECK BOX	**PURPOSE**
Spelling	Checks the presentation for spelling errors.
Visual clarity	Checks the presentation for appropriate font usage and for legibility of slide titles and body text.
Case and end punctuation	Checks the presentation for consistency of capitalization and end punctuation in slide titles and body text.

PowerPoint checks your presentation for spelling errors using a standard dictionary contained in the Microsoft Office group. This dictionary is shared with the other Microsoft Office applications such as Word and Excel. A **custom dictionary** is available if you want to add special words such as proper names, cities, and acronyms. When checking a presentation for spelling errors, PowerPoint opens the standard dictionary and the custom dictionary file, if one exists. When a word displays in the Spelling dialog box, you perform one of the actions listed in Table 1-4.

Table 1-4

ACTION	DESCRIPTION
Manually correct the word	Retype the word with the proper spelling in the Change to box and then click Change. PowerPoint continues checking the rest of the presentation.
Ignore the word	Click Ignore when the word is spelled correctly but not found in the dictionaries. PowerPoint continues checking the rest of the presentation.
Ignore all occurrences of the word	Click Ignore All when the word is spelled correctly but not found in the dictionaries. PowerPoint ignores all occurrences of the word and continues checking the rest of the presentation.
Select a different spelling	Click the proper spelling of the word from the list in the Suggestions box. Click Change. PowerPoint corrects the word and continues checking the rest of the presentation.
Change all occurrences of the misspelling to a different spelling	Click the proper spelling of the word from the list in the Suggestions box. Click Change All. PowerPoint changes all occurrences of the misspelled word and continues checking the rest of the presentation.
Add a word to the custom dictionary	Click Add. PowerPoint opens the custom dictionary, adds the word, and continues checking the rest of the presentation.
View alternative spellings	Click Suggest. PowerPoint lists suggested spellings. Click the correct word from the Suggestions box or type the proper spelling. Then click Change. PowerPoint continues checking the rest of the presentation.
Add spelling error to AutoCorrect list	Click AutoCorrect. PowerPoint adds the spelling error and its correction to the AutoCorrect list. Any future misspelling of the word is corrected automatically as you type.

The standard dictionary contains commonly used English words. It does not, however, contain proper names, abbreviations, technical terms, poetic contractions, or antiquated terms. PowerPoint treats words not found in the dictionaries as misspellings.

Starting Style Checker

Start Style Checker by clicking the Style Checker command on the Tools menu. Perform the following steps to start Style Checker.

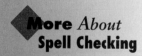

More *About* Spell Checking

To check a presentation for spelling errors without also checking the presentation for style errors, click the Spelling button on the Standard toolbar.

Steps To Start Style Checker

1 **Click Tools on the menu bar, and then point to Style Checker (Figure 1-55).**

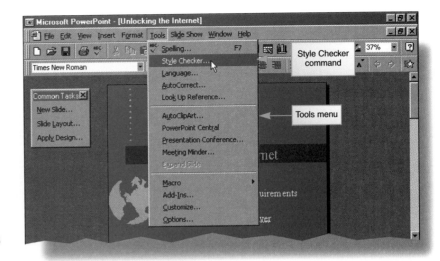

FIGURE 1-55

2 **Click Style Checker. When the Style Checker dialog box displays, click Case and end punctuation, and then point to the Start button.**

The Style Checker dialog box displays (Figure 1-56). Check marks display in the check box in front of Spelling and in front of Visual clarity. The check box in front of Case and end punctuation is blank to prevent Style Checker from automatically changing the capitalization of the company names in this presentation.

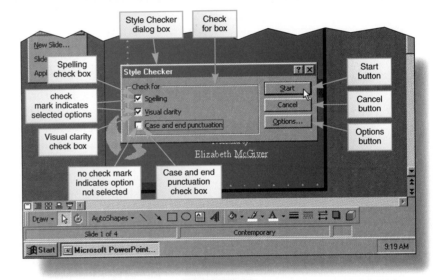

FIGURE 1-56

3 **Click the Start button.**

PowerPoint launches the spelling feature and displays the Spelling dialog box (Figure 1-57). McGiver displays in the Not in dictionary box. Depending on your custom dictionary, McGiver may not be recognized as a misspelled word.

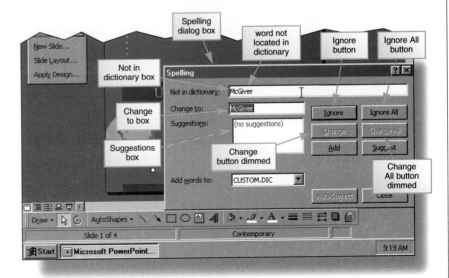

FIGURE 1-57

Click the Ignore button.

PowerPoint ignores the word
McGiver and continues searching
for additional misspelled words.
PowerPoint may stop on additional
words depending on your typing
accuracy. When PowerPoint has
checked all slides for misspellings, it
checks for style errors and displays
the Microsoft PowerPoint dialog box
(Figure 1-58).

 Click the OK button.

PowerPoint closes Style Checker
and returns to the current slide,
Slide 1, or to the slide where a
misspelled word occurred.

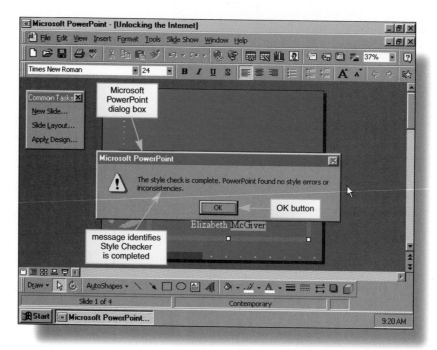

FIGURE 1-58

Other Ways

1. Press ALT+T, press Y, press C,
   press S; when finished,
   press ENTER

Table 1-5	
OPTION	*SETTING*
CASE	
Slide title style	**Title Case**
Body text style	**Sentence case.**
END PUNCTUATION	
Slide title periods	**Remove**
Body text periods	**Remove**
VISUAL CLARITY	
Number of fonts should not exceed	3
Title text size should be at least	36
Body text size should be at least	24
Number of bullets should not exceed	6
Number of lines per title should not exceed	2
Number of lines per bullet should not exceed	2
Check for title and placeholder text off slide	**Checked on**

If Style Checker identifies an error, it displays a message indicating the slide
number on which the error occurred. If you have punctuation errors, you can
click one of the buttons to ignore or change them. If you want to stop Style
Checker and return to the current slide, click the Cancel button.

If Style Checker identifies visual clarity inconsistencies, it
displays them in the Style Checker Summary dialog box. Write
the slide number and the message on a sheet of paper. Then
display the slide and correct the inconsistencies.

The Style Checker dialog box contains an **Options button**
(Figure 1-56 on the previous page), which when clicked, displays
the Style Checker Options dialog box. The **Style Checker Options
dialog box** has two tabbed sheets: Case and End Punctuation, and
Visual Clarity. Each tabbed sheet has several options that can be
changed to suit your design specifications. Table 1-5 identifies
each option available in Style Checker and each default setting.

Correcting Errors

After creating a presentation and running Style Checker, you may
find that you must make changes. Changes may be required
because a slide contains an error, the scope of the presentation
shifts, or Style Checker found a style inconsistency. This section
explains the types of errors that commonly occur when creating a
presentation.

Types of Corrections Made to Presentations

There usually are three types of corrections to text in a presentation: additions, deletions, and replacements.

▶ **Additions** — are necessary when you omit text from a slide and need to add it later. You may need to insert text in the form of a sentence, word, or single character. For example, you may want to add the rest of the presenter's first name on your title slide.

▶ **Deletions** — are required when text on a slide is incorrect or is no longer relevant to the presentation. For example, Style Checker identified too many bullets on Slide 3. Therefore, you may want to remove one of the bulleted paragraphs.

▶ **Replacements** — are needed when you want to revise the text in your presentation. For example, you may want to substitute the word, their, for the word, there.

Editing text in PowerPoint is basically the same as editing text in a word processing package. The following sections illustrate the most common changes made to text in a presentation.

Deleting Text

There are three methods for deleting text. One is to use the BACKSPACE key to remove text just typed. The second is to position the insertion point to the left of the text you wish to delete and then press the DELETE key. The third method is to drag through the text you wish to delete and press the DELETE key. (Use the third method when deleting large sections of text.)

Replacing Text into an Existing Slide

When you need to correct a word or phrase, you can replace the text by selecting the text to be replaced and then typing the new text. As soon as you press any key on the keyboard, the highlighted text is deleted and the new text displays.

PowerPoint inserts text to the left of the insertion point. The text to the right of the insertion point moves to the right (and shifts downward if necessary) to accommodate the added text.

Changing Line Spacing

The bulleted lists on Slides 2, 3, and 4 look crowded; yet, there is ample blank space that could be used to separate the paragraphs. You can adjust the spacing on each slide, but when several slides need to be changed, you should change the slide master. Each PowerPoint component (slides, title slides, audience handouts, and speaker's notes) has a **master**, which controls its appearance. Slides have two masters, title master and slide master. The **title master** controls the appearance of the title slide. The **slide master** controls the appearance of the other slides in your presentation.

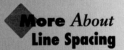

More *About* **Line Spacing**

Resist the temptation to regard blank space on a slide as wasted space. Blank space, added for directing the attention of the audience to specific text or graphics, is called white space. White space is a powerful design tool. Used effectively, white space improves audience attention.

Each design template has a specially designed slide master; so if you select a design template, but want to change one of its components, you can override that component by changing the slide master. Any change to the slide master results in changing every slide in the presentation, except the title slide. For example, if you change the line spacing to .5 inches before each paragraph on the slide master, each slide (except the title slide) changes line spacing after each paragraph to .5 inches. The slide master components more frequently changed are listed in Table 1-6.

Additionally, each view has its own master. You can access the master by holding down the SHIFT key while clicking the appropriate view button. For example, holding down the SHIFT key and clicking the Slide View button displays the slide master. To exit a master, click the view button to which you wish to return. To return to slide view, for example, click the Slide View button.

Table 1-6

COMPONENT	DESCRIPTION
Font	Defines the appearance and shape of letters, numbers, and special characters.
Font size	Specifies the size of the characters on the screen. Character size is gauged by a measurement system called points. A single point is about 1/72 of an inch in height. Thus, a character with a point size of eighteen is about 18/72 of an inch in height.
Text font style	Text font styles include plain, italic, bold, shadowed, and underlined. Text may have more than one font style at a time.
Text position	Position of text in a paragraph is left-aligned, right-aligned, centered, or justified. Justified text is proportionally spaced across the object.
Color scheme	A coordinated set of eight colors designed to complement each other. Color schemes consist of background color, line and text color, shadow color, title text color, object fill color, and three different accent colors.
Background items	Any object other than the title object or text object. Typical items include borders and graphics — such as a company logo, page number, date, and time.
Slide number	Inserts the special symbol used to print the slide number.
Date	Inserts the special symbol used to print the date the presentation was printed.
Time	Inserts the special symbol used to print the time the presentation was printed.

Displaying the Slide Master

Before you can change line spacing on the slide master, you first must display it. Perform the following steps to display the slide master.

 Steps To Display the Slide Master

1 **Drag the scroll box to display Slide 2. Press and hold down the SHIFT key and then point to the Slide View button.**

When you hold down the SHIFT key, the ScreenTip displays Slide Master (Figure 1-59).

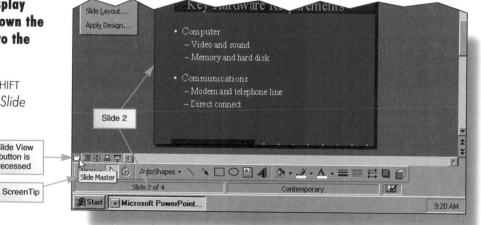

FIGURE 1-59

2 While holding down the SHIFT key, click the Slide Master button. Then release the SHIFT key.

The slide master displays (Figure 1-60). The Master toolbar displays. The Common Tasks toolbar changes to display a Master Layout button, which replaces the Slide Layout button in slide master.

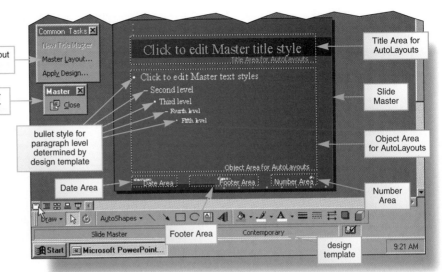

FIGURE 1-60

Changing Line Spacing on the Slide Master

Change line spacing by clicking the Line Spacing command on the Format menu. When you click the **Line Spacing command**, the Line Spacing dialog box displays. The Line Spacing dialog box contains three boxes, Line spacing, Before paragraph, and After paragraph, which allow you to adjust line spacing within a paragraph, before a paragraph, and after a paragraph, respectively.

In this project, you change the number in the amount of space box to increase the amount of space that displays before every paragraph, except the first paragraph, on every slide. For example, increasing the amount of space box to 0.75 lines increases the amount of space that displays before each paragraph. The first paragraph on every slide, however, does not change because of its position in the text placeholder. Perform the following steps to change the line spacing.

 Steps To Change Line Spacing on the Slide Master

1 Click the bulleted paragraph labeled, Click to edit Master text styles.

The insertion point displays at the point you clicked (Figure 1-61). The text object area is selected.

FIGURE 1-61

2 **Click Format on the menu bar and then point to Line Spacing (Figure 1-62).**

FIGURE 1-62

3 **Click Line Spacing.**

PowerPoint displays the Line Spacing dialog box (Figure 1-63). The default Before paragraph line spacing is set at 0.2 Lines.

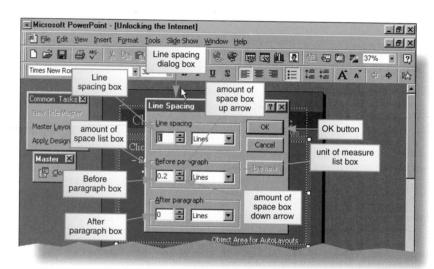

FIGURE 1-63

4 **Double-click the amount of space list box in the Before paragraph box. Then type** .75 **in the box.**

The amount of space list box displays 0.75 (Figure 1-64). The Preview button is available after a change is made in the Line Spacing dialog box.

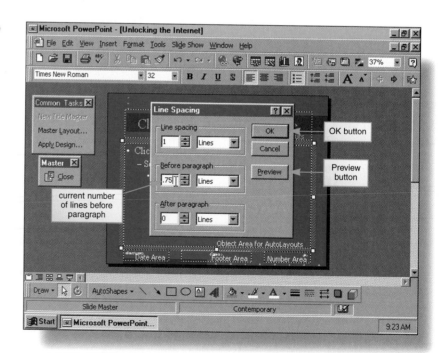

FIGURE 1-64

5 **Click the OK button.**

The slide master text placeholder displays the new line spacing (Figure 1-65). Depending on the video drivers installed, the spacing on your screen may appear slightly different than this figure.

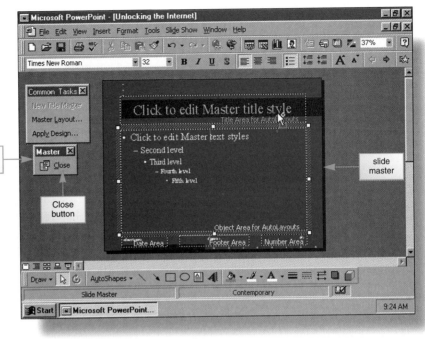

FIGURE 1-65

6 **Click the Close button on the Master toolbar to return to slide view.**

Slide 2 displays with the Before paragraph line spacing set to 0.75 lines (Figure 1-66).

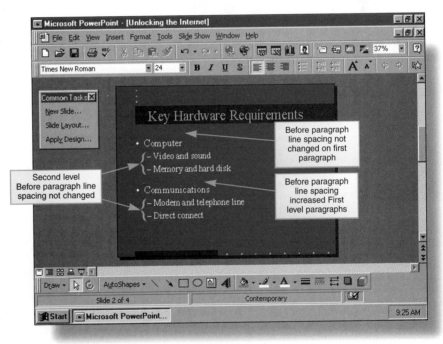

FIGURE 1-66

To display line spacing changes without making them permanent, click the Preview button in the Line Spacing dialog box. If you want to close the Line Spacing dialog box without applying the changes, click the Cancel button.

More *About*
Masters

To modify the attributes of the slide master or title master, display the master, and then use the buttons on the Formatting toolbar. To override a master attribute, change the attribute directly on a slide. For example, to italicize text not italicized on a master, select the text object and click the Italic button.

Before paragraph line spacing is controlled by establishing the number of units before a paragraph. Units are either lines or points; lines are the default unit. Points may be selected by clicking the down arrow next to the Before paragraph box (Figure 1-64 on page PP 1.48). Recall from page PP 1.20 that a single point is about 1/72 of an inch in height.

The Line spacing box and the After paragraph box each contain an amount of space list box and a unit of measure list box. To change the amount of space displaying between paragraphs, click the amount of space box up arrow or down arrow in the Line spacing box. To change the amount of space displaying after a paragraph, click the amount of space box up arrow or down arrow in the After paragraph box. To change the unit of measure from Lines to Points in either the Line spacing box or the After paragraph box, click the down arrow next to the unit of measure list box and then click Points.

The placeholder at the top of the slide master (Figure 1-65 on the previous page) is used to edit the Master title style. The large placeholder under the Master title placeholder is used to edit the Master text styles. Here you make changes to the various bullet levels. Changes can be made to line spacing, bullet font, text and line color, alignment, and text shadow. It is also the object area for AutoLayouts.

Displaying a Presentation in Black and White

This project explains how to print a presentation for the purpose of making transparencies. The **Black and White View button** allows you to display the presentation in black and white before you print. Table 1-7 identifies how PowerPoint objects display in black and white.

Table 1-7	
OBJECT	APPEARANCE IN BLACK AND WHITE VIEW
Text	Black
Text shadows	Hidden
Embossing	Hidden
Fills	Grayscale
Frame	Black
Pattern fills	Grayscale
Lines	Black
Object shadows	Grayscale
Bitmaps	Grayscale
Slide backgrounds	White

Perform the following steps to display the presentation in black and white.

Steps To Display a Presentation in Black and White

1 Point to the Black and White View button on the Standard toolbar (Figure 1-67).

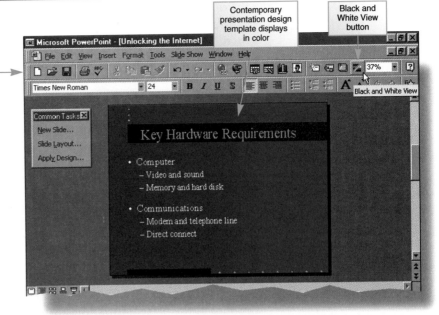

FIGURE 1-67

2 Click the Black and White View button.

The presentation displays in black and white (Figure 1-68). The Black and White View button is recessed. The Color box displays a miniature of the current slide in color.

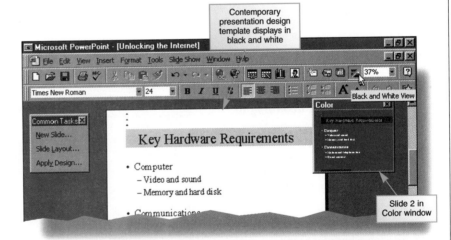

FIGURE 1-68

To return to the color view of the presentation, click the Black and White View button again.

Printing a Presentation

After you create a presentation, you often want to print it. A printed version of the presentation is called a **hard copy**, or **printout**. The first printing of the presentation is called a **rough draft**. The rough draft allows you to proofread the presentation to check for errors and readability. After correcting errors, you print the final copy of your presentation.

Saving Before Printing

Prior to printing your presentation, you should save your work in the event you experience difficulties with the printer. You occasionally may encounter system problems that can be resolved only by restarting the computer. In such an instance, you will need to reopen your presentation. As a precaution, always save your presentation before you print. Perform the following steps to save the presentation before printing.

TO SAVE A PRESENTATION BEFORE PRINTING

Step 1: Verify that your floppy disk is in drive A.
Step 2: Click the Save button on the Standard toolbar.

All changes made after your last save now are saved on a floppy disk.

Printing the Presentation

After saving the presentation, you are ready to print. Because you are in slide view, clicking the **Print button** on the Standard toolbar causes PowerPoint to print all slides in the presentation. Additionally, because you currently are viewing the presentation in black and white, the slides print in black and white, even if you have a color printer. Perform the following steps to print the presentation slides.

Steps **To Print a Presentation**

1 **Ready the printer according to the printer instructions. Then, click the Print button on the Standard toolbar.**

The mouse pointer momentarily changes to an hourglass. An animated printer icon displays on the status bar identifying which slide is being prepared (Figure 1-69). The printer icon, on the status bar, indicates there is a print job processing. After several moments, the presentation begins printing on the printer. When the presentation is finished printing, the printer icon on the status bar no longer displays.

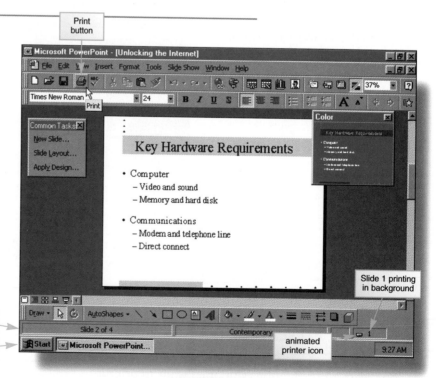

FIGURE 1-69

2 **When the printer stops, retrieve the printouts of the slides.**

The presentation, Unlocking the Internet, prints on four pages (Figure 1-70).

:
:
:

Key Internet Providers

• Online services
  – The Microsoft Network
  ...ine

...s

. . . .

(d)

:
:
:

Key Software Requirements

• Microsoft Corporation
  – Internet Explorer

• Netscape Communications Corporation
  – Netscape Navigator

• SPRY, CompuServe Internet
  – Internet In A Box

. . . . .

(c)

:
:
:

Key Hardware Requirements

• Computer
  – Video and sound

...hard disk

...ons

...telephone line

...ct

. . . .

(b)

Unlocking the Internet

World Wide Web Requirements
Presented by:
Elizabeth McGiver

. . . .

(a)

FIGURE 1-70

OtherWays

1. On File menu click Print
2. Press CTRL+P or press CTRL+SHIFT+F12

More *About*
Online Help

Prior versions of PowerPoint used to come with a thick manual. Most beginners had difficulty determining where to find the information they wanted. The extensive online Help shipped with PowerPoint replaces the manual and simplifies the process of finding helpful information.

Double-clicking the animated printer icon on the status bar cancels the printing process.

Making a Transparency

This project requires you to make overhead transparencies. You make transparencies using one of several devices. One device is a printer attached to your computer, such as an ink-jet printer or a laser printer. Transparencies produced on a printer may be in black and white or color, depending on the printer. Another device is a photocopier. A third device is a thermal copier. A thermal copier transfers a carbonaceous substance, like toner from a photocopier, from a paper master to an acetate film. Because each of the three devices requires a special transparency film, check the user's manual for the film requirement of your specific device, or ask your instructor.

PowerPoint Help

You can get assistance anytime while you are working in PowerPoint using online Help. When used effectively, online Help can increase your productivity and reduce the amount of time you spend learning how to use PowerPoint. Table 1-8 summarizes the five categories of online Help.

The following sections show examples of each of the online Help described in Table 1-8.

Table 1-8

HELP CATEGORY	SUMMARY	HOW TO START
Office Assistant	Answers your questions, offers tips, and provides help for a variety of PowerPoint features.	Click the Office Assistant button on the Standard toolbar.
Contents sheet	Groups Help topics by general categories. Use when you know, in general, what you want.	Click the Help menu, click Contents and Index, then click the Contents tab.
Index sheet	Alphabetical list of Help topics. Similar to an index in a book. Use when you know exactly what you want. For example, "adding footers."	Click the Help menu, click Contents and Index, then click the Index tab.
Find sheet	Searches the index for all phrases that include the term you specify. For example, "bullets."	Click the Help menu, click Contents and Index, then click the Find tab.
Question mark button	Provides an explanation of objects on the screen.	In a dialog box, click the Question mark button and then click a dialog box object. Click What's This? on the Help menu, then click an item on the screen.

Using Office Assistant

The **Office Assistant** answers your questions and suggests more efficient ways to complete a task. With the Office Assistant active, for example, you can type a word or phrase in a text box and the Office Assistant will provide immediate help on the subject. Also, as you create a presentation, the Office Assistant accumulates tips that suggest more efficient ways to complete the task you did in building a presentation, such as applying a design template, decreasing font size, printing, and saving. This tip feature is part of the IntelliSense technology that is built into PowerPoint, which understands what you are trying to do and suggests better ways to do it.

The following steps show how to use the Office Assistant to obtain information on footers in a presentation.

Steps To Obtain Help Using the Office Assistant

1 **If the Office Assistant is not on the screen, click the Office Assistant button on the Standard toolbar. If the Office Assistant is on the screen, click it. Type** footer **in the What would you like to do? box and then point to the Search button (Figure 1-71).**

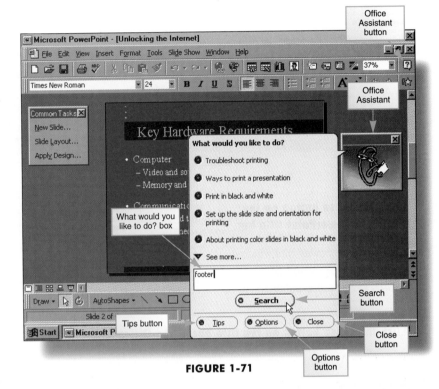

FIGURE 1-71

2 **Click the Search button and then point to the topic, Add or change the date, time, slide number, or footer text.**

The Office Assistant displays a list of topics relating to the word footer (Figure 1-72).

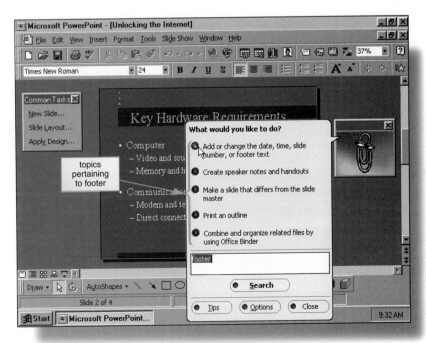

FIGURE 1-72

3 **Click Add or change the date, time, slide number, or footer text.**

The Office Assistant displays the **Microsoft PowerPoint window** *with Add or change the date, time, slide number, or footer text (Figure 1-73). The topics at the bottom of the window, preceded by a button, are* **links** *to topics related to Add or change the date, time, slide number, or footer text. When you move the mouse pointer over a link, it changes to a hand.*

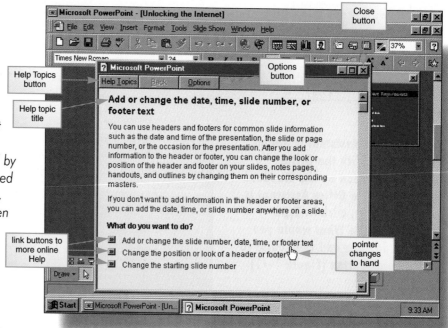

FIGURE 1-73

4 **Click the Close button on the Microsoft PowerPoint title bar.**

The Microsoft PowerPoint window no longer displays and control returns to the presentation.

5 **Click the Close button on the title bar of the Office Assistant window.**

The Office Assistant closes and no longer displays on the screen.

You can use the Office Assistant to search for online Help on any topic concerning PowerPoint. Once Help displays, you can read it, print it using the **Options button** or shortcut menu, or click one of the links to display a related topic. If you display a related topic, click the **Back button** to return to the previous screen. You also can click the **Help Topics button** to obtain Help through the Contents, Index, and Find tabs.

DISPLAYING TIPS If you click the Office Assistant Tips button (Figure 1-71 on the previous page), PowerPoint displays tips on how to work more efficiently. As you create and edit a presentation, PowerPoint adds tips to the list. Once a tip displays, you can move backward or forward through the list of accumulated tips (Figure 1-74). When you finish reading the tips, click the Close button to return to the presentation.

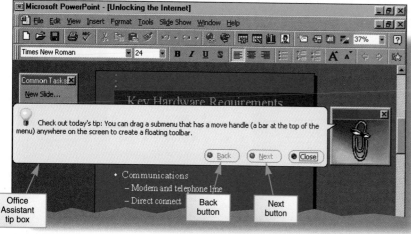

FIGURE 1-74

OFFICE ASSISTANT SHORTCUT MENU When you right-click the Office Assistant window, a shortcut menu displays (Figure 1-75). It allows you to change the look and feel of Office Assistant. You can hide the Office Assistant, display tips, change the way it works, change the icon representing the Office Assistant, or view the animation of the Office Assistant. These options also are available through the Options button that displays when you click the Office Assistant. Click Hide Assistant on the shortcut menu to remove the Office Assistant from the screen.

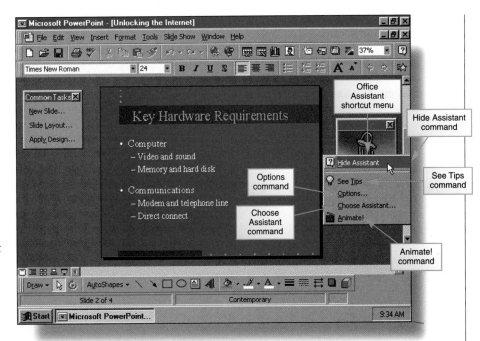

FIGURE 1-75

Using the Contents Sheet to Obtain Help

The **Contents sheet** in the Help Topics dialog box assists you in finding online Help about a specific subject. Use the Contents sheet in the same manner you use the table of contents in a book. Perform the following steps to use the Contents sheet to obtain Help on using the slide master to change the appearance of your presentation.

 To Obtain Help Using the Contents Sheet

1 Click Help on the menu bar and then point to Contents and Index.

The Help menu displays (Figure 1-76).

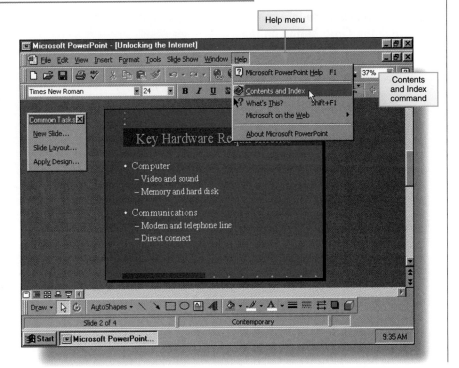

FIGURE 1-76

2 **Click Contents and Index. Click the Contents tab. Double-click Creating the Look of Your Presentation. Point to Ways to give my presentation a consistent look.**

The Help Topics: Microsoft PowerPoint dialog box displays (Figure 1-77). The Contents sheet displays with the Creating the Look of Your Presentation book open. An icon precedes each entry in the list. A book icon indicates there are subtopics. A question mark icon indicates information will display when the title is double-clicked.

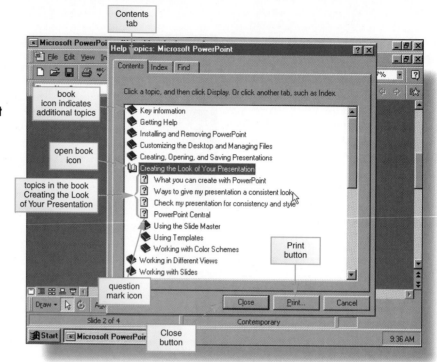

FIGURE 1-77

3 **Double-click the topic labeled Ways to give my presentation a consistent look.**

A Microsoft PowerPoint window displays information about Ways to give my presentation a consistent look (Figure 1-78).

4 **After reading the information, click the Close button on the Microsoft PowerPoint window.**

The Microsoft PowerPoint window closes.

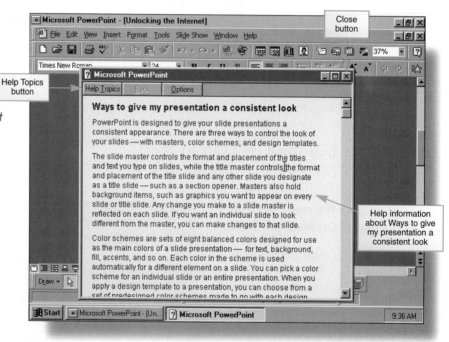

FIGURE 1-78

OtherWays

1. Press F1

As an alternative to double-clicking the topic name in the list, you can click it and then use the buttons at the bottom of the Microsoft PowerPoint window to display information about a topic or print information about a topic (Figure 1-78). Additionally, you can print information about a topic by pointing to the Help window, right-clicking, and then clicking Print Topic; or by clicking the Options button at the top of the Microsoft PowerPoint window, and then clicking Print Topic (Figure 1-78). To close or cancel the Microsoft PowerPoint window, click the Close button to return to PowerPoint, or click the Help Topics button to return to the Contents sheet.

Using the Index Sheet to Obtain Help

Use the Index sheet in the Help Topics: Microsoft PowerPoint dialog box when you know the term about which you are seeking Help. You can locate the term you are looking for by typing part or all of the word, or you can scroll through the alphabetical list and click the term. You use the Index sheet in the same manner you use an index at the back of a book.

Many of the online Help windows display jump boxes, which, when clicked, display a ScreenTip with information about that topic. For example, if you want to know how to create an interactive presentation to send on the World Wide Web, PowerPoint displays a window that contains three jump boxes. When you click one of the jump boxes, such as Start an interactive action, PowerPoint displays a ScreenTip that contains a detailed explanation of how to start an interactive action. Perform the following steps to obtain information about creating an interactive presentation that then could be sent on the World Wide Web.

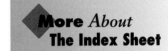

More *About*
The Index Sheet

The Index sheet works the same as the index in a book. However, instead of looking through a list of printed topics, you simply type the name of the topic. PowerPoint then searches for your information.

Steps **To Obtain Help Using the Index Sheet**

① **Click Help on the menu bar. Click Contents and Index. If necessary, click the Index tab to display the Index sheet.**

The Help Topics: Microsoft PowerPoint dialog box displays.

② **Type** Web **in the box labeled 1. Click Web in the box labeled 2.**

The term Web is highlighted in the box labeled 2 (Figure 1-79).

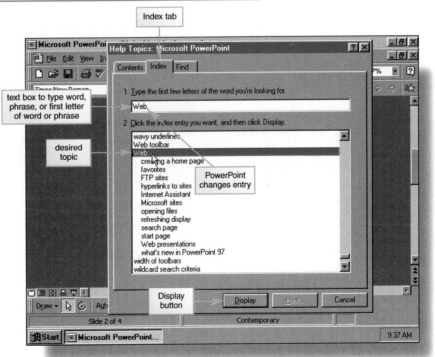

FIGURE 1-79

3 **Click the Display button.**

PowerPoint displays the Topics Found window (Figure 1-80). The About creating interactive presentation topic is highlighted.

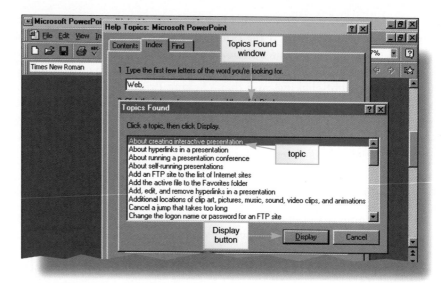

FIGURE 1-80

4 **Click the Display button in the Topics Found window. When the About creating interactive presentations Microsoft PowerPoint window displays, click Start an interactive action.**

PowerPoint displays a Microsoft PowerPoint window containing jump boxes that point to specific items on a slide. When you click the jump box labeled Start an interactive action, a ScreenTip displays containing information about starting an interactive action (Figure 1-81).

5 **After reading the information, click anywhere outside the ScreenTip to close it. Click the Close button in the upper-right corner of the Microsoft PowerPoint window to close it.**

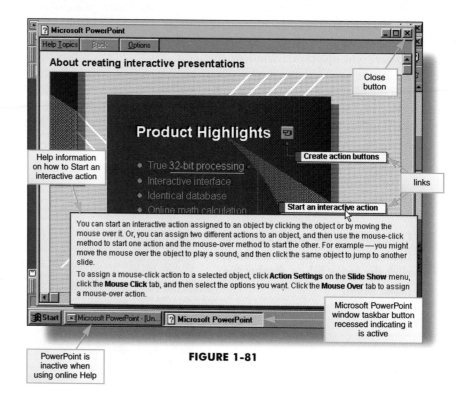

FIGURE 1-81

OtherWays

1. Press F1

Using the Find Sheet to Obtain Help

The Find sheet in the Help Topics: Microsoft PowerPoint dialog box locates the word or phrase you want. Use the Find sheet when you wish to find information about a term or a word contained within a phrase. The Find sheet displays a list of all topics pertaining to the specified term or phrase. You then can narrow your search by selecting words or phrases from the list. Perform the following steps to obtain information about changing the distance between bullets and text.

Steps To Obtain Help Using the Find Sheet

1 **Click the Help button on the menu bar, and then click Contents and Index.**

The Help Topics: Microsoft PowerPoint dialog box displays.

2 **If necessary, click the Find tab. Type** bulleted **in the box labeled 1. Then point to the topic in the box labeled 3, Add, change, or remove a bullet.**

Seven of the eight topics found that contain the word, bulleted, display in the box labeled 3. The topic, Add, change, or remove a bullet, is highlighted (Figure 1-82).

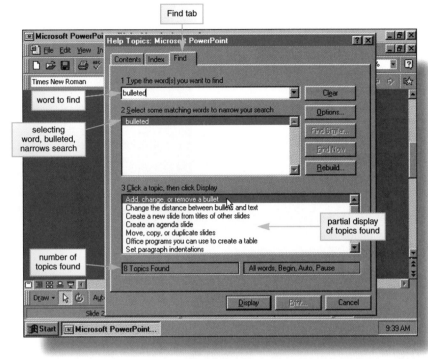

FIGURE 1-82

3 **Double-click the topic, Add, change, or remove a bullet, in the box labeled 3 on the Find sheet. When the Microsoft PowerPoint window displays the information about Add, change, or remove a bullet, point to the green underlined words, slide master, located at the middle of the Microsoft PowerPoint window.**

A Microsoft PowerPoint window displays information about changing the distance between bullets and text. The green underlined text at the middle of the Microsoft PowerPoint window identifies a jump to additional information (Figure 1-83).

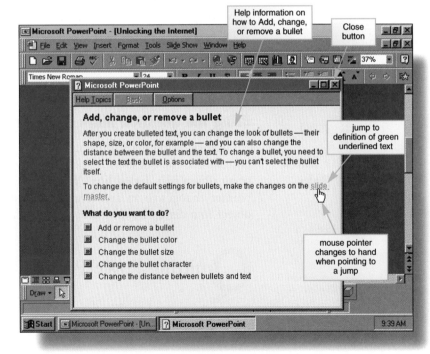

FIGURE 1-83

4 Click slide master.

Clicking the green underlined text displays a ScreenTip (Figure 1-84). The ScreenTip provides additional information about the word (often a definition).

5 Read the ScreenTip, and then click the Close button on the Microsoft PowerPoint window two times.

Clicking the Close button once closes the ScreenTip. Clicking the Close button a second time closes the Microsoft PowerPoint window and returns to PowerPoint.

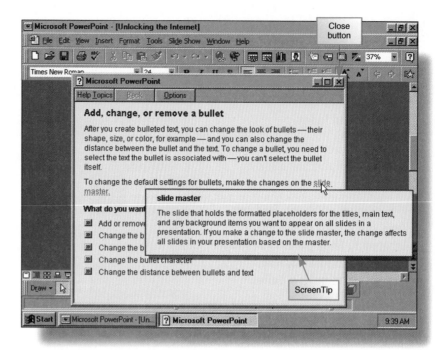

FIGURE 1-84

You may specify more than one word in the box labeled 1 (Figure 1-82 on the previous page) if you separate the words with a space. If you specify words in uppercase letters, then only uppercase occurrences of the words (within the Help Topics) are found. If you specify words in lowercase letters, however, both uppercase and lowercase occurrences of the words are found. Search options can be changed by clicking the Options button on the Find sheet.

Using the Question Mark Button to Obtain Online Help

The question mark button (Figure 1-82) is similar to the Office Assistant button. Use the question mark button when you are not certain about the purpose of an object in a dialog box. When you click the question mark button, the mouse pointer changes to an arrow with a question mark. Then, when you click an object in a dialog box, a ScreenTip displays.

Quitting PowerPoint

Project 1 is complete. The final task is to close the presentation and PowerPoint. Perform the following steps to quit PowerPoint.

TO QUIT POWERPOINT

Step 1: Click the Close button on the title bar.
Step 2: If prompted to save the presentation before closing PowerPoint, click the Yes button in the Microsoft PowerPoint dialog box.

More *About*
The Question Mark Button and Help Button

The Question Mark button in a dialog box and the Help button on the Standard toolbar display ScreenTips that provide a brief explanation of the object clicked when the pointer displays as an arrow with a question mark.

Project Summary

Project 1 introduced you to starting PowerPoint and creating a multi-level bulleted list presentation. You learned about PowerPoint design templates, objects, and attributes. This project illustrated how to create an interesting introduction to a presentation by changing the text font style to italic and decreasing font size on the title slide. Completing these tasks, you saved your presentation. Then, you created three multi-level bulleted list slides to explain the necessary requirements for connecting to the World Wide Web. Next, you learned how to view the presentation in slide show view. After which, you learned how to quit PowerPoint and how to open an existing presentation. Using Style Checker, you learned how to look for spelling errors and identify inconsistencies in design specifications. Using the slide master, you quickly adjusted the Before paragraph line spacing on every slide to make better use of white space. You learned how to display the presentation in black and white. Then, you learned how to print hard copies of your slides in order to make overhead transparencies. Finally, you learned how to use PowerPoint online Help.

What You Should Know

Having completed this project, you should be able to perform the following tasks:

▶ Add a New Slide Using the Bulleted List AutoLayout *(PP 1.26)*

▶ Add a New Slide with the Same AutoLayout *(PP 1.32)*

▶ Change Line Spacing on the Slide Master *(PP 1.47)*

▶ Change the Text Font Style to Italic *(PP 1.22)*

▶ Create Slide 3 *(PP 1.32)*

▶ Create Slide 4 *(PP 1.33)*

▶ Decrease Font Size *(PP 1.21)*

▶ Display a Presentation in Black and White *(PP 1.51)*

▶ Display the Slide Master *(PP 1.46)*

▶ Display the Slide Show View Popup Menu *(PP 1.37)*

▶ Enter a Slide Title *(PP 1.28)*

▶ Enter the Presentation Subtitle *(PP 1.19)*

▶ Enter the Presentation Title *(PP 1.18)*

▶ Manually Move Through Slides in a Slide Show *(PP 1.36)*

▶ Obtain Help Using the Contents Sheet *(PP 1.57)*

▶ Obtain Help Using the Find Sheet *(PP 1.61)*

▶ Obtain Help Using the Index Sheet *(PP 1.59)*

▶ Obtain Help Using the Office Assistant *(PP 1.55)*

▶ Open an Existing Presentation *(PP 1.40)*

▶ Print a Presentation *(PP 1.52)*

▶ Quit PowerPoint *(PP 1.39, 1.62)*

▶ Save a Presentation Before Printing *(PP 1.52)*

▶ Save a Presentation to a Floppy Disk *(PP 1.23)*

▶ Save a Presentation with the Same File Name *(PP 1.34)*

▶ Select a Text Placeholder *(PP 1.28)*

▶ Start a New Presentation *(PP 1.11)*

▶ Start Slide Show View *(PP 1.35)*

▶ Start Style Checker *(PP 1.43)*

▶ Type a Multi-level Bulleted List *(PP 1.29)*

▶ Type the Remaining Text for Slide 2 *(PP 1.31)*

▶ Use the Popup Menu to End a Slide Show *(PP 1.38)*

▶ Use the Vertical Scroll Bar to Move to Another Slide *(PP 1.34)*

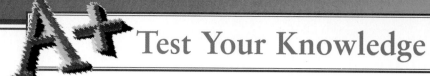

Test Your Knowledge

1 True/False

Instructions: Circle T if the statement is true or F if the statement is false.

T F 1. PowerPoint presentations can be run on a World Wide Web page.

T F 2. A wizard is a tutorial approach for quickly and efficiently creating a presentation.

T F 3. A PowerPoint document is called a slide show.

T F 4. A slide is the basic unit of a PowerPoint presentation.

T F 5. The name of the current presentation displays on the status bar.

T F 6. Toolbars consist of buttons that access commonly used PowerPoint tools.

T F 7. In PowerPoint, the Formatting toolbar contains tools for changing attributes of drawing objects.

T F 8. Press and hold down the SHIFT key and click the New Slide button to add a new slide to a presentation with the same AutoLayout as the current slide.

T F 9. PowerPoint assumes that every slide has a title.

T F 10. The slide indicator shows only the slide number.

2 Multiple Choice

Instructions: Circle the correct response.

1. When the mouse pointer is pointing to a button, it has the shape of a(n) _____.
   a. hand   b. hourglass   c. I-beam   d. left-pointing block arrow

2. _____ displays your slides as an electronic presentation on the full screen of your computer's monitor, looking much like a slide projector display.
   a. Slide view   b. Outline view   c. Slide sorter view   d. Slide show view

3. _____ are the properties or characteristics of an object.
   a. Wizards   b. Color schemes   c. Attributes   d. Design templates

4. Before you italicize a paragraph, you first must _____.
   a. underscore the paragraph to be formatted
   b. position the mouse pointer beside the first character in the paragraph to be formatted
   c. highlight the paragraph to be formatted
   d. highlight the first word in the paragraph to be formatted

5. PowerPoint automatically appends the extension _____ to a file name when you save a presentation.
   a. .DOC   b. .PPT   c. .TXT   d. .XLS

6. When you exit PowerPoint, _____.
   a. the presentation remains in memory
   b. the presentation is erased from the floppy disk
   c. control is returned to the desktop
   d. the presentation is saved automatically to a floppy disk

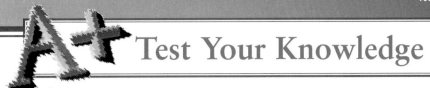

Test Your Knowledge

7. If you add objects to the slide master, they display on _____.
    a. every slide
    b. every slide except the title slide
    c. the slide master
    d. both b and c

8. Press the _____ key to remove characters to the right of the insertion point.
    a. BACKSPACE
    b. DELETE
    c. INSERT
    d. both a and b

9. To display online Help information that suggests more efficient ways to complete a task, use the
    _____.
    a. Office Assistant
    b. Contents sheet
    c. Find sheet
    d. Index sheet

10. To close a presentation and quit PowerPoint, click the Close button on the _____.
    a. menu bar
    b. title bar
    c. Standard toolbar
    d. Common Tasks toolbar

3 Understanding the PowerPoint Window

Instructions: In Figure 1-85, arrows point to the major components of the PowerPoint window. Identify the various parts of the window in the spaces provided.

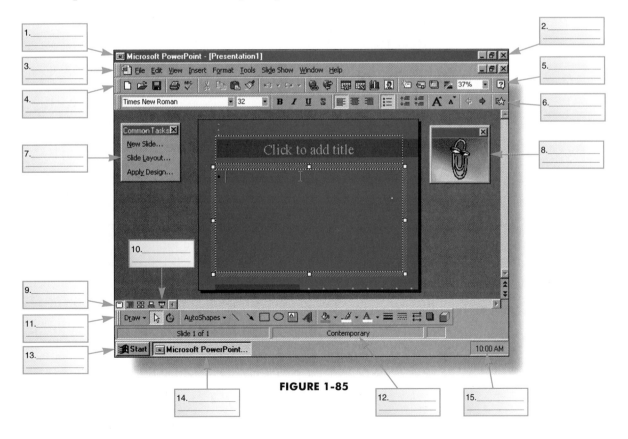

FIGURE 1-85

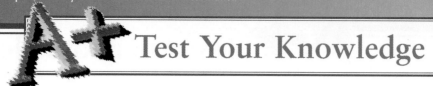

4 Understanding the PowerPoint Toolbars

Instructions: In Figure 1-86, arrows point to several buttons on the Standard and Formatting toolbars. Identify the buttons in the spaces provided.

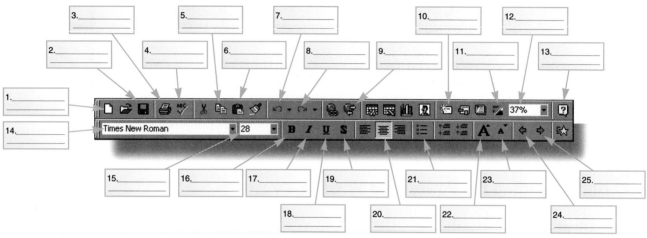

FIGURE 1-86

1 Reviewing Project Activities

Instructions: Perform the following tasks using a computer.

1. Start PowerPoint.
2. If the Office Assistant is on your screen, click it to display its balloon. If the Office Assistant is not on your screen, then click the Office Assistant button on the Standard toolbar.
3. Click Options in the Office Assistant balloon. Click the Gallery tab. Click the Next button to view each of the Office Assistants. Click the Back button to go to the Clippit Assistant and then click the Options tab. Review the different options for the Office Assistant. Close the Office Assistant dialog box.
4. Click the Office Assistant and type slide master in the What would you like to do? text box. Click the Search button.

Use Help

5. Click the link, Make a slide that differs from the slide master.

6. Read the information. Right-click the Help window to display a shortcut menu. Click Print Topic to print the information. Click the underlined green words, color scheme. Print the definition that displays by right-clicking the ScreenTip and then clicking Print Topic. Submit the printouts to your instructor.

7. Click the Close button in the Help window.

8. Click Help on the menu bar. Click Contents and Index. Click the Contents tab. Double-click Working with Slides. Double-click Make a new slide. Read and print the information. Click the Help Topics button to return the Contents sheet. Double-click Move, copy, or duplicate slides. Read and print the information. Click, read, and print the Help information for each of the three jumps at the bottom of the Help window. Submit the printouts to your instructor.

2 Expanding on the Basics

Instructions: Use PowerPoint online Help to better understand the topics listed below. Answer the questions on your own paper or submit the printed Help topic to your instructor.

1. Click the Office Assistant or the Office Assistant button on the Standard toolbar to display the Office Assistant balloon. Search for the topic, spelling. Click the link, Check spelling. When the Help window displays, answer the following questions by clicking the links. Close the Help window.
   a. How do you check spelling as you type? b. How do you check spelling at anytime? c. How do you temporarily hide spelling errors?

2. Click Contents and Index on the Help menu. Click the Index tab. Type line spacing in the top text box labeled 1. Use the Index sheet to display and print the answers to the following questions.
   a. How do you change the After paragraph line spacing? b. How do you change the amount of space within a paragraph?

3. Use the Find sheet in the Help Topics: Microsoft PowerPoint dialog box to display and then print information about keyboard shortcuts. Answer the following questions.
   a. Which key, or combination of keys, do you press to copy selected text? b. Which key, or combination of keys, do you press to move to the end of a line of text? c. Which key, or combination of keys, do you press to display a shortcut menu relevant to the selected object? d. Which key, or combination of keys, do you press to update the files listed in the Open or Save As dialog box? e. Which keys do you press to advance to the next slide during the running of a slide show?

4. Use the Find sheet in the Help Topics: Microsoft PowerPoint dialog box to display and then print the information about slide masters.
   a. How do you make a slide that is different from the slide master? b. What happens to a slide when its master changes? c. How do you make a slide with a different title or text format than the master?

Apply Your Knowledge

CAUTION: To ensure you have enough disk space to save your files, it is recommended that you create a copy of the Data Disk that accompanies this book. Then, delete folders from the copy of the Data Disk that are not needed for the application you are working on. Do the following: (1) Insert the Data Disk in drive A; (2) start Explorer; (3) right-click the 3½ Floppy (A:) folder in the All Folders side of the window; (4) click Copy Disk; (5) click Start and OK as required; (6) insert a floppy disk when requested; (7) delete all folders on the floppy disk you created except the PowerPoint folder; (8) remove the floppy disk from drive A and label it PowerPoint Data Disk.

1 Formatting a Multi-level Slide

Instructions: Start PowerPoint. Open the presentation Apply-1 from the PowerPoint folder on the Data Disk that accompanies this book. This slide lists features of a proposed insurance option. Perform the following tasks to change the slide so it looks like the one in Figure 1-87.

1. Press and hold down the SHIFT key, and then click the Slide View button to display the slide master. Click the paragraph, Click to edit Master text styles. Click Format on the menu bar and then click Line Spacing. Increase the Before paragraph line spacing to 0.6 lines. Click the OK button. Then click the Close button on the Master toolbar to return to slide view.
2. Select the title text. Click the Bold button on the Formatting toolbar.
3. Select the No paperwork paragraph. Click the Underline button on the Formatting toolbar.
4. Click the paragraph, Annual check-up, and then click the Demote button on the Formatting toolbar.
5. Click the paragraph, No out-of-pocket expense, and then click the Demote button on the Formatting toolbar.
6. Click File on the menu bar and then click Save As. Type `Preferred Provider Option` in the File name list box. If drive A is not already displaying in the Save in list box, click the Save in box arrow, and click drive A. Then, click the Save button.
7. Click the Black and White View button on the Standard toolbar to display the presentation in black and white.
8. Click the Print button on the Standard toolbar.
9. Click the Close button on the menu bar to exit PowerPoint.
10. Submit the printout to your instructor.

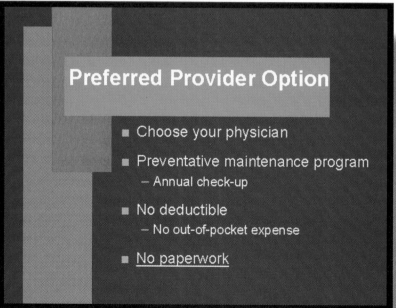

FIGURE 1-87

1 Designing and Creating a Presentation

Problem: You are the Director for the Career Development Center at Hammond College. You have been asked to speak as a guest lecturer in an undergraduate communications class. The course instructor suggests you discuss strategies for finding the right job. To prepare for the class, you create the presentation shown in Figure 1-88.

Instructions: Perform the following tasks.

1. Create a new presentation using the high voltage design template.
2. Using the typewritten notes illustrated in Figure 1-89, create the title slide shown in Figure 1-88 using your name in place of Leland Zoladz. Decrease the font size of the paragraph, Presented by:, to 24. Decrease the font size of the paragraphs, Director, Career Development, and Hammond College, to 28.
3. Using the typewritten notes in Figure 1-89, create the three bulleted list slides shown in Figure 1-88.
4. Click the Spelling button on the Standard toolbar. Correct any errors.
5. Save the presentation on a floppy disk using the file name, Finding the Right Job.
6. Display the presentation in black and white.
7. Print the black and white presentation. Quit PowerPoint.

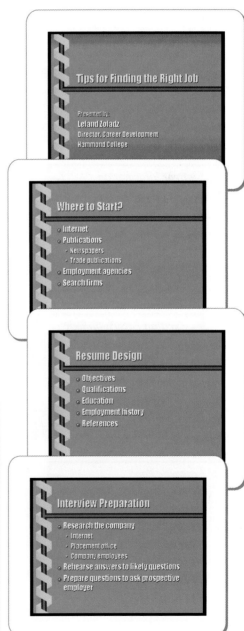

FIGURE 1-88

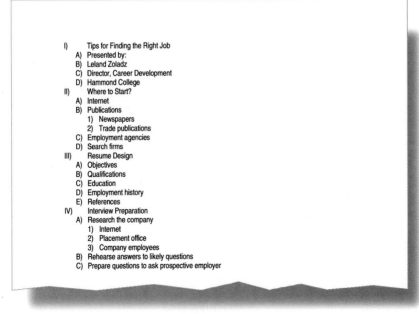

FIGURE 1-89

In the Lab

2 Modifying Masters to Override Design Template Attributes

Problem: You are the Festival Coordinator for the Annual Lakeview Autumn Festival. To promote this year's festival, you design a brief presentation. You select a design template but decide to modify it. *Hint*: Use Help to solve this problem.

Instructions: Perform the following tasks.

1. Create a new presentation using the Angles design template.
2. Using the notes in Figure 1-90, create the title slide shown in Figure 1-91, using your name in place of Tammaye Obuz. Decrease the font size of the paragraphs, Presented by:, and Festival Coordinator, to 24. Increase the font size of your name to 36.
3. Using the notes in Figure 1-90, create the three multi-level bulleted list slides shown in Figure 1-91.
4. Display the slide master. Click the paragraph, Click to edit Master title style. Click the Bold button, the Shadow button, and the Italic button on the Formatting toolbar.
5. Click the paragraph, Click to edit Master text styles. On the Format menu, click Line Spacing, and then increase the Before paragraph line spacing to 0.3 lines. Click the paragraph, Second level. On the Format menu, click Line Spacing, and then increase the After paragraph spacing to 0.15 lines.

FIGURE 1-91

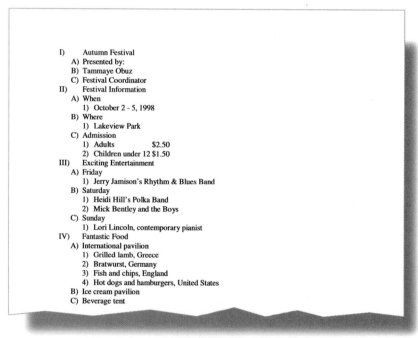

FIGURE 1-90

6. Drag the scroll box to display the title master. Click the paragraph, Click to edit Master title style. If necessary, click the Bold, Shadow, and Italic buttons on the Formatting toolbar.

7. Return to slide view. On the View menu, click Header and Footer. If necessary, click the Slide tab. Add the date (so it updates automatically), a slide number, and your name to the footer. Display the footer on all slides.

8. Drag the scroll box to display Slide 1. Click the Slide Show button to start slide show view. Then click to display each slide.

9. Save the presentation on a floppy disk using the file name, Autumn Festival. Display and print the presentation in black and white. Quit PowerPoint.

3 Creating a Training Presentation

Problem: You are the marketing manager for International Diamond and Jewels, a large jewelry wholesaler. Several people on your sales staff have requested presentation training. You decide to create a short presentation to emphasize the importance of rehearsing a presentation. *Hint:* Use Help to solve this problem.

Instructions: Using the list in Figure 1-92, design and create a presentation. The presentation must include a title slide and three bulleted list slides. Perform the following tasks.

1. Create a new presentation using the Whirlpool design template.

2. Create a title slide titled, Perfect Presentations. Include a subtitle, using your name in place of Roberto Cruz. Decrease the font size for paragraphs Presented by:, Marketing Manager, and International Diamond and Jewels to 24. Increase the font size of your name to 36. Italicize the paragraph, Presented by:.

3. Using Figure 1-92, create three multi-level bulleted list slides. On Slide 2, use numbers instead of bullets for the three Practice paragraphs.

4. Adjust Before paragraph and After paragraph line spacing to utilize the available white space.

5. Insert a footer on every slide except the title slide that includes the current date, your name, and the slide number.

6. View the presentation in slide show view to look for errors. Correct any errors.

7. Check the presentation for spelling errors.

8. Save the presentation to a floppy disk with the file name, Perfect Presentations. Print the presentation slides in black and white. Quit PowerPoint.

```
I)    Perfect Presentations
   A) Presented by:
   B) Roberto Cruz
   C) Marketing Manager
   D) International Diamond and Jewels
II)   Practice Makes Perfect
   A) Secrets for a successful presentation
            1. Practice
            2. Practice
            3. Practice
III)  Why Practice?
   A) Increase confidence
   B) Develop rhythm
      1) Pause for emphasis
   C) Improve articulation
      1) Vary pitch and inflection
   D) Identify problems
IV)   How To Practice
   A) Speak out loud
      1) Make a recording
      2) Look into a mirror
      3) Find a live audience
   B) Visit presentation site
      1) Inspect equipment
      2) Check environment
```

FIGURE 1-92

Cases and Places

200 MHz

The difficulty of these case studies varies: ▶ are the least difficult; ▶▶ are more difficult; and ▶▶▶ are the most difficult.

1 ▶ Maria Hernandez, coordinator for the Lincoln Elementary Fun Fair, has contacted Fun Fair Specialties to assist the school with this year's fun fair. Before finalizing plans, Ms. Hernandez needs approval from the parent-teacher association. She has prepared the notes in Figure 1-93 for a presentation that will be delivered at the next parent-teacher association meeting.

Ms. Hernandez has asked you to prepare a title slide and three additional slides that can be used on an overhead projector. Use the concepts and techniques introduced in this project to create the presentation.

> **Lincoln Elementary Fun Fair**
> Saturday, February 7, 1998
> 10:00 A.M. to 3:00 P.M.
>
> **Parent-Teacher Booths**
> • Bake sale
> • Clown face painting
> • Jelly bean contest
>   • Winner gets container of jelly beans
> • Raffle ticket sales
>   • Donated prizes
>
> **Fun Fair Specialties Booths**
> • Dunk the principal
>   • Teacher volunteers welcome
> • Fishing pond
> • Balloon animals
>
> **Fun Fair Goals**
> • Repair audio-visual equipment
> • Purchase five tumbling mats
> • Install telephone line for Internet access in library

FIGURE 1-93

2 ▶ Jackie Jacowski, a food technology instructor from Technology Tech High School, is delivering a presentation on how to make dinner in minutes. She has written out her recipe for baked pasta (Figure 1-94).

With this recipe, Mrs. Jacowski has asked you to prepare four slides that can be used on an overhead projector. She wants the title slide to introduce her and the recipe. Use the concepts and techniques introduced in this project to create the presentation.

> **Baked Pasta**
>
> **Preparation**
> • Cook ground meat in large skillet.
>   • Drain fat from meat.
> • Add cooked pasta, spaghetti sauce, and parmesan cheese.
>   • Stir mixture.
>   • Pour into 13 x 9 inch baking dish.
> • Sprinkle shredded mozzarella cheese over pasta mixture.
>
> **Ingredients**
> • 1 pound ground beef or ground turkey
> • 5 cups cooked pasta
> • 1 30 oz. jar of spaghetti sauce
> • ½ cup grated parmesan cheese
> • 1 8 oz. package shredded mozzarella cheese
>
> **Baking and Serving**
> • Put baking dish with pasta into oven.
> • Bake 20 minutes at 375° Fahrenheit.
>   • Remove from oven.
> • Serving Suggestion:
>   • Serve with tossed green salad and garlic bread.

FIGURE 1-94

Cases and Places

3 ▶▶ Party-Time is a store that specializes in parties. The consultants are trained to help clients in every aspect of party planning. Clients can stop by the store and pick up party favors; streamers; noise makers; and decorations for walls and windows. Party-Time also carries a complete line of paper and plastic items, such as plates, napkins, table-clothes, dinnerware, and serving utensils. Many clients consult Party-Time to help plan bridal showers, graduation receptions, and business meetings. The store is located in Logan's Mall, 621 West Logan Street, Thunder Bay, Ontario. For more information call 555-9979. Using the techniques presented in this project, prepare a title slide and three bulleted list slides to be used on an overhead projector.

4 ▶▶ After many months of hard work, you and your partner, Lydia Statton, finally open Paws Inn, an animal boarding resort. Your research found most pet owners want a home-like atmosphere for their furry friends. Pet owners want reassurance that their pet is treated with respect and cared for by compassionate, attentive individuals. All staff members are associate members of the Hillside Humane Society and have pets of their own. Paws Inn offers five living room suites, complete with pet couches, and five bedroom suites with day beds. For pets needing an outdoors atmosphere, cabins are available. Cabins include an enclosed exercise run, accessible through a door-gate. Additional Paws Inn facilities include an exercise area, a wading pool, and a grooming salon. A dietitian is available for special meal requirements. Veterinarian services are available 24 hours a day. Reservations are recommended. Paws Inn is located at 2144 Deer Creek Road, Hillside, New Hampshire. The telephone number is 555-PAWS. Using the concepts and techniques presented in this project, prepare a title slide and three bulleted list slides to be used on an overhead projector.

5 ▶▶▶ Many companies allow employees to work at home rather than commute to a central office. Some companies require the employee to present a work-at-home proposal to management before authorizing the work-at-home request. Research home-based offices using the Internet or a local library. Determine what is needed for the typical home-based office as well as the working environment. Using the concepts and techniques presented in this project, prepare a presentation to report your findings. Create a title slide and at least three additional slides that can be used with an overhead projector.

6 ▶▶▶ Credit card debt looms over millions of people everyday. Occasionally, people run out of money before all their financial obligations can be met. Financial planners write articles and often speak on television and radio about how to best handle this type of financial crisis. Contact a financial planner or a financial institution. Interview a financial consultant about what to do in a financial emergency and how to prevent a financial crisis in the future. Using the concepts and techniques presented in this project, prepare a presentation to report your findings. Create a title slide and at least three additional slides that can be used with an overhead projector

Cases and Places

200 MHz

7 ▶▶▶ Proper nutrition and exercise are necessary for a healthy body. But nutritionists often disagree on the daily requirements. Research the Internet for recommended daily portions for fruits, vegetables, grains, meats, dairy, and fats. Use more than one source to determine the daily requirements. Then, using the concepts and techniques presented in this project, prepare a presentation to report your findings. Create a title slide and at least three additional slides that can be used with an overhead projector.

Microsoft PowerPoint 97

Using Outline View and Clip Art to Create an Electronic Slide Show

Objectives:

You will have mastered the material in this project when you can:

▶ Create a presentation in outline view
▶ Describe the PowerPoint window in outline view
▶ Insert a blank line in a bulleted list
▶ Change the slide layout
▶ Move text between objects
▶ Insert clip art from Microsoft Clip Gallery 3.0
▶ Change clip art size
▶ Add a header and footer to outline pages
▶ Add slide transition effects
▶ Animate text
▶ Animate clip art
▶ Print a presentation outline
▶ Change printing options

Unsinkable:
Molly Brown and You!

On the clear, cold night of April 14, 1912, in the North Atlantic, the Titanic — called *unsinkable* by her builders — struck an iceberg, ripping a mortal 300-foot hole in her hull, well below the water line. In just under three hours, the remorseless sea claimed fifteen hundred lives as the Titanic plunged into the dark abyss. Only a few remember the names of those ill-fated passengers, but most know of heroic Molly Brown, immortalized on Broadway and in the subsequent movie, who refused to go down with the ship. This disaster also gave rise to the saying, "Tip of the iceberg," which now is universally understood as a metaphor describing any endeavor where the majority of the work or information is hidden. Figuratively, this term has found expression in other ways, such as that attributed to Vince Lombardi, "Spectacular success is preceded by unspectacular preparation."

Unsinkable

This certainly is true for all major entertainment events. To present a three-hour opera, an opera company books the stars a year or more in advance, creates sets that take hundreds of hours to build, and conducts hours of rehearsals. A circus that opens with a grand parade, then proceeds with two hours of performances in three rings takes thousands of hours in costume preparation, rigging, and animal training, not to mention lifetimes of dedication from acrobats and aerialists. A two-hour movie may have been in studio development for two years, plus another six months or more in shooting.

Plays, concerts, televised sporting events, Academy Awards, political conventions, and many other productions share a common thread: for even a chance at success, careful preparation is mandatory. In today's academic, scientific, and business arenas, the requirements are equally exacting. Often, the same people who demand top-notch operas, concerts, football games, and movies are decision-makers who sit for presentations in Melbourne, London, Toronto, and Atlanta. They are accustomed to the best and expect the best in business presentations, too.

Until recently, preparing a slide presentation was not a job for the faint-hearted. Writing and artwork were separate tasks, usually performed by specialists, then integrated by a graphics production company — at great expense. Changes were slow to make and costly. Relatively short presentations required days, even weeks of preparation.

Microsoft's PowerPoint 97 has changed all this by removing the mechanical impediments to producing slide shows, letting you concentrate on the creative content. With Pick a Look and AutoContent Wizards, you can use ready-made formats and speedily produce outstanding presentations. Build effects, clip art, drawings, graphs, logos, and a wide range of background, color, and style selections allow you to spice your message to suit the most sophisticated tastes.

At your next presentation, aided by PowerPoint, you, too, can be like the Titanic's Molly Brown: unsinkable.

Microsoft
PowerPoint 97

Using Outline View and Clip Art to Create an Electronic Slide Show

Case Perspective

Voyager Travel Tours is a travel agency promoting two new vacation packages. They are focusing on college students who want a great spring break vacation at a terrific price. After contacting several schools to learn how to reach the student community, your boss, Mr. Suarez, is asked if he would like to set up a booth at a spring break vacation fair. He accepts the offer. The vacation fair, however, is the day after tomorrow. To allow Mr. Suarez to finalize his travel arrangements, he asks you to put together a short electronic presentation. The purpose of the presentation is to entice students to buy one of the two vacation packages.

Voyager Travel Tour's marketing department supplies you with an outline to use in creating the presentation. The outline contains promotional information about the two new vacation packages — the Stargazer and the Castaway. You decide to call them Break Away Bargains.

To persuade students to buy one of the Break Away Bargains, you choose a design template with tropical colors. Then, to make the presentation more exciting, you add pictures and apply animation effects.

Creating a Presentation from an Outline

At some time during either your academic or business life, you probably will make a presentation. Most academic presentations are informative — providing detailed information about some topic. Business presentations, however, are usually sales presentations, such as selling a proposal or a product to a client, convincing management to approve a new project, or persuading the board of directors to accept the new fiscal budget. As an alternative to creating your presentation in slide view, as you did in Project 1, PowerPoint provides an outlining feature to help you organize your thoughts. When the outline is complete, it becomes the foundation for your presentation.

You create a presentation outline in outline view. When you create an outline, you type all of the text at one time, as if you were typing an outline on a sheet of paper. This is different than slide view where you type text as you create each individual slide. PowerPoint creates the presentation as you type the outline by evaluating the outline structure. Regardless of the view in which you build a presentation, PowerPoint automatically creates the views discussed in Project 1, such as slide view.

The first step in creating a presentation in outline view is to type a title for the outline. The **outline title** is the subject of the presentation and later becomes the presentation title slide. Then you type the remainder of the outline, indenting appropriately to establish a structure or hierarchy. Once the outline is complete, you make your presentation more persuasive by adding graphics. This project uses outlining to create the presentation and clip art graphics to visually support the text.

Project Two – Break Away Bargains

Project 2 uses PowerPoint to create the six-slide Break Away Bargains presentation shown in Figure 2-1. You create the presentation from the outline in Figure 2-2 on the next page.

Voyager Travel Tours

Announces

Break Away Bargains

FIGURE 2-1a

Two Dynamite Deals

➢ The Stargazer
  • All inclusive sand and sea adventure

➢ The Castaway
  • Self-designed sand and sun experience

FIGURE 2-1b

The Stargazer

➢ One incredible low price includes:
  • Round-trip airfare
  • Five-day cruise and two-day beach party
  • Sumptuous gourmet cuisine
  • Fabulous entertainment

FIGURE 2-1c

Time Is Running Out

➢ Contact Student Activities Office
  • Detter Hall, Room 225
  • Ext. 2772
➢ Call Voyager Travel Tours
  • 555-AWAY

FIGURE 2-1f

The Castaway

➢ Customized dream vacation
  • Luxurious oceanfront condominiums
    • Whirlpool
    • Daily maid service
  • Diverse dining opportunities
  • Countless recreational activities

FIGURE 2-1d

Both Deals Feature

➢ Balmy breezes   ➢ Neptune Beach
➢ Lucid azure pools   • Sunbathe, relax
➢ Starlit nights   ➢ Poseidon Bay
➢ Sunny days   • Sail, swim
➢ Tropical climate   ➢ Triton Reef
➢ White sand beaches • Scuba dive, snorkel

FIGURE 2-1e

More *About* **Electronic Slide Show**

Preparing an electronic slide show has several advantages. For example, you can add multimedia effects, such as sound and video, as well as animate text and graphics. You can add slide transitions and build text objects to control the pace of the presentation. Most important is the ability to make last minute changes.

More *About* **Presentation Design**

When designing a presentation, create your conclusion, or closing, first. Then design the rest of the presentation to reach the conclusion. This causes you to focus on the objectives of the presentation.

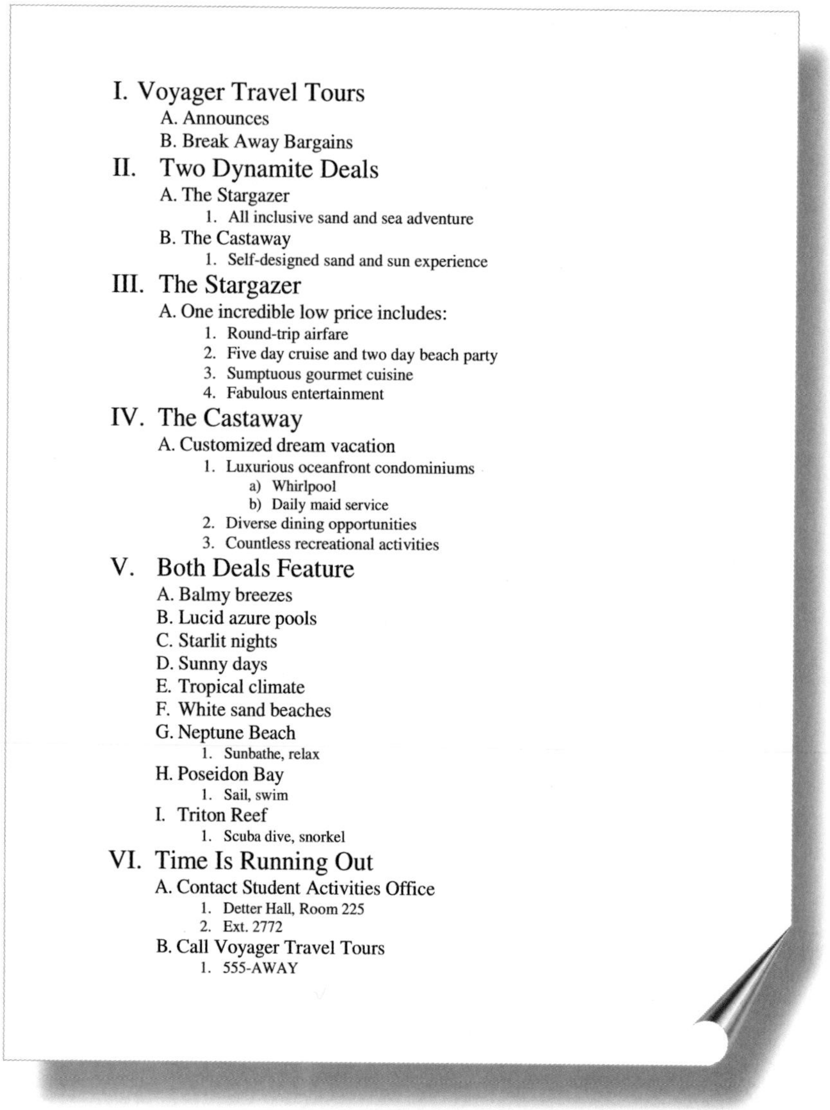

I. Voyager Travel Tours
  A. Announces
  B. Break Away Bargains
II. Two Dynamite Deals
  A. The Stargazer
    1. All inclusive sand and sea adventure
  B. The Castaway
    1. Self-designed sand and sun experience
III. The Stargazer
  A. One incredible low price includes:
    1. Round-trip airfare
    2. Five day cruise and two day beach party
    3. Sumptuous gourmet cuisine
    4. Fabulous entertainment
IV. The Castaway
  A. Customized dream vacation
    1. Luxurious oceanfront condominiums
      a) Whirlpool
      b) Daily maid service
    2. Diverse dining opportunities
    3. Countless recreational activities
V. Both Deals Feature
  A. Balmy breezes
  B. Lucid azure pools
  C. Starlit nights
  D. Sunny days
  E. Tropical climate
  F. White sand beaches
  G. Neptune Beach
    1. Sunbathe, relax
  H. Poseidon Bay
    1. Sail, swim
  I. Triton Reef
    1. Scuba dive, snorkel
VI. Time Is Running Out
  A. Contact Student Activities Office
    1. Detter Hall, Room 225
    2. Ext. 2772
  B. Call Voyager Travel Tours
    1. 555-AWAY

FIGURE 2-2

Presentation Preparation Steps

The preparation steps summarize how the slide presentation shown in Figure 2-1 on the previous page will be developed in Project 2. The following tasks will be completed in this project.

1. Start a new document and apply a design template.
2. Create a presentation in outline view.
3. Save the presentation.
4. Insert a blank line in the bulleted list on Slide 2.
5. Change the slide layout on Slide 5 to 2 Column Text and move text from the left column to the right column.
6. Change the slide layout on Slide 6 to Clip Art Text and insert a clip art picture into a clip art placeholder.
7. Insert clip art into Slide 3 and then move and reduce the size of the clip art picture.
8. Add header and footer text to the outline pages.
9. Add slide transition effects.

10. Add text and clip art animation effects.
11. Save the presentation.
12. Print the presentation outline and slides.
13. Quit PowerPoint.

The following pages contain a detailed explanation of these tasks.

Starting a New Presentation

Project 1 introduced you to starting a presentation document and applying a design template. The following steps summarize how to start a new presentation, apply a design template, and choose an AutoLayout. For a more detailed explanation, see pages PP 1.10 through PP 1.14 in Project 1. Perform the following steps to start a new presentation.

More *About*
Design Templates

You can build a presentation with the default design template and later select a different one. When you change design templates, PowerPoint automatically updates color scheme, font attributes, and location of slide objects on every slide in the presentation.

TO START A NEW PRESENTATION

Step 1: Click the Start button on the taskbar.
Step 2: Click New Office Document.
Step 3: Click the Presentation Designs tab. (Depending on your installation, the tab may display as Presentatio ... .) When the Presentation Designs sheet displays, scroll down the list of design templates until SERENE displays.
Step 4: Double-click SERENE.
Step 5: When the New Slide dialog box displays, click the OK button.
Step 6: If the Office Assistant displays, click the Office Assistant Close button.

PowerPoint displays the Title Slide AutoLayout and the Serene design template on Slide 1 in slide view (Figure 2-3).

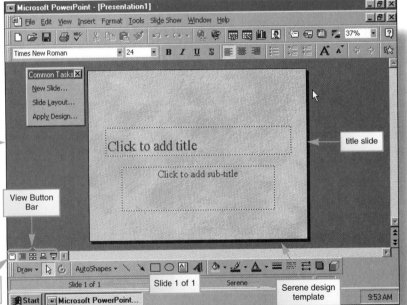

FIGURE 2-3

Using Outline View

Outline view provides a quick, easy way to create a presentation. Outlining allows you to organize your thoughts in a structured format. An outline uses indentation to establish a hierarchy, which denotes levels of importance to the main topic. An **outline** is a summary of thoughts, presented as headings and subheadings, often used as a preliminary draft when you create a presentation.

More *About*
Presentation Design

The key to a successful presentation is organization. Begin by jotting down your ideas. Next, look over your list and decide on three or four major topics. Then group the remaining ideas around the major topics selecting ideas that support the major topics and leaving out those that do not.

In outline view, title text displays at the left side of the window along with a slide icon and a slide number. Body text is indented under the title text. Graphic objects, such as pictures, graphs, or tables, do not display in outline view. When a slide contains a graphic object, the slide icon next to the slide title displays with a small graphic on it. The slide icon is blank when a slide does not contain graphics. The attributes for text in outline view are the same as in slide view except for color and paragraph style. PowerPoint displays the current slide in **Color View.** This allows you to see how the current slide will look in slide view and slide show view while you continue to work in outline view.

PowerPoint limits the number of heading levels to six. The first heading level is the slide title and is not indented. The remaining five heading levels are the same as the five indent levels in slide view. Recall from Project 1 that PowerPoint allows for five indent levels and that each indent level has an associated bullet.

The outline begins with a title on **heading level 1**. The title is the main topic of the slide. Text supporting the main topic begins on **heading level 2** and indents under heading level 1. **Heading level 3** indents under heading level 2 and contains text to support heading level 2. **Heading level 4, heading level 5,** and **heading level 6** indent under heading level 3, heading level 4, and heading level 5, respectively. Use heading levels 4, 5, and 6 as required. They generally are used for very detailed scientific and engineering presentations. Business and sales presentations usually focus on summary information and use heading level 1, heading level 2, and heading level 3.

PowerPoint initially displays in slide view when you start a new presentation. Change from slide view to outline view by clicking the Outline View button on the View Button Bar. Perform the following steps to change the view from slide view to outline view.

Steps **To Change the View to Outline View**

1 Point to the Outline View button located on the View Button Bar at the lower-left corner of the Microsoft PowerPoint window (Figure 2-4).

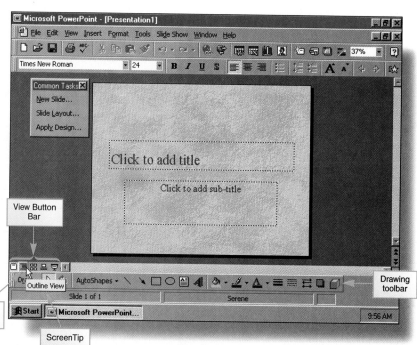

FIGURE 2-4

2 Click the Outline View button. If necessary, drag the Common Tasks toolbar to the right side of the Microsoft PowerPoint window as shown in Figure 2-5.

PowerPoint displays in outline view (Figure 2-5). PowerPoint displays the color view of Slide 1 in the Color View window.

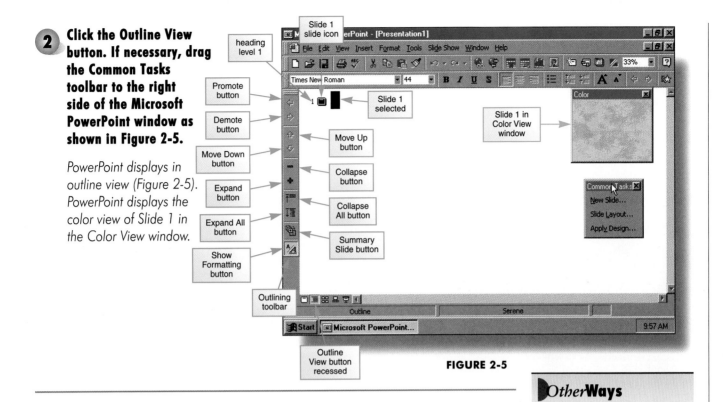

FIGURE 2-5

Other Ways

1. On View menu click Outline
2. Press ALT+V, press O

You can create and edit your presentation in outline view. Outline view also makes it easy to sequence slides and to relocate title text and body text from one slide to another. In addition to typing text to create a new presentation in outline view, PowerPoint can produce slides from an outline created in Microsoft Word or another word processor, if you save the outline as an RTF file or as a plain text file. The file extension **RTF** stands for **R**ich **T**ext **F**ormat.

The PowerPoint Window in Outline View

The PowerPoint window in outline view differs from the window in slide view because the Outlining toolbar displays but the Drawing toolbar does not (Figures 2-4 and 2-5). Table 2-1 on the next page describes the buttons on the Outlining toolbar.

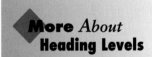

More *About*
Heading Levels

You may overwhelm the audience if a slide contains too much detail and requires more than six heading levels with which to explain the topic. Decompose large topics into two or more subtopics. Then, create a new slide for each group of subtopics.

Table 2-1

BUTTON	BUTTON NAME	DESCRIPTION
⇦	Promote	The Promote button moves the selected paragraph up one level in the outline hierarchy each time you click the button. Promoting a paragraph outdents or moves it to the left until your reach heading level 1.
⇨	Demote	The Demote button moves the selected paragraph down one level in the outline hierarchy each time you click the button. Demoting a paragraph indents or moves it to the right. You only can demote down to heading level 6.
⇧	Move Up	The Move Up button moves selected text above the preceding displayed paragraph while maintaining its hierarchical heading level and text style. The selected text changes position with the paragraph located above it.
⇩	Move Down	The Move Down button moves selected text below the following displayed paragraph while maintaining its hierarchical heading level and text style. The selected text changes position with the paragraph located below it.
▬	Collapse	The Collapse button hides all heading levels except the title of the selected slide. The button is useful when you want to collapse one slide in your outline. Hidden text displays as a gray line.
✚	Expand	The Expand button displays all heading levels and text for the selected slide. The button is useful when you want to expand one slide in your outline.
↑≣	Collapse All	The Collapse All button hides all heading levels to show only the slide titles of the entire presentation. This button is useful when you are looking at the organization of your presentation and do not care to see the details. Hidden text displays as gray lines below the title.
↓≣	Expand All	Expands all heading levels to display the slide title and text for all slides.
▣	Summary Slide	Creates a bulleted list slide from the titles of the slides selected in slide sorter view or outline view, and then inserts that slide in front of the first selected slide.
A≣	Show Formatting	The Show Formatting button is a toggle that displays or hides the text attributes. This is useful when you want to work with plain text as opposed to working with bolded, italicized, or underlined text. When printing your outline, plain text often speeds up the printing process.

Creating a Presentation in Outline View

Outline view enables you to view title and body text, add and delete slides, **drag and drop** slide text, drag and drop slides to change slide order, promote and demote text, save a presentation, print an outline, print slides, copy and paste slides or text to and from other presentations, apply a design template, and import an outline.

Developing a presentation in outline view is quick because you type the text for all slides on one screen. Once you type the outline, the presentation fundamentally is complete. If you choose, you then can go to slide view to enhance your presentation with graphics.

Creating a Title Slide in Outline View

Recall from Project 1 that the title slide introduces the presentation to the audience. In addition to introducing the presentation, Project 2 uses the title slide to capture the attention of the audience by using a design template with tropical colors. Remember that Voyager Travel Tours is trying to sell vacation packages. They want the audience to focus on getting away to a warm, tropical climate for an exciting vacation; consequently, they use an appropriate design template. Perform the following steps to create a title slide in outline view.

More *About*
**Creating
Presentations in
Outline View**

A method some presenters use to create a presentation is to create a list of the main topics for a presentation in outline view. Developing the list of main topics generates all presentation slides because each topic becomes the title for a slide. The presenter then completes each slide with relevant subtopics.

Steps **To Create a Title Slide in Outline View**

1 **Type** Voyager Travel Tours **and press the ENTER key.**

*Voyager Travel Tours displays as the title for Slide 1 and is called heading level 1. A slide icon displays to the left of each slide title. The font for heading level 1 is Times New Roman and the font size is 44 points. In outline view, the default Zoom setting is 33% of the actual slide size. Depending on the **resolution** of your computer monitor (the number of pixels displaying per unit of measurement, such as a centimeter or an inch), your Zoom setting may be different. Pressing the ENTER key moves the insertion point to the next line and maintains the same heading level. The insertion point, therefore, is in position for typing the title for Slide 2 (Figure 2-6).*

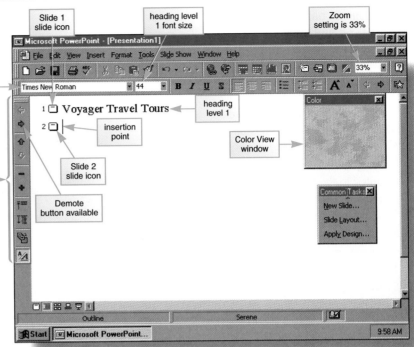

FIGURE 2-6

2 **Point to the Demote button on the Outlining toolbar.**

The Demote ScreenTip displays (Figure 2-7).

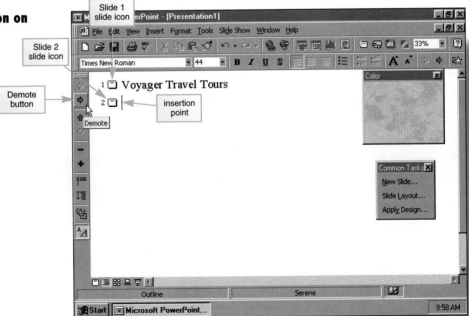

FIGURE 2-7

3 **Click the Demote button. Type** Announces **and press the ENTER key. Type** Break Away Bargains **and press the ENTER key.**

The Slide 2 slide icon does not display (Figure 2-8). The paragraphs, Announces and Break Away Bargains, are subtitles on the title slide (Slide 1) and demote to heading level 2. Heading level 2 is indented to the right under heading level 1. The heading level 2 font is Times New Roman and the heading level 2 font size is 32 points.

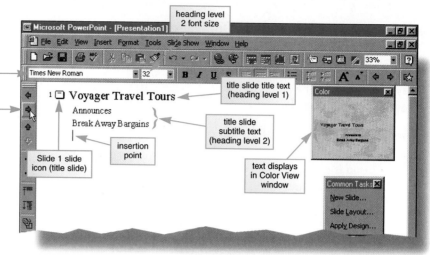

FIGURE 2-8

The title slide text for the Voyager Travel Tours presentation is complete. The next section explains how to add a slide in outline view.

Adding a Slide in Outline View

Recall from Project 1 that when you add a new slide, PowerPoint defaults to the Bulleted List AutoLayout layout. This is true in outline view as well. One way to add a new slide in outline view is to promote a paragraph to heading level 1 by clicking the Promote button until the insertion point or the paragraph displays at heading level 1. A slide icon displays when the insertion point or paragraph reaches heading level 1. Perform the following steps to add a slide in outline view.

Steps **To Add a Slide in Outline View**

1 **Point to the Promote button on the Outlining toolbar.**

The insertion point still is positioned at heading level 2 (Figure 2-9).

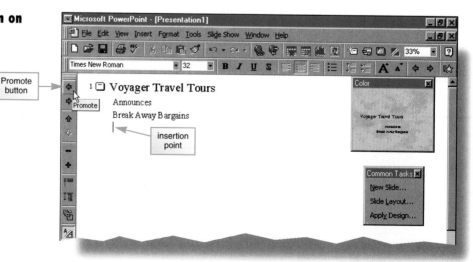

FIGURE 2-9

2 **Click the Promote button.**

The Slide 2 slide icon displays indicating a new slide is added to the presentation (Figure 2-10). The insertion point is in position to type the title for Slide 2 at heading level 1.

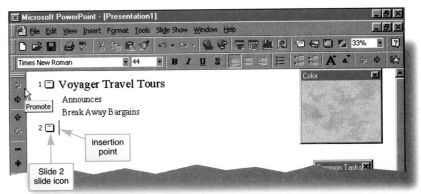

FIGURE 2-10

After you add a slide, you are ready to type the slide text. The next section explains how to create a multi-level bulleted list slide in outline view.

Creating Multi-level Bulleted List Slides in Outline View

To create a multi-level bulleted list slide, you demote or promote the insertion point to the appropriate heading level and then type the paragraph text. Recall from Project 1 that when you demote a paragraph, PowerPoint adds a bullet to the left of each heading level. Depending on the design template, each heading level has a different bullet font. Also recall that the design template determines font attributes, including the bullet font.

Slide 2 is the first **informational slide** for Project 2. Slide 2 introduces the main topic — two vacation packages offered by Voyager Travel Tours. Each vacation package displays as heading level 2, and each **supportive paragraph** displays as heading level 3. The following steps explain how to create a multi-level bulleted list slide in outline view.

Other Ways

1. On Standard toolbar, click New Slide button, click OK button in New Slide dialog box
2. On Insert menu click New Slide, click OK button in New Slide dialog box
3. Press ALT+I, press N, press ENTER
4. Press CTRL+M, press ENTER
5. Press and hold SHIFT, press TAB until paragraph or insertion point displays at heading level 1, release TAB

 Steps To Create a Multi-level Bulleted List Slide in Outline View

1 **Type** Two Dynamite Deals **and press the ENTER key. Then click the Demote button to demote to heading level 2.**

The title for Slide 2, Two Dynamite Deals, displays and the insertion point is in position to type the first bulleted paragraph (Figure 2-11). A leaf shaped bullet displays to the left of the insertion point.

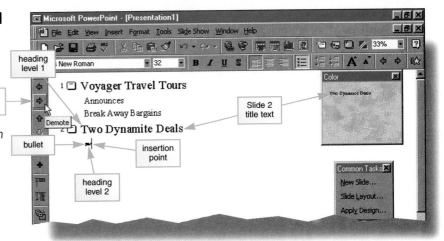

FIGURE 2-11

2 **Type** The Stargazer **and press the ENTER key. Then click the Demote button to demote to heading level 3.**

Slide 2 displays three heading levels: the title, Two Dynamite Deals, on heading level 1, the bulleted paragraph, The Stargazer, on heading level 2, and the insertion point on heading level 3 (Figure 2-12). The bullet for heading level 2 is a leaf. The bullet for heading level 3 is a dot.

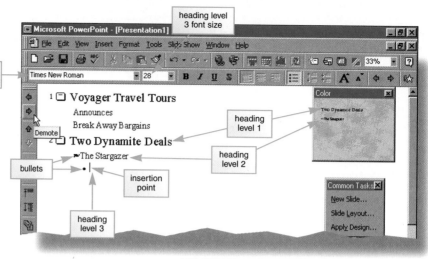

FIGURE 2-12

3 **Type** All inclusive sand and sea adventure **and press the ENTER key. Then click the Promote button.**

Pressing the ENTER key begins a new paragraph at the same heading level as the previous paragraph. Clicking the Promote button moves the insertion point left and elevates the paragraph from heading level 3 to heading level 2 (Figure 2-13).

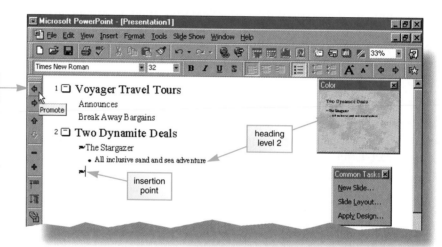

FIGURE 2-13

4 **Type** The Castaway **and press the ENTER key. Click the Demote button. Type** Self-designed sand and sun experience **and press the ENTER key (Figure 2-14).**

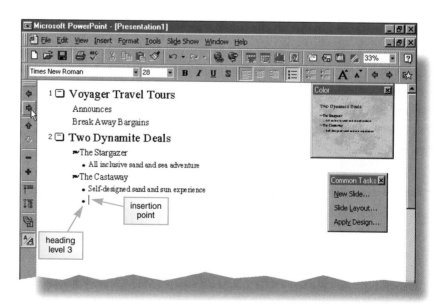

FIGURE 2-14

Creating a Subordinate Slide

When developing your presentation, begin with a main topic and follow with **subordinate slides**, slides to support the main topic. Placing all your information on one slide may overwhelm your audience. Decompose your presentation, therefore, into several slides with three to six bullets per slide or per object. The following steps explain how to create a subordinate slide that further explains the vacation package, The Stargazer, first introduced on Slide 2. This new slide, Slide 3, provides additional information that supports the first heading level 2 on Slide 2. Later in this project, you create another subordinate slide to support the second heading level 2 on Slide 2, The Castaway.

TO CREATE A SUBORDINATE SLIDE

Step 1: Click the Promote button two times so that Slide 3 is added to the end of the presentation.

Step 2: Type The Stargazer and press the ENTER key.

Step 3: Click the Demote button to demote to heading level 2.

Step 4: Type One incredible low price includes: and press the ENTER key.

Step 5: Click the Demote button to demote to heading level 3.

Step 6: Type Round-trip airfare and press the ENTER key.

Step 7: Type Five-day cruise and two-day beach party and press the ENTER key.

Step 8: Type Sumptuous gourmet cuisine and press the ENTER key.

Step 9: Type Fabulous entertainment and press the ENTER key.

The screen displays as shown in Figure 2-15.

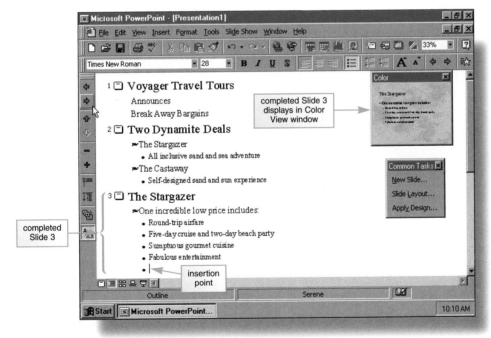

FIGURE 2-15

More *About*
Outline View

When working in outline view, many people prefer to use keyboard keys instead of toolbar buttons. This way their hands never leave the keyboard and their typing is finished quickly. For example, instead of clicking the Demote button to demote text, press the TAB key.

More *About*
Subordinate Slides

When reviewing a presentation, look for slides containing more information than the audience can quickly grasp. When a slide gets complicated, simplify the presentation by clicking the Expand Slide command on the Tools menu. This generates a new slide for each bulleted item on the original slide.

More *About*
Subordinate Slides

Subordinate items must directly support the main topic under which they are placed. This means that they must be less important in meaning while being logically related. Indentation identifies levels of importance. The more important the item, the closer it displays to the left margin.

Creating a Second Subordinate Slide

The next step is to create the slide that supports The Castaway, which is the second heading level 2 on Slide 2. Perform the following steps to create this subordinate slide.

TO CREATE A SECOND SUBORDINATE SLIDE

Step 1: Click the Promote button two times so that Slide 4 is added to the end of the presentation. Type The Castaway and press the ENTER key.

Step 2: Click the Demote button to demote to heading level 2. Type Customized dream vacation and press the ENTER key.

Step 3: Click the Demote button to demote to heading level 3. Type Luxurious oceanfront condominiums and press the ENTER key.

Step 4: Click the Demote button to demote to heading level 4. Type Whirlpool and press the ENTER key. Type Daily maid service and press the ENTER key.

Step 5: Click the Promote button to promote to heading level 3. Type Diverse dining opportunities and press the ENTER key. Type Countless recreational activities and press the ENTER key.

The screen displays as shown in Figure 2-16.

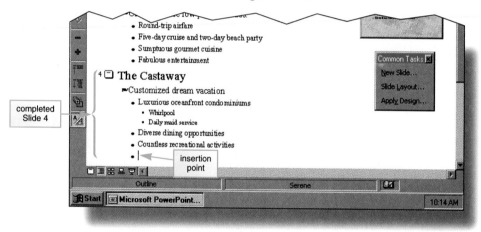

FIGURE 2-16

Creating a Slide with Multiple Text Objects in Outline View

All of the slides you have created to this point consist of a title object and one text object. Occasionally, you need to provide the audience with a long list of items. If you use the Bulleted List slide layout, Style Checker will identify the slide as having too many bullets. Recall from Project 1 that Style Checker checks a presentation for spelling, visual clarity, case, and end punctuation. One of the design standards Style Checker looks for is too many bullets in an object.

In order to create a slide with more than six bulleted paragraphs and still comply with design standards, break the list into two or more objects. When you divide the text into multiple objects, each object complies with PowerPoint's default settings for visual clarity in Style Checker, as long as the number of bullets per object is less than or equal to six. Six is the default setting for the number of bullets per object.

Because you are creating the presentation in outline view, type the text for this slide as a bulleted list. Later in this project, you convert the bulleted list slide into a multiple object slide by changing views, changing slide layout, and moving some of the text from the bulleted list to another object. Perform the following steps to create a slide with multiple text objects in outline view.

TO CREATE A SLIDE WITH MULTIPLE TEXT OBJECTS IN OUTLINE VIEW

Step 1: Click the Promote button two times so that Slide 5 is added to the end of the presentation. Type Both Deals Feature as the slide title and press the ENTER key.

Step 2: Click the Demote button to demote to heading level 2. Type Balmy breezes and press the ENTER key. Type Lucid azure pools and press the ENTER key. Type Starlit nights and press the ENTER key. Type Sunny days and press the ENTER key. Type Tropical climate and press the ENTER key. Type White sand beaches and press the ENTER key. Type Neptune Beach and press the ENTER key.

Step 3: Click the Demote button to demote to heading level 3. Type Sunbathe, relax and press the ENTER key.

Step 4: Click the Promote button to promote to heading level 2. Type Poseidon Bay and press the ENTER key.

Step 5: Click the Demote button to demote to heading level 3. Type Sail, swim and press the ENTER key.

Step 6: Click the Promote button to promote to heading level 2. Type Triton Reef and press the ENTER key.

Step 7: Click the Demote button to demote to heading level 3. Type Scuba dive, snorkel and press the ENTER key.

The screen displays as shown in Figure 2-17.

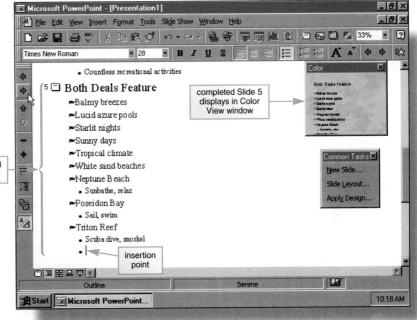

FIGURE 2-17

Creating a Closing Slide in Outline View

The last slide in your presentation is the closing slide. A **closing slide** gracefully ends a presentation. Often used during a question and answer session, the closing slide usually remains on the screen to reinforce the message delivered during the presentation. Professional speakers design the closing slide with one or more of the methods on the next page.

1. List important information. Tell the audience what to do next.
2. Provide a memorable illustration or example to make a point.
3. Appeal to emotions. Remind the audience to take action or accept responsibility.
4. Summarize the main points of the presentation.
5. Cite a quotation that directly relates to the main points of the presentation. This is most effective if the presentation started with a quotation.

The closing slide in this project combines listing important information and providing an illustration. Because Voyager Travel Tours wants students to buy one of the tropical island vacations, they combine telling students what to do next with providing a list of telephone numbers on the Serene design template. Perform the following steps to create this closing slide.

TO CREATE A CLOSING SLIDE IN OUTLINE VIEW

Step 1: Click the Promote button two times so that Slide 6 is added to the end of the presentation. Type `Time Is Running Out` as the slide title and press the ENTER key.

Step 2: Click the Demote button to demote to heading level 2. Type `Contact Student Activities Office` and press the ENTER key.

Step 3: Click the Demote button to demote to heading level 3. Type `Detter Hall, Room 225` and press the ENTER key. Type `Ext. 2772` and press the ENTER key.

Step 4: Click the Promote button to promote to heading level 2. Type `Call Voyager Travel Tours` and press the ENTER key.

Step 5: Click the Demote button to demote to heading level 3. Type `555-AWAY` but do not press the ENTER key.

Slide 6 displays as shown in Figure 2-18.

More *About*
Closing Slides

Keep the closing slide brief. It should be a conclusion, not a complete restatement of the entire presentation. Remember that the audience is ready to leave, so keep your closing slide simple.

The outline now is complete and the presentation should be saved. The next section explains how to save the presentation.

Saving a Presentation

Recall from Project 1 that it is wise to frequently save your presentation. Because you have created all the text for your presentation, you should save your presentation now. For a detailed explanation of the following summarized steps, refer to pages PP 1.23 through PP 1.25 in Project 1.

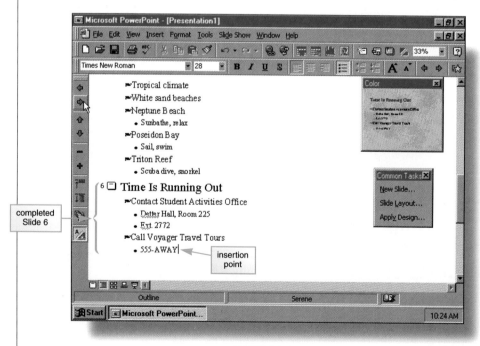

FIGURE 2-18

TO SAVE A PRESENTATION

Step 1: Insert a formatted floppy disk in drive A and then click the Save button on the Standard toolbar.

Step 2: Type Break Away Bargains in the File name box. Do not press the ENTER key.

Step 3: Click the Save in box arrow. Click 3½ Floppy (A:) in the Save in list.

Step 4: Click the Save button.

The presentation is saved to drive A under the file name Break Away Bargains. The file name displays in the title bar.

Reviewing a Presentation in Slide Sorter View

In Project 1, you displayed slides in slide show view to evaluate the presentation. Slide show view, however, restricts your evaluation to one slide at a time. Outline view is best for quickly reviewing all the text for a presentation. Recall from Project 1 that slide sorter view allows you to look at several slides at one time, which is why it is the best view to use to evaluate a presentation for content, organization, and overall appearance. Perform the following step to change from outline view to slide sorter view.

 Steps To Change the View to Slide Sorter View

1 **Click the Slide Sorter View button on the View Button Bar at the bottom of the PowerPoint window.**

PowerPoint displays the presentation in slide sorter view (Figure 2-19). Slide 6 is selected because it was the current slide in outline view.

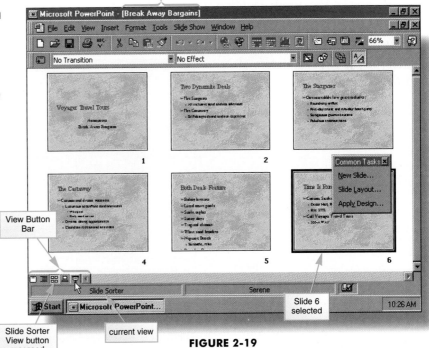

FIGURE 2-19

OtherWays

1. On View menu click Slide Sorter
2. Press ALT+V, press D

Because there are only six slides in this presentation and the Zoom setting is 66%, you can review all slides in one window. Notice that all slides have a significant amount of white space and that the text on Slide 5 exceeds the length of the slide. These observations indicate a need to adjust line spacing to make better use of the slide. Recall that Slide 5 will be corrected by changing the slide layout to one that displays text in two text objects. Additionally, the presentation lacks excitement. To make the presentation more interesting, you may wish to add graphics, such as clip art. The next several sections explain how to improve the presentation by adding a blank line in a bulleted list, changing slide layouts, and adding clip art.

Adding a Blank Line to a Bulleted List

The first improvement to this presentation is adding a blank line to Slide 2. In order to increase white space between paragraphs, add a blank line after the heading level 3 paragraph, All inclusive sand and sea adventure. Recall that a paragraph begins when you press the ENTER key and ends when you again press the ENTER key. Also recall that PowerPoint adds a bullet in front of every new paragraph in a bulleted list. Thus, to create a blank line in a bulleted list, you also must remove the bullet.

You can make changes to text in both slide view and outline view. It is best, however, to change the view to slide view when making changes that impact white space so that you can see the result of editing the text object. Perform the following steps to change the view to slide view.

More About
White Space

Do not crowd a slide with text. White space allows the reader's eye to relax and then focus on the next line of text. Balance text, graphics, and white space to create an appealing slide.

Steps To Change the View to Slide View

① **Point to the slide miniature of Slide 2 (Figure 2-20).**

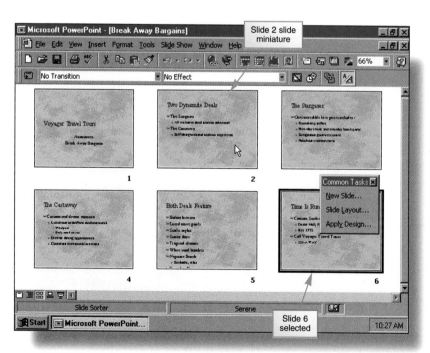

FIGURE 2-20

2 **Double-click the Slide 2 slide miniature.**

Slide 2 displays in slide view (Figure 2-21). The Slide View button is recessed on the View Button Bar.

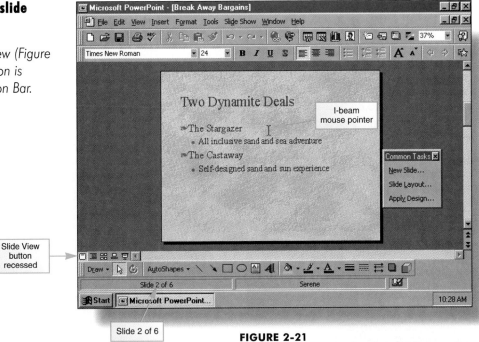

FIGURE 2-21

The next section explains how to add a blank line to Slide 2.

Adding a Blank Line to Slide 2

Now that Slide 2 displays in slide view, you are ready to add a blank line after the paragraph, All inclusive sand and sea adventure. Perform the following steps to add a blank line.

 Steps To Add a Blank Line

1 **Position the I-beam mouse pointer to the right of the second letter e in the word adventure in the paragraph All inclusive sand and sea adventure. Then click the left mouse button.**

PowerPoint selects the text object and positions the insertion point after the second e in the word, adventure (Figure 2-22). The mouse pointer displays as an I-beam when located in a text object.

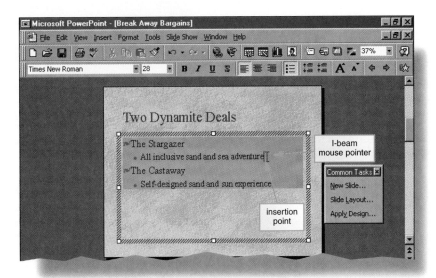

FIGURE 2-22

2 **Press the ENTER key.**

PowerPoint inserts a new paragraph (Figure 2-23). The new paragraph has the same attributes as the previous paragraph. The Bullets button is recessed on the Formatting toolbar.

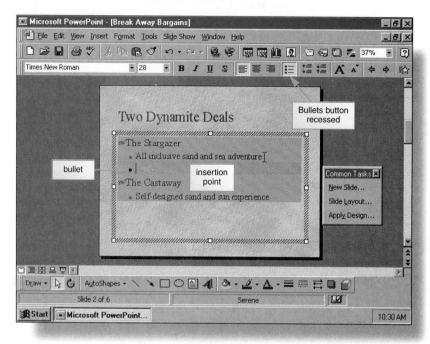

FIGURE 2-23

3 **Click the Bullets button to remove the bullet.**

The line displays blank because the bullet does not display (Figure 2-24). The Bullets button is not recessed.

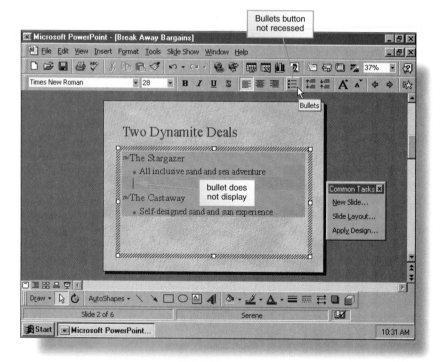

FIGURE 2-24

Positioning the insertion point at the end of a paragraph and then pressing the ENTER key two times also creates a blank paragraph. The bullet, however, displays dimmed on the screen and the Bullets button displays recessed on the Formatting toolbar. If you click a paragraph other than the blank paragraph, the bullet does not display. Additionally, the dimmed bullet does not display when you run the presentation in slide show view.

To display a bullet on a selected paragraph, click the Bullets button on the Formatting toolbar.

Changing Slide Layout

Recall from Project 1 that when you add a new slide, PowerPoint displays the New Slide dialog box from which you choose one of the slide AutoLayouts. After creating a slide, you can change its layout by clicking the **Slide Layout button** on the Common Tasks toolbar. The Slide Layout dialog box then displays. Like the AutoLayout dialog box, the Slide Layout dialog box allows you to choose one of the 24 different slide layouts.

When you change the layout of a slide, PowerPoint retains the text and graphics and repositions them into the appropriate placeholders. Using slide layouts eliminates the need to resize objects because PowerPoint automatically sizes the object to fit the placeholder.

To keep your presentation interesting, PowerPoint includes several slide layouts to combine text with nontext objects, such as clip art. The placement of the text, in relationship to the nontext object, depends on the slide layout. The nontext object placeholder may be to the right or left of the text, above the text, or below the text. Additionally, some slide layouts are constructed with two nontext object placeholders. Refer to Project 1 for a list of the available slide layouts (Figure 1-27 on PP 1.25). The following steps explain how to change the slide layout from a bulleted list to two columns of text.

Steps To Change Slide Layout

<table>
<tr>
<td valign="top">

1 **Drag the scroll box on the vertical scroll bar to display Slide 5 (Figure 2-25).**

</td>
<td>

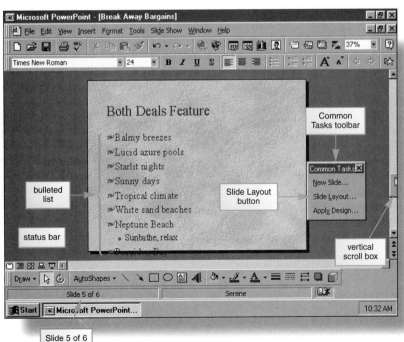

FIGURE 2-25

</td>
</tr>
</table>

2 Click the Slide Layout button on the Common Tasks toolbar. When the Slide Layout dialog box displays, click the 2 Column Text slide layout located in row one, column three.

The Slide Layout dialog box displays (Figure 2-26). The 2 Column Text slide layout is selected. When you click a slide layout, its name displays in the box at the lower-right corner of the Slide Layout dialog box.

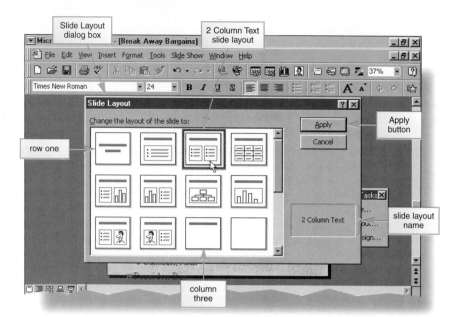

FIGURE 2-26

3 Click the Apply button.

Slide 5 displays the bulleted list in the left column text object (Figure 2-27). The right column text placeholder displays the message, Click to add text.

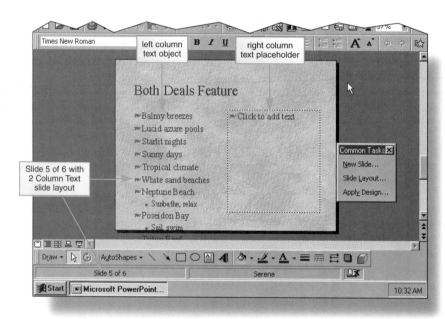

FIGURE 2-27

The text in the left column of Slide 5 is too lengthy to fit into the text object. The next section explains how to move the text at the bottom of the left column to the top of the right column text placeholder.

Moving Text

Because the bulleted list on Slide 5 contains more paragraphs than will fit in the left column text object, select a portion of the list and move it to the right column text placeholder. Perform the following steps to select a portion of the text in the left column and then move it to the right column.

 **To Move Text**

1 Position the I-beam mouse pointer immediately to the left of the N in Neptune. Drag to the right and down so that the last six bulleted paragraphs are selected. If necessary, click the vertical scroll bar down arrow to display all the bulleted items.

The six bulleted paragraphs, Neptune Beach, Sunbathe, relax; Poseidon Bay, Sail, swim; and Triton Reef, Scuba dive, snorkel are selected (Figure 2-28).

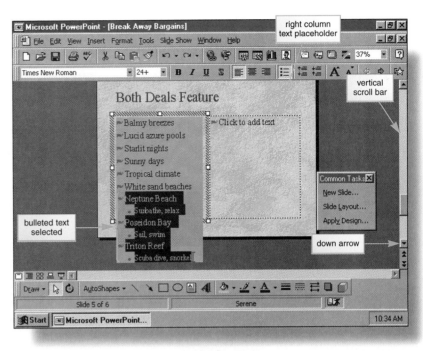

FIGURE 2-28

2 Point to the selected text. If the mouse pointer displays as a four-headed arrow, move the mouse pointer to the right of the bullets so that it is positioned over the text. Then drag the selected text to the right column text placeholder.

As you drag the text, the mouse pointer displays as a block arrow with a small dotted box around the arrow shaft. The six selected paragraphs are moved to the right column text placeholder (Figure 2-29). When you insert text into a text placeholder, it becomes a text object.

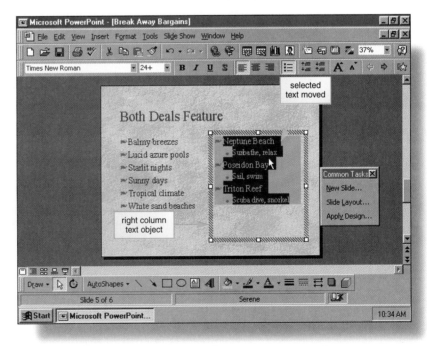

FIGURE 2-29

Because Slide 5 contains two bulleted text objects, it now complies with the default Style Checker design rules of no more than six bullets per object.

▶**Other Ways**

1. Right-click selected text, click Cut, right-click new text location, click Paste

2. Select text, click Cut button, click new text location, click Paste button

Adding Clip Art to a Slide

Clip art offers a quick way to add professional-looking graphic images to your presentation without creating the images yourself. One clip art source is the Microsoft Clip Gallery 3.0. **Microsoft Clip Gallery 3.0** is a tool that accompanies Microsoft Office 97 that allows you to insert clip art, pictures, audio clips, and video clips to a presentation. It contains a wide variety of clip art images and is shared with other Microsoft Office applications. Microsoft Clip Gallery 3.0 combines topic-related clip art images into categories, such as Animals, Household, and People at Work.

Table 2-2 gives you an idea of the organization of Microsoft Clip Gallery 3.0 that accompanies PowerPoint. The table contains four of the categories from Microsoft Clip Gallery 3.0 and keywords of the clip art contained therein. Clip art images have one or more keywords that associate an image with various entities, activities, labels, and emotions. In most instances, the keyword does not contain the name of the physical object. For example, an image of a magnifying glass in the Academic category has keywords of Focus Investigation Identify Small. As a result, you may find it necessary to scroll through several categories to find an appropriate picture.

Table 2-2	
CATEGORY	CLIP ART KEYWORDS
Academic	Reward Accomplishment, Reward Accomplishment Milestone Guarantee, Focus Investigation Identify Small, Leadership Information Test Communication Listen Dictate
Cartoons	Anger Demanding, Stress Frustration Anger Chaos, Reward Agreeable, Success Victory Accomplishment Result Invincible Milestone Superior
Gestures	Success Impress, Harmony Trust Compromise Consensus Guarantee Synergy, Trust Protect, Success Invincible, Failure
Transportation	Performance Fast Sports Car, War Battle Powerful Battleship Navigate, Performance Fast War Battle Plane, Performance Ship Navigate, Priority Traffic Light

Depending on the installation of Microsoft Clip Gallery 3.0 on your computer, you may not have the clip art pictures used in this project. Contact your instructor if you are missing clip art when you perform the following steps.

Using AutoLayouts to Add Clip Art

PowerPoint simplifies adding clip art to a slide by providing AutoLayouts designed specifically for clip art. Recall from Project 1 that an AutoLayout is a collection of placeholders for the title, text, clip art, graphs, tables, and media clips. A clip art placeholder contains instructions to open Microsoft Clip Gallery 3.0. Double-clicking the clip art placeholder activates the instructions. When you use an AutoLayout placeholder to add an object to a slide, such as clip art, PowerPoint automatically sizes the object to fit the placeholder. If the object is in landscape orientation, PowerPoint sizes it to the width of the placeholder. If the object is in portrait orientation, PowerPoint sizes it to the height of the placeholder.

Adding clip art to Slide 6 requires two steps. First, change the slide layout to Clip Art & Text. Then insert clip art into the clip art placeholder. The next two sections explain how to add clip art into an AutoLayout placeholder.

More *About*
Clip Art

Humor and interest are just two of several reasons to add clip art to your presentation. People have limited attention spans. A carefully placed humorous clip art image can spark attention and interest. When interest is high, it greatly increases the chance that your concept or idea will be remembered.

Changing Slide Layout to Clip Art & Text

Before you insert clip art into an AutoLayout placeholder, you first must select one of the slide layouts that includes a clip art placeholder. The clip art placeholder on the left side of Slide 6 will hold clip art. Perform the following steps to change the slide layout to Clip Art & Text.

 Steps **To Change the Slide Layout to Clip Art & Text**

1 Drag the scroll box on the vertical scroll bar to display Slide 6 (Figure 2-30).

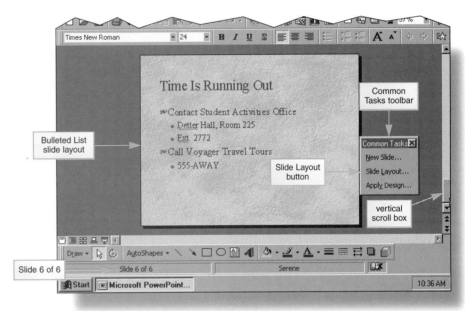

FIGURE 2-30

2 Click the Slide Layout button on the Common Tasks toolbar. When the Slide Layout dialog box displays, click the Clip Art & Text slide layout located in row three, column two. Then point to the Apply button.

The Clip Art & Text slide layout is selected in the Slide Layout dialog box (Figure 2-31).

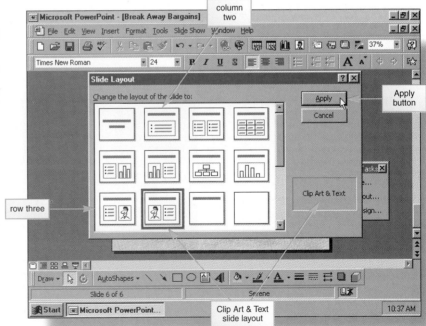

FIGURE 2-31

Click the Apply button.

Slide 6 displays the Clip Art & Text slide layout (Figure 2-32). PowerPoint moves the text object and automatically resizes the text to fit the object.

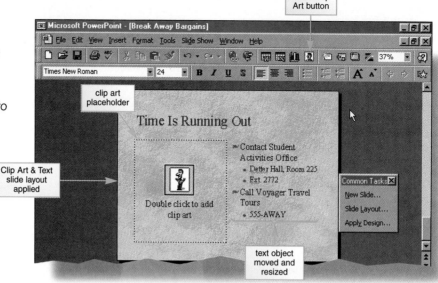

FIGURE 2-32

Other Ways

1. Right-click slide anywhere except text or object place-holders, click Slide Layout, double-click Clip Art & Text slide layout

2. Press ALT+L, press arrow keys to select Clip Art & Text slide layout, press ENTER

3. Press ALT+O, press L, press arrow keys to select Clip Art & Text slide layout, press ENTER

You can use an AutoLayout placeholder to insert clip art even if the AutoLayout does not have a clip art placeholder. For example, to insert clip art into the object placeholder of the Object AutoLayout, click the placeholder to select it, click the Insert Clip Art button on the Standard toolbar, and then select a clip art picture.

Inserting Clip Art into a Clip Art Placeholder

Now that the Clip Art & Text placeholder is applied to Slide 6, you insert clip art into the clip art placeholder. Perform the following steps to insert clip art to the clip art placeholder on Slide 6.

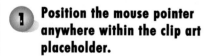 **To Insert Clip Art into a Clip Art Placeholder**

Position the mouse pointer anywhere within the clip art placeholder.

The mouse pointer is positioned inside the clip art placeholder (Figure 2-33). The mouse pointer becomes a four-headed arrow. It is not necessary to point to the picture inside the placeholder.

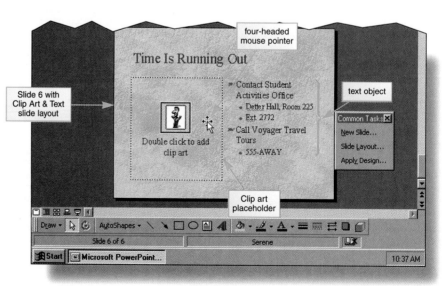

FIGURE 2-33

2 **Double-click the clip art placeholder on the left side of Slide 6.**

PowerPoint displays the Microsoft Clip Gallery 3.0 dialog box (Figure 2-34). The Clip Art list box displays clip art images by category. When you open Microsoft Clip Gallery 3.0, All Categories is the selected category on the Clip Art sheet. The selected clip art image in this figure is a diploma. Your selected image may be different depending on the clip art installed on your computer.

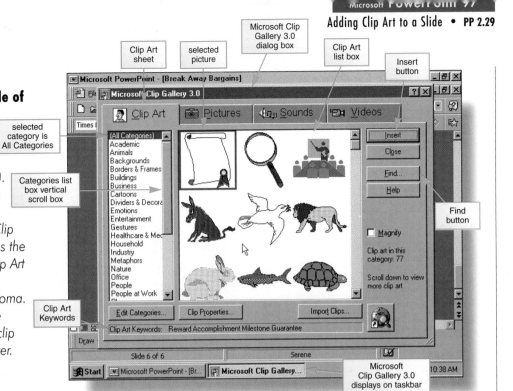

FIGURE 2-34

3 **Click the Find button.**

The Find Clip dialog box displays three boxes in which you enter clip art search criteria (Figure 2-35). The Keywords text box is selected and contains the keyword, All Keywords. Use the Keywords text box to find clip art when you know one of the words associated with the clip art image. Use the File name containing text box when you know the name of the file containing the desired clip art image. Use the Clip type list box when you want to find clip art saved in a specific format.

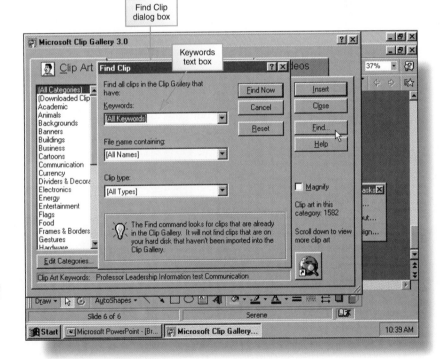

FIGURE 2-35

4 **Type** time **in the Keywords text box and point to the Find Now button.**

The Keywords text box contains time (Figure 2-36). You do not need to type the full keyword because the Find feature of Microsoft Clip Gallery 3.0 searches for all pictures containing the consecutive letters typed in the Keywords text box. The Find Now button initiates the clip art search. The Reset button resets the Keywords, File name containing, and Clip type boxes. Click the Reset button when you wish to begin a new search.

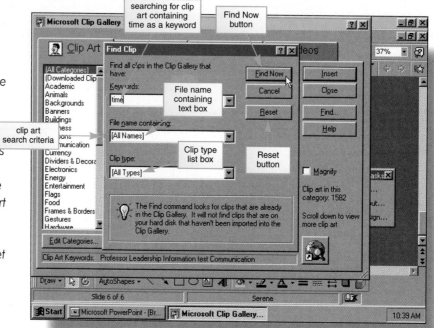

FIGURE 2-36

5 **Click the Find Now button. If necessary, scroll to display the clip art with the keywords, Timeline Schedule Clock Wait Procrastinate. Click the clock clip art to select it.**

The Microsoft Clip Gallery searches for all pictures that contain time in the keywords. All pictures that contain the keyword display in the Pictures box (Figure 2-37). The picture of a clock is selected. The selected category changes to Results of Last Find. Timeline Schedule Clock Wait Procrastinate displays at the bottom of the Microsoft Clip Gallery 3.0 dialog box as the keywords of the selected picture. Your selected picture may be different depending on the clip art installed on your computer.

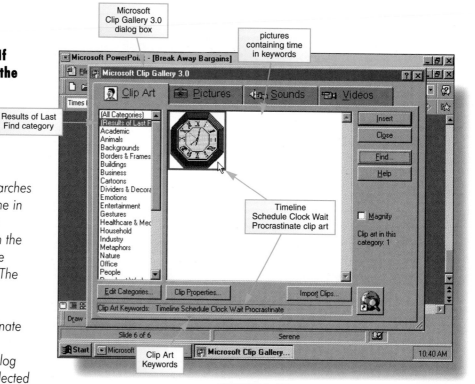

FIGURE 2-37

6 Click the Insert button.

The selected picture is inserted into the clip art placeholder on Slide 6 (Figure 2-38). PowerPoint automatically sizes the picture to best fit the placeholder. In this instance, the picture is taller than it is wide (portrait orientation), so PowerPoint sizes the picture to fit the height of the placeholder. When a picture is in landscape orientation, PowerPoint sizes the picture to fit the width of the placeholder.

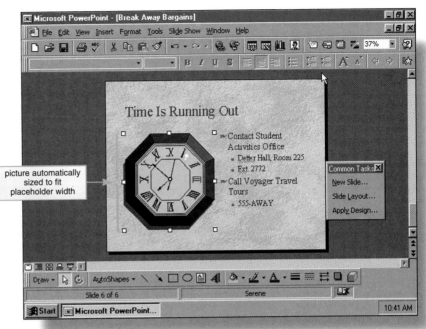

FIGURE 2-38

In addition to the clip art images in Microsoft Clip Gallery 3.0, other sources for clip art include retailers specializing in computer software, the Internet, bulletin board systems, and online information systems. Some popular online information systems are The Microsoft Network, America Online, CompuServe, and Prodigy. A **bulletin board system** is a computer system that allows users to communicate with each other and share files. Microsoft has created a special page on their World Wide Web site where you can add new clips to the Clip Gallery.

Besides clip art, you can insert pictures into your presentation. These may include scanned photographs, line art, and artwork from compact discs. To insert a picture into a presentation, the picture must be saved in a format that PowerPoint can recognize. Table 2-3 identifies some of the formats PowerPoint recognizes.

PowerPoint converts pictures saved in the formats listed in Table 2-3 by using filters. These filters are shipped with the PowerPoint installation software and must be installed before PowerPoint can properly convert files.

Table 2-3

FORMAT	FILE EXTENSION
AutoCAD Format 2-D	*.dxf
Computer Graphics Metafile	*.cgm
CorelDRAW	*.cdr
Encapsulated PostScript	*.eps
Graphics Interchange Format	*.gif
JPEG File Interchange Format	*.jpg
Kodak Photo CD	*.pcd
Macintosh PICT	*.pct
Micrografx Designer/Draw	*.drw
PC Paintbrush	*.pcx
Portable Network Graphics	*.png
Tagged Image File Format	*.tif
Targa	*.tga
Windows Bitmaps	*.bmp, .rle, .dib
Windows Enhanced Metafile	*.emf
Windows Metafile	*.wmf
WordPerfect Graphics	*.wpg

More *About*
Clip Art

Clip art serves a purpose in a
presentation – it conveys a message. Clip art should contribute
to the understandability of the
slide. It should not be used dec-
oratively. Before adding clip art
to a presentation, ask yourself:
"Does the clip art convey a message or support the slide topic?"
If the answer is yes, put the clip
art on the slide.

Inserting Clip Art on a Slide without a Clip Art Placeholder

PowerPoint does not require you to use an AutoLayout containing a clip
art placeholder to add clip art to a slide. You can insert clip art on any slide
regardless of its slide layout. On Slide 3, you are adding a picture of a sailboat
to illustrate the type of sailing vessel used in The Stargazer vacation package.
Recall that the slide layout on Slide 3 is the Bulleted List slide layout. Because the
Bulleted List AutoLayout does not contain a clip art placeholder, you click the
Insert Clip Art button on the Standard toolbar to start Microsoft Clip Gallery
3.0. The picture for which you are searching is a sailing ship. Its keywords are
Performance Ship Navigate. Perform the following steps to insert the picture of a
ship on a slide that does not have a clip art placeholder.

TO INSERT CLIP ART ON A SLIDE WITHOUT A CLIP ART PLACEHOLDER

Step 1: Drag the scroll box on the vertical scroll bar until Slide 3, titled The
Stargazer, displays in the slide indicator.

Step 2: Click the Insert Clip Art button on the Standard toolbar (Figure 2-32
on page PP 2.28).

Step 3: Click the Find button. When the Find Clip dialog box displays, type
navigate in the Keywords text box. Click the Find Now button.

Step 4: If necessary, when the Microsoft Clip Gallery 3.0 dialog box displays
the results, click the down arrow on the Pictures box scroll bar until
the sailboat displays. If the sailboat is not installed on your computer,
see your instructor for an appropriate replacement picture.

Step 5: Double-click the picture of the sailboat that has the keywords Performance Ship Navigate.

*The sailboat displays on Slide 3 (Figure 2-39). A selection box indicates the
clip art is selected.*

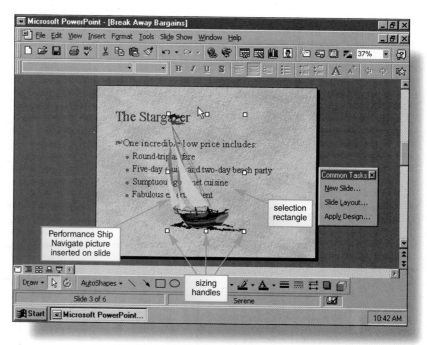

FIGURE 2-39

Moving Clip Art

After you insert clip art on a slide, you may want to reposition it. The picture of the sailboat on Slide 3 overlays the bulleted list. Moving the picture to the lower-right corner of the slide places the sailboat away from the text. Because you want to align the sailboat mast under the letter b in the word beach on the second heading level 2, you first move the picture and then change its size. You change the size of the sailboat later in this project. Perform the steps below to move the sailboat to the lower-right corner of the slide.

> ### More *About* Clip Art
>
> When used appropriately, clip art reduces misconceptions. If a presentation consists of words alone, the audience creates its own mental picture. The mental picture created may be different from the concept you are trying to convey. The audience better understands the concept when a graphic is included.

Steps To Move Clip Art

1 If the picture of the sailboat is not already selected, use the mouse pointer to point to the sailboat and then click.

2 Press and hold down the left mouse button. Drag the picture of the sailboat past the bottom of the slide and then to the right until the top-left corner of the dotted box aligns below the b in beach. Release the left mouse button.

When you drag an object, a dotted box displays. The dotted box indicates the new position of the object. When you release the left mouse button, the picture of the sailboat displays in the new location (Figure 2-40). Sizing handles appear at the corners and along the edges of the selection box.

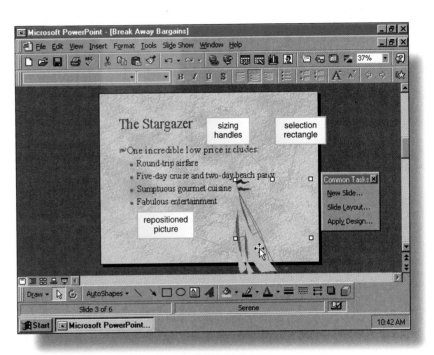

FIGURE 2-40

> ### Other**Ways**
>
> 1. Select clip art, press arrow keys to move to new position

Changing the Size of Clip Art

Sometimes it is necessary to change the size of clip art. For example, on Slide 3, the sailboat displays off the slide. In order to make the picture fit onto the slide, you reduce its size. To change the size of a clip art picture by an exact percentage, use the **Format Picture command**. The Format Picture dialog box contains five sheets with several options for formatting a picture. The **Size sheet** contains options for changing the size of a picture. You either enter the exact height and width in the Size and rotate area, or enter the height and width as a percentage of

> ### More *About* Sizing Objects
>
> The Preview button in the Format Picture dialog box allows you to check the object's new size without applying it. When you want to make an object bigger, increase the number in the Height box or the Width box. To make an object smaller, decrease the number.

the original picture in the Scale area. When the **Lock aspect ratio check box** displays a check mark, the height and width settings change to maintain the aspect ratio of the original picture. **Aspect ratio** is the relationship between the height and width of an object. For example, a picture 3 inches high by 5 inches wide scaled to fifty percent would become 1½ inches high by 2½ inches wide. Perform the following steps to reduce the size of the sailboat.

Steps To Change the Size of Clip Art

1 Right-click the sailboat picture. When the shortcut menu displays, point to Format Picture (Figure 2-41).

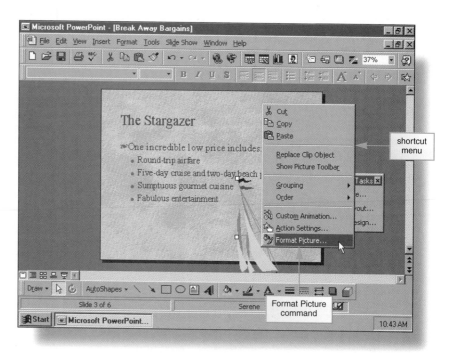

FIGURE 2-41

2 Click Format Picture. If necessary, when the Format Picture dialog box displays, click the Size tab.

The Format Picture dialog box displays the Size sheet (Figure 2-42). The Height and Width text boxes in the Scale area display the current percentage of the sailboat picture, 100. Check marks display in the Lock aspect ratio and Relative to original picture size check boxes.

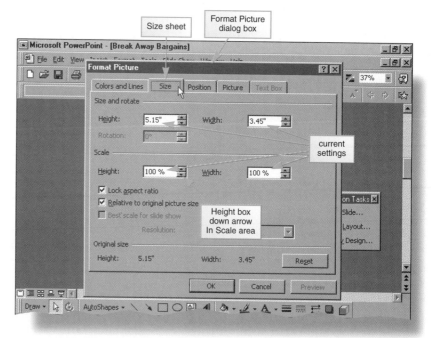

FIGURE 2-42

3 **Click the Height box down arrow in the Scale area until 70 displays. Then point to the OK button.**

Both the Height and Width text boxes in the Scale area display 70% (Figure 2-43). PowerPoint automatically changes the Height and Width text boxes in the Size and rotate area to reflect changes in the Scale area.

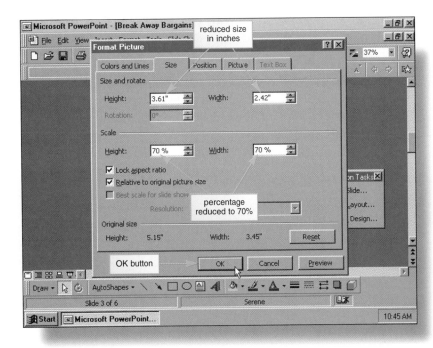

FIGURE 2-43

4 **Click the OK button.**

PowerPoint displays the reduced sailboat picture and closes the Format Picture dialog box (Figure 2-44).

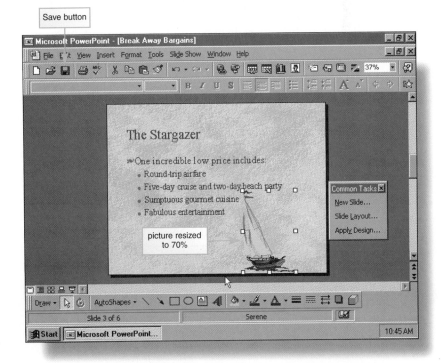

FIGURE 2-44

More *About*
Headers and Footers

Consider placing footers on slides that are used for making overhead transparencies. A slide number and presentation name help keep the presentation organized. The slide number can be a great time saver in the event you drop your transparencies.

Saving the Presentation Again

To preserve the work completed this far, save the presentation again.

TO SAVE A PRESENTATION

Step 1: Click the Save button on the Standard toolbar.

The changes made to the presentation after the previous save are saved to a floppy disk.

A default setting in PowerPoint allows for **fast saves**, which saves only the changes made since the last time you saved. If you want to **full save** a copy of the complete presentation, on the menu bar click Tools, click Options on the Tools menu, click the Save tab and then remove the check mark in the Allow fast saves check box by clicking the check box. Then click the OK button.

Adding a Header and Footer to Outline Pages

A printout of the presentation outline often is used as an audience handout. Distributing a copy of the outline provides the audience with paper on which to write notes or comments. Another benefit of distributing a copy of the outline is to help the audience see the text on the slides when lighting is poor or the room is too large. To help identify the source of the printed outline, add a descriptive header and footer.

Using the Notes and Handouts Sheet to Add Headers and Footers

Add headers and footers to outline pages by clicking the Notes and Handouts sheet in the Header and Footer dialog box and entering the information you wish to print. Perform the following steps to add the current date, a header, the page number, and a footer to the printed outline.

Steps To Use the Notes and Handouts Sheet to Add Headers and Footers

1 **Click View on the menu bar. Point to Header and Footer (Figure 2-45).**

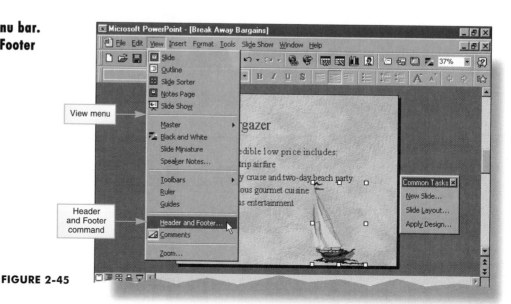

FIGURE 2-45

2 **Click Header and Footer. If necessary, click the Notes and Handouts tab.**

The Header and Footer dialog box displays the Notes and Handouts sheet (Figure 2-46). Check marks display in the Date and time, Header, Page number, and Footer check boxes. The Fixed option button is selected.

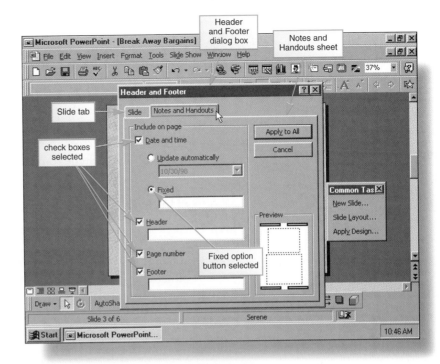

FIGURE 2-46

3 **Click the Update automatically option button. Click the Header text box. Type** Break Away Bargains **in the Header text box. Type** Voyager Travel Tours **in the Footer text box. Then point to the Apply to All button (Figure 2-47).**

4 **Click the Apply to All button.**

PowerPoint applies the header and footer text to the outline, closes the Header and Footer dialog box, and displays Slide 3. You cannot see header and footer text until you print the outline.

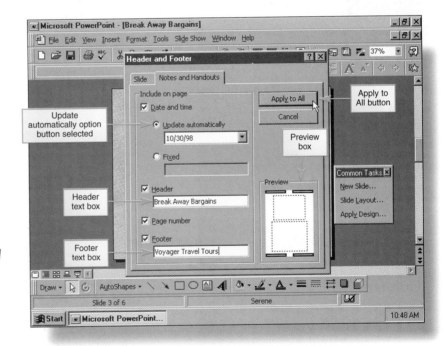

FIGURE 2-47

Checking the Presentation for Spelling and Style Errors

Now that the individual slide changes have been made, you should run Style Checker to identify errors in your presentation. Recall from Project 1 that Style Checker identifies possible errors in spelling, visual clarity, case, and end punctuation. Perform the following steps to run Style Checker.

TO RUN STYLE CHECKER

Step 1: Click Tools on the menu bar.
Step 2: Click Style Checker.
Step 3: When the Style Checker dialog box displays, click the Case and end punctuation check box.
Step 4: Click the Start button.

Step 5: Correct spelling errors and ignore correct spellings of words not located in the standard dictionary.
Step 6: If Style Checker lists visual clarity inconsistencies in the Style Checker Summary dialog box, write the slide number and the message on a sheet of paper.
Step 7: When the Microsoft PowerPoint dialog box displays, press the OK button.

FIGURE 2-48

PowerPoint closes Style Checker and displays the slide containing the last word not in the dictionaries, Slide 6 (Figure 2-48). Ext., the abbreviation for extension, is not found in the standard dictionary and therefore displays highlighted.

This presentation contains no visual clarity inconsistencies. If Style Checker identifies visual clarity inconsistencies, review the steps for correcting the identified slide. Then make the appropriate corrections. For more information about Style Checker, see page PP 1.41 in Project 1.

More *About* Animation

To keep your audience from reading ahead while making a point related to the current item on your slide, use animation effects to build the slide.

Adding Animation Effects

PowerPoint provides many animation effects to make your slide show presentation look professional. In this project you use slide transition and custom animation. **Slide transition effects** define special effects for progressing from one slide to the next in a slide show. **Custom animation effects** define animation, sound effects, and timing for objects on a slide. The following pages discuss each of these animation effects in detail.

Adding Slide Transitions to a Slide Show

PowerPoint allows you to control the way you advance from one slide to the next by adding slide transitions to an on-screen slide show. Slide transitions are visual effects that display when you move one slide off the screen and bring the next one on. PowerPoint has 46 different slide transitions. The name of the slide transition characterizes the visual effect that displays. For example, the slide transition effect, Split Vertical In, displays the next slide by covering the previous slide with two vertical boxes moving toward the center of the screen until the two boxes meet. The effect is similar to closing draw drapes over a window.

PowerPoint requires you to select at least one slide before applying slide transition effects. In this presentation, you apply slide transition effects to all slides except the title slide. Because Slide 6 already is selected, you must select Slides 2 through 5. The technique used to select more than one slide is the **SHIFT+click technique**. To perform the SHIFT+click technique, press and hold down the SHIFT key as you click each slide. After you click the slides to which you want to add animation effects, release the SHIFT key.

In the Break Away Bargains presentation, you wish to display the Box Out slide transition effect between slides. That is, all slides begin stacked on top of one another, like a deck of cards. As you click the mouse to view the next slide, the new slide enters the screen by starting at the center of the slide and exploding out toward the edges of the slide while maintaining a box shape. Perform the following steps to apply the Box Out slide transition effect to the Break Away Bargains presentation.

 Steps **To Add Slide Transitions to a Slide Show**

1 **Click the Slide Sorter View button on the View Button Bar at the bottom of the Microsoft PowerPoint – [Break Away Bargains] screen.**

PowerPoint displays the presentation in slide sorter view (Figure 2-49). Slide 6 is selected. Slide 6 currently does not have a slide transition effect as noted in the Slide Transition Effects list box on the Slide Sorter toolbar.

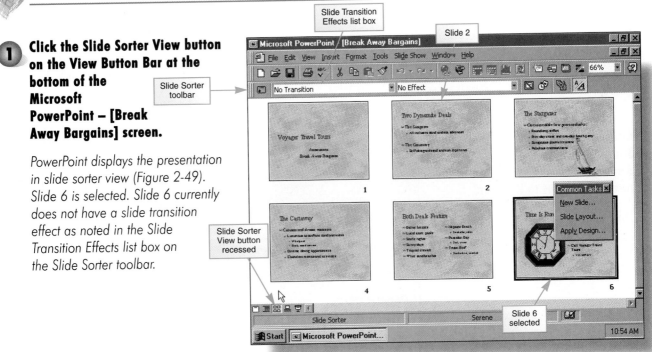

FIGURE 2-49

2 Press and hold down the SHIFT key and click Slide 2, Slide 3, Slide 4, and Slide 5. Release the SHIFT key.

Slides 2 through 6 are selected, as indicated by the heavy border around each slide (Figure 2-50).

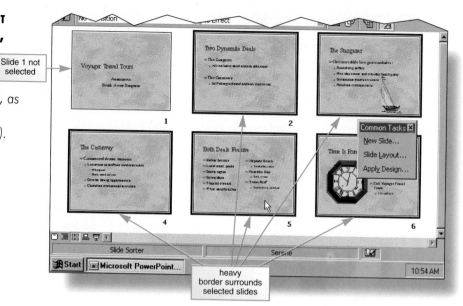

FIGURE 2-50

3 Point to Slide 5 and right-click. When a shortcut menu displays, point to Slide Transition (Figure 2-51).

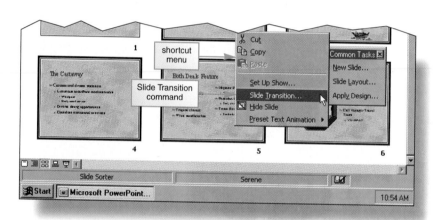

FIGURE 2-51

4 Click Slide Transition. When the Slide Transition dialog box displays, click the Effect box arrow and point to Box Out.

The Slide Transition dialog box displays (Figure 2-52). The Effect list displays available slide transition effects.

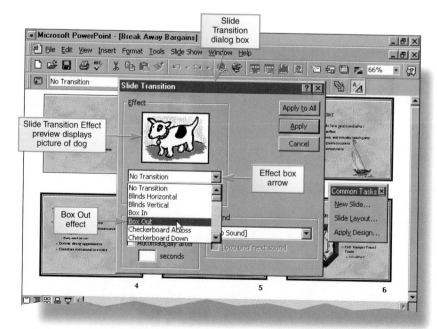

FIGURE 2-52

Click Box Out.

The Slide Transition Effect preview demonstrates the Box Out effect (Figure 2-53). To see the demonstration again, click the picture in the Slide Transition Effect preview.

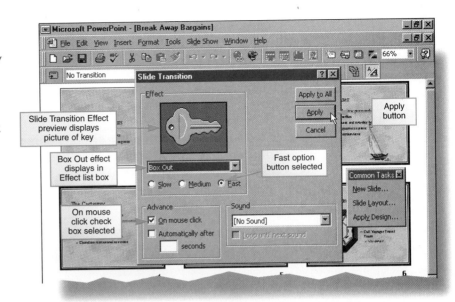

FIGURE 2-53

 Click the Apply button.

PowerPoint displays the presentation in slide sorter view (Figure 2-54). A slide transition icon displays under each selected slide, which indicates that slide transition effects have been added to those slides. The current slide transition effect, Box Out, displays in the Slide Transition Effects box.

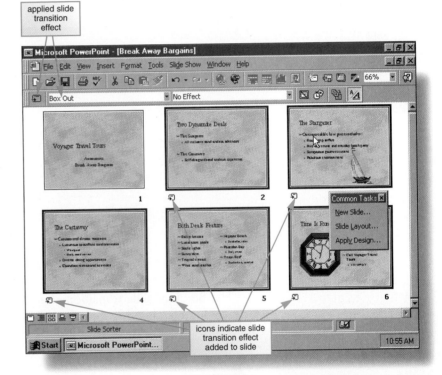

FIGURE 2-54

To apply slide transition effects to every slide in the presentation, select a slide, choose the desired slide transition effect and then click the Apply to All button in the Slide Transition dialog box.

To remove slide transition effects when displaying the presentation in slide sorter view, select the slides to which slide transition effects are applied, right-click one of the selected slides, click the Effect box arrow, select No Transition, and then click the Apply button.

Other Ways

1. Select slides, right-click selected slide, click Slide Transition, click Effect box arrow, select slide transition effect, click Apply button

2. Select slides, on Slide Show menu click Slide Transition, click Effect box arrow, select slide transition effect, click Apply button

Slide Sorter Toolbar

PowerPoint provides you with multiple methods for accomplishing most tasks. Generally, the fastest method is to right-click to display a shortcut menu. Another frequently used method is to click a toolbar button. For example, you can apply slide transition effects by clicking the Slide Transition Effects list box on the Slide Sorter toolbar.

The Slide Sorter toolbar displays only when you are in slide sorter view. It displays beneath the Standard toolbar, in place of the Formatting toolbar. The Slide Sorter toolbar contains tools to help you quickly add animation effects to your slide show. Table 2-4 explains the function of the buttons and boxes on the Slide Sorter toolbar.

Table 2-4

BUTTON/BOX	BUTTON/BOX NAME	FUNCTION
	Slide Transition	Displays the Slide Transition dialog box, which lists special effects used for slide changes during a slide show.
Box Out	Slide Transition Effects	Displays a list of slide transition effects. Selecting a slide transition effect from the list applies it to the selected slide(s) and demonstrates it in the preview box.
	Text Preset Animation	Displays a list of text animation effects.
	Hide Slide	Excludes a slide from the presentation without deleting it.
	Rehearse Timings	Runs your slide show in rehearsal mode, in which you can set or change the timing of your electronic slide show.
	Summary Slide	Creates a bulleted list slide from the titles of the slides selected in slide sorter view or outline view, and then inserts that slide in front of the first selected slide.
	Show Formatting	Displays or hides character formatting attributes in outline view. In slide sorter view, switches between showing all text and graphics on each slide and displaying titles only.

The Box Out slide transition effect has been applied to the presentation. The next step in creating this slide show is to add animation effects to individual slides.

Applying Animation Effects to Bulleted Slides

Animation effects can be applied to text as well as to objects, such as clip art. When you apply animation effects to bulleted text, you progressively disclose each bulleted paragraph. As a result, you build the slide, paragraph by paragraph during the running of a slide show to control the flow of information. PowerPoint has 55 custom animation effects and the capability to dim the paragraphs already displaying on the slide when the new paragraph is displayed.

More About
Custom Animation Effects

The After animation list box contains eight colors and four commands controlling what happens after animation effects display. By default, Don't Dim is selected. To change the color of the previous bulleted text, click one of the eight listed colors from the applied design template. To display additional colors, click More Colors. To hide text as soon as its animation effect displays, click Hide after Animation. To hide text when you click the mouse, click Hide on Next Mouse click.

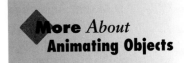
The next step is to apply the Zoom In From Screen Center animation effect to Slides 2, 3, 4, 5, and 6 in the Break Away Bargains presentation. All slides, except the title slide will have the Zoom In From Screen Center animation effect. Recall from Project 1, that when you need to make a change that affects all slides, make the change to the slide master. Perform the following steps to apply animation effects to the bulleted paragraphs in this presentation.

More *About*
Animating Objects

Used sparingly, animated objects add interest to a presentation. Overused animated objects are distracting and minimize the message of the presentation.

 Steps **To Use the Slide Master to Apply Animation Effects to All Bulleted Slides**

1 **Press and hold down the SHIFT key and then click the Slide Master button on the View Button Bar.**

The slide master displays. If necessary, drag the Master toolbar onto the screen as shown in Figure 2-55.

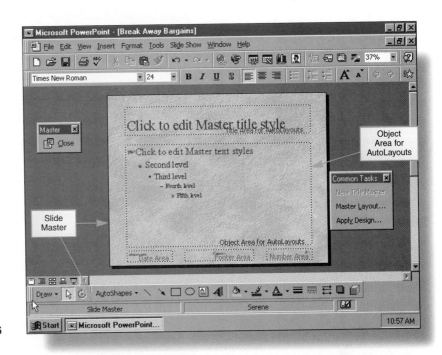

FIGURE 2-55

2 **Right-click the slide master. When a shortcut menu displays, point to Custom Animation (Figure 2-56).**

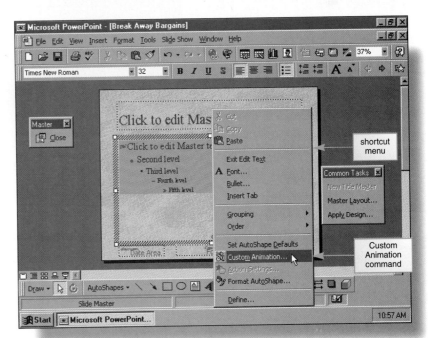

FIGURE 2-56

3 Click Custom Animation. If necessary, when the Custom Animation dialog box displays, click the Effects tab.

The Custom Animation dialog box displays (Figure 2-57).

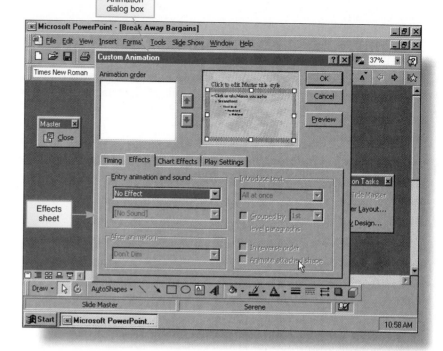

FIGURE 2-57

4 Click the Entry animation and sound box arrow. Scroll down the list until Zoom In From Screen Center displays. Then point to Zoom In From Screen Center (Figure 2-58).

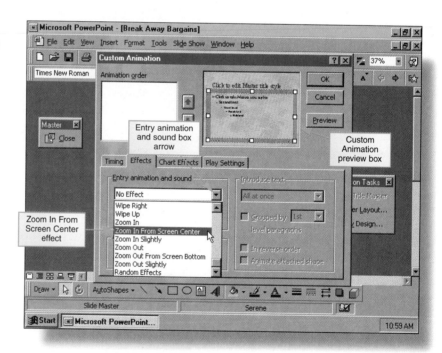

FIGURE 2-58

5 **Click Zoom In From Screen Center. Then point to the Grouped by level paragraphs box arrow.**

The Entry animation and sound list box displays Zoom In From Screen Center (Figure 2-59). A check mark displays in the Grouped by level paragraphs list box.

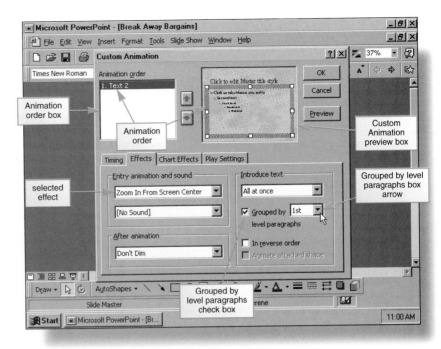

FIGURE 2-59

6 **Click the Grouped by level paragraphs box arrow and then point to 3rd.**

3rd is highlighted in the Grouped by level paragraphs list (Figure 2-60).

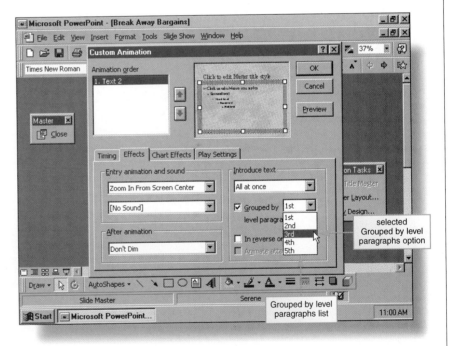

FIGURE 2-60

7 **Click 3rd and then click the OK button.**

PowerPoint applies the animation effects to the slide master, closes the Custom Animation dialog box, and then displays the slide master (Figure 2-61).

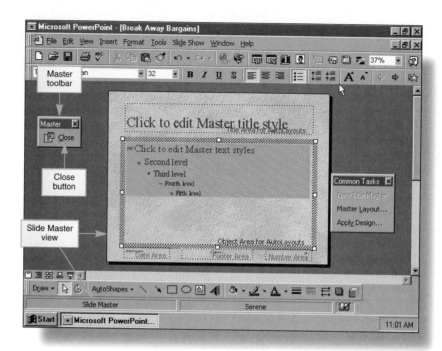

FIGURE 2-61

8 **Click the Close button on the Master toolbar.**

PowerPoint closes the slide master and returns to slide sorter view (Figure 2-62).

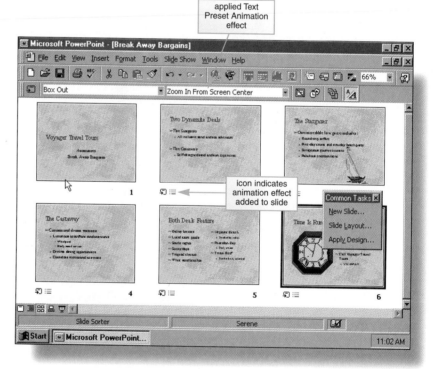

FIGURE 2-62

The Zoom In From Screen Center animation effect displays for each bulleted paragraph on paragraph level 1, 2, or 3 on Slides 2 through 6 during the running of an electronic slide show.

To remove animation effects from the slide master, press and hold down the SHIFT key, click the Slide View button, release the SHIFT key, right-click the slide master, click Custom Animation, click the Entry animation and sound box arrow, click No effect in the Entry animation and sound list, click the OK button, and then click the Close button on the Master toolbar.

Animating Clip Art Objects

Animating a clip art object takes several steps. First display the slide containing the clip art in slide view (Slide 3 in this project). Then select the clip art object and display the Custom Animation dialog box. Next, select the animation effect. Finally, apply the animation effect as described in the following sections.

Displaying a Slide in Slide View

PowerPoint requires you to display a slide in slide view before adding animation effects to clip art. Before continuing with the animation of the sailboat on Slide 3, display the slide in slide view as described in the following step.

TO DISPLAY A SLIDE IN SLIDE VIEW

Step 1: Double-click Slide 3.

Slide 3 displays in slide view.

With Slide 3 displaying in slide view, you are ready to animate the sailboat clip art as explained in the next section.

Animating Clip Art

PowerPoint allows you to animate clip art by selecting an animation effect from a list. Because Slide 3 features The Stargazer vacation package, you want to emphasize the slow, gentle cruise by displaying the sailboat slowly across the bottom of the slide. Perform the steps on the next page to add the Crawl From Right animation effect to the sailboat on Slide 3.

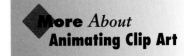

More *About*
Animating Clip Art

When animating a clip art object, consider adding sound effects to communicate a concept. Select an appropriate sound from the list in the Entry animation and sound list box on the Effects sheet in the Custom Animation dialog box.

Steps **To Animate Clip Art**

1 **Right-click the sailboat clip art object and then click Custom Animation on the shortcut menu. If necessary, click the Effects tab.**

The Custom Animation dialog box displays (Figure 2-63). The sailboat is selected in the preview box. Text 2, the bulleted list on Slide 3, is listed in the Animation order box because of the text animation applied to the slide master earlier in this project.

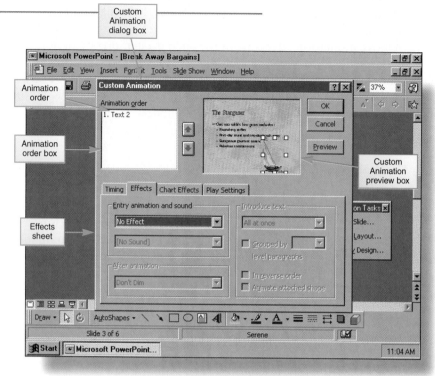

FIGURE 2-63

2 **Click the Entry animation and sound box arrow. Scroll down the list until Crawl From Right displays and then point to Crawl From Right (Figure 2-64).**

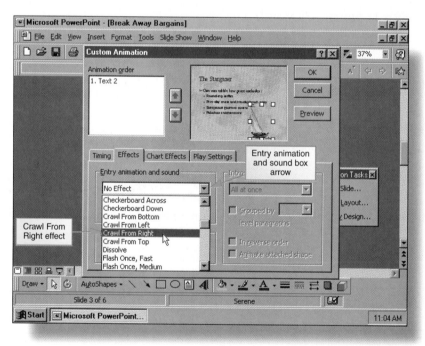

FIGURE 2-64

3 **Click Crawl From Right and then point to the OK button.**

Crawl From Right displays in the Entry animation and sound list box (Figure 2-65). Object 3, the sailboat, displays as number 2 in the Animation order box.

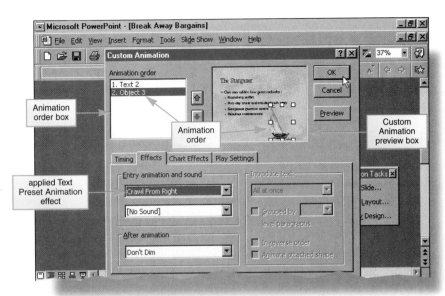

FIGURE 2-65

4 **Click the OK button.**

PowerPoint applies Crawl From Right animation effects to the clip art and closes the Custom Animation dialog box (Figure 2-66). Slide 3 displays in slide view.

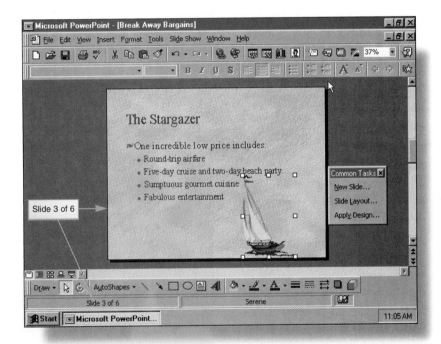

FIGURE 2-66

During the running of the slide show, the sailboat slowly will move across the bottom of the slide as if it was sailing across water. The sailboat will begin moving from the right side of the slide and stop at the position at which it was placed when you inserted the sailboat onto Slide 3.

Other**Ways**

1. Click clip art, on Slide Show menu click Custom Animation, click Effects tab, click Entry animation and sound box arrow, click desired animation effect, click OK

2. Press TAB until clip art is selected, press ALT+D, press M, press right arrow key to select Effects tab, press down arrow until desired animation effect selected, press ENTER

More *About*
Animating a Title Slide

Choose title slide animation effects carefully. Choose traditional effects, such as Fly From Left, when addressing a serious topic. Choose flashy, fun animation effects, such as Spiral, for lighter, less serious topics.

Formatting and Animating a Title Slide

The title slide of every presentation should seize the attention of the audience. In order to excite the audience with the Break Away Bargains presentation, you want to intensify the subtitle object on the title slide. First, you italicize the word Announces and then increase the size of the words in the subtitle, Break Away Bargains. Finally, you add animation effects to the subtitle.

The first step is to display Slide 1 and then format the title slide subtitle. Perform the following steps to format the subtitle object on Slide 1.

TO CHANGE TEXT FONT STYLE TO ITALIC AND INCREASE FONT SIZE

Step 1: Drag the vertical scroll box to display Slide 1.
Step 2: Double-click the word, Announces, and then click the Italic button on the Formatting toolbar.
Step 3: Triple-click the paragraph, Break Away Bargains.
Step 4: Click the Increase Font Size button three times until 44 displays in the Font Size list box on the Formatting toolbar.

The formatted subtitle on Slide 1 displays (Figure 2-67). The word, Announces, displays the italic font style and the paragraph, Break Away Bargains, displays in font size 44.

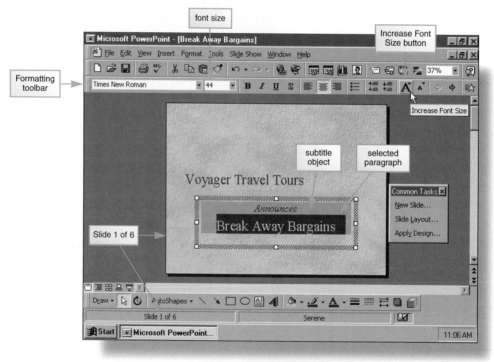

FIGURE 2-67

The next step is to apply the Spiral animation effect to the subtitle text. Perform the following steps to animate the paragraphs in the subtitle object on Slide 1.

TO ANIMATE TEXT

Step 1: Right-click the subtitle object and then click Custom Animation on the shortcut menu.

Step 2: If necessary, click the Effects tab in the Custom Animation dialog box.

Step 3: Click the Entry animation and sound box arrow.

Step 4: Scroll down the list until Spiral displays and then click Spiral.

Step 5: Click the OK button.

The subtitle object, Text 2, displays in the Animation order box and is selected in the preview box. Spiral displays in the Entry animation and sound list box. By default, the subtitle text is grouped by first level paragraphs. PowerPoint applies the animation effect, closes the Custom Animation dialog box, and then displays Slide 1.

Animation effects are complete for this presentation. You now are ready to review the presentation in slide show view.

Saving the Presentation Again

The presentation is complete. Save the finished presentation to a floppy disk before running the slide show.

TO SAVE A PRESENTATION TO A FLOPPY DISK

Step 1: Click the Save button on the Standard toolbar.

PowerPoint saves the presentation to your floppy disk by saving the changes made to the presentation since the last save.

Running an Animated Slide Show

Project 1 introduced you to using slide show view to look at your presentation one slide at a time. This project introduces you to running a slide show with slide transition effects and text and object animation effects. When you run a slide show with slide transition effects, PowerPoint displays the slide transition effect when you click the mouse button to advance to the next slide. When a slide has text animation effects, each paragraph level displays as determined by the animation settings. Animated clip art objects display the selected animation effect in the sequence established in the Custom Animation dialog box. Perform the steps on the next page to run the animated Break Away Bargains slide show.

Steps To Run an Animated Slide Show

1 **With Slide 1 displaying, click the Slide Show button on the View Button Bar. When Slide 1 displays in slide show view, click the slide anywhere except on the Popup Menu buttons.**

PowerPoint first displays the Serene design template and then displays the title slide title object, Voyager Travel Tours (Figure 2-68). Recall the Popup Menu buttons display when you move the mouse pointer during a slide show.

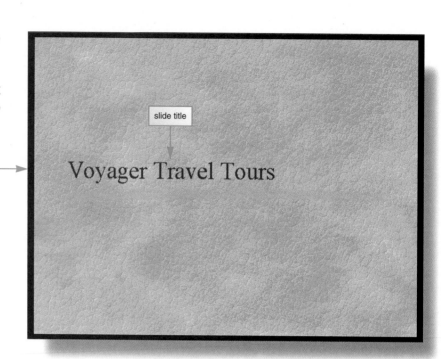

FIGURE 2-68

2 **Click the slide anywhere except on the Popup Menu buttons.**

PowerPoint displays the first heading level 1 subtitle paragraph using the Spiral animation effect (Figure 2-69).

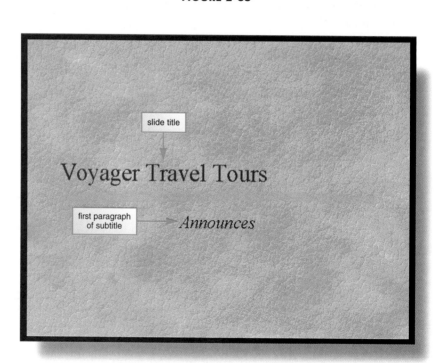

FIGURE 2-69

3 **Click the slide anywhere except on the Popup Menu buttons.**

PowerPoint displays the second heading level 1 subtitle paragraph beneath the first heading level 1 subtitle paragraph. PowerPoint again uses the Spiral animation effect (Figure 2-70).

4 **Click the slide anywhere except on the Popup Menu buttons. Continue clicking to finish running the slide show and return to slide sorter view.**

Each time a new slide displays, PowerPoint first displays the Box Out slide transition effect and then displays only the slide title. Then, PowerPoint builds each slide based on the animation settings. When you click the slide after the last paragraph displays on the last slide of the presentation, PowerPoint exits slide show view and returns to slide sorter view.

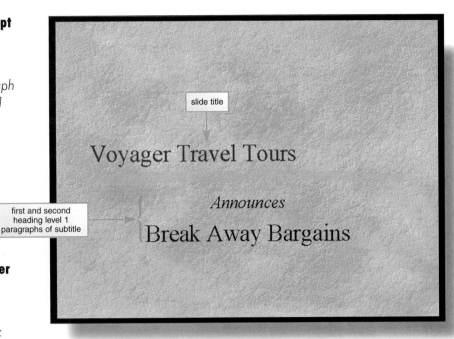

FIGURE 2-70

Now that the presentation is complete and you have tested the animation effects, the last step is to print the presentation outline and slides.

Printing in Outline View

When you click the Print button on the Standard toolbar, PowerPoint prints a hard copy of the presentation component last selected in the Print what box in the Print dialog box. To be certain to print the component you want, such as the presentation outline, use the Print command located on the File menu. When the Print dialog box displays, you can select the appropriate presentation component in the Print what box. The next two sections explain how to use the Print command to print the presentation outline and the presentation slides.

Printing an Outline

During the development of a lengthy presentation, it often is easier to review your outline in print rather than on-screen. Printing your outline also is useful for audience handouts or when your supervisor or instructor wants to review your subject matter before you fully develop your presentation.

Other Ways

1. On Slide Show menu click View Show, click slide until slide show ends
2. Press ALT+D, press V, press ENTER until slide show ends

Recall that the Print dialog box displays print options. When you wish to print your outline, select Outline View in the Print what list located in the Print dialog box. The outline, however, prints as last viewed in outline view. This means that you must select the Zoom setting to display the outline text as you wish it to print. If you are uncertain of the Zoom setting, you should return to outline view and review it prior to printing. Perform the following steps to print an outline from slide view.

Steps **To Print an Outline**

1 **Ready the printer according to the printer manufacturer's instructions. Click File on the menu bar and then point to Print.**

The File menu displays (Figure 2-71).

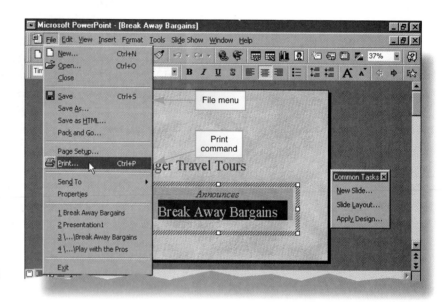

FIGURE 2-71

2 **Click Print.**

The Print dialog box displays (Figure 2-72).

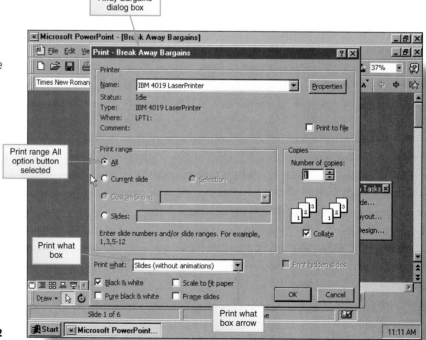

FIGURE 2-72

3 **Click the Print what box arrow and then point to Outline View.**

Outline View displays highlighted in the Print what list (Figure 2-73).

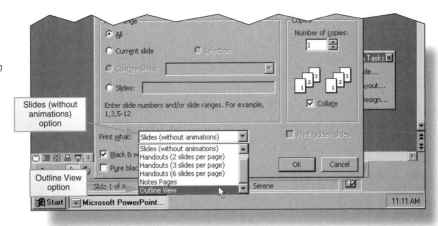

FIGURE 2-73

4 **Click Outline View and then point to the OK button (Figure 2-74).**

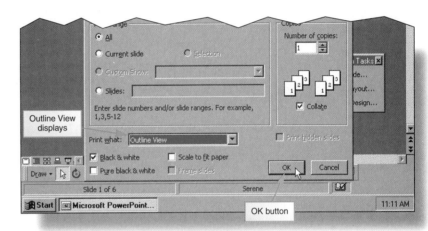

FIGURE 2-74

5 **Click the OK button.**

PowerPoint momentarily displays a message in the Print Status dialog box explaining that the outline is printing as last viewed (Figure 2-75). To cancel the print request, click the Cancel button.

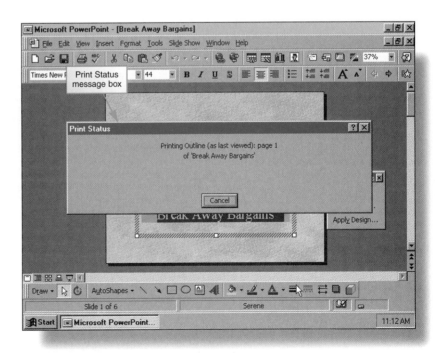

FIGURE 2-75

6 **When the printer stops, retrieve the printout of the outline (Figure 2-76).**

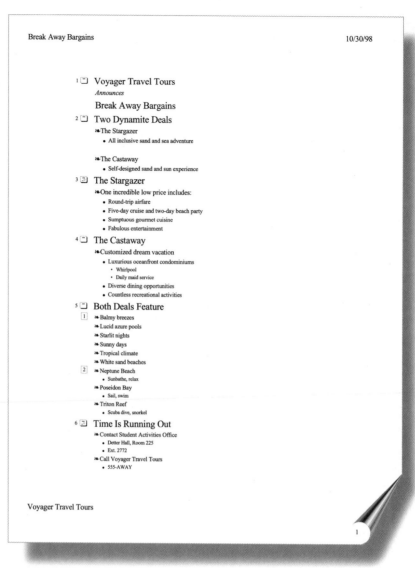

FIGURE 2-76

You may select the Print command from the File menu while in any view except slide show view.

Printing Presentation Slides

After correcting errors, you will want to print a final copy of your presentation. If you made any changes to your presentation since your last save, be sure to save your presentation before you print.

Perform the following steps to print the presentation.

TO PRINT PRESENTATION SLIDES

Step 1: Ready the printer according to the printer manufacturer's instructions.

Step 2: Click File on the menu bar and then click Print.

Step 3: When the Print dialog box displays, click the Print what box arrow.

Step 4: Click Slides (without animations).

Step 5: Click the OK button. When the printer stops, retrieve the slide printouts.

The printouts should look like the slides in Figure 2-77.

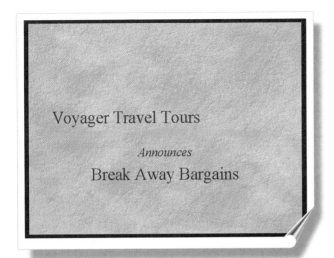

FIGURE 2-77a

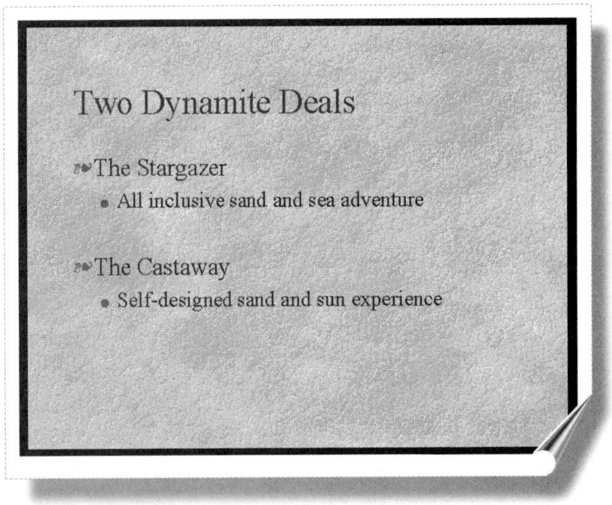

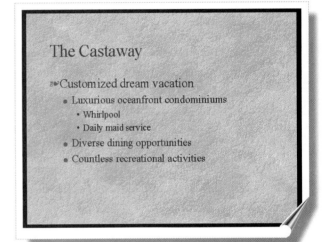

FIGURE 2-77b

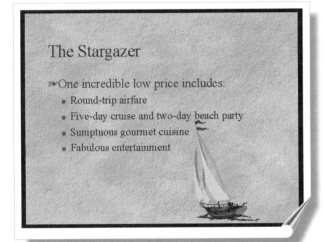

FIGURE 2-77c

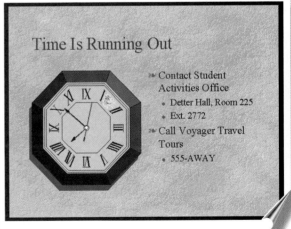

FIGURE 2-77d

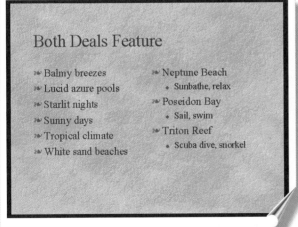

FIGURE 2-77e

FIGURE 2-77f

The Print what list in the Print dialog box contains options for printing two, three, or six slide images per page. These options are labeled as Handouts (2 slides per page), Handouts (3 slides per page), and Handouts (6 slides per page). Printing handouts is useful for reviewing a presentation because you print several slides on one page. Additionally, many businesses distribute handouts of the slide show before a presentation so the attendees can refer to a copy.

Saving and Quitting PowerPoint

If you made any changes to your presentation since your last save, you should save it again before quitting PowerPoint. For more details on quitting PowerPoint, refer to page PP 1.38 in Project 1. Perform the following steps to save changes to the presentation and quit PowerPoint.

TO SAVE CHANGES AND QUIT POWERPOINT

Step 1: Click the Close button on the title bar.
Step 2: If prompted, click the Yes button in the Microsoft PowerPoint dialog box.

PowerPoint saves any changes made to the presentation since the last save and then quits PowerPoint.

Project Summary

Project 2 introduced you to outline view, clip art, and animation effects. You created a slide presentation in outline view where you entered all the text in the form of an outline. You arranged the text using the Promote and Demote buttons. Once your outline was complete, you changed slide layouts and added clip art to a clip art placeholder. After adding clip art to another slide without using a clip art placeholder, you moved and sized the picture. You added slide transition effects and text animation effects. Then you applied animation effects to clip art. You learned how to run an animated slide show demonstrating slide transition and animation effects. Finally, you printed the presentation outline and slides using the Print command.

What You Should Know

Having completed this project, you now should be able to perform the following tasks:

▶ Add a Blank Line *(PP 2.21)*
▶ Add a Slide in Outline View *(PP 2.12)*
▶ Add Slide Transitions to a Slide Show *(PP 2.39)*
▶ Animate Clip Art *(PP 2.48)*
▶ Animate Text *(PP 2.51)*
▶ Change Slide Layout *(PP 2.23)*
▶ Change the Size of Clip Art *(PP 2.34)*
▶ Change the Slide Layout to Clip Art & Text *(PP 2.27)*
▶ Change the View to Outline View *(PP 2.8)*
▶ Change the View to Slide Sorter View *(PP 2.19)*
▶ Change the View to Slide View *(PP 2.20)*
▶ Change Text Font Style to Italic and Increase Font Size *(PP 2.50)*
▶ Create a Closing Slide in Outline View *(PP 2.18)*
▶ Create a Multi-level Bulleted List Slide in Outline View *(PP 2.13)*
▶ Create a Second Subordinate Slide *(PP 2.16)*
▶ Create a Slide with Multiple Text Objects in Outline View *(PP 2.17)*
▶ Create a Subordinate Slide *(PP 2.15)*

▶ Create a Title Slide in Outline View *(PP 2.11)*
▶ Display a Slide in Slide View *(PP 2.47)*
▶ Insert Clip Art into a Clip Art Placeholder *(PP 2.28)*
▶ Insert Clip Art on a Slide without a Clip Art Placeholder *(PP 2.32)*
▶ Move Clip Art *(PP 2.33)*
▶ Move Text *(PP 2.25)*
▶ Print an Outline *(PP 2.54)*
▶ Print Presentation Slides *(PP 2.56)*
▶ Run an Animated Slide Show *(PP 2.52)*
▶ Run Style Checker *(PP 2.38)*
▶ Save a Presentation *(PP 2.19, 2.36)*
▶ Save a Presentation to a Floppy Disk *(PP 2.51)*
▶ Save Changes and Quit PowerPoint *(PP 2.58)*
▶ Start a New Presentation *(PP 2.7)*
▶ Use the Notes and Handouts Sheet to Add Headers and Footers *(PP 2.36)*
▶ Use the Slide Master to Apply Animation Effects to All Bulleted Slides *(PP 2.43)*

A+ Test Your Knowledge

1 True/False

Instructions: Circle T if the statement is true or F if the statement is false.

T F 1. An outline is a summary of thoughts presented as headings, subheadings, and pictures.

T F 2. Graphic objects, such as pictures, graphs, and tables, do not display in outline view.

T F 3. When in outline view, Microsoft PowerPoint displays the current slide in black-and-white view so you can see how the slide will look in both slide view and slide show view.

T F 4. Each time you click the Demote button the selected paragraph moves down one level in the outline hierarchy.

T F 5. Resolution is the number of pixels per unit of measurement displaying on your computer monitor.

T F 6. The slide that gracefully ends a presentation is the ending slide.

T F 7. Microsoft Clip Gallery 3.0 accompanies Microsoft Office 97 and is a tool that allows you to insert clip art, pictures, audio clips, and video clips into Microsoft Office documents.

T F 8. Right-clicking a clip art placeholder activates instructions to open the Microsoft Clip Gallery 3.0.

T F 9. PowerPoint inserts clip art only into clip art placeholders.

T F 10. Double-clicking a slide miniature in slide sorter view displays that slide in slide view.

2 Multiple Choice

Instructions: Circle the correct response.

1. Outline view provides a quick, easy way to _____.
   a. add animation effects
   b. create a presentation
   c. insert clip art
   d. display slide miniatures

2. An outline _____.
   a. is a summary of thoughts
   b. uses indentation to establish a hierarchy to denote levels of importance
   c. allows you to organize your thoughts in a structured format
   d. all of the above

3. When viewing a presentation in outline view, you know which slides contain graphic objects because _____.
   a. slide icons display blank when a slide contains graphics
   b. all graphics display in outline view
   c. slide icons display a small graphic when a slide contains graphics
   d. none of the above

(continued)

A+ Test Your Knowledge

Multiple Choice (continued)

4. In PowerPoint, a presentation outline begins with a title on _____.
   a. heading level 0
   b. heading level 1
   c. heading level 2
   d. none of the above

5. Clicking the _____ button moves selected text above the preceding displayed paragraph while maintaining its hierarchical heading level and text style.
   a. Promote
   b. Demote
   c. Move Up
   d. Move Down

6. Microsoft Clip Gallery 3.0 _____.
   a. is shared with PowerPoint and other Microsoft Office 97 applications
   b. combines topic-related images into categories
   c. is a tool that allows you to insert clip art, pictures, audio clips, and video clips into a presentation
   d. all of the above

7. The relationship between the height and width of an object is its _____.
   a. height-to-width ratio
   b. aspect ratio
   c. size
   d. scale

8. The animation effect that displays when one slide moves off the screen and another slide displays on the screen is _____.
   a. custom animation
   b. clip art animation
   c. text animation
   d. slide transition

9. The default PowerPoint setting that allows for saving only the changes made to a presentation since the last save is called a(n) _____.
   a. intermediate save
   b. full save
   c. fast save
   d. all of the above

10. Clicking the Print button on the Standard toolbar when displaying the presentation in outline view instructs PowerPoint to print the presentation in _____.
    a. outline view
    b. slide view
    c. slide sorter view
    d. the view last printed

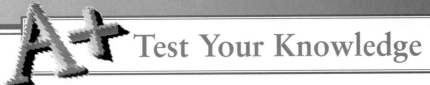

Test Your Knowledge

_3_ Understanding a Microsoft PowerPoint Window in Outline View

Instructions:
Arrows in Figure 2-78 point to the major components of a Microsoft PowerPoint window in outline view. Identify the various parts of the window in the spaces provided.

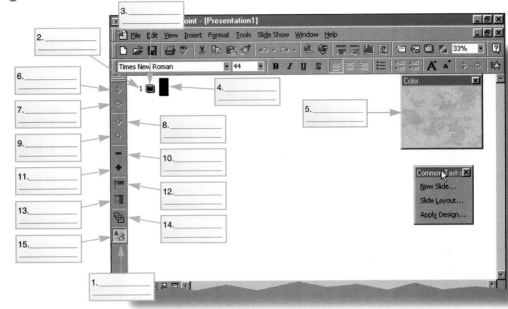

FIGURE 2-78

_4_ Understanding the Custom Animation Dialog Box

Instructions: In Figure 2-79, arrows point to several of the components in the Custom Animation dialog box. Identify the various parts of the dialog box in the spaces provided.

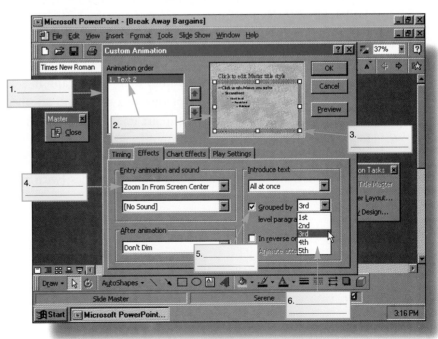

FIGURE 2-79

Use Help

1 Learning More about PowerPoint

Instructions: Perform the following tasks using a computer.

1. If PowerPoint is not started already, start a new PowerPoint presentation and select any AutoLay-out. If necessary, click the Office Assistant to display the What would you like to do? box.
2. Type outline view in the What would you like to do? text box and then click the Search button. Click the topic Ways to organize my content in outline view. When the Microsoft PowerPoint window displays, read the information, right-click within the dialog box, and click Print Topic. When the Print dialog box displays, click the OK button. Click the Help Topics button to return to the Help Topics: Microsoft PowerPoint dialog box. If necessary, click the Find tab.
3. Type outline in box 1. Double-click the Change the order of slides in a presentation topic displayed in box 3. When the Microsoft PowerPoint window displays, read and print the information. Click the Help Topics button to return to the Help Topics: Microsoft PowerPoint dialog box.
4. Scroll the topics listed in box 3 to display File formats for saving presentations. Double-click File formats for saving presentations. When the Microsoft PowerPoint window displays, read and print the information. Click the Close button to exit Help. Submit the printouts to your instructor.

2 Expanding on the Basics

Instructions: Use PowerPoint online Help to better understand the topics listed below. Begin each of the following by clicking the Office Assistant button on the Standard toolbar. If you cannot print the Help information, answer the question on a separate piece of paper.

1. When in outline view, how do you change the color of a bullet for all slides in a presentation?
2. How do you change the bullet character from a dot to an open file folder?
3. How do you add a period to the end of every paragraph in a list?
4. How do you replace one clip art picture in a slide with another picture?
5. How do you build a slide with a clip art image that appears to fly onto the slide?
6. How do you add sound to animation effects?
7. How do you change the order animated objects display on a slide?
8. What happens when you print slides using the Slides (with animations) option?

Apply Your Knowledge

1 Intensifying a Presentation by Applying a Design Template, Changing Slide Layout, Inserting Clip Art, and Applying Animation Effects

Instructions: Start PowerPoint. Open the presentation, Apply-2, from the PowerPoint folder on the Data Disk that accompanies this book. Perform the following tasks to change the presentation to look like Figure 2-80 on the next page.

1. Apply the Blush design template. Add the current date, slide number, and your name to the footer. Display the footer on all slides and on notes and handouts.
2. On Slide 1, insert one blank paragraph after the November 14, 1998 paragraph. Insert the runner clip art image shown in Figure 2-80 that has the keywords, Victory Performance Fast Invincible. Scale the clip art to 65% using the Format Picture command. Drag the runner clip art image to align the upper-left corner of the dotted box below the letter o in the word Triathlon, as shown in Figure 2-80. Apply the Zoom In From Screen Center custom animation effect to the clip art. Italicize the paragraph, Sponsored by:, and then decrease the font size to 24 points.
3. Go to Slide 3. Change the slide layout to 2 Column Text. Move the six male categories to the right column placeholder.
4. Go to Slide 4. Change the slide layout to Text & Clip Art. Insert the trophy clip art image shown in Figure 2-80 that has the keywords, Goal Success Reward Accomplishment Impress Trophy. Change the size of the trophy clip art image to 105%. Change the line spacing for the heading level 1 bullets to 0.75 lines before each paragraph.
5. Go to Slide 5. Change the slide layout to Clip Art & Text. Insert the directional post clip art image shown in Figure 2-80 that has the keywords, Direction Alternative Solution. Change the line spacing for the heading level 1 bullets to 1 line before each paragraph.
6. Add the Box Out slide transition effect to all slides except the title slide.
7. Save the presentation to a floppy disk using the file name, Southwestern Triathlon.
8. Print the presentation in black and white. Print the presentation outline.
9. Quit PowerPoint.

(continued)

Apply Your Knowledge

Intensifying a Presentation by Applying a Design Template, Changing Slide Layout, Inserting Clip Art, and Applying Animation Effects *(continued)*

FIGURE 2-80a

FIGURE 2-80b

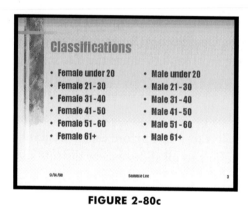

FIGURE 2-80c

FIGURE 2-80d

FIGURE 2-80e

In the Lab

1 Adding Clip Art and Animation Effects to a Presentation Created in Outline View

Problem: You are enrolled in Psychology 401. Your professor assigns a research paper and requires you to present your findings during a five-minute presentation. Your topic is positive mental attitude. You create the outline shown in Figure 2-81 to prepare your presentation. You use the outline to create the slide show shown in Figure 2-82 on the next page. Because of your research findings, you create a unique closing slide.

Instructions: Perform the following tasks.

1. Create a new presentation using the high voltage design template.

2. Using the outline shown in Figure 2-81, create the title slide shown in Figure 2-82. Use your name instead of the name Chelsea Ihalainen. Increase the font size of your name to 36 points.

3. Using the outline in Figure 2-81, create the three bulleted list slides shown in Figure 2-82.

4. Change the slide layout on Slide 2 to Clip Art & Text. Using the clip art placeholder, insert the clip art shown in Figure 2-82 that has the keywords, Success Victory Accomplishment Result Invincible Milestone Superior. Increase the bulleted list font size to 36 points.

```
1) Positive Mental Attitude
   a) Chelsea Ihalainen
   b) Psychology 401
2) Positive Attitude Characteristics
   a) Cheerful
   b) Considerate
   c) Courteous
   d) Friendly
   e) Neat
   f) Thoughtful
3) How to Improve Your Attitude
   a) Associate with positive people
   b) Speak well of others
   c) Isolate negative thoughts
   d) Treat others with respect
   e) Forgive and forge on
4) Attitude is Everything. . .
   a) Anything is possible with a positive attitude
```

FIGURE 2-81

5. Change the slide layout on Slide 3 to Text & Clip Art. Using the clip art placeholder, insert the clip art shown in Figure 2-82 that has the keywords, Consensus Cooperate Guarantee Synergy Agreeable. Increase the bulleted list line spacing to 0.4 lines before each paragraph.

6. On Slide 4, change the font size of Anything is possible with a positive attitude, to italic, 72 points. Center the bulleted text and then remove the bullet.

7. Add the slide number and your name to the slide footer. Display the footer on all slides. Add your name to the outline header and your school's name to the outline footer.

(continued)

In the Lab

Adding Clip Art and Animation Effects to a Presentation Created in Outline View *(continued)*

8. Apply the Strips Right-Down slide transition effect to all slides. Apply the Wipe Right custom animation effect to all heading level 1 paragraphs on Slide 2 and Slide 3.
9. Check the presentation for errors.
10. Save the presentation on a floppy disk using the file name, Positive Attitude.
11. Print the presentation outline. Print the black and white presentation.
12. Quit PowerPoint.

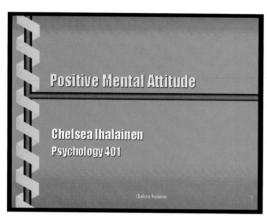

FIGURE 2-82a

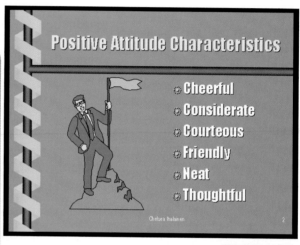

FIGURE 2-82b

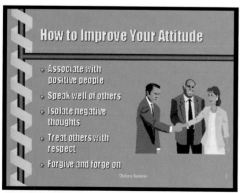

FIGURE 2-82c

FIGURE 2-82d

FIGURE 2-82

In the Lab

2 Animating a Slide Show

Problem: You are the marketing director for Clarity Health Products, a manufacturer of vitamins and other nutritional supplements. Experience tells you that sales are related directly to the quality of the sales presentation. Sales quotas are higher than last year and you want to make sure your sales staff understands the importance of practicing the delivery of a presentation. After much research, you prepare the outline shown in Figure 2-83. When you practice your presentation, you decide to add animation effects to the slide show. The completed slide show is shown in Figure 2-84.

Instructions: Perform the following tasks. *Hint:* Use Help to solve this problem.

1. Create a new presentation using the Ribbons design template and the outline shown in Figure 2-83.

2. On the title slide, use your name instead of the name Anna Douglas. Decrease the font size of Presented by: to 20 points. Decrease the font size of Marketing Director and Clarity Health Products to 24 points.

3. On Slide 2, increase the font size of the heading level 1 bullets to 36 points and heading level 2 bullets to 32 points. Increase the line spacing for heading level 2 bullets to 0.75 lines before each paragraph. Using Figure 2-84 as a reference, insert the clip art that has the keyword, Leadership. Scale the clip art to 95% and drag it to the lower-right corner of the slide as shown in Figure 2-84.

4. On Slide 3, insert the clip art shown in Figure 2-84 that has the keywords, Surprise Incomprehensible Incredible. Scale the clip art to 90%. Drag the clip art to the right side of the slide.

I. Polishing Your Presentation
   A. Presented by:
   B. Anna Douglas
   C. Marketing Director
   D. Clarity Health Products
II. Practice Makes Perfect
   A. Three key factors for a successful presentation
      1. Practice
      2. Practice
      3. Practice
III. Why Practice?
   A. Increase confidence
   B. Develop rhythm
      1. Pause for emphasis
   C. Improve articulation
      1. Vary pitch and inflection
   D. Establish timings
   E. Identify problems
IV. How To Practice
   A. Speak out loud
      1. Make a recording
         a) Video
         b) Audio
      2. Look into a mirror
      3. Find a live audience
         a) Friend or co-worker
         b) Group or team
   B. Go to delivery site
      1. Inspect equipment
         a) Audio-visual
         b) Lectern
      2. Check environment
         a) Noise
         b) Lighting
         c) Room temperature
V. Practice Makes Perfect

FIGURE 2-83

(continued)

In the Lab

Animating a Slide Show *(continued)*

5. On Slide 4, change the slide layout to 2 Column Text. Drag the text into the right column place-holder so your slide looks like Slide 4 in Figure 2-84. Increase the line spacing to 0.5 lines before each paragraph.

6. On Slide 5, change the slide layout to Object. Insert the clip art that has the keywords, Target Incredible.

7. Add the current date, slide number, and your name to the slide footer. Display the footer on all slides. Include the current date and your name on the outline header. Include Clarity Health Products and the page number on the outline footer.

8. Apply the Strips Right-Up slide transition effect to all slides. Apply the Fly From Bottom custom animation effect to bulleted text on Slides 1 through 4. Introduce text grouped by 3rd level paragraphs.

9. Animate the clip art on Slide 2 using the Fly From Bottom-Right custom animation effect so it displays immediately after the slide title when you run the slide show. Animate clip art on Slide 5 using the Zoom In From Screen Center custom animation effect.

10. Save the presentation on a floppy disk using the file name, Polishing Your Presentation.

11. Print the presentation outline. Print the presentation slides without animations in black and white.

12. Quit PowerPoint.

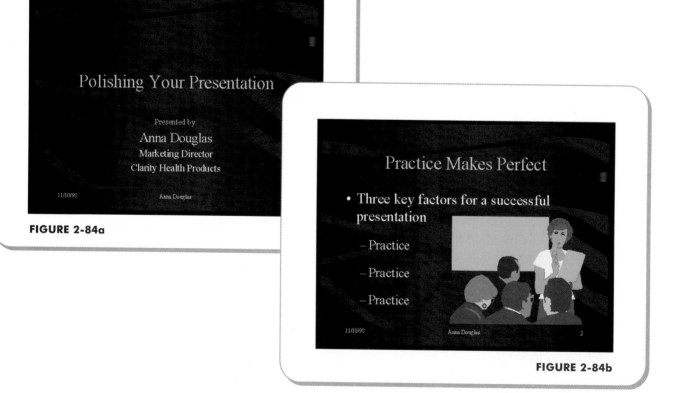

FIGURE 2-84a

FIGURE 2-84b

In the Lab

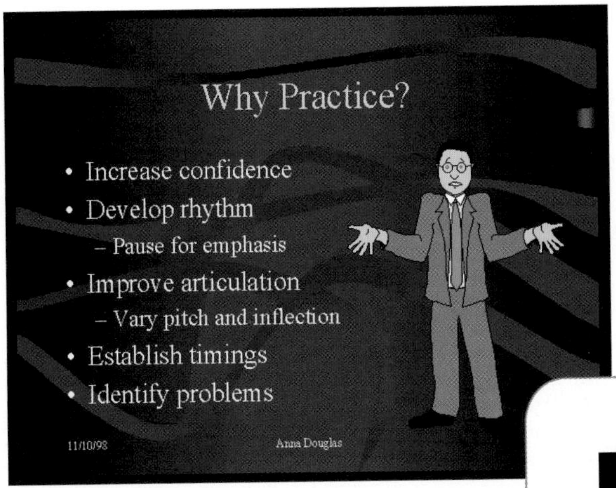

FIGURE 2-84c

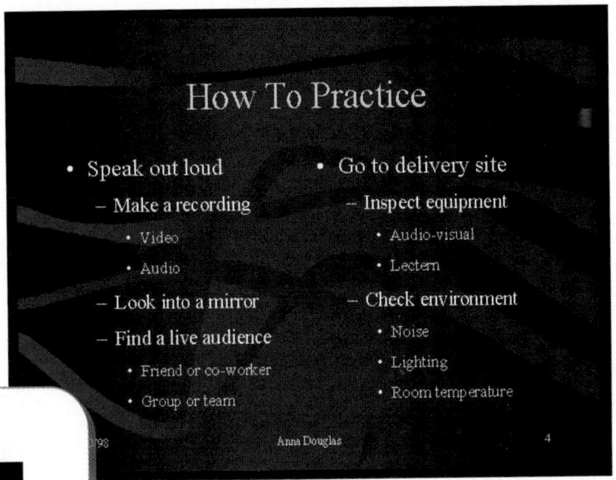

FIGURE 2-84d

FIGURE 2-84e

In the Lab

3 Creating a Presentation in Outline View, Inserting and Moving Clip Art, and Applying Slide Transition and Animation Effects

Problem: You are Maurice Barber, the Director of Career Development and Placement at Mercedes Valley College. A local middle school principal has asked you to speak to his eighth grade students about career opportunities. You create the presentation using the outline shown in Figure 2-85. You then refine the presentation using clip art, slide transitions, and animation effects to create the slide show shown in Figure 2-86. *Hint*: Use Help to solve this problem.

Instructions: Perform the following tasks.

1. Create a new presentation using the Zesty design template and the outline in Figure 2-85.

2. On the title slide, animate the subtitle with the Zoom In From Screen Center custom animation effect.

3. Use Figure 2-86 as a reference. Change the slide layout on Slide 2 to Clip Art & Text. Then insert clip art that has the keywords, Opportunity Knocks. Increase line spacing to 1 line before paragraph on heading level 1.

4. Change the slide layout on Slide 3 to Clip Art & Text. Insert clip art that has the keywords, Focus Investigation Diagnose.

5. On Slide 4, insert the clip art that has the keywords, Surprise Incomprehensible Incredible. Scale the clip art to 75%. Move the clip art to the right edge of the slide as shown in Figure 2-86.

6. Add the slide number and your name to the slide footer. Display the footer on all slides. Display your name to the outline header, and the page number, and the name of the school, Mercedes Valley College, to the outline footer.

7. Check the presentation for spelling errors.

I.	Future Considerations
	A. What Will You Be When You Grow Up?
II.	What Is In Your Future?
	A. Education
	1. College
	2. Technical School
	3. Apprenticeship
	B. Work
	1. On the job training
III.	Investigate Options
	A. Engineer
	B. Entertainer
	C. Florist
	D. Machinist
	E. Nurse
	F. Programmer
	G. Teacher
	H. Veterinarian
IV.	How Do You Choose?
	A. Consider likes and dislikes
	1. Reading and writing
	2. Working with people
	3. Working with animals
	4. Working with computers
	5. Working with your hands

FIGURE 2-85

In the Lab

8. Apply the Box In slide transition effect to all slides. Apply the Strips Right-Down custom animation effect to all 2nd level paragraphs on Slides 2 through 4. Apply the Peek From Left custom animation effect to clip art on Slide 3 and then change animation order so the clip art displays before the bulleted text.

9. Save the presentation on a floppy disk using the file name, Future Considerations.

10. Run the electronic slide show.

11. Print the presentation outline. Print the presentation slides without animations in black and white.

12. Quit PowerPoint.

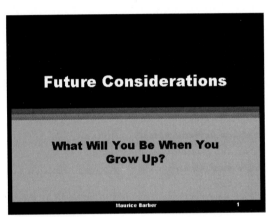

FIGURE 2-86a

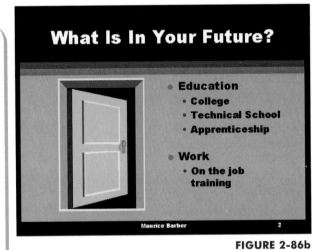

FIGURE 2-86b

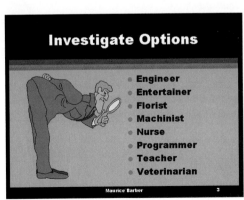

FIGURE 2-86c

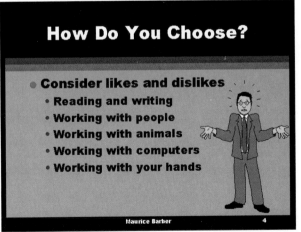

FIGURE 2-86d

Cases and Places

The difficulty of these case studies varies: ▶ are the least difficult; ▶▶ are more difficult; and ▶▶▶ are the most difficult.

1 ▶ AAA Accounting and Tax Consultants is a privately owned accounting firm. Marshall Weatherbee, president of the firm, is one of several Certified Public Accountants conducting short presentations at a financial planning seminar. The purpose of the seminar is to inform people about their financial options and to promote the services of the presenters. To prepare for the presentation, Mr. Weatherbee created the following outline.

Using the concepts and techniques introduced in this project, together with Mr. Weatherbee's outline, develop slides for an electronic slide show. Include clip art and animation effects to add interest. Print the outline so that it can be distributed to the audience at the conclusion of the presentation.

FIGURE 2-87

I. AAA Accounting and Tax Consultants
   A. We listen to you and work as a team to meet your financial goals.
   B. Marshall Weatherbee, President
II. Prepare for Retirement, Now
   A. Follow 20/80 rule for current income
      1. Live on 20%
      2. Save 80%
   B. Eliminate all debt
   C. Establish financial plan
III. Financial Plan
   A. Establish monthly budget
   B. Develop investment strategy
      1. High-risk investments
      2. Low-risk investments
      3. Savings
   C. Consult with certified financial planner
IV. AAA Accounting and Tax Consultants
   A. Comprehensive financial planning
      1. Financial and estate
      2. Retirement
      3. Education
      4. Investments
      5. Insurance
   B. Additional services
      1. Tax strategies
      2. Tax preparation
      3. Tax audit representation
      4. Debt reduction strategies
      5. Business planning

Cases and Places

2 ▶ First Class Limousine advertises their services at bridal fairs, county fairs, and business conventions. Next week is the 1998 Stone Mountain bridal fair. You have been asked to create a professional-looking presentation from the outline developed by the company owner, Margo Quinn.

Using the concepts and techniques introduced in this project along with the following outline, create an electronic presentation for First Class Limousine. Include appropriate clip art and animation effects. Ms. Quinn would like a printed outline that can be distributed to the audience at the conclusion of the presentation.

I.   First Class Limousine
  A. The ultimate in luxury, comfort, and affordability
  B. A special ride for your special day
II. Affordable Packages
  A. Debutante
    1. Luxury transportation at reasonable rates
  B. Princess
    1. Pampered conveyance in style
  C. Royalty
    1. A once-in-a-lifetime adventure
III. Debutante
  A. The basic package includes:
    1. Six passenger sedan
    2. Courteous, licensed driver
    3. Soft drinks
IV. Princess
  A. The most popular package offers:
    1. Eight passenger luxury sedan
    2. Courteous, licensed driver in chauffeur's cap
    3. Refreshments
      a) Soft drinks and hors d'oeuvres
    4. Twelve-speaker CD sound system

V.   Royalty
  A. The aristocratic package features:
    1. Ten or twelve passenger stretch limousine
    2. Courteous, licensed driver in top hat and tails
    3. Refreshments
      a) Soft drinks and hors d'oeuvres
      b) Lobster salad or prime rib sandwiches
    4. Live music
      a) Concert violinist performs customized selection
            of songs
VI. Luxury Limousines
  A. New 6, 8, and 12 passenger sedans
  B. TV, VCR, and mood lights
  C. Beverages
  D. Glass and privacy partitions
  E. Cellular telephone
VII. Travel First Class Limousine
  A. Telephone
    1. 555-LIMO
  B. Ask about our FREE hour special

FIGURE 2-88

Cases and Places

3 ▶▶ Diver Dan's Dive Shop sells equipment for SCUBA divers. SCUBA is the acronym for Self-Contained Underwater Breathing Apparatus. Dan, the store's owner, is frequently asked for information about three SCUBA certification programs, PATI, NAUI, and YMCA. Each program has different teaching approaches and certification standards. Dan wants you to create a presentation that compares and contrasts the three programs. He also wants the presentation to be animated and include clip art. Research the three certification programs and then using the concepts and techniques introduced in this project, create the presentation. Create handouts from the presentation outline.

4 ▶▶ Goals are often divided into four categories: spiritual, family, career, and self. A 1973 Yale University economics study concluded that three-percent of the 1953 Yale graduating class had written goals and defined a plan with which to reach them. Twenty years later, the same three-percent had achieved a net worth greater than the rest of the entire class combined. Using the techniques introduced in the project, create a presentation about yourself. Provide a brief biography. Develop a list of your goals. Under each goal category, identify two or more goals. One goal should be a short-term goal, something that will take less than a year to achieve. Another goal would be a long-term goal, something that will take longer than one year to achieve. Include appropriate clip art and animation effects.

5 ▶▶▶ In addition to Microsoft PowerPoint, other presentation graphics software packages include Persuasion, Compel, Freelance Graphics, and Harvard Graphics. Visit a software vendor and try one of these or another presentation graphics package. Using current computer magazines or other resources, learn more about the package you tested. Based on what you have discovered, together with the concepts and techniques introduced in this project, prepare a presentation comparing and contrasting the package you tested against Microsoft PowerPoint. Contrast the capabilities, strengths, weaknesses, ease of use, and cost of each package. End by noting which package you prefer and your reasons why. Enhance the presentation with clip art and custom animation. Print the outline of the presentation.

6 ▶▶▶ Recent economic changes have forced many organizations to alter their business focus from manufacturing to service. To be successful, service-oriented businesses must be able to clearly and convincingly explain how they can benefit prospective clients. Visit a local business that provides a service and learn all you can about the service and the people to whom it is being offered. Using the results of your visit, along with the concepts and techniques introduced in this project, prepare a presentation promoting the company's services. Embellish the presentation with clip art and custom animation effects. Print the presentation and the presentation outline.

7 ▶▶▶ Are people born with great leadership skills, or do ordinary people develop into great leaders? Leadership expert and author, John Maxwell, states in his book, *The Success Journey*; "Success is not a destination thing, it is a daily thing." Go to the library or use the World Wide Web to research some of the world's great leaders. What qualities do they share? Why are these people considered to be great leaders? Using the results of your research, together with the concepts and techniques introduced in this project, prepare a presentation about leadership. Feature one of the leaders you researched. Enhance the presentation with clip art and custom animation.

Importing Clip Art from the Microsoft Clip Gallery Live Web Site

INTEGRATION FEATURE

Case Perspective

Because of the success of the Break Away Bargains promotion, Mr. Hayes, your boss at Voyager Travel Tours, decides to run the promotion at several schools. After reviewing the presentation, you suggest he replace the clock clip art on Slide 6 to something more persuasive, like a sun, radiating sun rays into the audience. Mr. Hayes agrees and asks you to find a picture of a sun. You look at Microsoft Clip Gallery 3.0, but don't find clip art that you like. Knowing that World Wide Web access was built into Microsoft Clip Gallery 3.0, you decide to browse the Microsoft Clip Gallery Live Web site for clip art. You find several sun clip art images on the Web. You decide to open the clip art into the Microsoft Clip Gallery 3.0 and then insert it into Slide 6.

Your suggestion to Mr. Hayes is to animate the sun to make sure the audience remembers it when they leave the presentation. You decide the best animation effect for the sun is Swivel.

Introduction

As you become more experienced with PowerPoint, you realize that Microsoft Clip Gallery 3.0 has a limited amount of clip art. There are times when you cannot locate an appropriate clip art image in Microsoft Clip Gallery 3.0, or other times when you just want something different. Microsoft, fortunately, created a source for additional clip art, called Microsoft Clip Gallery Live, which is conveniently located on the World Wide Web. To make accessing the Web site easy, Microsoft added a button to the Microsoft Clip Gallery 3.0 dialog box, which, when clicked, connects you directly to the Microsoft Clip Gallery Live start page (Figure 1 on the next page).

In this integration feature, you modify the presentation created in Project 2 by replacing the clock clip art on Slide 6 with clip art from the Web as shown in Figure 2 on the next page.

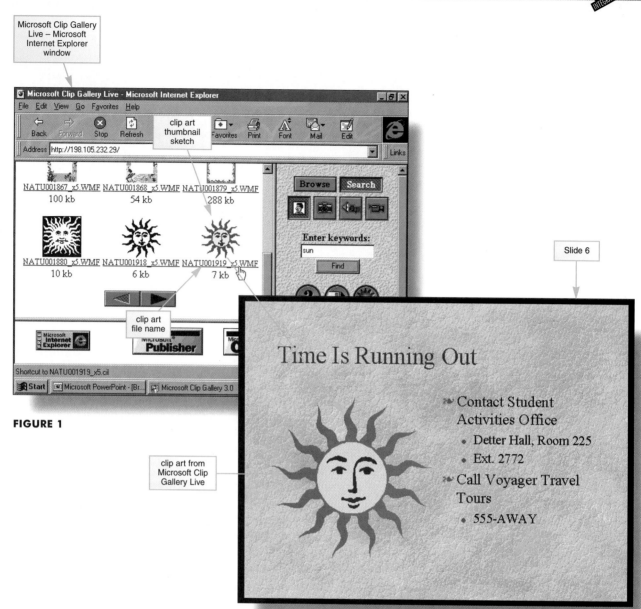

FIGURE 1

FIGURE 2

Opening an Existing Presentation and Saving it with a New File Name

Because you are replacing clip art in the Break Away Bargains presentation created in Project 2, the first step is to open the presentation. To ensure that the original Break Away Bargains presentation remains intact, you save the presentation with a new name: Break Away Bargains Sun. Then, you connect to the World Wide Web and import clip art. The following pages illustrate these steps.

Opening an Existing Presentation

Before making changes to the clip art in the Break Away Bargains presentation, you first must open it. Perform the following steps to open the Break Away Bargains presentation.

TO OPEN AN EXISTING PRESENTATION

Step 1: Insert your floppy disk into drive A that contains the Break Away Bargains presentation created in Project 2.

Step 2: Click the Start button on the taskbar. Click Open Office Document. Click 3½ Floppy (A:) in the Look in list box.

Step 3: Double-click the presentation, Break Away Bargains.

PowerPoint opens and displays the presentation in the view in which it was last saved. Project 2 last saved the presentation in slide view.

Saving a Presentation with a New File Name

Because you want to preserve the original Break Away Bargains presentation, you save the open presentation with a new file name. Then, you make the changes to the new presentation. Essentially, you are making a duplicate copy of a file. Perform the following steps to save the Break Away Bargains presentation with a new file name using the Save As command.

TO SAVE A PRESENTATION WITH A NEW FILE NAME

Step 1: Click File on the menu bar. Click Save As.

Step 2: Type Break Away Bargains Sun in the File name text box.

Step 3: Click the Save button.

The Break Away Bargains presentation is saved with the file name Break Away Bargains Sun. The new file name displays in the title bar.

Moving to Another Slide

When creating or editing your presentation, you often want to display a slide other than the current one. Dragging the vertical scroll bar box up or down displays the slide indicator. Recall the slide indicator displays the slide number and title of the slide you are about to display. Once you see the number of the slide you wish to display, release the left mouse button. Perform the step on the next page to move to Slide 6 using the vertical scroll box.

More *About*
Custom Slide Shows

When you need slightly different presentations for separate audiences, consider creating a custom slide show instead of several individual presentations. A custom slide show allows you to group slides common to all audiences with slides unique to an individual audience. For details on creating a custom slide show, see Create a custom show in PowerPoint online Help.

Steps **To Move to Another Slide**

1 **Drag the vertical scroll bar down until Slide: 6 of 6 Time Is Running Out displays in the slide indicator.**

Slide 6 displays (Figure 3).

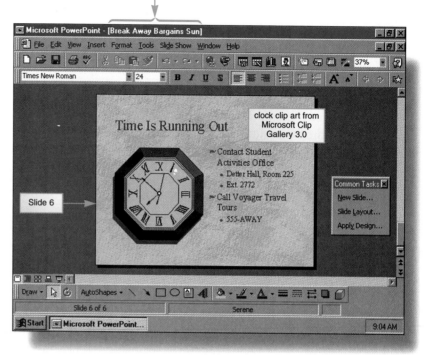

FIGURE 3

Importing Clip Art from Microsoft Clip Gallery Live on the World Wide Web

Recall from Project 2 that one source for additional clip art images is the World Wide Web. Many companies provide clip art images on the Web; some free of cost, some charge a fee. Microsoft maintains a Web site called **Microsoft Clip Gallery Live** that contains files for clip art, photographs, sounds, and videos.

Because Microsoft Clip Gallery 3.0 has a limited amount of clip art, you sometimes cannot find an image that best enhances your slide. At those times, you may want to connect to the Microsoft Clip Gallery Live Web site to search for additional clip art files. To use the Microsoft Clip Gallery Live Web site you must have access to the World Wide Web and Web browser software. You access the World Wide Web through an **Internet service provider**, called an **ISP**. This project, for example, uses **The Microsoft Network** to access the Web and uses **Microsoft Internet Explorer** for the Web browser. If you do not have an ISP, your instructor will provide the clip art file used in this project.

To simplify connecting to the Microsoft Clip Gallery Live Web site, the Microsoft Clip Gallery 3.0 dialog box contains a **Connect to Web for additional clips** button. When you click the Connect to Web for additional clips button, a network Sign In window displays. Depending on your ISP, the Sign In window will vary.

More *About*
Clip Art Web Sites

Searching the World Wide Web for sources of clip art can supplement clip art available in the Microsoft Clip Gallery or the Microsoft Clip Gallery Live Web site. Use one of the search engines to search for public domain clip art. Search for the following keywords: clip art and clip+art.

Opening Microsoft Clip Gallery 3.0

A clip art image on a slide maintains a **link** to Microsoft Clip Gallery 3.0. When you double-click a clip art image, Microsoft Clip Gallery 3.0 opens and the Clip Art sheet displays. In this project you want to replace the clock clip art image on Slide 6 with an image of the sun to improve the closing slide. A picture of the sun reinforces the warm tropical vacations of the Break Away Bargains promotion.

Perform the following step to open Microsoft Clip Gallery 3.0.

 Steps To Open Microsoft Clip Gallery 3.0

1 **Double-click the clock clip art image on Slide 6.**

Microsoft Clip Gallery 3.0 opens and displays the Clip Art sheet (Figure 4).

 Clip Art sheet

Microsoft Clip Gallery 3.0 dialog box

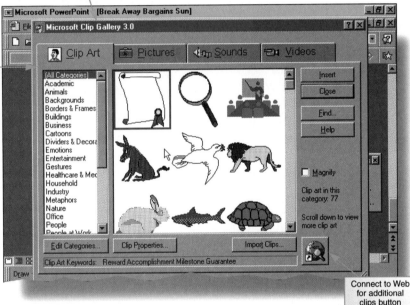

FIGURE 4

 Connect to Web for additional clips button

Connecting to the Microsoft Clip Gallery Live World Wide Web Site

When you are ready to access clip art in Microsoft Clip Gallery Live, you click the Connect to Web for additional clips button. A Sign In window for your ISP displays if you are required to identify yourself with a name and password. Some schools by-pass this window because of the school's Web connection setup. See your instructor for your school's requirements. If you are connecting to the Web at a location other than school, you must know the ISP's sign in requirements.

Once you connect to the Web, the Microsoft Clip Gallery Live start page displays. A **start page** is a specially designed page that serves as a starting point for a Web site.

Perform the step on the next page to connect to the World Wide Web and display the Microsoft Clip Gallery Live start page.

More *About*
Connecting to Microsoft Clip Gallery Live

To connect to the Microsoft Clip Gallery Live Web page using a browser other than Internet Explorer, such as Netscape, start the browser and type http://www.microsoft.com/clipgallerylive in the Location text box, and then press the ENTER key.

Steps **To Connect to the Microsoft Clip Gallery Live World Wide Web Site**

1 **Click the Connect to Web for additional clips button in the Microsoft Clip Gallery 3.0 dialog box. Connect to the World Wide Web as required by your browser software and ISP. When the Microsoft Clip Gallery Live start page displays, read the End-User License Agreement for Microsoft Software. Click the Accept button.**

If you are using a modem, Microsoft Clip Gallery 3.0 displays a dialog box that connects you to the World Wide Web via your ISP. If you are directly connected to the World Wide Web through a computer network, the dialog box does not display. Once connected to the World Wide Web, the Microsoft Clip Gallery Live start page displays the End-User License Agreement. When you click the

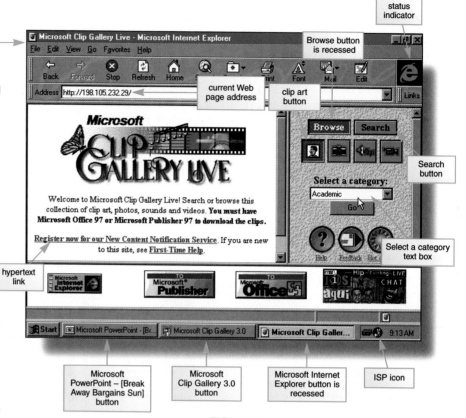

FIGURE 5

Accept button, the End-User License Agreement area no longer displays. The area now displays buttons to locate clip art, photo, sound, and video clips (Figure 5). The Browse button and the Clip Art button are recessed indicating the current mode is set to browse the Clip Art category listed in the Select a category text box. Underlined text is a hypertext link to other Web pages.

Searching for Microsoft Clip Gallery Live Clip Art

Microsoft Clip Gallery Live is similar to Microsoft Clip Gallery 3.0 in that you can search for clip art by keywords. This project is looking for a clip art image of the sun, so you want to search Microsoft Clip Gallery Live using the keyword, sun. Perform the following steps to search for clip art in Microsoft Clip Gallery Live.

Steps To Search for Microsoft Clip Gallery Live Clip Art

1 **Click the Search button. Click the Enter keywords text box. Type** sun **in the Enter keywords text box. Point to the Find button.**

When you click the Search button, the Enter keywords text box replaces the Select a category text box (Figure 6).

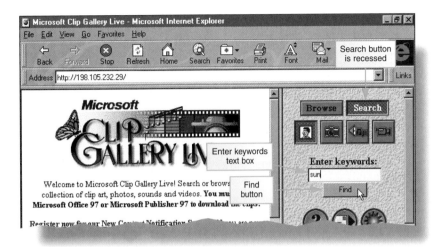

FIGURE 6

2 **Click the Find button.**

After a few moments, the result of the search displays in the left side of the page (Figure 7). Search status displays at the top of the area, such as the number of images that match the search criteria. Below the search status information is the number of images that display in this page. The underlined text below each image is its file name and a hypertext link used to import the image. The number below the file name is the file size.

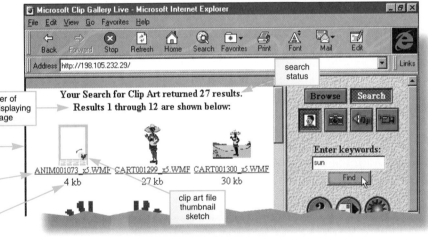

FIGURE 7

3 **Scroll down the search results area until the orange and yellow sun with the file name NATU001919_x5.WMF displays. Then point to the file name hypertext link NATU001919_x5.WMF (Figure 8).**

FIGURE 8

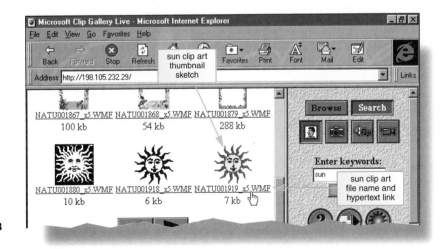

4 **Click NATU001919_x5. When the Internet Explorer dialog box displays, click the Open it option button. Then click the OK button.**

Microsoft Internet Explorer displays a dialog box cautioning that viruses could be transmitted when this file is sent to your computer. The Open it option button is selected. By default, a check mark displays in the Always ask before opening this type of file check box. The file extension for the clip art file is cil, which stands for Clip Gallery Download Package. The NATU001919_x5.WMF file is added to the Microsoft Clip Gallery 3.0 in the Downloaded Clips category (Figure 9). Keywords for this clip art display at the bottom of the Clip Art sheet.

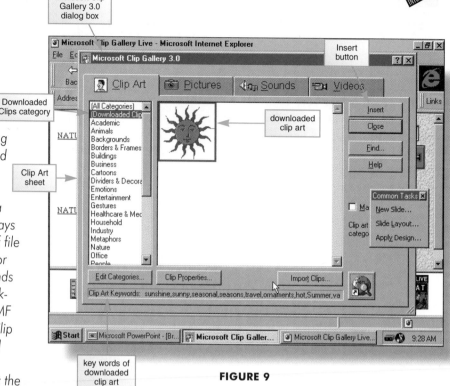

FIGURE 9

5 **Click the Insert button.**

The clip art displays on Slide 6 and replaces the clock clip art (Figure 10). Microsoft Clip Gallery Live still is open and you still are connected to the ISP.

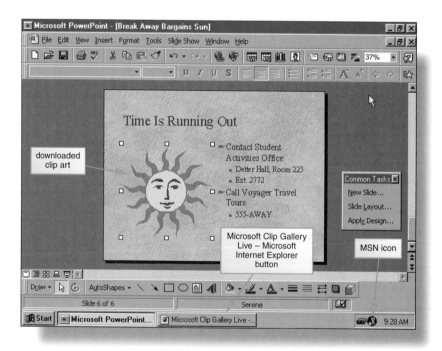

FIGURE 10

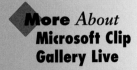
If you click the Save it to disk option button in the Internet Explorer dialog box in Step 4 above, you download the file to disk. If you save clip art to disk, you must double-click the file name in Explore to decompress the file and insert it into the Microsoft Clip Gallery 3.0.

Quitting a Web Session

Once you have downloaded your clip art, you want to quit your Web session. Because Windows 95 displays buttons on the taskbar for each open application, you quickly can quit an application by right-clicking an application button and then clicking the Close button on the shortcut menu. Perform the following steps to quit your current Web session.

TO QUIT A WEB SESSION

Step 1: Right-click the Microsoft Clip Gallery Live – Microsoft Internet Explorer button on the taskbar. If you are not using Microsoft Internet Explorer, right-click the button for your browser.

Step 2: Click Close on the shortcut menu.

Step 3: When The Microsoft Network dialog box displays, click the Yes button to disconnect. If you are using a different ISP, click the Yes button to disconnect.

The browser software closes and the ISP connection is terminated.

Adding Animation Effects

To draw attention to the sun clip art on Slide 6, you apply animation effects. In this project you add the Swivel custom animation effect as described in the following steps.

TO ANIMATE CLIP ART

Step 1: Right-click the sun clip art object and then click Custom Animation on the shortcut menu. If necessary, click the Effects tab.

Step 2: Click the Entry animation and sound box arrow. Drag the Entry animation and sound list scroll box until Swivel displays.

Step 3: Click Swivel.

Step 4: Click the OK button.

PowerPoint applies Swivel animation effects to the sun clip art and closes the Custom Animation dialog box.

Saving the Presentation

The changes to the presentation are complete. Perform the following step to save the finished presentation to a floppy disk before running the slide show.

More *About*
Microsoft Clip Gallery Live

Click the Hot Clips button in the Microsoft Clip Gallery Live Web page to open a sample of the latest clip art images available for the selected media type, such as clip art. Microsoft updates this Web site regularly.

More *About*
Animation Effects

Animation effects help direct the eyes to follow an object. The goal is to assist the audience in understanding the content supported by the graphic object. The more efficiently you control the eye movement of the audience, the more effective the presentation.

TO SAVE A PRESENTATION

Step 1: Click the Save button on the Standard toolbar.

PowerPoint saves the presentation by saving the changes made to the presentation since the last save.

Running an Animated Slide Show

To verify that the presentation looks like expected, run the presentation in slide show view. Perform the following steps to run the revised Break Away Bargains Sun slide show.

TO RUN AN ANIMATED SLIDE SHOW

Step 1: Drag the vertical scroll bar to display Slide: 1 of 6 Voyager Travel Tours.

Step 2: Click the Slide Show button on the View Button Bar. When Slide 1 displays in slide show view, click the slide anywhere except on the Popup Menu buttons.

Step 3: Continue clicking the slides to finish running the slide show and return to slide view.

The presentation displays the animation effects in slide show view and returns to slide view when finished.

Now that the presentation is complete, the last step is to print the presentation slides.

Printing Presentation Slides

Perform the following steps to print the revised presentation.

TO PRINT PRESENTATION SLIDES

Step 1: Click File on the menu bar and then click Print.

Step 2: When the Print dialog box displays, click the Print what box arrow.

Step 3: Click Slides (without animations) and then click the OK button.

Quitting PowerPoint

The changes to this presentation are saved. The last step is to quit PowerPoint. Perform the following steps to quit PowerPoint.

TO QUIT POWERPOINT

Step 1: Click the Close button on the title bar.

Step 2: If the Microsoft PowerPoint dialog box displays, click the Yes button to save changes made since the last save.

PowerPoint closes.

Project Summary

This integration feature introduced importing clip art to Microsoft Clip Gallery 3.0 from Microsoft Clip Gallery Live on the World Wide Web. You began by opening an existing presentation, Break Away Bargains, and then saving the presentation with a new file name. Next you opened Microsoft Clip Gallery 3.0 by double-clicking the clip art on Slide 6. You then accessed the Microsoft Clip Gallery Live start page on the World Wide Web by clicking the Connect to Web for additional clips button. Once connected to the Microsoft Clip Gallery Live start page, you searched for clip art with the keyword, sun. Then you imported the clip art file to the Microsoft Clip Gallery 3.0 by downloading the file from the Web page. To insert the sun clip art into Slide 6, you double-clicked the imported clip art. You then quit the Web session by closing the browser software and disconnecting from the ISP. Next you applied the Swivel animation effect to the sun clip art. Finally, you saved the presentation, ran the presentation in slide show view to check for continuity, printed the presentation slides, and quit PowerPoint.

What You Should Know

Having completed this project, you now should be able to perform the following tasks:

▶ Animate Clip Art *(PPI 1.10)*
▶ Connect to the Microsoft Clip Gallery Live World Wide Web Site *(PPI 1.6)*
▶ Move to Another Slide *(PPI 1.4)*
▶ Open an Existing Presentation *(PPI 1.3)*
▶ Open Microsoft Clip Gallery 3.0 *(PPI 1.5)*
▶ Print Presentation Slides *(PPI 1.11)*
▶ Quit a Web Session *(PPI 1.9)*

▶ Quit PowerPoint *(PPI 1.11)*
▶ Run an Animated Slide Show *(PPI 1.10)*
▶ Save a Presentation *(PPI 1.10)*
▶ Save a Presentation with a New File Name *(PPI 1.3)*
▶ Search for Microsoft Clip Gallery Live Clip Art *(PPI 1.7)*

In the Lab

1 Using Help

Instructions: Perform the following tasks using a computer.

1. Open an existing presentation. Click Office Assistant. Type web in the What would you like to do? box. Click the Search button. Click Presentations on the Internet. Click the hypertext link, Internet. Read and print the information. Read and print the other seven hypertext links on this Microsoft PowerPoint Help window. Click the Help Topics button.

2. Click the Index tab. Type internet in box 1. Double-click Microsoft Web sites in box 2. Double-click Additional locations of clip art, pictures, music, sound, video clips, and animations. Read and print the online Help information. Click the Help Topics button.

(continued)

In the Lab

In the Lab 1 *(continued)*

3. Double-click Microsoft Web sites. Double-click Connect to Microsoft technical resources. Read and print the online Help information. Click the hypertext link for Microsoft Knowledge Base (KB). Read and print the information. Click the hypertext link for Microsoft Software Library (MSL). Read and print the information.

4. Click the Close button. Click the Office Assistant Close button. Quit PowerPoint.

2 Importing Clip Art

Problem: You are the manager of Holiday Getaways travel agency. You need to find a piece of clip art for a sports-lover vacation presentation you are developing. In order to open easily Microsoft Clip Gallery 3.0 and search the Web for clip art, you create a one slide presentation using the Text & Clip Art AutoLayout. You then search the Web for appropriate clip art and download it into your slide.

Instructions: Open the presentation Sports Holiday from the PowerPoint folder on the Data Disk that accompanies this book. Perform the following tasks.

1. Double-click the clip art placeholder. Click the Connect to Web for additional clips button. After connecting to the Microsoft Internet Explorer and the World Wide Web, click the Accept button, if necessary. Click the Search button. Type sports in the Enter keywords text box and then click the Find button.

2. Download one of the clip art files listed in the results area of the Microsoft Clip Gallery Live page. Double-click the downloaded clip art when it displays in the Microsoft Clip Gallery 3.0.

3. Disconnect from the Web.

4. Add your name in the slide footer.

5. Save the presentation as Play with the Pros. Print the slide in black and white. Quit PowerPoint.

3 Importing and Animating Clip Art

Problem: The marketing manager at Mega-Money Management, Mr. Money, conducts financial seminars at which he displays graphics to illustrate his topic. He recently learned that you could create a PowerPoint presentation and include graphics from the World Wide Web. He asks you to create a PowerPoint presentation and find clip art for his upcoming debt reduction seminar.

Instructions: Perform the following tasks.

1. Open the presentation Debt from the PowerPoint folder on the Data Disk that accompanies this book.

2. Insert clip art into the clip art placeholder on Slide 2 by searching Microsoft Clip Gallery Live for clip art with the keyword, dollars. Import the file, BUSI001193_x5.WMF to Microsoft Clip Gallery 3.0. Disconnect from the Web.

3. Animate the clip art with the Zoom In Slightly animation effect.

4. Add your name in the footer on all slides.

5. Save the presentation as Debt Reduction. Print the presentation in black and white. Quit PowerPoint.

Microsoft PowerPoint 97

Microsoft PowerPoint 97

Using Embedded Visuals to Enhance a Slide Show

Objectives:

You will have mastered the material in this project when you can:

▶ Import an outline created in Microsoft Word
▶ Create a slide background using a picture
▶ Embed an Excel chart
▶ Create and embed an organization chart
▶ Move text
▶ Embed a picture
▶ Resize objects
▶ Create a PowerPoint clip art object
▶ Scale objects
▶ Ungroup clip art
▶ Apply slide transition and text preset animation effects
▶ Print handouts

Presentations Provide Fuel for *Top Performance*

Amoco Corporation is one of the world's leading integrated petroleum and chemical companies, with revenues of approximately $30 billion a year and operations in 40 countries. Amoco's operating strategies are based on financial performance, core business leadership, environmental leadership, improvement.

The Company's 17 business sectors: exploration and chemicals.

Exploration Amoco exp focusing potent Egypt Unite

Gasoline. Sportswear. Carpeting. Cassette tapes. Paint. Tires. Home insulation. On first glance, these products seem unrelated. But they are all manufactured from petroleum and chemicals developed and marketed by the Amoco Corporation, one of the world's largest industrial organizations. More than 40,000 employees in 40 countries worldwide implement Amoco's cutting-edge technologies, and once a year the corporation's 350 top executives travel to one location from all corners of the globe to determine strategies that will help keep Amoco an international leader.

Central to this three-day Worldwide Senior Management event is a $100,000 multimedia presentation combining Microsoft PowerPoint slides with video, audio, and special effects. The slide show is produced by the Presentation Graphics team at Amoco's Graphic Resources department in Chicago. The department offers complete project management, including graphic design of publications and manuals, displays for exhibits, photography, printing, writing assistance, and new media, such as intranets and the Internet.

The department creates more than 60 new presentations annually. When Amoco employees contact Graphic Resources with a project idea, the Graphics team first determines the users' needs. Previously, users wanted 35mm slides, but now they request computer presentations incorporating multimedia and overhead transparencies. The team uses PowerPoint and other drawing and graphics programs to design and produce presentations, color overheads, and color prints. The presentations incorporate text, video, music, animation, and graphics that are saved on a CD-ROM distributed throughout the corporation.

The Graphic Resources department often imports Microsoft Word files, just as you will import the Internet Training Outline file in Project 3. These Word documents often are written by Amoco corporate writers or speech writers. Then the presentations can be enhanced by photos supplied by the employees and digitized by passing the pictures through a scanner. In addition, the department can select clip art and computer graphics from its digital library, which has files dating back to Amoco's first graphics computer system installed more than 15 years ago at a cost of one million dollars.

In addition to creating new slide shows, the Presentation Graphics team updates and enhances many files. If information on a previous slide show needs to be changed, employees can modify the information themselves or bring the data disk containing the presentation to the Graphic Resources department for revisions.

Occasionally, employees come to the department with original PowerPoint slide shows they have created themselves. If their layouts are not pleasing, Graphics team members suggest using different templates, slide masters, colors, type sizes, or fonts. You will make similar changes to the slide show in Project 3 when you create a slide background using a digitized photograph and apply the Contemporary Portrait design template. Graphics personnel also suggest style changes, such as using uppercase letters in the main title text, and they recommend dividing some slides into two different slides for a less-cluttered appearance.

Amoco sells more gasoline than any other company, and the presentations produced by the Graphic Resources department help steer top executives and employees down the road to a productive future.

Project 3

Microsoft
PowerPoint 97

Using Embedded Visuals to Enhance a Slide Show

Case Perspective

Computers are found in nearly 40 million households in the United States, and that number is expected to double by the end of the decade. About one-half of these computers have modems, which allow users to connect to the Internet — a collection of networks that allows you to do research, shop, send messages, and converse with other computer users throughout the world.

Thousands of new Internet users, or newbies, come online each month. Even though the Internet has become more user-friendly recently, these people need training to help them learn the various components of the Internet. The Net-Train Corporation specializes in Internet training, and company executives have asked you to produce a presentation to help them market their upcoming seminar scheduled for the Presidents' Day weekend in Park City, Utah, which is the site of the 2002 Winter Olympics.

Net-Train employees use an outline created in Microsoft Word for their advertisements and sales promotions, and they have modified it to reflect this seminar's content. You use this outline to develop the marketing presentation. Then you enhance the presentation by creating a custom background, embedding an Excel chart showing Internet use, creating and embedding an organization chart, and inserting pictures and clip art.

Create Exciting Presentations Using Embedded Visuals

Bulleted lists and simple graphics are the starting point for most presentations, but they can become boring. Advanced PowerPoint users want exciting presentations — something to impress their audiences. With PowerPoint, it is easy to develop impressive presentations by creating a custom background, embedding graphs and organization charts, inserting pictures, and creating new graphics.

One problem you may experience when developing a presentation is finding the proper graphic to convey your message. One way to overcome this obstacle is to modify clip art from the Microsoft Clip Gallery. Another solution is to import charts created in another application, such as Microsoft Excel. PowerPoint design templates offer a limited number of slide backgrounds and allow you to create your own background using a picture or clip art.

This project introduces several techniques to make your presentations more exciting.

Project Three – Internet Training Seminar

Project 3 expands on the basic PowerPoint presentation features by importing existing files and embedding objects. This project creates a presentation that is used to promote the Internet Training Seminar. The workshop provides intense training sessions for various Internet components, including electronic mail, the World Wide

Web, newsgroups, chat rooms, netiquette, search engines, creating Web pages, and privacy issues. The project begins by building the presentation from an outline created in Microsoft Word and saved as a Rich Text Format (RTF) file. Then, several objects are inserted to customize the presentation. These objects include an Excel chart, an organization chart, and pictures.

Slide Preparation Steps

The preparation steps summarize how the slide presentation shown in Figures 3-1a through 3-1e will be developed in Project 3. The following tasks will be completed in this project.

1. Start PowerPoint.
2. Import the Training Outline file from the PowerPoint folder on the Data Disk that accompanies this book.
3. Apply a design template.
4. Save the presentation as Internet Training.
5. Insert a picture to create a slide background (Figure 3-1a).
6. Embed an Excel chart on Slide 2 (Figure 3-1b).
7. Create and embed an organization chart on Slide 3 (Figure 3-1c).
8. Insert a picture in Slide 4 (Figure 3-1d).
9. Insert clip art and ungroup pieces of this art (Figure 3-1e).

FIGURE 3-1a

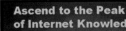
FIGURE 3-1b

FIGURE 3-1c

FIGURE 3-1d

FIGURE 3-1e

10. Apply slide transition and text preset animation effects.
11. Save the presentation again.
12. Print handouts.
13. Close PowerPoint.

Importing Outlines Created in Another Application

You may be asked to present the findings of a research paper. Instead of typing the presentation outline, you can import the outline from the research paper. If you did not create an outline for the research paper, you can create it by first saving the research paper document as an RTF file, removing all text except topic headings, and then saving the RTF file again. Once the research paper outline is saved as an RTF file, you can import the outline into PowerPoint.

You also can create a presentation by opening an outline created in Microsoft Word or another word processing program. The advantage of using an outline saved as a Microsoft Word document or as an RTF file is the text attributes and outline heading levels are maintained. Documents saved as plain text (.txt) files can be opened in PowerPoint but do not maintain text attributes and outline heading levels. Consequently, each paragraph becomes a slide title.

To create a presentation using an existing outline, select All Outlines from the Files of type box in the Open dialog box. When you select All Outlines, PowerPoint displays a list of outlines. Next, you select the file that contains the outline. PowerPoint then creates a presentation using your outline. Each major heading in your outline becomes a slide title, and subheadings become a bulleted list.

Opening an Existing Outline Created in Another Application

After starting PowerPoint, the first step in this project is to open an outline created in Microsoft Word. PowerPoint can produce slides from an outline created in Microsoft Word or another word processing program if the outline was saved in a format that PowerPoint can recognize. The outline created by the workshop organizing team was saved as an RTF file.

Opening an outline into PowerPoint requires two steps. First, you must tell PowerPoint you are opening an existing presentation. Then, to open the outline, you need to select the proper file type from the Files of type box in the Open dialog box. The following steps explain how to start PowerPoint and to open an outline created in Microsoft Word.

Note: The Data Disk that accompanies this book contains a PowerPoint folder with three executable files that include compressed versions of the files for Projects 3 and 4 and the Integration Feature of PowerPoint. Some of these files are required if you plan to step through the PowerPoint projects on a PC. The other files are required for the exercises at the end of the projects. It is recommended that you copy the executable file for a project to a blank floppy disk and then expand it. The paragraph below explains how to expand the files for Project 3. To expand the files for Project 4 and the Integration Feature, replace Project3 with Project4 or Integrat.

To expand the executable file for Project 3, do the following: (1) insert the Data Disk in drive A; (2) start Windows Explorer and, if necessary, click the Restore button so that part of the desktop displays; (3) click the plus sign to the left of the 3½ Floppy (A:) icon in the All Folders side of the window and then click the PowerPoint icon; (4) right-drag Project3 on to the desktop and click Copy Here on the shortcut menu; (5) insert a blank floppy disk in drive A; (6) right-drag Project3 from the desktop on to the 3½ Floppy (A:) icon in the All Folders side of the window and then click Move Here on the shortcut menu; (7) double-click Project3 in the Contents of '3½ Floppy (A:)' side of the window and then click the Proceed button when the PowerPoint 97 Project3 Data Disk dialog box displays (do not change the folder location unless installing to a hard disk); (8) If necessary, click Yes to create the new folder; (9) right-click Project3 and click Delete on the shortcut menu, and then click the Yes button in the Confirm File Delete dialog box; (10) clearly label the newly created floppy disk as PowerPoint 97 Project3 Data Disk.

Steps To Start PowerPoint and Open an Outline

1 Insert your PowerPoint 97 Project 3 Data Disk into drive A. Click the Start button on the taskbar. Point to Programs on the Start menu. Click Microsoft PowerPoint on the Programs submenu.

2 When the PowerPoint startup dialog box displays, click Open an existing presentation. Click the OK button.

The Open dialog box displays (Figure 3-2). The current folder is My Documents. The current file type is Presentations and Shows as displayed in the Files of type box.

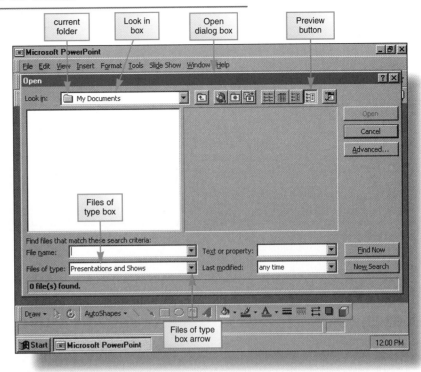

FIGURE 3-2

3 Click the Look in box arrow, and then click 3½ Floppy (A:). Double-click the PowerPoint folder in the list box. Click the Files of type box arrow, and then scroll down and click All Outlines.

A list displays the types of files that PowerPoint can open. Your list may be different depending on the software installed on your computer.

4 Double-click Training Outline in the list box.

PowerPoint opens Training Outline and displays it in Outline View (Figure 3-3). The title on Slide 1 is highlighted. The outline text displays

FIGURE 3-3

bulleted, indicating the slide layout is Bulleted List. The position of the elevator on the scroll bar indicates more outline text exists than can display in the Outline View window. The current design template is Default Design as identified on the status bar.

More *About*
Font Color

If you want to change the text back to its original default color, highlight the text, click the Font Color button arrow on the Drawing toolbar and then click Automatic.

When opening a file created in another presentation graphics program, such as Harvard Graphics or Aldus Persuasion, PowerPoint picks up the outline structure from the styles used in the file (heading level one becomes a title, heading level two becomes the first level of text, and so on). If the file does not contain heading styles, PowerPoint uses paragraph indents to create the outline. For **plain text files**, which are files saved without formatting, PowerPoint uses the tabs at the beginning of paragraphs to define the outline structure.

Imported outlines can have up to nine outline levels, whereas PowerPoint outlines can have only six (one for titles and five for text). When you import an outline, all text in outline levels six through nine is treated as outline level six.

Changing the Font Color of the Existing Outline

Colored type can make your presentation visually interesting. Perform the following steps to change the font color of all the text in the outline from black to gold.

Steps To Change the Font Color of the Entire Outline

1 **Click Edit on the menu bar and then click Select All.**

The characters in the outline are selected (Figure 3-4).

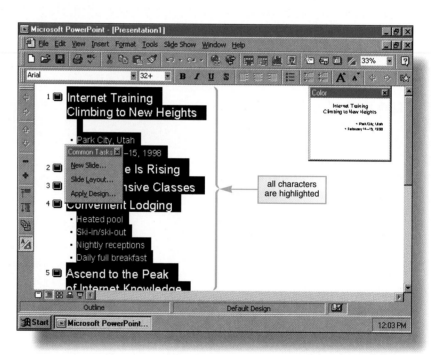

FIGURE 3-4

2 **Right-click the selection. Click Font on the shortcut menu. In the Font dialog box, click the Color box arrow and then point to More Colors.**

PowerPoint displays the Font dialog box (Figure 3-5). In the Font dialog box, you can set the font typeface, font style, font size, effects, and color of characters. More Colors is highlighted in the Color list.

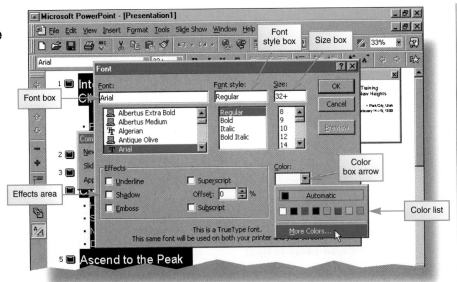

FIGURE 3-5

3 **Click More Colors. When the Colors dialog box displays, if necessary, click the Standard tab and then click the color gold as shown in Figure 3-6.**

The Colors dialog box displays the Standard sheet (Figure 3-6). The color gold is selected. Colors on the Standard sheet are arranged in varying shades of the color groups. White, black, and varying shades of gray display at the bottom of the Standard sheet. The preview box at the lower-right corner of the Standard sheet displays the new color and the current color. The object color on the slide does not change until you click the OK button.

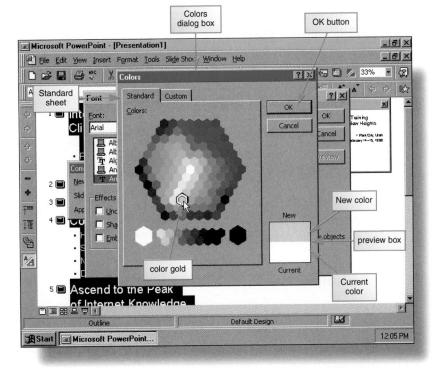

FIGURE 3-6

4 **Click the OK button in the Colors dialog box.**

The Font dialog box displays. The gold font color displays in the Color box.

5 **Click the OK button.**

The outline text displays in the gold font in the Color View window.

Changing Presentation Design Templates

Recall that **design templates** format the look of your presentation. You can change the design template any time you wish to change the appearance of your presentation, not just when you create a new presentation. The current design template is Default Design. Applying the Contemporary Portrait design template complements the custom slide background you will create later in this project. Perform these steps to change design templates.

Steps To Change Design Templates

1 **Point to the Apply Design button on the Common Tasks toolbar (Figure 3-7).**

2 **Click the Apply Design button. Click the Preview button if it is not already recessed. Click Contemporary Portrait in the list box.**

The Apply Design dialog box displays. The Preview button is recessed (refer to the location of the Preview button as shown in Figure 3-2 on page PP 3.9). Contemporary Portrait is highlighted in the list box and a preview of the Contemporary Portrait design template displays in the preview area.

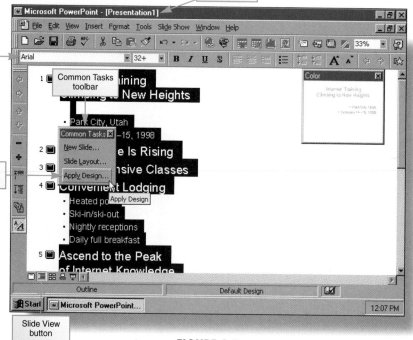

FIGURE 3-7

3 **Click the Apply button.**

PowerPoint applies the Contemporary Portrait design template as indicated by the change to the font and bullets.

OtherWays

1. Click Apply Design button on Standard toolbar, click Contemporary Portrait, click Apply button

Recall that slide attributes change when you select a different design template. The Contemporary Portrait design template format determines the slide attributes of the slide master and the title master. For example, when you compare Figure 3-3 on page PP 3.9 to your screen, you see the font changed from Arial to Arial Black and Tahoma and the bullets changed from small squares to large rectangles.

Saving the Presentation

You now should save your presentation because you created a presentation from an RTF file and changed the design template. The following steps summarize how to save a presentation.

TO SAVE A PRESENTATION

1. Click the Save button on the Standard toolbar.
2. Type Internet Training in the File name text box.
3. Click the Save button.

The presentation is saved with the file name, Internet Training. The presentation title, Internet Training, displays on the title bar, instead of the default, Presentation.

Creating a Custom Background

PowerPoint has 17 design templates in the Presentation Designs folder. Sometimes you want a background, however, that is not found in one of the design templates, such as the picture of the mountains in Figures 3-1a through 3-1e on page PP 3.7. PowerPoint allows you to create that background by inserting a picture. PowerPoint also allows you to customize the background color, shading, pattern, and texture.

You perform two tasks to create the customized background for this presentation. First, you change the layout of Slide 1 to the Title Slide AutoLayout. Then, you create the slide background by inserting a picture of mountains.

The next two sections explain how to create a slide background using a picture.

Changing the Slide Layout to Title Slide

When you import an outline to create a presentation, PowerPoint assumes the text is bulleted text. Because Slide 1 is the title slide for this presentation, you want to change the AutoLayout to the Title Slide layout. You cannot change the slide layout in Outline View, however. Therefore, you want to change to Slide View and then change the AutoLayout.

The following steps summarize how to change to Slide View and change the layout of Slide 1 to the Title Slide layout.

TO CHANGE SLIDE LAYOUT TO TITLE SLIDE

1. Click the Slide View button.
2. Click the Slide Layout button on the Common Tasks toolbar.
3. Double-click Title Slide, the first layout in the Slide Layout dialog box.

Slide 1 displays in Slide View with the Contemporary Portrait design template (Figure 3-8).

More *About*
Saving Files

PowerPoint file names can have one of five extensions: .ppt saves as a typical presentation, .wmf as a graphic, .rtf as an outline, .pot as a template, and .pps as a slide show.

More *About*
Custom Font Colors

If you desire a text color that does not appear in the color scheme, you can mix your own color by clicking the Custom tab in the Colors dialog box. Then you can adjust the hue, saturation (intensity), luminance (brightness), and amounts of red, green, and blue.

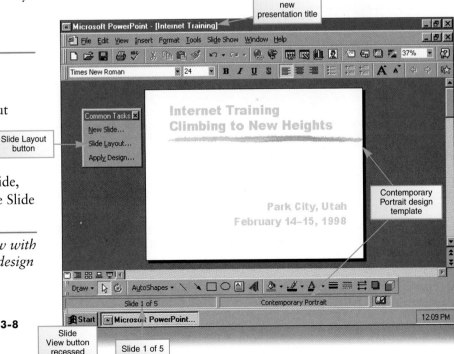

FIGURE 3-8

◆ **More** *About*
Slide Layouts

When audience members view your slides, they scan the material. First they look at simple shapes, such as circles and squares. Then they focus on more complex shapes, such as text.

PowerPoint provides two alternative methods to double-clicking the Auto-Layout in Step 3 on the previous page. The first alternative is to type the layout number of one of the 24 AutoLayouts and press the ENTER key. A layout number corresponds to each AutoLayout, with the four slides in the first row numbered one through four from left to right, the next row of AutoLayouts numbered five through eight, and so on. The second alternative is to type the layout number and click the Apply button. PowerPoint interprets the number you type as the corresponding AutoLayout and applies it when you press the ENTER key (alternative one) or click the Apply button (alternative two). For example, the Title Slide AutoLayout is layout number one. When the Slide Layout dialog box displays, you would type 1 and press the ENTER key instead of double-clicking the Title Slide layout.

Inserting a Picture to Create a Custom Background

The next step in creating the Internet Training presentation is to insert a picture to create a custom background. In PowerPoint, a **picture** is any graphic created in another application. Pictures usually are saved in one of two **graphic formats**: bitmap or vector.

A **bitmap graphic** is a piece of art that has been stored as a pattern of dots called pixels. A **pixel**, short for **picture element**, is one dot in a grid. A picture that is produced on the computer screen or on paper by a printer is composed of thousands of these dots. Just as a bit is the smallest unit of information a computer can process, a pixel is the smallest element that can display or that print hardware and software can manipulate in creating letters, numbers, or graphics. For example, the letter A shown in Figure 3-9 actually is made up of a pattern of pixels in a grid.

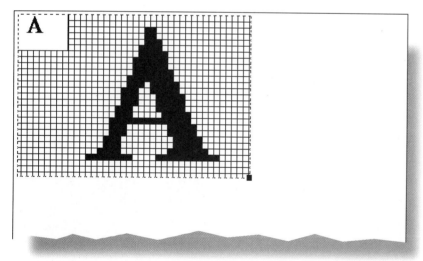

FIGURE 3-9

Bitmap graphics are created in paint programs such as Microsoft Paint. Bitmap graphics also can be produced from **digitizing** art, pictures, or photographs by passing the artwork through a scanner. A **scanner** is a hardware device that converts lines and shading into combinations of the binary digits 0 and 1 by sensing different intensities of light and dark. The scanner shines a beam of light on the picture being scanned. The beam passes back and forth across the picture, sending a digitized signal to the computer's memory. A **digitized signal** is the conversion of input, such as the lines in a drawing, into a series of discrete units represented by the binary digits 0 and 1. **Scanned pictures** are bitmap pictures and have jagged edges. The jagged edges are caused by the individual pixels that create the picture. Bitmap graphics also are known as **raster images**. Additionally, bitmap files cannot be ungrouped into smaller object groups.

The other graphic format in which pictures are stored is vector graphics. A **vector graphic** is a piece of art that has been created by a drawing program such as CorelDRAW! or AutoCAD. Vector graphic objects are created as a collection of lines instead of patterns of individual dots (pixels), as are bitmap graphics. Vector graphic files store data either as picture descriptions or as calculations. These files describe a picture mathematically as a set of instructions for creating the objects in the picture. These mathematical descriptions determine the position, length, and direction in which the lines are to be drawn. These calculations allow the drawing program to re-create the picture on the screen as necessary. Because vector graphic objects are described mathematically, they also can be layered, rotated, and magnified with relative ease. Vector graphics also are known as **object-oriented pictures**. Clip art pictures in the Microsoft Clip Gallery that have the file extension of **.wmf** are examples of vector files. Vector files can be ungrouped and manipulated by their component objects.

PowerPoint allows you to insert vector files because it uses **graphic filters** to convert the various graphic formats into a format PowerPoint can use. These filters are installed with the initial PowerPoint installation or can be added later by running the Setup program.

The Internet Training presentation will be used to help Net-Train market its seminar in Park City, Utah, so you want to emphasize the beautiful mountain scenery. To create the desired effect, you insert a picture of mountains to cover the Contemporary Portrait design template.

Perform the following steps to create a custom background.

More *About*
Graphic Filters

PowerPoint allows you to directly insert many graphic file formats in your presentation. No separate filter is needed for these graphics types: Enhanced Metafile (.emf), Joint Photographic Experts Group (.jpg), Portable Network Graphics (.png), Windows Bitmap (.bmp, .rle, .dib), and Windows Metafile (.wmf). A separate filter is needed for all other file formats.

More *About*
Adding Colors

A maximum of eight additional colors you have added will display on the Line Color list. If you select additional colors, the more recent ones display and the oldest ones drop off.

Steps To Insert a Picture to Create a Custom Background

1 **Right-click anywhere on Slide 1 except the title object or subtitle object. Click Background on the shortcut menu. When the Background dialog box displays, point to the down arrow in the Background fill area.**

The Background dialog box displays (Figure 3-10).

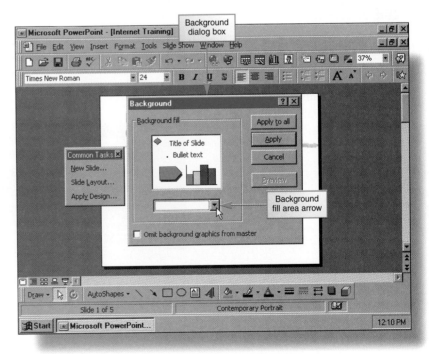

FIGURE 3-10

2 **Click the down arrow. When the list displays, point to Fill Effects.**

The list contains options for filling the slide background (Figure 3-11). The current background fill is Automatic, which is the Contemporary Portrait design template default. Fill Effects is highlighted.

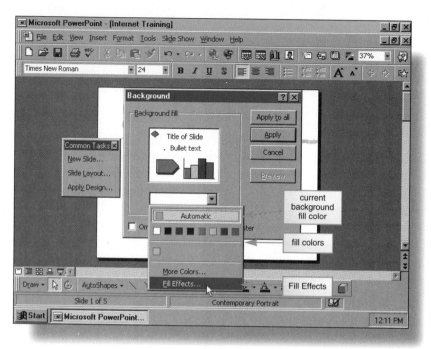

FIGURE 3-11

3 **Click Fill Effects. Click the Picture tab and then click the Select Picture button. Click the Preview button if it is not recessed. Click Mountains in the list box.**

The Select Picture dialog box displays (Figure 3-12). The Preview button is recessed. The selected file, Mountains, displays in the preview box.

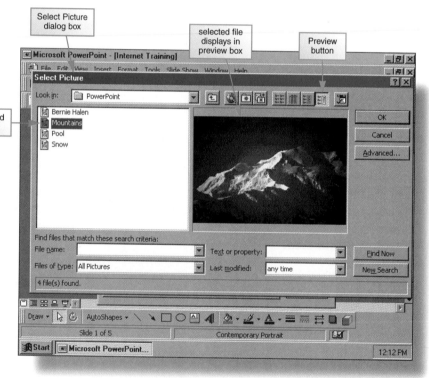

FIGURE 3-12

4 **Click the OK button. When the Fill Effects dialog box displays, click the OK button. When the Background dialog box displays, point to the Apply to all button.**

The Background dialog box displays the Mountains picture in the Background fill area (Figure 3-13a).

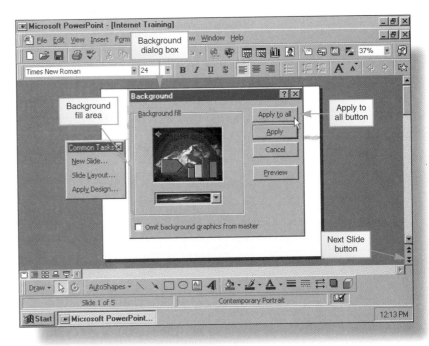

FIGURE 3-13a

5 **Click the Apply to all button.**

Slide 1 displays the Mountains picture as the slide background (Figure 3-13b). Although not shown in this figure, the Mountains picture is the background for all slides in the presentation. The Contemporary Portrait design template text attributes display on the slide.

FIGURE 3-13b

When you customize the background, the design template text attributes remain the same, but the slide background changes. For example, inserting the Mountains picture for the slide background changes the appearance of the slide background but maintains the text attributes of the Contemporary Portrait design template.

The next section explains how to embed an Excel chart into the presentation.

Embedding an Existing Excel Chart

PowerPoint allows you to embed many types of objects into a presentation. In this project, you embed an existing Excel chart into the slide. The Excel chart is located in the PowerPoint folder on the Data Disk that accompanies this book.

Embedding an existing Excel chart is similar to embedding other objects. Because the Excel chart already exists, you must retrieve it from the file in which it was saved instead of opening the supplementary application and creating the object. Then you embed and edit the Excel chart.

Changing Slide Layouts

Before you embed the Excel chart, you need to display Slide 2 and change the slide layout to the Object layout.

OtherWays

1. Move scroll bar elevator downward to display Object layout, double-click Object layout

TO DISPLAY THE NEXT SLIDE AND CHANGE THE SLIDE LAYOUT

1️⃣ Click the Next Slide button to display Slide 2.

2️⃣ Click the Slide Layout button on the Common Tasks toolbar.

3️⃣ When the Slide Layout dialog box displays, type 16 to select the Object layout from the 24 available AutoLayouts. Click the Apply button.

Slide 2 displays the slide title and subtitle object.

Slide 2 now displays the title of the slide and a subtitle object. The next section explains how to embed an Excel chart.

Embedding an Excel Chart

The next step in modifying the PowerPoint object for Slide 2 is to embed an Excel chart. The Excel chart already is created and saved on the Data Disk. The following steps explain how to embed an existing Excel chart.

Steps **To Embed an Excel Chart**

1️⃣ **Double-click the object placeholder in the middle of Slide 2. Click the Create from file option button.**

The Insert Object dialog box displays (Figure 3-14). Drive A is the current drive and PowerPoint is the current folder.

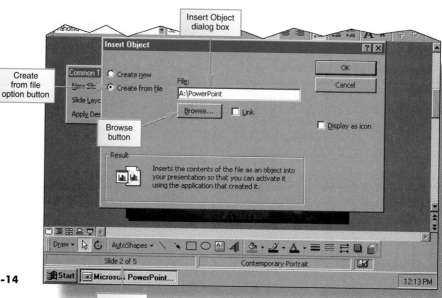

FIGURE 3-14

2 **Click the Browse button. When the Browse dialog box displays, click Internet Use.**

The Browse dialog box displays the files in the PowerPoint folder on the Data Disk (Figure 3-15). Internet Use is the Excel file you will embed into Slide 2, and it displays in the preview box.

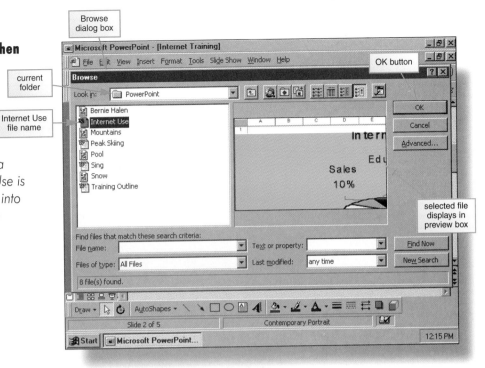

FIGURE 3-15

3 **Click the OK button. When the Insert Object dialog box displays, point to the OK button.**

The Insert Object dialog box now displays A:\PowerPoint\Internet Use.xls in the File text box (Figure 3-16).

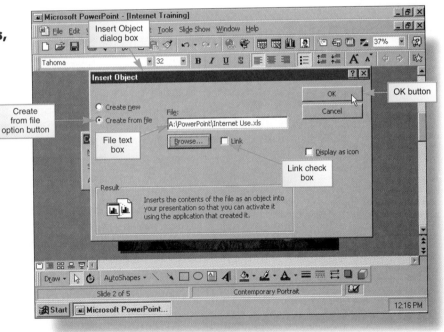

FIGURE 3-16

4 **Click the OK button.**

After a short time, Slide 2 displays a blue rectangle, which is part of the background of the Internet Use Pie chart (Figure 3-17).

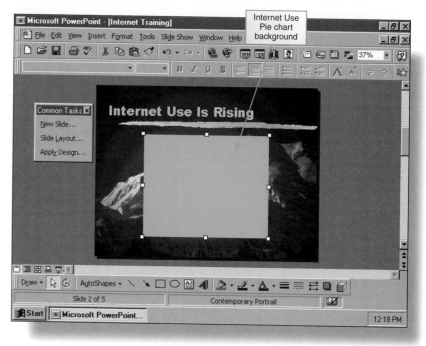

FIGURE 3-17

OtherWays

1. On Insert menu click Object, click Create from file, click Browse button, click Internet Use, click OK button in Browse dialog box, click OK button

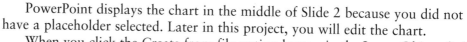

More *About* **Embedding Visuals**

If you embed a chart or photograph obtained from another source, you should acknowledge this source either on the slide or when you verbally give the presentation. The same plagiarism rules apply to slide shows and written documents.

PowerPoint displays the chart in the middle of Slide 2 because you did not have a placeholder selected. Later in this project, you will edit the chart.

When you click the Create from file option button in the Insert Object dialog box, the dialog box changes. The File box replaces the Object type box. Another change to the dialog box is the addition of the **Link check box**. If the Link check box is selected, the object is inserted as a linked, instead of an embedded, object. Like an embedded object, a **linked object** also is created in another application; however, the linked object maintains a connection to its source. If the original object is changed, the linked object on the slide also changes. The linked object is stored in the source file where it was created.

For example, the Excel chart you inserted into the slide is stored in the Internet Use file from the PowerPoint folder on the Data Disk that accompanies this book. If you were to link the Internet Use file to your presentation, every time the Internet Use file changed in Excel, the changes would display on the chart in Slide 2. Your PowerPoint presentation stores a representation of the original Internet Use file and information about its location. Therefore, if later you move or delete the source file, the link will be broken, and the object will not be available. Hence, if you make a presentation on a computer other than the one on which the presentation was created and the presentation contains linked objects, be certain to include a copy of the source files. The source files must be stored in the exact location as originally specified when you linked them to your presentation.

When you select a source file from the Browse dialog box, PowerPoint associates the file with a specific application, which is based on the file extension. For example, if you select a source file with the file extension .DOC, PowerPoint recognizes the file as a Microsoft Word file. Additionally, if you select a source file with the file extension **.xls**, PowerPoint recognizes the file as a Microsoft Excel file.

Slide 2 now displays the title of the slide and the upper-left corner of the embedded Internet Use Pie chart object. The next section explains how to edit the Excel chart so the entire chart object displays.

Editing an Excel Chart

The next step in creating Slide 2 is to edit the embedded Excel Pie chart. The following steps explain how to edit the embedded Excel chart object.

 To Edit an Embedded Excel Chart

1 **Double-click the blue rectangle in the center of the slide, which is the upper-left corner of the Internet Use Pie chart object. Point to the right center sizing handle on the right side of the object.**

PowerPoint starts Excel and opens the Internet Use Pie chart object for editing (Figure 3-18). The mouse pointer displays as a two-headed arrow.

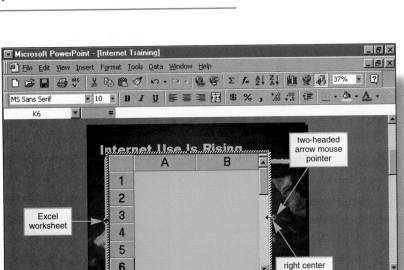

FIGURE 3-18

2 Drag the mouse pointer to the black border along the right edge of the slide (Figure 3-19).

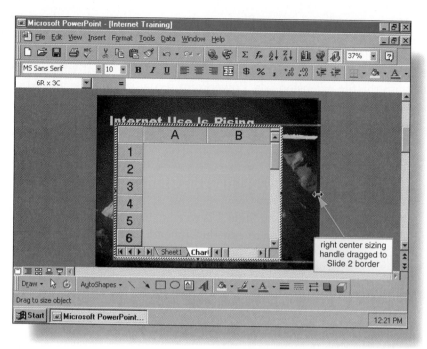

FIGURE 3-19

3 Click anywhere along the right edge of the Excel object border, which looks like rope (Figure 3-20a).

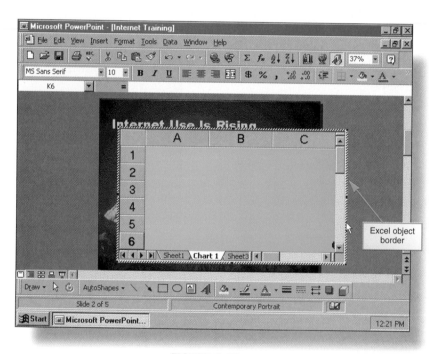

FIGURE 3-20a

4 **Click anywhere on the slide other than the Excel chart.**

The Excel Pie chart displays in Slide 2 (Figure 3-20b).

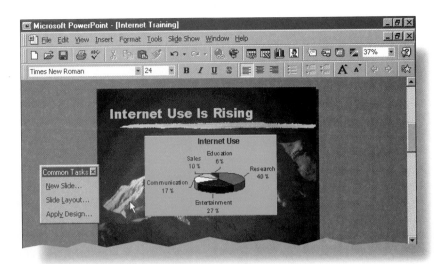

FIGURE 3-20b

You now will position the Excel chart object in a more desirable area of the slide.

Positioning an Embedded Object

Now that the Excel Pie chart object displays in its entirety, you need to move it downward to a more central area of the slide. The steps on the next page explain how to position the embedded Excel chart object.

Steps **To Position an Embedded Excel Chart Object**

1 **Right-click the Internet Use Pie chart object. Click Format Object on the shortcut menu.**

2 **Click the Position tab in the Format Object dialog box. Triple-click the Horizontal text box in the Position on slide area. Type 1.9 and then triple-click the Vertical text box in the Position on slide area. Type 2.8 as the entry.**

The Format Object dialog box displays (Figure 3-21a). The upper-left corner of the Internet Use Pie chart object will be positioned at 1.9 inches to the right of the top left corner and 2.8 inches down from the top of the slide.

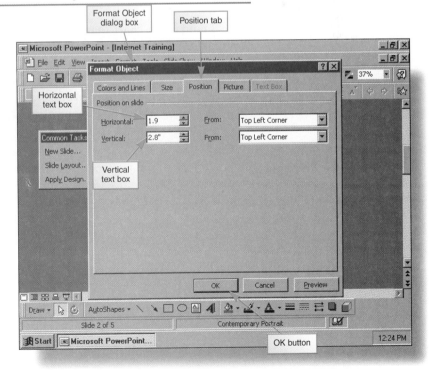

FIGURE 3-21a

3 **Click the OK button. Click above or to the left of the Pie chart.**

The Excel Pie chart object displays in the center of Slide 2 (Figure 3-21b).

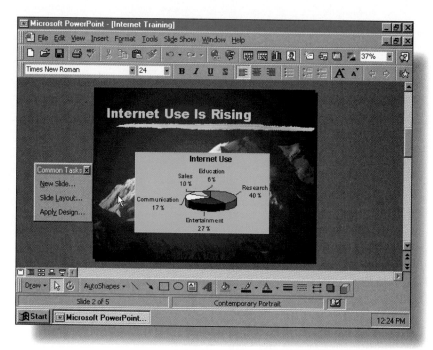

FIGURE 3-21b

PowerPoint displays the embedded chart in the center of Slide 2. This slide is now complete. The next section describes how to embed an organization chart in a slide.

Creating and Embedding an Organization Chart

Slide 3 contains a chart that elaborates on the daily schedule for the Internet Training seminar as shown in Figure 3-22. This type of chart is called an **organization chart,** which is a hierarchical collection of elements depicting various functions or responsibilities that contribute to an organization or to a collective function. Typically, an organization chart is used to show the structure of people or departments within an organization, hence the name, organization chart.

Figure 3-23 illustrates how a company uses an organization chart to describe the relationships between the company's departments. In the information sciences, organization charts often are used to show the decomposition of a process or program. When used in this manner, the chart is called a **hierarchy chart.**

PowerPoint contains a supplementary application called **Microsoft Organization Chart 2.0** that allows you to create an organization chart. When you open Microsoft Organization Chart, its menus, buttons, and tools are available to you directly in the PowerPoint window. Microsoft Organization Chart is an object linking and embedding (OLE) application. The organization chart you create for Slide 3 (Figure 3-22) is an embedded object because it is created in an application other than PowerPoint.

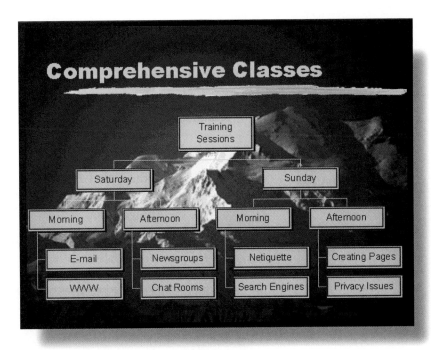

FIGURE 3-22

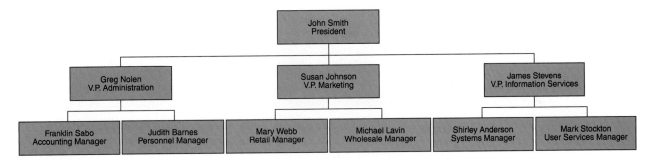

FIGURE 3-23

Creating an organization chart requires several steps. First, you display the slide that will contain the organization chart in Slide View and change the AutoLayout to the Organization Chart layout. Then, you open the Microsoft Organization Chart application. Finally, you enter and format the contents of the boxes in the organization chart window.

Perform the steps on the following pages to create the organization chart for this project.

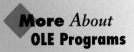

More *About*
OLE Programs

When you install PowerPoint, you install four OLE programs to help you create embedded objects. Microsoft Organization Chart 2.0, Microsoft Photo Editor 3.0 Photo, Microsoft Graph 97 Chart, and Microsoft Equation 3.0 (Equation Editor) all allow you to share information between programs. To verify these programs exist on your system, click Object on the Insert menu, and then scroll down through the Object type list.

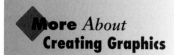

More *About* Creating Graphics

Large companies employ graphic artists to help corporate writers communicate complex information. The artists advise the writers on what slide layout would be effective, where objects should appear on slides, and which type of object, such as a Bar chart, Pie chart, or table, would best communicate information to viewers.

Changing Slide Layouts

Before you open Microsoft Organization Chart 2.0, you need to display Slide 3 and change the AutoLayout to the Organization Chart layout.

TO DISPLAY THE NEXT SLIDE AND CHANGE THE SLIDE LAYOUT

1. Click the Next Slide button.
2. Click the Slide Layout button on the Common Tasks toolbar.
3. When the Slide Layout dialog box displays, type 7 to select the Organization Chart layout from the 24 available AutoLayouts. Click the Apply button.

Slide 3 displays the organization chart placeholder and the slide title (Figure 3-24).

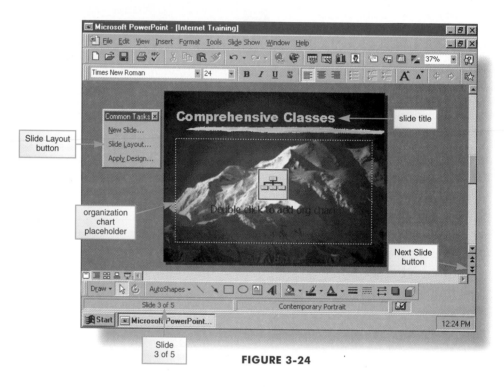

FIGURE 3-24

OtherWays

1. Move scroll bar elevator downward to display Organization Chart layout, double-click Organization Chart layout

Slide 3 now displays the placeholder for the organization chart. The next section explains how to open the Microsoft Organization Chart application.

Opening the Microsoft Organization Chart Application

To create the organization chart on Slide 3, you first must open the organization chart application, Microsoft Organization Chart 2.0, which is included within PowerPoint. Recall that when this supplementary application is active, the menus, buttons, and tools in the organization chart application are made available in the PowerPoint window. Once active, Microsoft Organization Chart displays a sample four-box organization chart in a work area in the middle of the PowerPoint window, as explained in the following step.

Steps **To Open Microsoft Organization Chart**

1 **Double-click the Organization Chart placeholder in the middle of Slide 3.**

Organization Chart displays the Microsoft Organization Chart - [Object in Internet Training] window in a work area in the PowerPoint window (Figure 3-25). Notice the sample organization chart is composed of four boxes connected by lines. When Microsoft Organization Chart is active, the first line of the top box automatically is selected. Depending on the version of Microsoft Organization Chart installed on your computer, the display on the screen may vary slightly.

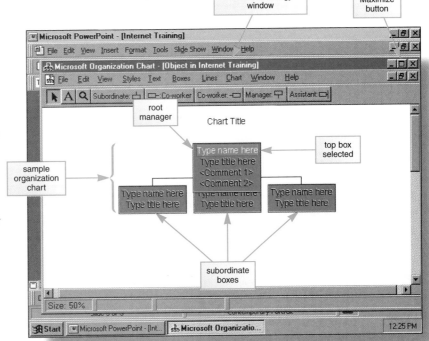

FIGURE 3-25

Microsoft Organization Chart displays a sample organization chart to help you create your chart. The sample is composed of one **manager box**, located at the top of the chart, and three **subordinate boxes**. A manager box has one or more subordinates. The topmost manager is called the **root manager**. A subordinate box is located at a level lower than its manager. A subordinate box has only one manager. When a lower-level subordinate box is added to a higher-level subordinate box, the higher-level subordinate box becomes the manager of the lower-level subordinate box.

Maximizing the Microsoft Organization Chart Window

When Microsoft Organization Chart is active, the Microsoft Organization Chart window is not maximized. Maximizing the Microsoft Organization Chart window makes it easier to create your organization chart because it displays a larger area in which to view the chart.

TO MAXIMIZE THE MICROSOFT ORGANIZATION CHART WINDOW

1 Click the Maximize button in the upper-right corner of the Microsoft Organization Chart window.

The Microsoft Organization Chart window fills the desktop. Clicking the Restore button returns the Microsoft Organization Chart window to its original size.

More *About* **Delivering Presentations**

If you are delivering your PowerPoint presentation in front of a group, consider using a laser pointer to direct the audience's attention to objects projected on the screen. Some laser pointer models have dot, underline, and arrow images. Other features are clocks and countdown timers that beep at set intervals, such as five minutes prior to the scheduled slide show ending time.

Creating the Title for the Root Manager Box

In this presentation, the organization chart is used to communicate the daily training schedule. The topmost box, the root manager, identifies the purpose of this organization chart: Comprehensive Classes. Recall that when Microsoft Organization Chart became active, the first line in the root manager box was selected. The following step explains how to create the title for the root manager box.

Steps To Create the Title for the Root Manager Box

1 **Type** Training **in the root manager box on level one and then press the** ENTER **key. Type** Sessions **on the second line.**

Training Sessions displays in the root manager box (Figure 3-26). <Comment 1> and <Comment 2> prompts display in brackets under the root manager box title.

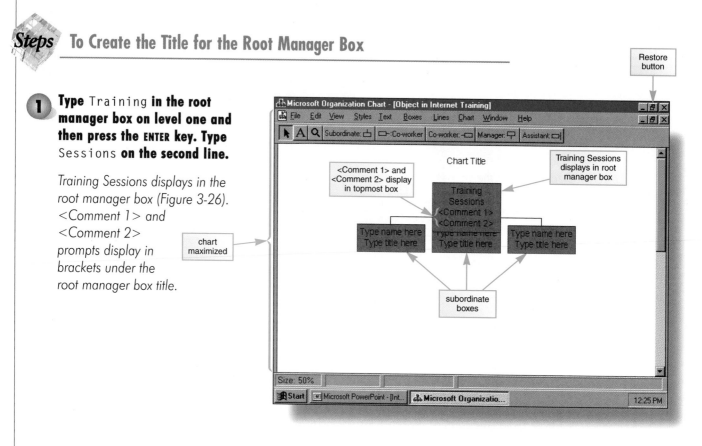

FIGURE 3-26

Deleting Subordinate Boxes

The organization chart in this presentation has two boxes on level 2 immediately below the root manager. The schedules for both days of the training are similar, so you create the schedule for Saturday, copy it, and make editing changes. Before proceeding with the remaining boxes for Saturday, you want to delete the level 2 unnecessary boxes as shown in the following steps.

Steps  **To Delete Subordinate Boxes**

1 **Click the level 2 middle subordinate box located directly under the root manager box.**

2 **Press and hold the SHIFT key. Then click the rightmost subordinate box in level 2. Release the SHIFT key.**

The middle and right subordinate boxes are selected (Figure 3-27). <Comment 1> and <Comment 2> do not display in the root manager box because text was not entered at their prompts. Name and title prompts, however, display in the subordinate boxes without entering text at their prompts. The technique of selecting more than one object by pressing and holding the SHIFT key while clicking the objects is called SHIFT+click.

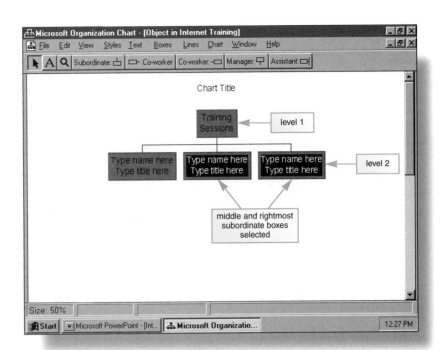

FIGURE 3-27

3 **Press the DELETE key.**

Microsoft Organization Chart displays two boxes: the root manager and one subordinate (Figure 3-28).

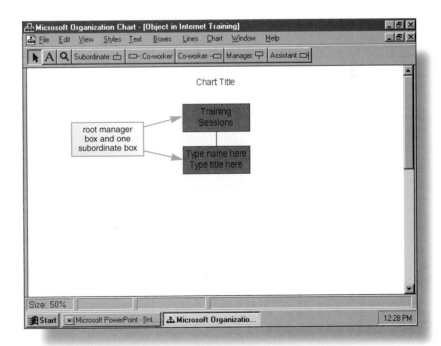

FIGURE 3-28

Titling the Subordinate Box

The process of adding a title to a subordinate box is the same as adding the title to the root manager box except that you first must select the subordinate box. The following step explains how to title a subordinate box.

 Steps **To Title a Subordinate Box**

1 **Click the subordinate box. Type** Saturday **and then press the ENTER key. Press the DELETE key.**

Saturday displays as the title for the subordinate box (Figure 3-29). You pressed the DELETE key because only one line of text is needed.

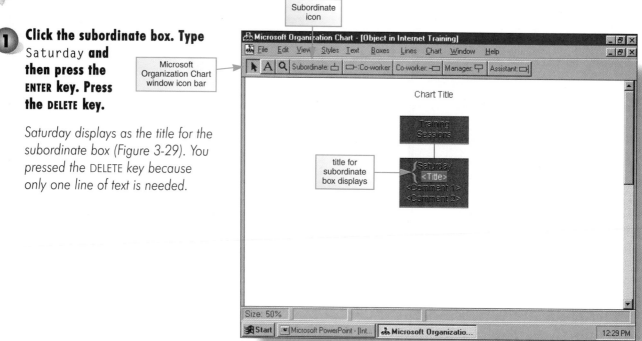

FIGURE 3-29

Adding Subordinate Boxes

Microsoft Organization Chart has five **types of boxes** you can add to a chart. Each box type has a corresponding **box tool** on the Microsoft Organization Chart window **icon bar**. Because the daily activities for the workshop in this project are divided into morning and afternoon sessions, you need to add two subordinate boxes to Saturday's schedule.

To add a single subordinate box, click the **Subordinate icon** and then click the box on the organization chart to which the subordinate reports. When you want to add several subordinate boxes, you can click the Subordinate icon once for each box you want to add to the organization chart. For example, if you want to add two subordinate boxes, click the Subordinate icon two times. If the Subordinate icon is recessed and you decide not to add subordinate boxes, you can deselect the Subordinate icon by clicking the Selection Arrow icon on the Microsoft Organization Chart window icon bar or pressing the ESC key.

The following steps explain how to use the Subordinate box tool to add two subordinate boxes to the Saturday box.

Steps **To Add Multiple Subordinate Boxes**

1 **Click the Subordinate icon on the Microsoft Organization Chart window icon bar two times. Point to the Saturday box.**

The Subordinate icon is recessed (Figure 3-30). The status bar displays the number of subordinate boxes Microsoft Organization Chart is creating, which is two. The mouse pointer shape changes to a subordinate box.

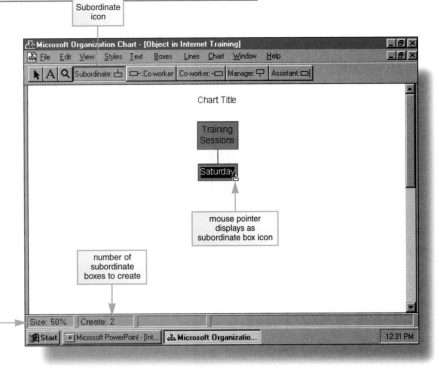

FIGURE 3-30

2 **Click the Saturday box.**

Two subordinate boxes display below the Saturday box (Figure 3-31). The new subordinate boxes display one level lower than the box to which they are attached. Saturday is now the manager to the new subordinate boxes. The left subordinate box on level 3 is selected.

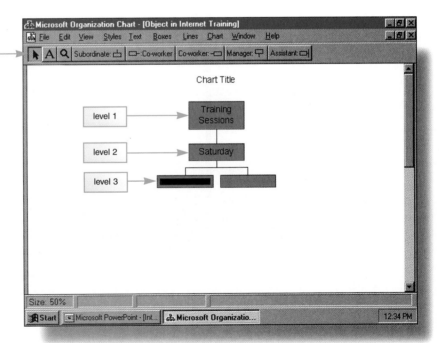

FIGURE 3-31

Adding Another Level of Subordinate Boxes

To further develop the organization chart in this project, you need to add a fourth level of subordinate boxes for the workshop sessions. This workshop presents two classes during the morning session and two classes during the afternoon session. Workshop participants must decide which four-hour class they want to attend. For example, a participant can attend the E-mail session on Saturday morning and then attend the Netiquette session on Sunday morning. The same decision will need to be made for the afternoon sessions.

The following steps summarize adding multiple subordinate boxes to a higher-level box.

TO ADD ANOTHER LEVEL OF SUBORDINATE BOXES

1 Click the Subordinate icon on the icon bar two times, and then click the left subordinate box on level 3.

2 Click the Subordinate icon two times, and then click the right subordinate box on level 3.

Two subordinate boxes display under each level 3 subordinate box (Figure 3-32).

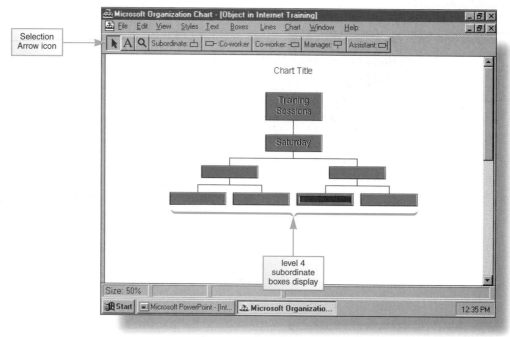

FIGURE 3-32

The structure of the organization chart is complete. The next step is to add titles to the boxes in the chart.

Adding Names to the Subordinate Boxes

To complete the organization chart, you must add names to all boxes subordinate to the Saturday box. Before you can add the names, however, you must deactivate the Subordinate box tool and activate the Selection Arrow tool. When the **Selection Arrow tool** is active, the mouse pointer displays as a left-pointing block arrow. Because the subordinate boxes in this project have names but do not have titles, the Title, Comment 1, and Comment 2 prompts display in brackets under the box name when the box is selected. The brackets indicate the label is optional, and it displays only when replaced by text. The following steps summarize adding a title to each level 4 subordinate box.

TO ADD NAMES TO SUBORDINATE BOXES

1 Click the left subordinate box on level 3. Type `Morning` in the subordinate box.

2 Click the right subordinate box on level 3. Type `Afternoon` in the subordinate box.

3 Click the left subordinate box under the Morning box. Type `E-mail` in the subordinate box.

4 Click the right subordinate box under the Morning box. Type `WWW` in the subordinate box.

5 Click the left subordinate box under the Afternoon box. Type `Newsgroups` in the subordinate box.

6 Click the right subordinate box under the Afternoon box. Type `Chat Rooms` in the subordinate box.

All level 4 subordinate boxes under the Saturday box display session names (Figure 3-33).

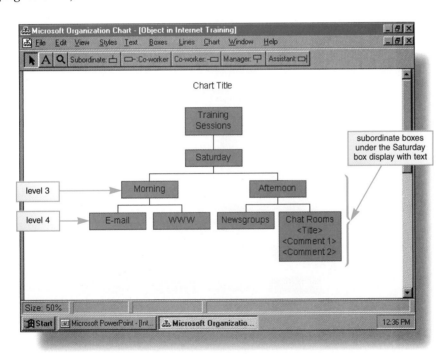

FIGURE 3-33

Changing Organization Chart Styles

Now that the boxes for the Saturday branch are labeled, you want to change the way the organization chart looks. With the addition of each new box, the chart expanded horizontally. Before you add Sunday's schedule, you must change the style of selected boxes from horizontal to vertical.

Steps | To Change the Organization Chart Style

1 Click anywhere outside the Organization Chart boxes. Press and hold the SHIFT key. Click the four lowest-level boxes: E-mail, WWW, Newsgroups, and Chat Rooms. Release the SHIFT key.

The four lowest-level boxes are selected (Figure 3-34).

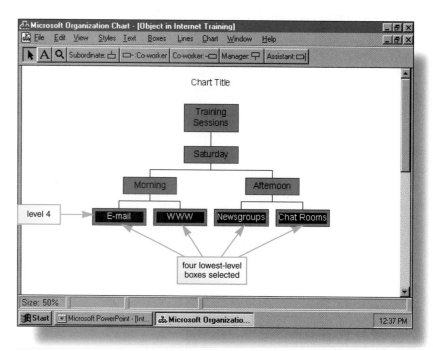

FIGURE 3-34

2 Click Styles on the menu bar and then point to the vertical style icon (row 1, column 2) in the top set of Groups styles.

*The default group style is selected, which is indicated by the recessed icon (Figure 3-35). The verticle style icon is highlighted. The **Styles menu** icons allow you to change the arrangement of boxes in your chart. The top set of styles changes the arrangement of boxes in a group. The middle style creates assistant boxes. The bottom style is used to show co-managers.*

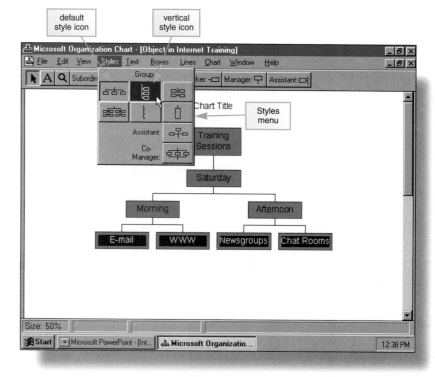

FIGURE 3-35

3 **Click the vertical style icon.**

The organization chart displays the two morning sessions and the two afternoon sessions vertically (Figure 3-36). The Morning box and the Afternoon box still display horizontally under the Saturday box because only the selected boxes change styles.

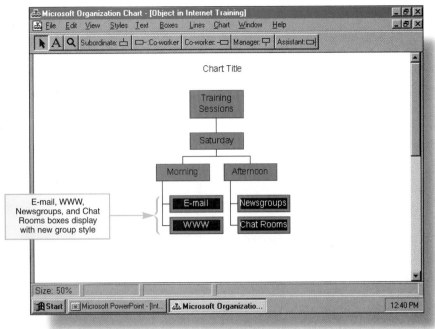

FIGURE 3-36

If you select the wrong group style or decide to retain the previous style, immediately click Undo Chart Style on the Edit menu.

Copying a Branch of an Organization Chart

Saturday's schedule is complete, and Sunday's schedule is similar. Instead of creating Sunday's schedule by adding and labeling boxes, you can copy Saturday's schedule and add it under the Training Sessions box. When you work with a whole section of an organization chart, it is referred to as working with a branch, or an appendage, of the chart. The following steps explain how to copy a branch of the chart.

More *About*
Delivering
Presentations

Use the "one-person-per-two-inch-rule" when deciding the maximum number of audience members who should view your slide show on a monitor. One person can comfortably view the screen for every two diagonal inches on the monitor. For example, 16 people can be seated comfortably around a 32-inch monitor.

Steps **To Copy a Branch of an Organization Chart**

1 **Press and hold the SHIFT key. Click the Saturday box, the Morning box, and the Afternoon box. If not already selected, click the E-mail box, the WWW box, the Newsgroups box, and the Chat Rooms box. Release the SHIFT key (Figure 3-37).**

2 **Right-click one of the selected boxes and then click Copy on the shortcut menu.**

*Microsoft Organization Chart copies the Saturday branch of the organization chart to the Clipboard. Recall that the **Clipboard** is a temporary Windows storage area.*

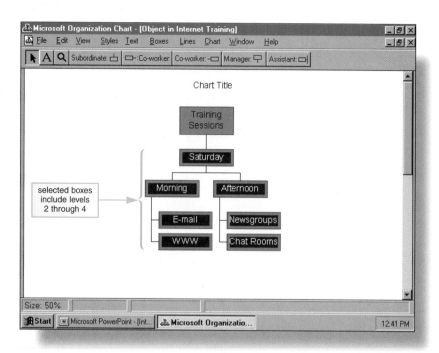

FIGURE 3-37

The next section explains how to paste the Saturday branch of the organization chart to another location on the chart.

Pasting a Branch of an Organization Chart

Now that a copy of the Saturday branch of the organization chart is on the Clipboard, the next step is to paste it from the Clipboard to the Comprehensive Classes slide.

Steps **To Paste a Branch of an Organization Chart**

1 **Right-click the root manager box labeled Training Sessions and then point to Paste Boxes on the shortcut menu.**

Paste Boxes is highlighted on the shortcut menu (Figure 3-38). The Training Sessions box is selected.

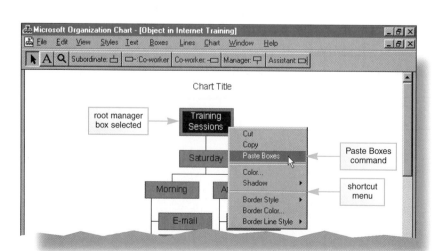

FIGURE 3-38

2 **Click Paste Boxes on the shortcut menu.**

The organization chart displays two Saturday branches (Figure 3-39).

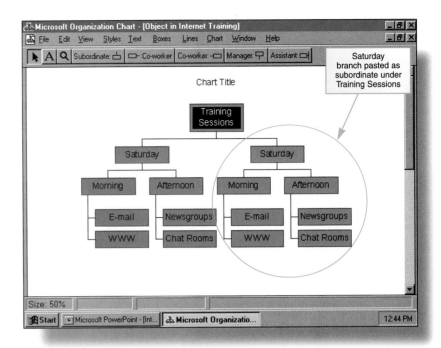

FIGURE 3-39

Editing an Organization Chart

After you have copied and pasted a branch of the organization chart, you need to **edit** the title of the first subordinate level so it displays as Sunday. You also need to edit the four sessions scheduled for Sunday. Editing a box requires you first to select the box and then make your edits.

 To Edit Text in an Organization Chart

1 **Click the Saturday box at the top of the right branch of the organization chart. Type** Sunday **in the subordinate box.**

The word Sunday replaces the word Saturday (Figure 3-40).

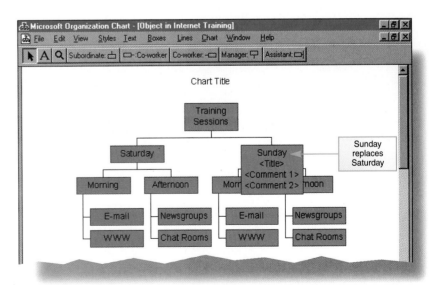

FIGURE 3-40

2 Click the E-mail box under the Sunday morning branch of the organization chart. Type Netiquette **in the subordinate box. For the other Sunday classes, type** Creating Pages **to replace Newsgroups, type** Search Engines **to replace WWW, and type** Privacy Issues **to replace Chat Rooms. Click anywhere outside the organization chart boxes.**

The Sunday training sessions schedule is revised (Figure 3-41).

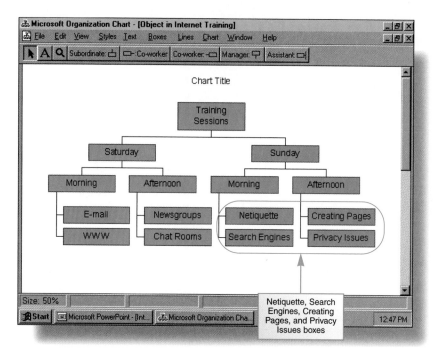

FIGURE 3-41

The text on the organization chart is complete. The next section explains how to format an organization chart.

Formatting an Organization Chart

Microsoft Organization Chart allows you to format a box simply by selecting it. To make your organization chart look like the chart shown in Figure 3-22 on page PP 3.25, you must add shadow effects and a border to every box. Then, you change the color of the boxes and the lines connecting the boxes. The following sections explain how to select all the boxes in the chart, change the box attributes to shadow and border, and then change the color of the organization chart boxes and lines.

Steps To Select All Boxes in an Organization Chart

1 Click Edit on the menu bar, point to Select, and then point to All (Figure 3-42).

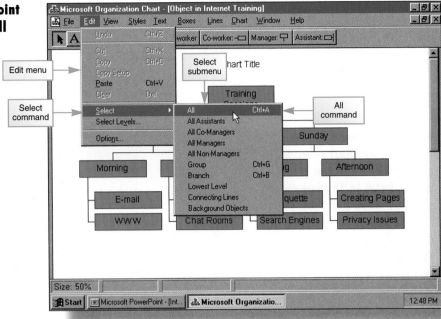

FIGURE 3-42

2 Click All on the submenu.

Microsoft Organization Chart selects all the boxes in the chart (Figure 3-43).

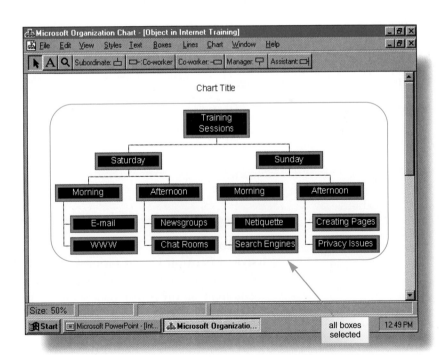

FIGURE 3-43

Other Ways

1. Press CTRL+A

Adding Shadow Effects to the Boxes in an Organization Chart

Now that all the boxes are selected, you can add shadow effects. Microsoft Organization Chart has eight shadow effects from which to choose. One style is None, which has no shadow. The following steps explain how to add shadow effects to all the boxes in an organization chart.

Steps To Add Shadow Effects to the Boxes in an Organization Chart

1 **With all the boxes in the organization chart selected, right-click one of the selected boxes. Point to Shadow on the shortcut menu and then point to the shadow style in row 2, column 2 on the Shadow submenu.**

Microsoft Organization Chart displays the Shadow submenu (Figure 3-44). The default shadow style for Microsoft Organization Chart is None. The desired shadow style is highlighted.

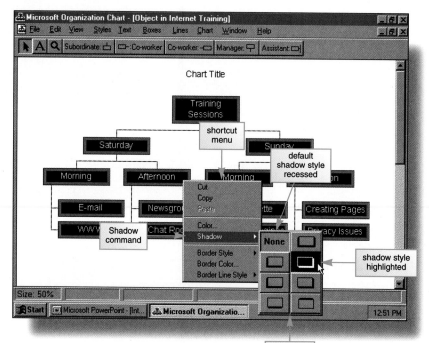

FIGURE 3-44

2 **Click the highlighted shadow style on the Shadow submenu.**

Microsoft Organization Chart adds the shadow effect to all the boxes in the organization chart.

Changing Border Styles in an Organization Chart

To enhance the boxes in the organization chart, you must change the border style. Microsoft Organization Chart has 12 border styles from which to choose. One style is None, which has no border. The default border style is a thin line. The steps on the next page explain how to change border styles.

Steps **To Change the Border Style**

1 **With all the boxes in the organization chart selected, right-click one of the selected boxes. Point to Border Style on the shortcut menu and then point to the border style in row 4, column 1 on the Border Style submenu.**

Microsoft Organization Chart displays the Border Style submenu (Figure 3-45). The default border style for Microsoft Organization Chart is recessed in row 2, column 1. The desired border style is highlighted.

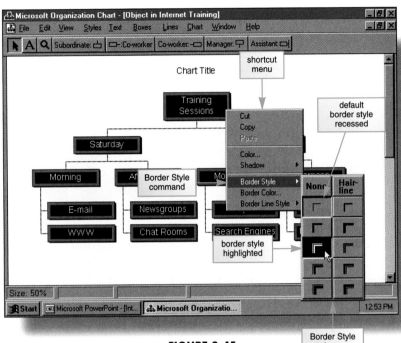

FIGURE 3-45

2 **Click the highlighted border style on the Border Style submenu.**

Microsoft Organization Chart applies the new border style to all the boxes in the organization chart.

Changing Box Color in an Organization Chart

To enhance the boxes in the organization chart, you need to change their color. Microsoft Organization Chart uses orange as the default box color, but you can choose 31 other colors. The following steps explain how to change box colors.

Steps To Change the Box Color

1 **With all the boxes in the organization chart still selected, right-click one of the selected boxes. Click Color on the shortcut menu.**

Microsoft Organization Chart displays the Color dialog box with a palette of 32 colors for the boxes (Figure 3-46). Orange is selected as the default box color.

2 **Point to the color gold in row 1, column 4.**

3 **Click the gold box and then click the OK button.**

Microsoft Organization Chart applies the new color to all boxes in the organization chart.

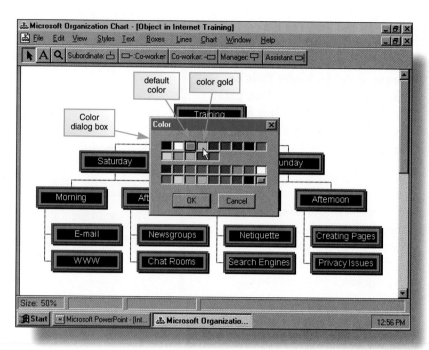

FIGURE 3-46

More About Chart Lines

Solid lines on an organization chart represent a formal chain of command between the boxes, as when one person is a direct supervisor of another person. On the other hand, dotted or dashed lines represent an open line of communication for reporting out of the chain of authority.

Changing Line Color in an Organization Chart

To enhance the lines connecting the boxes in the organization chart, you need to change their color. Microsoft Organization Chart uses black as the default line color, but you can choose 30 other colors. The steps on the next page explain how to change line colors.

Steps To Change the Line Color

1 With all the boxes in the organization chart still selected, click Lines on the menu bar and then click Color.

2 Click the color gold in row 1, column 4, which is the same color you selected for the box color. Click the OK button.

Microsoft Organization Chart applies the new color gold to all lines in the organization chart (Figure 3-47).

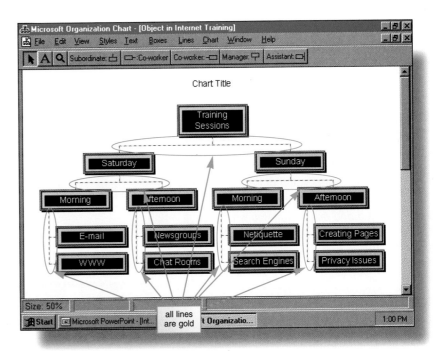

FIGURE 3-47

The organization chart now is complete. The next step is to return to the PowerPoint window.

Quitting Microsoft Organization Chart and Returning to the PowerPoint Window

After you create and format an organization chart, you quit Microsoft Organization Chart and return to the PowerPoint window. The steps on the next page explain how to return to the PowerPoint window.

More *About* **Organization Chart**

If you want to modify your organization chart object after you have inserted it in your PowerPoint slide, just double-click it. PowerPoint will open Microsoft Organization Chart and allow you to make your changes. When you click the Close button, you will return to the PowerPoint window.

Steps **To Quit Microsoft Organization Chart and Return to the PowerPoint Window**

1 **Click the Close button on the Microsoft Organization Chart - [Object in Internet Training] title bar. When the Microsoft Organization Chart dialog box displays, point to the Yes button.**

The Microsoft Organization Chart dialog box warns you that the organization chart object has changed and asks you if you want to update the object in the PowerPoint presentation, Internet Training, before proceeding (Figure 3-48).

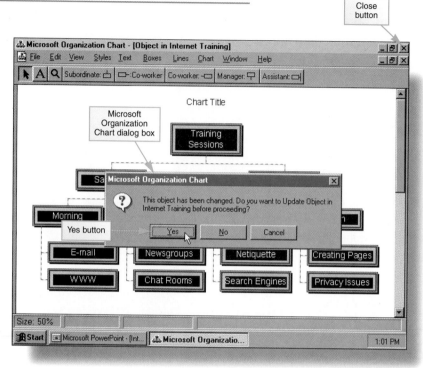

FIGURE 3-48

2 **Click the Yes button.**

Microsoft Organization Chart updates the organization chart object and closes, and then PowerPoint displays the organization chart on Slide 3 (Figure 3-49).

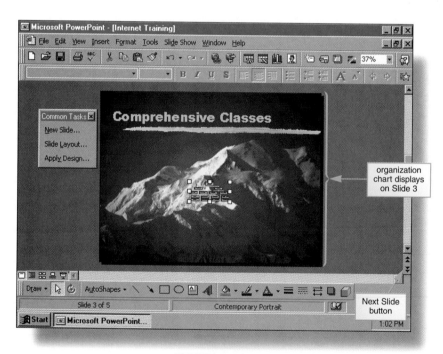

FIGURE 3-49

Scaling an Organization Chart Object

The organization chart on Slide 3 is sized to fit the Organization Chart placeholder. The organization chart would be easier to read if it were enlarged. The **Scale command** allows you to enlarge or reduce an object by very precise amounts while retaining the object's original proportions.

Perform the following steps to scale an organization chart object.

TO SCALE AN ORGANIZATION CHART OBJECT

1 Right-click the selected organization chart object and then click Format Object on the shortcut menu.

2 Click the Size tab. In the Scale area, triple-click the Height text box. Type 110 as the entry.

3 Click the OK button.

The organization chart is scaled to 110 percent of its original size (Figure 3-50).

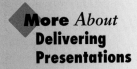

FIGURE 3-50

Moving the Organization Chart

Now that the organization chart is scaled to a readable size, you need to move it onto the slide. The following step explains how to move the organization chart.

Steps **To Move the Organization Chart**

1 Drag the organization chart onto the middle of the blank area of Slide 3 (Figure 3-51).

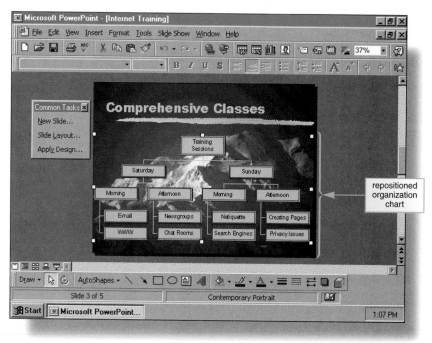

FIGURE 3-51

Slide 3 now is complete. The next section introduces you to moving text and embedding a picture into a slide.

FIGURE 3-52

Moving Text and Embedding a Picture into a Slide

Slide 4 is included in this presentation to inform prospective attendees that convenient lodging and social activities are included in their workshop package. You list features of the weekend seminar package and insert a picture of the hotel and heated outdoor pool to reinforce that message. Another graphic object often inserted into a slide is a picture. Slide 4 contains a bulleted list and an embedded picture as shown in Figure 3-52. Recall that a **picture** is any graphic image from another application.

Moving Text in a Slide

The first step is to display the next slide and to move the bulleted list to the right side of the slide.

Perform these steps to move the text.

 Steps **To Move Text in a Slide**

---

1 **Click the Next Slide button to display Slide 4.**

Slide 4 displays the Bulleted List layout (Figure 3-53).

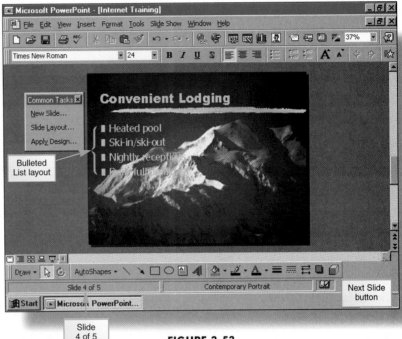

FIGURE 3-53

2 **Click any of the bulleted list text.**

All the text becomes highlighted and a border displays around the subtitle object (Figure 3-54).

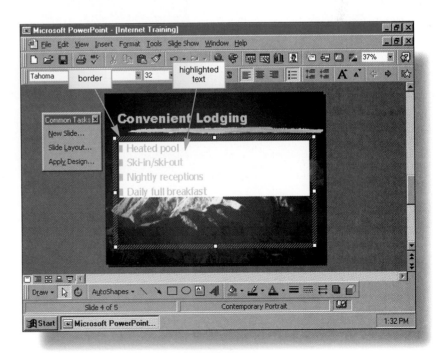

FIGURE 3-54

3 Click the bottom right fill handle and drag it diagonally so the border frames the text (Figure 3-55).

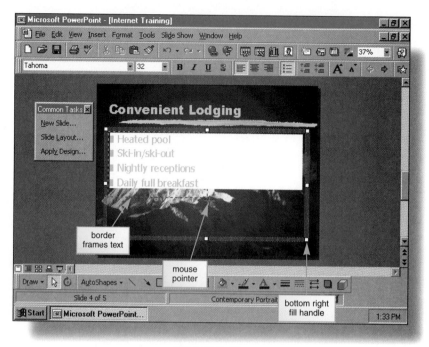

FIGURE 3-55

4 Point to the border around the subtitle object. Drag the border to the lower-right quadrant of the slide so the right and bottom borders align with the edges of the slide (Figure 3-56).

5 Click anywhere outside the box.

The border disappears.

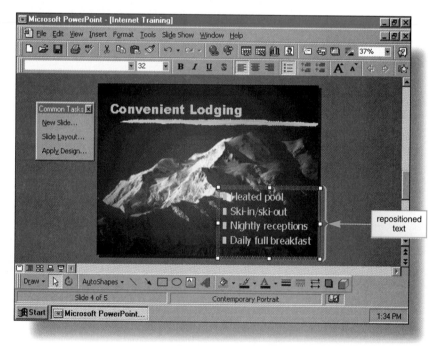

FIGURE 3-56

Inserting a Picture

The picture you insert on Slide 4 is a scanned picture that has been stored as a bitmap graphic and saved as a TIF file. The Pool file is from the PowerPoint folder on the Data Disk that accompanies this book.

Perform the following steps to insert this picture.

Steps **To Insert a Picture**

1 **Click Insert on the menu bar, point to Picture, and then point to From File (Figure 3-57).**

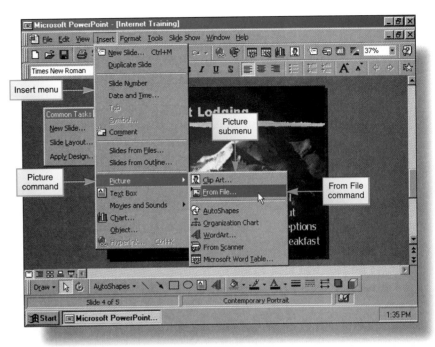

FIGURE 3-57

2 **Click From File. When the Insert Picture dialog box displays, if necessary, click 3½ Floppy (A:) in the Look in box. Double-click Pool in the list box.**

The Pool.tif file displays on Slide 4 (Figure 3-58).

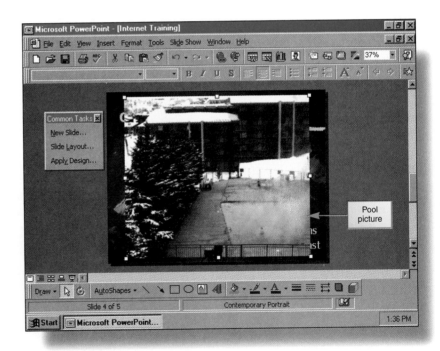

FIGURE 3-58

When the Insert Picture dialog box displays, PowerPoint does not require that you specify which format your picture is in. The default includes all the formats installed on your system that PowerPoint recognizes.

Resizing a Picture

PowerPoint automatically placed the picture in the middle of Slide 4 because a placeholder was not selected. To balance the text object and the picture, you must drag the picture to the left of the bulleted list. **Balance** means that the slide possesses a harmonious, or satisfying, arrangement of proportions of its objects. The height of the picture is not in balance with the bulleted text. To correct this, you need to change the proportions of the picture.

PowerPoint allows you to **constrain**, or control, resizing an object from its center by holding down the CTRL key while dragging a sizing handle. This method of constraining is called **resizing about center**.

Perform the following steps to resize a picture about its center.

Steps To Resize a Picture

1 **Point to the right center sizing handle on the right side of the picture.**

The mouse pointer shape changes to a two-headed arrow when it is positioned on a sizing handle (Figure 3-59).

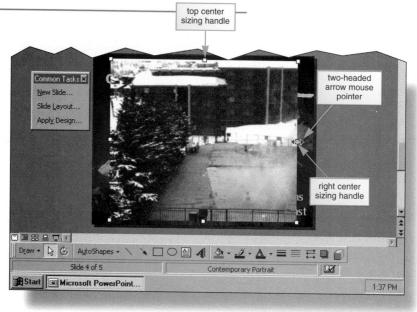

top center
sizing handle

two-headed
arrow mouse
pointer

right center
sizing handle

FIGURE 3-59

2 **Press and hold the CTRL key. Drag the mouse pointer inward toward the middle of the picture until the right edge of the picture aligns with the swimmer in the pool. Release the mouse button. Then, release the CTRL key (Figure 3-60).**

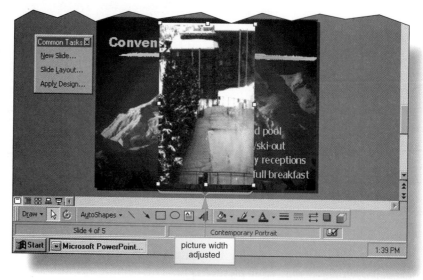

picture width
adjusted

FIGURE 3-60

3 Point to the top center sizing handle. Press and hold the CTRL key. Drag the mouse pointer inward toward the middle of the picture until the top edge of the picture aligns with the bottom of the gold line at the top of the slide. Release the mouse button. Then, release the CTRL key.

The picture is resized about its center (Figure 3-61). Resize about center means changing the size of an object proportionally from its center.

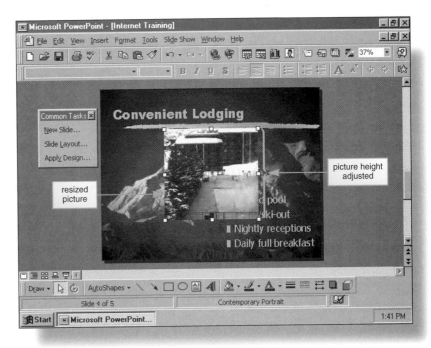

FIGURE 3-61

4 Drag the picture to the bottom-left corner of the slide (Figure 3-62).

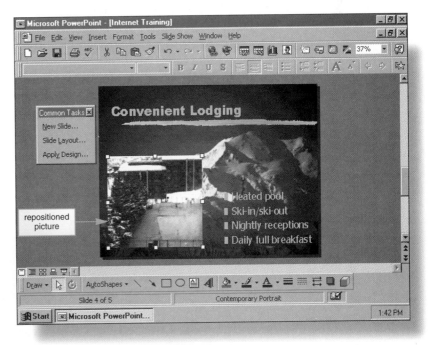

FIGURE 3-62

Caution should be exercised when resizing an object about its center. In Step 3, releasing the CTRL key before releasing the left mouse button does not resize about center; it resizes only the bottom of the picture. To correct this error, click the Undo button on the Standard toolbar and perform Steps 2 and 3 again, making certain first to release the mouse button and then release the CTRL key.

Table 3-1

METHOD	CONSTRAINING WITH RESIZING AN OBJECT
SHIFT+drag a corner sizing handle	Resizes a selected object proportionally from a corner
CTRL+drag a sizing handle	Resizes a selected object vertically, horizontally, or diagonally from the center outward
CTRL+SHIFT+drag a corner sizing handle	Resizes a selected object proportionally from the center
ALT+drag a sizing handle	Resizes a selected object while temporarily overriding the settings for the grid and guides

PowerPoint has other methods of constraining objects when resizing. Table 3-1 explains the various constraining methods.

You can **restore** a resized object to its original proportions by selecting and then right-clicking the object to produce a shortcut menu. Click Format Picture on the shortcut menu, click the Size tab, click Reset in the Original size area, and then click the OK button.

Changing the size of the object can be achieved simply by dragging a sizing handle. This action resizes the picture in the direction toward which you drag. Dragging a sizing handle, however, changes the proportions of the picture. Recall that evenly resizing the object from a center point in the object is called resizing about center. This method of resizing the picture maintains the object's proportions.

Adding a Border to the Picture

The next step is to add a border to the picture. A **border** is the visible line around the edge of an object. The border draws attention to the object by defining its edges. A border has line style and line color attributes. The **line style** determines the line thickness and line appearance of the border. For example, you could choose a thick, solid line for your border. **Line color** determines the color of the line that forms the border. The picture illustrated in Figure 3-52 on page PP 3.46 has a three-line white border.

Perform these steps to format the picture by adding a three-line border.

Steps **To Add a Border to a Picture**

1 **Verify the picture is selected. Click the Line Style button on the Drawing toolbar.**

The Line Style list displays (Figure 3-63).

2 **Click the last line style in the list, which is the 6 pt thin-thick-thin three-line style.**

A three-line style displays around the picture.

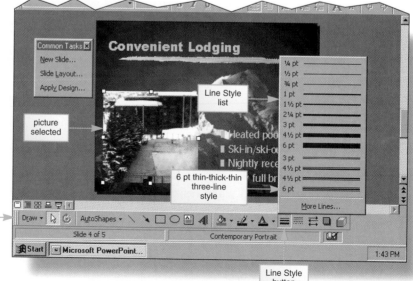

FIGURE 3-63

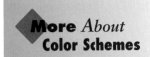

Changing the Border Line Color

To draw the attention of the audience to the picture, you can add color to the lines of the border. Recall that the design template establishes the attributes of the title master and the slide master. When you click the Line Color button arrow on the Drawing toolbar, a list displays line colors. A portion of the list contains the eight colors used to create the design template. One of the colors is identified as the line color and is labeled Automatic.

Perform the following steps to add the Contemporary Portrait design template default line color to the border around the picture on Slide 4.

More *About*
Color Schemes

Whenever you select a color other than one present in the color scheme, that new color is added to all color menus. As a result, the color can be used for text, lines, backgrounds, and other effects, such as shadows and bullets.

 To Change the Border Line Color

1 **Click the Line Color button arrow on the Drawing toolbar.**

The Line Color list displays (Figure 3-64a). The current line color is black.

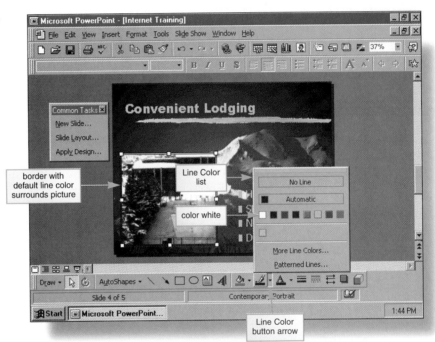

FIGURE 3-64a

2 **Click the color white, which is the first box in the row of available colors.**

A white border displays around the pool picture (Figure 3-64b).

3 **Click the Save button on the Standard toolbar to save the presentation again.**

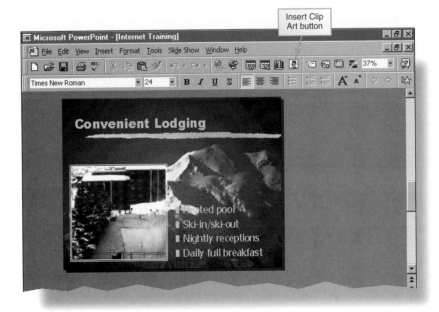

FIGURE 3-64b

Slide 4 now is complete. The next section describes how to ungroup clip art and insert pieces of it in your closing slide in the onscreen slide show.

Creating a PowerPoint Clip Art Object

A **clip art picture** is composed of many objects grouped together to form one object. PowerPoint allows you to alter clip art by disassembling the objects. **Disassembling** a clip art object, also called **ungrouping**, separates one object into multiple objects. Once ungrouped, you can manipulate the individual objects as needed to form a new object. When you ungroup a clip art picture in PowerPoint, it becomes a **PowerPoint object** and loses its link to the Microsoft Clip Gallery. Therefore, you cannot double-click the new picture to open the Microsoft Clip Gallery.

Slide 5 contains a modified version of the Opportunity Challenge Difficult Objective picture from the Microsoft Clip Gallery. You may want to modify clip art for various reasons. Many times you cannot find clip art that precisely illustrates your topic. For example, you might want a picture of a man and woman shaking hands, but the only available clip art picture has two men and a woman shaking hands.

Occasionally, you may want to remove or change a portion of a clip art picture or you may want to combine two or more clip art pictures. For example, you can use one clip art picture for the background and another picture as the foreground. Still other times, you may want to combine clip art with another type of object. The types of objects you can combine with clip art depend on the software installed on your computer. The Object type list box in the Insert Object dialog box identifies the types of objects you can combine with clip art.

Modifying the clip art picture on Slide 5 requires several steps. First, you display Slide 5. Then, you change the AutoLayout to Object. Next, you insert the Opportunity Challenge Difficult Objective clip art into the object placeholder. Then, you scale the clip art to increase its size. Then, you ungroup the clip art and delete unwanted pieces. The steps on the following pages explain in detail how to insert, scale, and ungroup clip art.

Inserting Clip Art

The first step in modifying a clip art picture is to insert the picture on a slide. You insert the Opportunity Challenge Difficult Objective clip art from the Microsoft Clip Gallery. In later steps, you modify the clip art.

The following steps explain how to insert the Opportunity Challenge Difficult Objective clip art onto Slide 5 of this presentation.

TO INSERT CLIP ART

1. Click the Next Slide button to display Slide 5.
2. Click the Slide Layout button on the Common Tasks toolbar. Type 16 to select the Object AutoLayout. Press the ENTER key.
3. Click the object placeholder to select it.
4. Click the Insert Clip Art button on the Standard toolbar. Then, click the Find button in the Microsoft Clip Gallery 3.0 dialog box.
5. When the Find Clip dialog box displays, type Opportunity Challenge Difficult Objective in the Keywords text box.

(6) Click the Find Now button.

(7) Click the Insert button in the Microsoft Clip Gallery 3.0 dialog box.

Slide 5 displays the Opportunity Challenge Difficult Objective clip art picture (Figure 3-65).

Scaling Clip Art

Now that the clip art picture is inserted onto Slide 5, you must increase its size by **scaling**. Perform the following steps to scale the clip art picture.

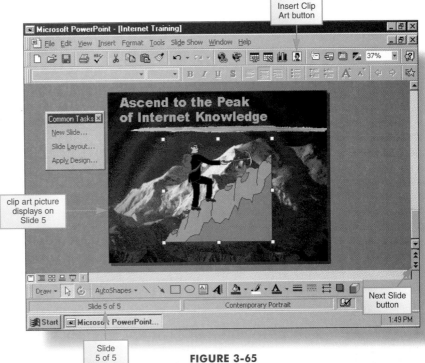

FIGURE 3-65

TO SCALE CLIP ART

(1) Making sure the Opportunity Challenge Difficult Objective clip art picture still is selected, right-click the clip art picture.

(2) Click Format Picture on the shortcut menu.

(3) If necessary, click the Size tab.

(4) In the Scale area, triple-click in the Height text box. Type 175 and then click the OK button.

The Opportunity Challenge Difficult Objective clip art picture is scaled to 175 percent of its original size (Figure 3-66).

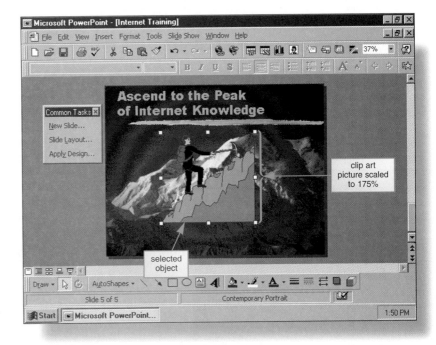

FIGURE 3-66

Ungrouping Clip Art

The next step is to ungroup the Opportunity Challenge Difficult Objective clip art picture in Slide 5. When you **ungroup** a clip art picture, PowerPoint breaks it into its component objects. These new groups can be ungrouped repeatedly until they decompose into individual objects. A clip art picture may be composed of a few individual objects or several complex groups of objects.

The steps on the next page explain how to ungroup clip art.

Steps **To Ungroup Clip Art**

1 **With the Opportunity Challenge Difficult Objective clip art picture selected, right-click the clip art. Point to Grouping on the shortcut menu. Click Ungroup on the Grouping submenu.**

A Microsoft PowerPoint dialog box displays explaining that this clip art object is an imported object and that converting it to a Microsoft Office drawing permanently discards any embedded data or linking information it contains. Finally, you are asked if you want to convert the object to a Microsoft Office drawing.

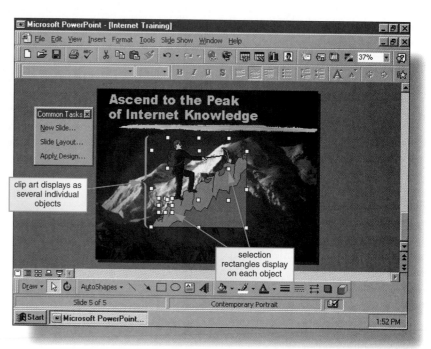

FIGURE 3-67

2 **Click the Yes button.**

*The clip art picture now displays as several PowerPoint objects (Figure 3-67). Selection rectangles display around the ungrouped objects. Recall that a **selection rectangle** is the box framed by the sizing handles when a graphic is selected.*

Other Ways

1. On Draw menu click Ungroup

When you ungroup a clip art object and click the Yes button in the Microsoft PowerPoint information box (Step 2 above), PowerPoint converts the clip art object to a PowerPoint object. Recall that a PowerPoint object is an object *not* associated with a supplementary application. As a result, you lose the capability to double-click the clip art picture to open the Microsoft Clip Gallery. To replace a PowerPoint object with a clip art object, click the Insert Clip Art button on the Standard toolbar or click Insert on the menu bar. Click Object and then click Microsoft Clip Gallery. If for some reason, you decide not to ungroup the clip art picture, click the No button in the Microsoft PowerPoint dialog box. Clicking the No button terminates the Ungroup command, and the clip art picture displays on the slide as a clip art object.

Because clip art is a collection of complex groups of objects, you may need to ungroup a complex object into less complex objects before being able to modify a specific object.

If you accidentally ungroup an object, you immediately can **regroup** it by clicking Group on the Grouping submenu. If only one composite object is selected or you made changes to the composite objects, you can regroup the composite objects using the **Regroup command** on the Grouping submenu.

Recall that clip art is an object imported from the Microsoft Clip Gallery. Disassembling imported, embedded, or linked objects eliminates the embedding data or linking information the object contains that ties it back to its original source.

Use caution when objects are not completely regrouped. Dragging or scaling affects only the selected object, not the entire collection of objects.

Deselecting Clip Art Objects

All of the ungrouped objects in Figure 3-67 are selected. Before you can manipulate an individual object, you must **deselect** all selected objects to remove the selection rectangles, and then you must select the object you want to manipulate. For example, in this slide you will remove the clip art mountains under the man. The following step explains how to deselect objects.

TO DESELECT A CLIP ART OBJECT

1 Click outside the clip art area.

Slide 5 displays without selection rectangles around the objects.

The Opportunity Challenge Difficult Objective clip art picture now is ungrouped into many objects. The next two sections explain how to drag a PowerPoint object and delete unwanted objects.

Moving a PowerPoint Object

To make deleting the unwanted clip art mountains easier, you must move the mountain climber away from the other clip art objects. Perform the following steps to move a PowerPoint object.

 Steps To Move a PowerPoint Object

 Click the torso of the mountain climber object.

A selection rectangle displays around the mountain climber object (Figure 3-68). If you inadvertently select a different object, click the center of the mountain climber object.

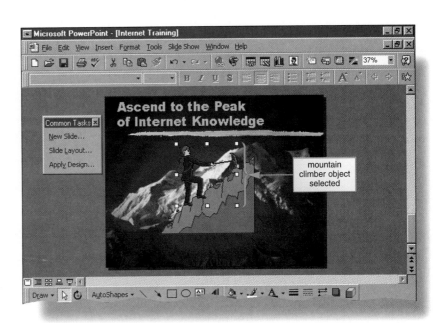

FIGURE 3-68

2 Drag the mountain climber object downward and away from the clip art mountain so his pick is reaching into a mountain peak in the mountain photograph (Figure 3-69).

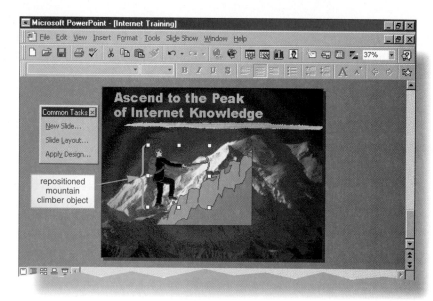

FIGURE 3-69

You moved the mountain climber object away from the other objects to make it easier to delete the unwanted objects.

Deleting PowerPoint Objects

Now that the mountain climber object is separated from the other objects in the Opportunity Challenge Difficult Objective clip art picture, you can delete the mountain objects that are part of this clip art. Perform the following steps to delete unwanted PowerPoint objects.

 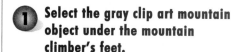

To Delete PowerPoint Objects

1 Select the gray clip art mountain object under the mountain climber's feet.

A selection rectangle displays around the mountain object (Figure 3-70). If you inadvertently select a different object, click the center of the mountain object.

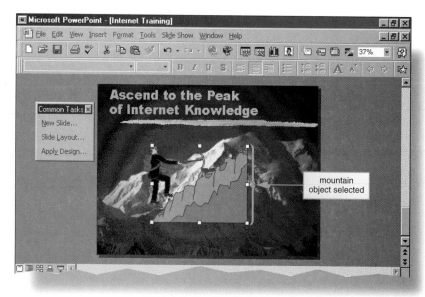

FIGURE 3-70

2 **Press the DELETE key.**

The mountain object is deleted (Figure 3-71).

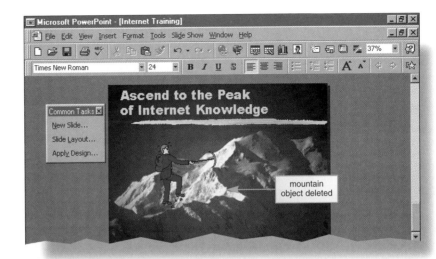

FIGURE 3-71

Slide 5 now is complete. The next section shows you how to add effects for switching from one slide to the next when you give your presentation.

Adding Slide Transition and Text Preset Animation Effects

The final step in preparing the Internet Training presentation is to add slide transition and text preset animation effects. Perform the following steps to add the slide transition and text preset animation effects.

TO ADD SLIDE TRANSITION AND TEXT PRESET ANIMATION EFFECTS

1 Click the Slide Sorter View button.

2 Press and hold the SHIFT key. Click Slide 2, Slide 3, and Slide 4. Release the SHIFT key.

3 Click the Slide Transition Effects box arrow. Click Box In.

4 Click Slide 1. Press and hold the SHIFT key and then click Slide 4. Release the SHIFT key.

5 Click the Text Preset Animation box arrow. Scroll down and click Spiral.

The presentation displays in Slide Sorter View (Figure 3-72). Slides 1 and 4 are selected. Text preset animation effects are applied to Slides 1 and 4. Slide transition effects are applied to Slides 2, 3, 4, and 5.

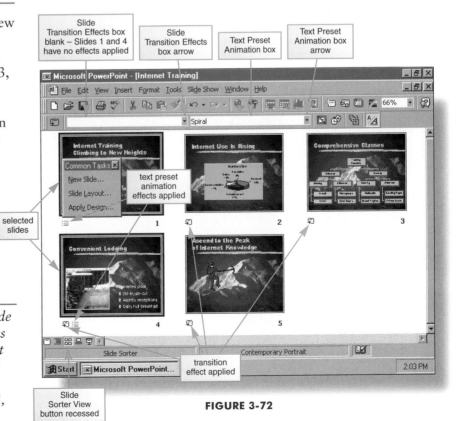

FIGURE 3-72

Printing Slides as Handouts

Perform the following steps to print the presentation slides as handouts, six slides per page.

 Steps **To Print Slides as Handouts**

1 Click File on the menu bar and then click Print. When the Print dialog box displays, click the Print what box arrow and click Handouts (6 slides per page) in the Print what list box. Then click Scale to fit paper (Figure 3-73).

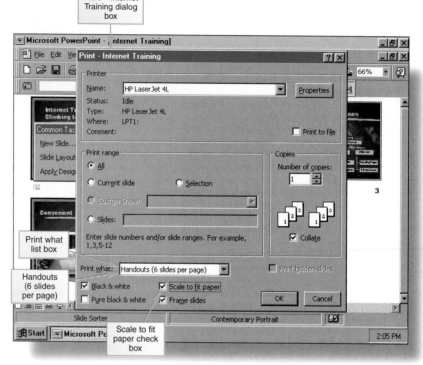

FIGURE 3-73

More *About*
Electronic
Presentations

PowerPoint allows you to change slides quickly and effortlessly. As a result, presenters often need to develop three times as many slides for their speeches than they would have needed had they been using overhead transparencies or 35mm slides.

2 **Click the OK button to begin printing.**

The handout prints as shown in Figure 3-74.

FIGURE 3-74

Project Summary

Project 3 introduced you to several methods of enhancing a presentation with embedded visuals. You began the project by creating the presentation from an outline that was created in Word. Then, you learned how to create a special slide background using a picture. When you created Slide 2, you learned how to embed an existing Excel chart. Slide 3 introduced you to creating and embedding an organization chart using the supplementary application Microsoft Organization Chart 2.0. You then learned how to embed a picture on Slide 4. Then, you learned how to ungroup objects for Slide 5. Finally, you learned how to print your presentation slides as handouts.

What You Should Know

Having completed this project, you now should be able to perform the following tasks:

- Add a Border to a Picture *(PP 3.52)*
- Add Another Level of Subordinate Boxes *(PP 3.32)*
- Add Multiple Subordinate Boxes *(PP 3.31)*
- Add Names to Subordinate Boxes *(PP 3.33)*
- Add Shadow Effects to Boxes in an Organization Chart *(PP 3.40)*
- Add Slide Transition and Text Preset Animation Effects *(PP 3.59)*
- Change the Box Color *(PP 3.42)*
- Change the Border Line Color *(PP 3.53)*
- Change the Border Style *(PP 3.41)*
- Change Design Templates *(PP 3.12)*
- Change the Font Color of the Entire Outline *(PP 3.10)*
- Change the Line Color *(PP 3.43)*
- Change the Organization Chart Style *(PP 3.34)*
- Change Slide Layout to Title Slide *(PP 3.13)*
- Copy a Branch of an Organization Chart *(PP 3.36)*
- Create the Title for the Root Manager Box *(PP 3.28)*
- Delete PowerPoint Objects *(PP 3.58)*
- Delete Subordinate Boxes *(PP 3.29)*
- Deselect a Clip Art Object *(PP 3.57)*
- Display the Next Slide and Change the Slide Layout *(PP 3.18, 3.26)*
- Edit an Embedded Excel Chart *(PP 3.21)*
- Edit Text in an Organization Chart *(PP 3.37)*
- Embed an Excel Chart *(PP 3.18)*
- Insert a Picture *(PP 3.49)*
- Insert a Picture to Create a Custom Background *(PP 3.15)*
- Insert Clip Art *(PP 3.54)*
- Maximize the Microsoft Organization Chart Window *(PP 3.27)*
- Move a PowerPoint Object *(PP 3.57)*
- Move Text in a Slide *(PP 3.47)*
- Move the Organization Chart *(PP 3.46)*
- Open Microsoft Organization Chart *(PP 3.27)*
- Paste a Branch of an Organization Chart *(PP 3.36)*
- Position an Embedded Excel Chart Object *(PP 3.23)*
- Print Slides as Handouts *(PP 3.60)*
- Quit Microsoft Organization Chart and Return to the PowerPoint Window *(PP 3.44)*
- Resize a Picture *(PP 3.50)*
- Save a Presentation *(PP 3.13)*
- Scale an Organization Chart Object *(PP 3.45)*
- Scale Clip Art *(PP 3.55)*
- Select All Boxes in an Organization Chart *(PP 3.39)*
- Start PowerPoint and Open an Outline *(PP 3.9)*
- Title a Subordinate Box *(PP 3.30)*
- Ungroup Clip Art *(PP 3.56)*

A+ Test Your Knowledge

1 True/False

Instructions: Circle T if the statement is true or F if the statement is false.

T F 1. RTF is an abbreviation for Real Text Font.
T F 2. The default design template is named Auto Design.
T F 3. You can change presentation design templates when you are creating a presentation and also any time you wish to change the look of your presentation.
T F 4. Bitmap and vector are the two types of graphic formats used to save pictures.
T F 5. The smallest element that can display or that print hardware and software can manipulate is called a pixel.
T F 6. A linked object on a slide does not change if the original object changes.
T F 7. An organization chart shows various functions or responsibilities that contribute to an organization or to a collective function.
T F 8. In Microsoft Organization Chart, the top box is called the root manager.
T F 9. To resize an object about its center, press and hold the CTRL key and double-click the object.
T F 10. When a PowerPoint object is disassembled, it becomes a clip art picture.

2 Multiple Choice

Instructions: Circle the correct response.

1. When PowerPoint opens an outline created in Microsoft Word and saved as a(n) _____ file, the text attributes and outline heading levels are maintained.
   a. Microsoft Word
   b. PowerPoint
   c. Rich Text Format (RTF)
   d. plain text (.txt)
2. Which slide attributes can change when a different design template is selected?
   a. font
   b. bullets
   c. color
   d. all of the above
3. A(n) _____ is a piece of art that has been stored as a pattern of dots called pixels.
   a. graphic filter
   b. vector graphic
   c. digitized signal
   d. bitmap graphic

(continued)

Multiple Choice *(continued)*

4. A(n) _____ object is created in another application but maintains a connection to its source.
   a. inserted
   b. linked
   c. extended
   d. related

5. To select more than one object, such as two subordinate boxes, press and hold the _____ key while clicking the objects.
   a. ALT
   b. CTRL
   c. SHIFT
   d. TAB

6. To resize a picture about its center, press and hold the _____ key while dragging a sizing handle.
   a. ALT
   b. CTRL
   c. ESC
   d. TAB

7. A(n) _____ object can be embedded in a PowerPoint slide.
   a. Excel chart
   b. clip art
   c. picture
   d. all of the above

8. The _____ attribute(s) of an organization chart can be formatted.
   a. box color
   b. border style
   c. shadow effects
   d. all of the above

9. The OLE application used to create an organization chart is called _____.
   a. Microsoft Organization Chart
   b. Microsoft Hierarchy Chart
   c. Microsoft Embedded Chart
   d. Microsoft Department Chart

10. A PowerPoint sample organization chart has _____ boxes.
    a. two
    b. three
    c. four
    d. five

Test Your Knowledge

3 Understanding PowerPoint Menus and Commands

Instructions: Identify the menus and commands that carry out the operation or cause the dialog box to display and allow you to make the indicated changes.

	MENU	COMMAND
1. Add slide transition effects	_____	_____
2. Change design templates	_____	_____
3. Change AutoLayout to Title Slide	_____	_____
4. Delete subordinate boxes	_____	_____
5. Insert a picture	_____	_____
6. Insert clip art	_____	_____
7. Open an outline	_____	_____
8. Open Microsoft Organization Chart	_____	_____
9. Print slides as handouts	_____	_____
10. Scale an Organization Chart object to 110 percent	_____	_____

4 Working with an Organization Chart

Instructions: Write the step numbers below to indicate the sequence necessary to create the organization chart shown in Figure 3-75. Assume Microsoft Organization Chart is active, the design template and Organization Chart layout are selected, and the title text already is created. Label levels 1 and 2 before adding the level 3 subordinate boxes. Label new level 3 subordinate boxes before changing the chart style. Then add the level 4 subordinate boxes. Finally, format all the box border styles.

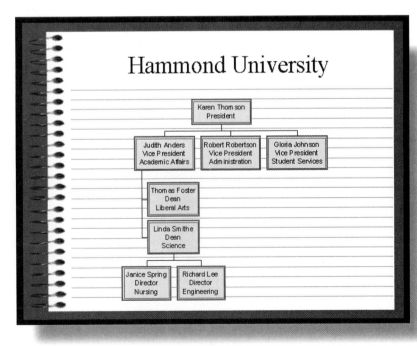

FIGURE 3-75

(continued)

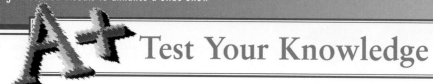

Test Your Knowledge

Working with an Organization Chart *(continued)*

Step _____: Click the box to the right of the Thomas Foster subordinate box. Type `Linda Smithe` and then press the ENTER key. Type `Dean` and then press the ENTER key. Type `Science` in the box.

Step _____: Click Styles on the menu bar and then click the vertical style icon in the Groups styles.

Step _____: On the Boxes menu, click Border Color. Click brown (row 3, column 2 in the Color dialog box). Click the OK button.

Step _____: Click the Subordinate icon on the Microsoft Organization Chart window icon bar two times. Click the left subordinate box labeled Judith Anders. Type `Thomas Foster` and then press the ENTER key. Type `Dean` and then press the ENTER key. Type `Liberal Arts` in the box.

Step _____: Click the Close button. Click the Yes button in the Microsoft Organization Chart dialog box.

Step _____: On level 2, click the left subordinate box. Type `Judith Anders` and then press the ENTER key. Type `Vice President` and then press the ENTER key. Type `Academic Affairs` in the box. Next, click the middle subordinate box. Type `Robert Robertson` and then press the ENTER key. Type `Vice President` and then press the ENTER key. Then, type `Administration` in the box. Click the right subordinate box. Type `Gloria Johnson` and then press the ENTER key. Type `Vice President` and then press the ENTER key. Type `Student Services` in the box.

Step _____: Click the box to the right of the Nursing subordinate box. Type `Richard Lee` and then press the ENTER key. Type `Director` and then press the ENTER key. Type `Engineering` in the box.

Step _____: Type `Karen Thomson` in the root manager box and then press the ENTER key. Type `President` in the root manager box.

Step _____: On the Microsoft Organization Chart Edit menu, point to Select and then click All on the Select submenu.

Step _____: Press and hold the SHIFT key. Click the two lowest-level boxes — Liberal Arts and Science. Release the SHIFT key.

Step _____: Double-click the organization chart placeholder.

Step _____: Click the Subordinate icon on the Microsoft Organization Chart window icon bar two times. Click the bottom subordinate box labeled Linda Smithe. Type `Janice Spring` and then press the ENTER key. Type `Director` and then press the ENTER key. Type `Nursing` in the box.

Use Help

1 Learning More about the Microsoft Clip Gallery

Instructions: Perform the following tasks using a computer.

1. Start PowerPoint. When the PowerPoint startup dialog box displays, double-click Blank presentation. Type 10 to select the Clip Art & Text AutoLayout. Click the OK button.
2. Double-click the Clip Art placeholder. When the Microsoft Clip Gallery 3.0 window displays, click the Help button and then click the Index tab.
3. In the Help Topics: Microsoft Clip Gallery 3.0 window, click Adding Clips from the Clip Gallery to a document. Click Display. When the Topics Found window displays, click What's the difference between clip art and pictures? Click the Display button and then read the information. Right-click in the dialog box, and click Print Topic on the shortcut menu. Click the OK button.
4. Click the Help Topics button. Scroll down and then click Pictures. Click Display. Scroll down and then click What if I can't find the clip I'm looking for? Click the Display button. Read and then print the information. Click How and read the information. Print the Import clips from Clip Gallery Live into the Clip Gallery information.
5. Click the Help Topics button. Double-click Properties of clips. In the Topics Found window, double-click What is a keyword? When the Help menu displays, read and then print the information.
6. Click the Help Topics button. Double-click Searching for clips. Display the Find a specific clip in the Clip Gallery information. Read and then print the information.
7. Click the Microsoft Clip Gallery 3.0 Help window Close button. Click the Microsoft Clip Gallery 3.0 window Close button. When the Microsoft PowerPoint – [Presentation1] window displays, click the Close button.
8. When the Microsoft PowerPoint window displays, quit PowerPoint without saving the presentation.
9. Hand in the printouts to your instructor.

2 Expanding on the Basics

Instructions: Use PowerPoint Help to better understand the topics listed below. Begin each of the following by clicking the Office Assistant button on the Standard toolbar. If you cannot print the Help information, answer the question on a separate piece of paper.

1. How do you recolor an organization chart?
2. How do you remove a border?
3. In what ways can you modify a picture in your presentation?
4. How do you edit an organization chart?
5. What is the default font for organization charts?
6. How can you rotate or flip a clip art object?
7. How do you change a slide background picture?
8. How can you crop or trim a picture?

Apply Your Knowledge

1 Creating a Presentation from an Outline, Inserting Clip Art, and Changing the Slide Background

Instructions: Start PowerPoint. Open the outline, Peak Skiing, from the PowerPoint folder on the Data Disk that accompanies this book.

1. Apply the Whirlpool design template.
2. Change the AutoLayout for Slide 1 to Title Slide (Figure 3-76a).
3. Create the custom background shown in Figure 3-76a using the Snow picture file from the Data Disk.
4. Change the AutoLayout for Slide 2 to Text & Clip Art. Move the bulleted text to look like Figure 3-76b. Insert the Screen Beans People Happy Joy clip art. Scale the height of the clip art picture to 110 percent.
5. Apply the Dissolve slide transition effect. Apply the Peek From Left text preset animation effect.
6. Save the presentation with the file name, Ski School.
7. Print the presentation.
8. Quit PowerPoint.

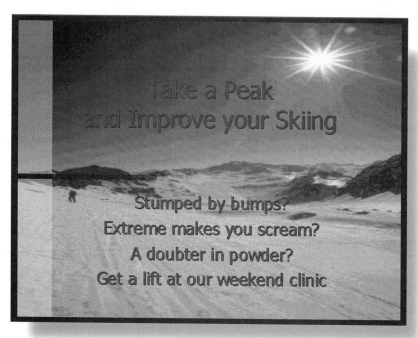

FIGURE 3-76a

FIGURE 3-76b

1 Creating a Custom Slide

Problem: You are the marketing manager for a new office building. One of the benefits of working in that building is the convenient parking lot next door. You are creating a sales presentation to persuade the business community to lease space from your company. You want a title slide with a rendering of office buildings and the parking lot. You modify various clip art objects to create this presentation.

Instructions: Perform the following tasks to create the slide shown in Figure 3-77.

1. Start PowerPoint, choose the Object AutoLayout, and apply the high voltage design template.
2. Type Park Close to the Office for the slide title. Change the font size to 48 and the text color to black.
3. Change the slide background color to light green.
4. Insert the clip art picture from the Microsoft Clip Gallery with a description Skyscraper Large Tall. Resize the clip art about center to increase the width of the buildings as shown in Figure 3-77.
5. Ungroup the Skyscraper Large Tall picture. Delete the purple building in the front row of buildings.
6. Insert the clip art picture with the description Success Victory Accomplishment Result. Ungroup the Success picture and delete everything in the clip art except the flag, flagpole, and hand. Scale the flag, flagpole, and hand height to 65 percent. Move the flag, flagpole, and hand to the right side of the orange building. Ungroup the flag, flagpole, and hand. Delete the hand from the flagpole. Color the flag red.
7. Change the fill effect of the pink building to Green marble in the Texture sheet in the Fill Effects dialog box.
8. Insert the clip art picture with the description Performance Fast Sports Car. Scale the car to a height of 25 percent. Then move the car into the vacant lot where the purple building originally stood.
9. Group the PowerPoint objects.
10. Save the presentation with the file name Park Close.
11. Print the slide using the Black & white option.
12. Quit PowerPoint.

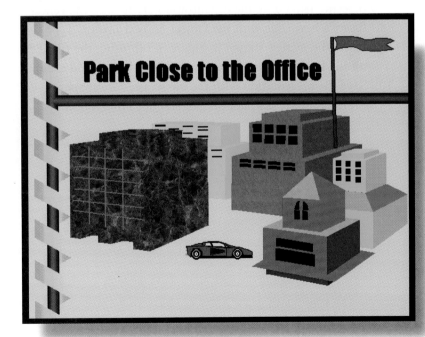

FIGURE 3-77

In the Lab

2 Embedding an Organization Chart and Inserting a Picture

Problem: You are the news editor of the *Observer*, the student newspaper at Hammond University. You want to print an organization chart in the *Observer* that will familiarize the campus with the student editors. You decide to use PowerPoint to create the organization chart shown in Figure 3-78a and the fact sheet about the editor shown in Figure 3-78b.

Instructions: Perform the following tasks.

1. Start PowerPoint. Click Blank presentation to create a new presentation. Apply the Organization Chart layout. Apply the Professional design template.
2. Type Hammond University in the slide title and then press the ENTER key. Type Observer Staff on the second line.
3. Create the organization chart shown in Figure 3-78a. Type your name in the News Editor text box.
4. Change the box color for the editor to red (row 1, column 9). Change the box color for the assistant editor to purple (row 2, column 5). Change the box color for the four news staff members to yellow (row 2, column 1). Change the box color for the two sports staff members to lime green (row 2, column 2). Change the box color for the three business staff members to light blue (row 2, column 3).
5. Add borders to all boxes. Use the border style in column 1, row 6 on the Border Style submenu. Change the border color for all boxes to royal blue (column 4, row 2).
6. Change the line color to red (column 9, row 1).
7. Quit Microsoft Organization Chart and return to Slide 1. Scale the organization chart to 115 percent. Then drag the organization chart onto the center of the blank area under the title object.
8. Insert a new slide with the Object & Text layout. Type the text shown in Figure 3-78b.
9. Insert the picture shown in Figure 3-78b using the file, Bernie Halen, from the PowerPoint folder on the Data Disk that accompanies this book. Add a border to the picture using the 3 pt single line.
10. Save the presentation with the file name, Newspaper.
11. Print handouts (2 slides per page). Quit PowerPoint.

In the Lab

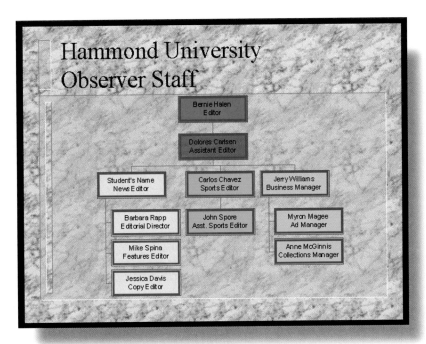

FIGURE 3-78a

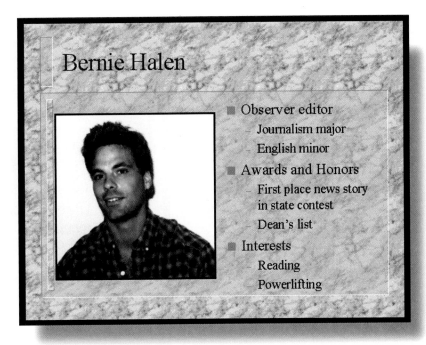

FIGURE 3-78b

In the Lab

3 Opening an Existing Outline and Creating a New Clip Art Picture

Problem: You are in charge of recruiting new choir members for an informal choral group at school. The choir director has asked you to create a presentation to show to students enrolled in music and drama classes. Create the opening slide of the presentation from the outline developed for your program. Because you cannot find clip art of a choir, you create the object shown in Figure 3-79.

Instructions: Perform the following tasks.

1. Start PowerPoint. Open the Sing outline from the PowerPoint folder on the Data Disk that accompanies this book.
2. Apply the Blush design template. Change the AutoLayout to Text & Clip Art.
3. Select the title text and change the font size to 54.
4. Insert the clip art picture with the description of Leadership Information Test Communication Listen Dictate. Ungroup the clip art picture.
5. Delete the table and screen from the clip art. Move the people so they form a half-circle around the choir director.
6. Change the color of the choir director to the same color as the title text. Change the color of the baton to limegreen.
7. Change the color of the two end singers to yellow. Change the color of the middle two people to light blue. Change the color of the two remaining people to lime green, which is the same color as the baton.
8. Add a lime green border around the bulleted text using a ¼ pt line.
9. Group all the individual objects in the clip art picture into one object.
10. Scale the object to 110 percent.
11. Place the date, your name, and the slide number in the slide footer.
12. Save the presentation with the file name, Choir Practice. Print the presentation. Quit PowerPoint.

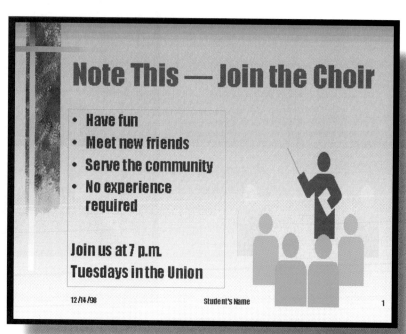

FIGURE 3-79

Cases and Places

The difficulty of these case studies varies: ❘ are the least difficult; ❘❘ are more difficult; and ❘❘❘ are the most difficult.

1 ❘ "I'll have a caffe latte macchiato extra-tall non." What's that? A coffee connoisseur would know it is an extra-large cup of nonfat steamed milk with a small amount of full-bodied coffee. Cappuccino, espresso, mocha, and latte are standard lingo for many coffee drinkers. Visit a coffeehouse or gourmet food store to learn the definitions and recipes for these drinks. Prepare a presentation that describes the various types of coffee beverages, the amounts of caffeine and calories in an eight-ounce serving, and price. Create a custom background. Include a title slide and clip art.

2 ❘ Skis, tennis rackets, and golf clubs have changed shape dramatically in recent years to help the infrequent or average user enjoy the sport. For instance, the parabolic shape of the new super-sidecut skis helps average skiers carve turns with ease. Visit a sporting goods store, read sports magazines, or use the Internet to learn about one of these new pieces of equipment. Find out why this new style makes using this equipment much easier than the traditional shape. What materials comprise this item? What are some of the leading brands? How much does this equipment cost? Use a word processing program to outline your research findings. Create a presentation from this outline. Design a custom background and add pictures or clip art. Use a title slide and apply slide transition and text preset animation effects.

3 ❘❘ When one thinks of leaders, President Bill Clinton, Gen. George Patton, and Lee Iacocca might come to mind. Leadership is defined as the process of exerting social influence on others in an attempt to obtain voluntary participation in efforts to reach a goal. Consider the student leaders at your school, such as the student government president, football team captain, or newspaper editor. Interview one of these individuals and create a presentation profiling major accomplishments and strategies on leading others successfully. Create a title slide with a bordered picture of this person, if possible.

4 ❘❘ Athletic organizations have a hierarchy of coaches and managers that often is highly specialized. In softball and baseball, for instance, hitting, pitching, catching and first base coaches and assistants may report to an infield coach who, in turn, reports to a manager. Visit the athletic department of your school and obtain the names and titles of coaches and managers associated with one sport. Then create a presentation that includes a hierarchy chart explaining this chain of command. Format the hierarchy chart to highlight the team's divisions. Include a slide showing the team's record for the past three years, a short biography of the team captain, and appropriate clip art or pictures.

Cases and Places

5 ▶▶ Treadmills are one of the more quickly selling products in the home-exercise market today. They provide an efficient means of burning calories and giving an aerobic workout. These machines vary widely in price, features, and guarantees. Visit a sporting goods store, read a fitness magazine, or use the Internet to examine the diverse treadmill market. Group the treadmills in three categories according to price: low-, middle-, and high-end. Compare features, such as walking surface size, speed, incline, motor horsepower, guarantee, and programming. Create a presentation comparing various treadmills on the basis of price and features. Use a title slide and apply slide transition and text preset animation effects.

6 ▶▶▶ Whether it is a high-rise condominium overlooking New York City's Central Park, a beach house in Tahiti, or an isolated cabin in the Colorado Rockies, we all dream of the ideal place to live. Use the Internet, magazines, or a travel agent to gather information about this dream house and then create a presentation. Include geographical information and a map. Scan a picture of this place and use it for the background of your title slide. Include another picture to depict one of the features of this location, such as a carriage ride through Central Park. Apply slide transition and text preset animation effects.

7 ▶▶▶ We eat, on average, one-third of our meals away from home. Often restaurants and fast-food places serve portions that are large enough to satisfy two or three people. For example, the U.S. Department of Agriculture classifies a serving of pancakes as two or three medium-sized pancakes, but many restaurants serve up to four large pancakes in an order. Obtain the standard serving size of three breakfast, lunch, dinner, and snack food items you normally consume away from home, such as bagels, french fries, pizza, and ice cream. You can find these serving sizes by looking at nutrition books or at the labels of these items in supermarkets. Then visit the restaurants where you typically eat these products and determine the serving sizes. Create a presentation that compares the official serving sizes to the restaurant serving sizes. Insert clip art and apply slide transition and text preset animation effects where appropriate.

Creating a Presentation Containing Interactive OLE Documents

Objectives:

You will have mastered the material in this project when you can:

▶ Open an existing presentation and save it with a new file name
▶ Create a custom background
▶ Modify a color scheme
▶ Draw an object
▶ Add a special text effect
▶ Embed an object into the slide master
▶ Change the organization chart formatting
▶ Create a slide using action buttons and hyperlinks
▶ Add text to a slide
▶ Use guides to position and size an object
▶ Modify PowerPoint options to end a presentation with a black slide
▶ Hide a slide
▶ Animate an object
▶ Run a slide show to display a hidden slide and activate an interactive document

Project 4

Order in the High-Tech Court

Lawyers in today's courtrooms are using different types of cases that do not involve plaintiffs and defendants. Instead, these cases are the ones used to carry their notebook computers. They are installing presentation software on these notebooks to develop and project carefully prepared slide shows to juries.

Perry Mason, Clarence Darrow, and F. Lee Bailey are known for the art of effective lawyering, with jurors regularly influenced by their compelling and persuasive opening and closing arguments. Not every lawyer or every case, however, has the flair and drama to rest on mere words alone.

With a generation of jurors raised on MTV and VCRs, attorneys realize they need to turn to technology to enhance their messages.

One of their technological tools is a notebook computer equipped with electronic presentation software, such as Microsoft PowerPoint. They realize that convincing a jury means more than merely creating a presentation and running it on the computer. Their slide show must be

overhead

impressive, which means having effective design, color, graphics, photographs, animation effects, and transitions. The PowerPoint projects in this textbook have illustrated the techniques for creating powerful presentations. The More About features provide insight on delivering these slide shows. Lawyers follow these same principles to make their presentations effective and ensure that the jurors feel comfortable with the new courtroom technology.

Using this hardware in court presents special challenges. First, the attorneys usually need to seek permission and make arrangements with the appropriate personnel. Once approval is granted, they then have to examine the courtroom to determine where the electrical outlets are located, what type of lighting exists, and where to place a projection screen or monitor. Some courtrooms are equipped with televisions and videotape recorders to play taped depositions for the jury, so lawyers can plug their notebook computers into the jacks in this equipment. Many courtrooms also have overhead projectors, so attorneys can connect their computers into an LCD presentation panel that rests on top of the overhead projector.

Lawyers know they must expect the unexpected, so they come to court with extra extension cords, batteries, disks, and bulbs. If time permits, they rehearse in the courtroom to adjust the lighting and determine electrical loads. In addition, they prepare a set of overhead transparencies that duplicate the PowerPoint slides, just in case their notebook computers fail. They can make these overheads by placing transparency film sheets in color printers or copiers.

Lawyers are using the power of PowerPoint beyond the courtroom. They frequently prepare PowerPoint presentations to educate general community groups and such specialized audiences as insurance agents on the intricacies of estate planning, charitable giving, and life insurance products. Some firms then convert their presentations to HTML documents and post them on the World Wide Web or the firm's intranet.

As the computers gain acceptance in the courtroom, juries soon may be hearing, "Your Honor, my digital co-counsel and I rest our case."

Microsoft
PowerPoint 97

Creating a Presentation Containing Interactive OLE Documents

Case Perspective

The next Net-Train Corporation Internet Training seminar will be held in San Francisco, California. Company executives have asked you to modify the Internet presentation created for the Park City, Utah, seminar. You want to change design templates, but you cannot find one that exemplifies the California spirit and has a light, colorful background. You find a design template, however, on the Microsoft site on the Internet and decide to change the color scheme. You draw the company logo and insert it onto the title slide. You decide to animate the logo to fly across the title slide. You replace the convenient-housing picture with a picture of the Golden Gate Bridge. Finally, you add a slide to demonstrate two components of the Internet Training workshop: e-mail and the World Wide Web. Then you decide to display that slide only if time permits.

Introduction

Because every presentation is created for a specific audience, subsequent deliveries of the same presentation may require changes. These changes are necessary to accommodate the knowledge base or interest level of the audience. Sometimes, when running a slide show, you want to open another application to show the audience the effect of a change. For example, when presenting next year's projected sales, you may want to perform a what-if analysis during the slide show without leaving PowerPoint. PowerPoint allows you to do so using interactive documents. An **interactive document** is a file created in another application, such as Microsoft Word, and then opened during the running of a slide show. Other times you may want to refrain from showing one or more slides because you are short on time or the slides are not applicable to a particular audience.

PowerPoint has the capability of hiding slides. As the presenter, you decide whether to display them. Occasionally, you need to change the look of your presentation by adding special graphics, such as a company logo, adding borders to objects and text, adding shadow effects to objects, or changing the overall color scheme. Project 4 customizes the Internet Training seminar presentation created in Project 3 (see Figures 3-1a through 3-1e on page PP 3.7).

Slide Preparation Steps

The preparation steps are an overview of how the slide presentation shown in Figures 4-1a through 4-1h (shown on this and the next page) will be developed in Project 4. The following tasks will be completed in this project.

1. Start PowerPoint.
2. Open an existing presentation, save it with a new file name, and apply a new design template.
3. Select a new color scheme and then modify it.
4. Create a logo using drawing tools.
5. Embed the logo into the slide master.
6. Link Word and PowerPoint documents to create a slide containing interactive documents.
7. Replace the text and picture on the slide titled, Convenient Activities.
8. Change the PowerPoint options to end the presentation with a blank slide.
9. Hide a slide.
10. Animate two slides.
11. Save the presentation.
12. Run the slide show to display the hidden slide and activate the interactive documents.
13. Quit PowerPoint.

FIGURE 4-1a

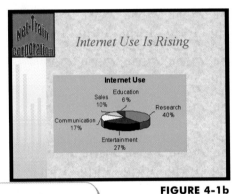

FIGURE 4-1b

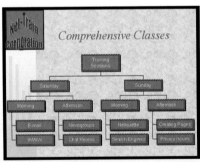

FIGURE 4-1c

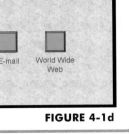

FIGURE 4-1d

hyperlinked file

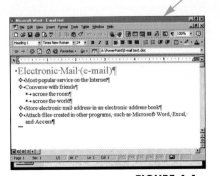

FIGURE 4-1e

(slide show continued on next page)

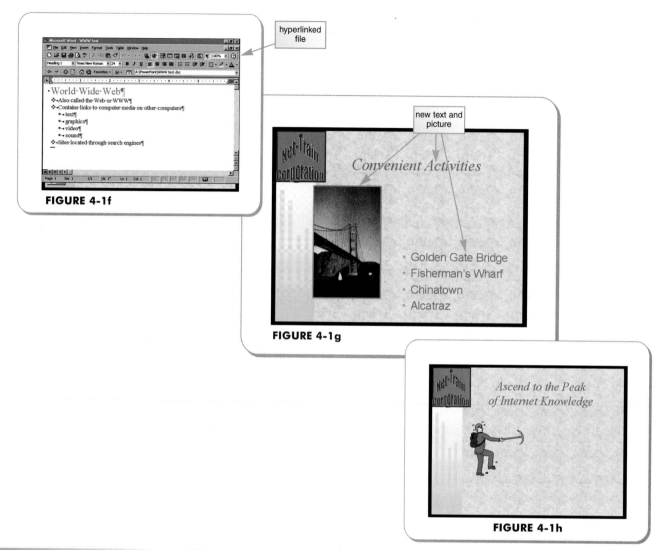

FIGURE 4-1f

FIGURE 4-1g

FIGURE 4-1h

Project Four – Customizing an Existing Presentation

Because you are customizing the Internet Training seminar presentation created in Project 3, the first step in this project is to open the Internet Training file. To ensure that the original presentation remains intact, you must save it with a new file name, Internet Training San Fran. Later in this project, you will modify the new presentation's slides by changing the design template, selecting a new color scheme, replacing a picture and bulleted text, and adding one new slide. The following steps illustrate these procedures.

Opening a Presentation and Saving It with a New File Name

After starting PowerPoint, the first step in this project is to open the Internet Training presentation saved in Project 3 and save it with the file name, Internet Training San Fran. This procedure should be done immediately to prevent inadvertently saving the presentation with the original file name. Perform the following steps to open an existing presentation and save it with a new file name. If you did not complete Project 3, see your instructor for a copy of the presentation.

TO OPEN A PRESENTATION AND SAVE IT WITH A NEW FILE NAME

1. Insert your PowerPoint 97 Project3 Data Disk into drive A.
2. Start Windows Explorer and, if necessary, click the Restore button so that part of the desktop displays.
3. Click the plus sign to the left of the 3½ Floppy (A:) icon in the All Folders side of the window, and then click the PowerPoint icon.
4. Right-drag Internet Training onto the desktop and click Copy Here on the shortcut menu.
5. Insert your PowerPoint 97 Project4 Data Disk into drive A.
6. Right-drag Internet Training from the desktop onto the 3½ Floppy (A:) icon on the All Folders side of the window, and then click Move Here on the shortcut menu.
7. Click the Close button on the Windows Explorer title bar.
8. Click the Start button on the taskbar, and then click Open Office Document.
9. When the Open Office Document dialog box displays, click the Look in box arrow, and then click 3½ Floppy (A:). Double-click Internet Training.
10. Click File on the menu bar, and then click Save As. If necessary, click the Look in box arrow, and then click 3½ Floppy (A:). Double-click the PowerPoint folder in the list.
11. Type Internet Training San Fran in the File name text box.
12. Click the Save button.

The presentation is saved on the PowerPoint 97 Project4 Data Disk in drive A with the file name, Internet Training San Fran (Figure 4-2).

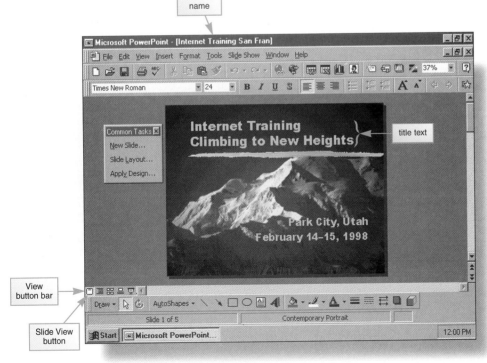

FIGURE 4-2

More *About*
Pack and Go Wizard

If you are going to display your slide show on another computer, the Pack and Go Wizard allows you to compress and save the file so you can transfer it to a floppy disk. All linked documents and multimedia files are included in the file. If you pack the presentation with the PowerPoint Viewer, the slide show will run on practically any computer, even one without PowerPoint installed.

More *About*
Kiosk Presentations

You can set your slide show to display automatically in a kiosk situation. With this option, viewers can start the slide show presentation themselves, or you can start the presentation and have it repeat after the last slide has displayed.

Editing Text

Because the location of the Internet Training seminar is changing, you must change the title and subtitle text on the title slide. Recall that text objects that display on a slide can be edited in slide view or outline view. Perform the following steps to display the title slide in slide view, and then revise the title and subtitle text.

TO CHANGE TEXT

1) If necessary, click the Slide View button on the View button bar.
2) Double-click the title text and then drag through the text, Climbing to New Heights, to select it.
3) Type Bridging to the 21st Century in place of the highlighted text.
4) Triple-click Park City, Utah.
5) Type San Francisco, CA in place of the highlighted text.
6) Double-click February.
7) Type March in place of the highlighted text.
8) Click anywhere on the slide other than the title or subtitle objects.

Slide 1 displays the updated title and subtitle text (Figure 4-3).

Changing Design Templates

The Internet Training seminar organizing team has requested that you change the Contemporary Portrait design template used in Project 3. You examine the design templates included in Office 97, but none has a colorful, lively feeling to correlate with a California setting. You search the Microsoft site on the Internet and find the design template, speed. The speed design template is located in the PowerPoint folder on the Data Disk that accompanies this book. Perform the following steps to change the design template.

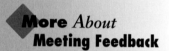

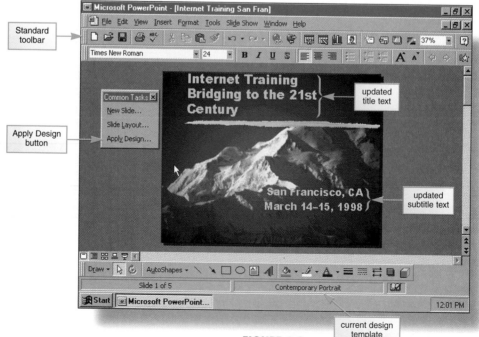

FIGURE 4-3

TO CHANGE THE DESIGN TEMPLATE

① Click the Apply Design button on the Common Tasks toolbar.

② When the Apply Design dialog box displays, click the Look in box arrow, click 3½ Floppy (A:), and double-click the PowerPoint folder in the list.

③ Double-click speed in the list.

Several messages will display before Slide 1 displays the new design template, speed, with the title master background graphics (Figure 4-4).

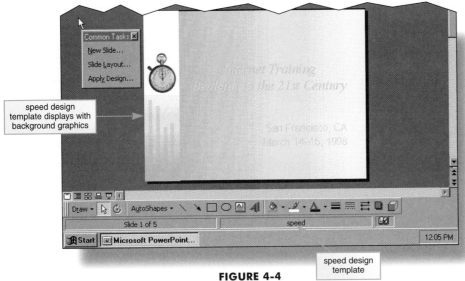

FIGURE 4-4

Creating a Custom Background

Sometimes it is difficult to find a design template that has all the attributes your presentation requires. For example, you may find a design template with a pleasing design and attractive fonts, but you do not like the background objects or texture. Recall in Project 3, you modified the background by adding a picture of mountains. In this project, you want to modify the background by changing the texture. Perform the following steps to create a custom background.

TO CREATE A CUSTOM BACKGROUND

① Right-click Slide 1 anywhere except the title or subtitle object. Click Background on the shortcut menu.

② Click the Background fill area box arrow. Click Fill Effects in the list.

③ Click the Texture tab in the Fill Effects dialog box. Click the Bouquet texture (row 3, column 4).

④ Click the OK button and then click the Apply to all button in the Background dialog box.

When you customize the background, the design template text attributes remain the same, but the slide background changes (Figure 4-5 on the next page). Inserting the Bouquet texture for the slide background changes the appearance of the slide background but maintains the text attributes of the speed design template.

Clicking the Apply to all button applies the new background texture to every slide in the presentation. Clicking the Apply button in the Background dialog box, however, applies the new background texture only to the current slide or to any selected slides. If you click the Apply button by mistake, you can correct the error immediately by clicking the Undo button on the Standard toolbar and then reapplying the background texture to all slides.

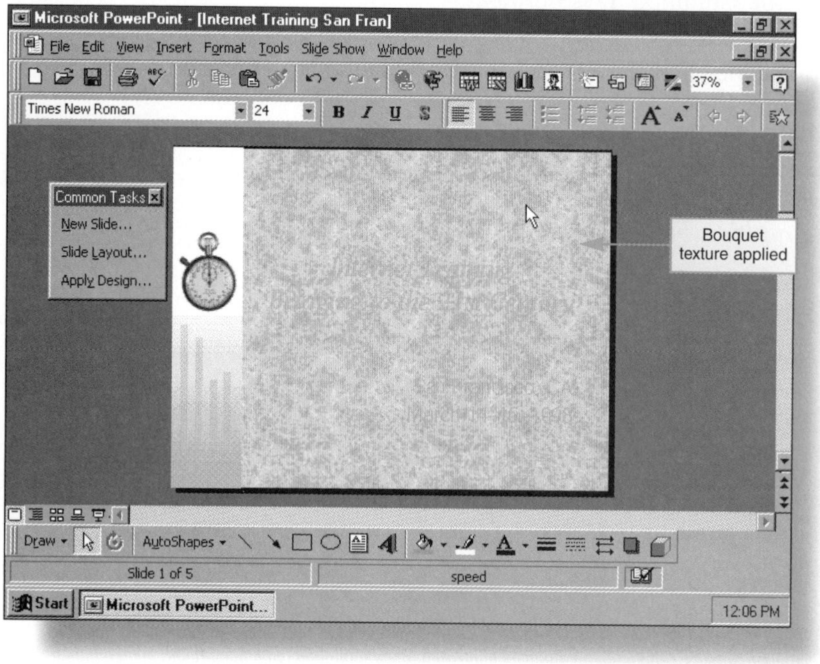

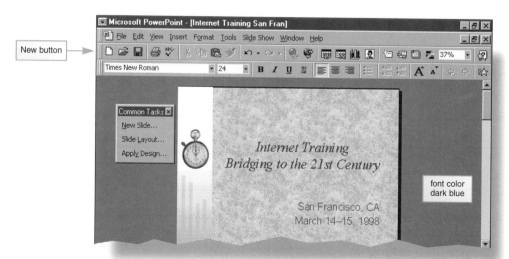

FIGURE 4-5

Modifying the Font Color

The gold text is difficult to read against the new Bouquet texture background, so you want to change the font color of the text. Recall in Project 3, you changed the text to the color gold. Now you want to change it to dark blue to complement the Bouquet texture background. Perform the following steps to change the font color of all text in the PowerPoint presentation from gold to dark blue.

More About Color Schemes

If you develop a color scheme for one slide that you would like to use on another slide, click the Slide Sorter View button on the View button bar, click the Format Painter button on the Standard toolbar, and click the slide to which you want to apply the color scheme. You also can use this technique to copy a color scheme from one presentation to another. With both presentations open, on the Window menu, click Arrange All, and then follow the above steps.

TO CHANGE THE FONT COLOR

1. Click the Outline View button on the View button bar.
2. Click Edit on the menu bar, and then click Select All.
3. Right-click the selection. Click Font on the shortcut menu. Click the Color box arrow in the Font dialog box.
4. Click the Follow Title Text Scheme Color dark blue box (row 1, column 4).
5. Click the OK button.
6. Click the Slide View button on the View button bar.

Slide 1 displays the font color changes to the title and subtitle text (Figure 4-6).

FIGURE 4-6

The eight color samples in row 1 in the Color list in the Font dialog box represent the color scheme associated with the speed design template. A **color scheme** is a set of eight balanced colors you can apply to all slides, an individual slide, notes pages, or audience handouts. A color scheme consists of colors for a background, text and lines, shadows, title text, fills, accent, accent and hyperlink, and accent and followed hyperlink. Table 4-1 explains the components of a color scheme.

Table 4-1

COMPONENT	DESCRIPTION
Background color	The background color is the fundamental color of a PowerPoint slide. For example, if your background color is white, you can place any other color on top of it, but the fundamental color remains white. The white background shows everywhere you do not add color or other objects. The background color on a slide works the same way.
Text and lines color	The text and lines color contrasts with the background color of the slide. Together with the background color, the text and lines color sets the tone for a presentation. For example, a gray background with a black text and lines color sets a dreary tone. In contrast, a red background with a yellow text and lines color sets a vibrant tone.
Title text color	The title text color contrasts with the background color in a manner similar to the text and lines color. Title text displays in the title placeholder on a slide.
Shadow color	The shadow color is applied when you color an object. This color is usually a darker shade of the background color.
Fill color	The fill color contrasts with both the background color and the text and lines color. The fill color is used for graphs and charts.
Accent colors	Accent colors are designed as colors for secondary features on a slide. Additionally, accent colors are used as colors on graphs.

Creating a Logo

Many companies establish presentation standards to which every presentation must adhere. Very often, a company logo is part of those standards. Net-Train managers have asked you to create a new logo for the corporation (Figure 4-8 on the next page) and to display it on the title slide.

Creating and displaying the Net-Train Corporation logo requires several steps. First, you must open a new presentation and draw the square object. Next, you apply a border. Then, you use the company name to create a graphic text object using WordArt. The drawing and graphic text objects then are combined into one logo object. Finally, after copying the logo object onto the Clipboard, you paste it on the Internet Training San Fran title slide. The next several sections explain how to create the Net-Train Corporation logo.

Opening a New Presentation

Because you may want to reuse the Net-Train Corporation logo in other presentations, you should create it in a new presentation. Perform the steps on the next page to open a new presentation.

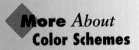

More *About*
Color Schemes

If you change color schemes, the colors you have added previously will remain displayed on the list. This feature is useful if you have mixed custom colors and need to display them on several slides.

TO OPEN A NEW PRESENTATION

1 Click the New button on the Standard toolbar.
2 Type 12 to select the Blank AutoLayout.
3 Click the OK button.
4 If necessary, click the Maximize button to maximize the PowerPoint window.

Slide 1 displays the Blank AutoLayout in a new presentation titled, Presentation1 (Figure 4-7).

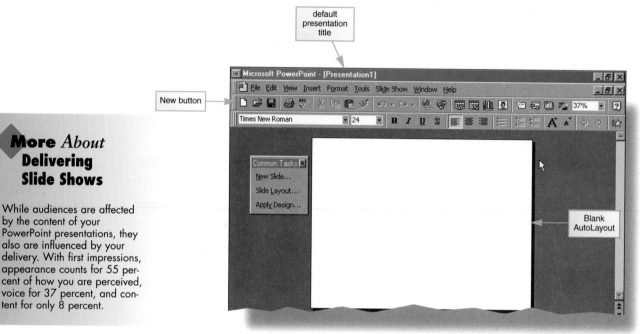

FIGURE 4-7

Drawing a Logo

The Net-Train Corporation logo is a square enclosing the company name. The logo is actually two objects, a square object and a text object. You create the square object using PowerPoint's drawing tools. Drawing the square object requires several steps. To help you draw the square object, display the horizontal and vertical rulers and guides to assist in aligning the objects. Next, increase the zoom percentage to see the detail of small objects better. Then, draw the outline of the square object using the Rectangle button on the Drawing toolbar. Finally, you add a border and change its line style. You will create the text object later in this project. The next several sections explain how to draw the square object shown in Figure 4-8.

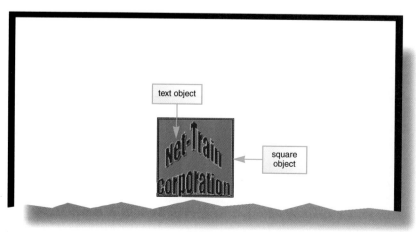

FIGURE 4-8

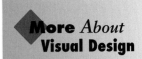
Displaying the Rulers

To help you align objects, PowerPoint provides two **rulers**: a horizontal ruler and a vertical ruler. The **horizontal ruler** displays at the top of the slide window. The **vertical ruler** displays at the left side of the slide window. When the zoom percentage is 25 or 33 percent, **tick marks** display in one-half-inch segments. When the zoom percentage is 50 percent or greater, tick marks display in one-eighth-inch segments. When you move the mouse pointer, a **pointer indicator** traces the position of the mouse pointer and displays its exact location on both rulers. You will use the rulers and pointer indicator later in this project when you draw the square object. In preparation for creating the logo, you display the rulers now. Perform the following steps to display the horizontal and vertical rulers.

More *About*
Visual Design

Where you place objects affects how viewers scan your slides. Arranging the objects in circles, rectangles, and triangles focuses attention, as does using shapes that mirror letters of the alphabet, particularly L, T, U, and Z.

Steps To Display the Rulers

1 **Right-click anywhere on the blank slide, and then point to Ruler on the shortcut menu (Figure 4-9).**

2 **Click Ruler.**

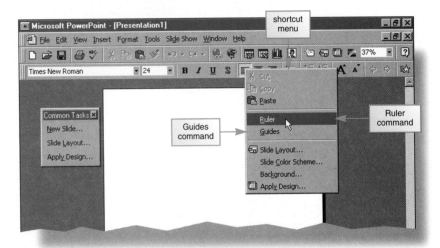

FIGURE 4-9

*Other***Ways**
1. On View menu click Ruler
2. Press ALT+V, press R

When the **Ruler command** is active, a check mark displays in front of the Ruler command on both the shortcut menu and the View menu. When you want to prohibit the rulers from displaying in the PowerPoint window, you hide them. To hide the rulers, right-click anywhere in the PowerPoint window except on an object, and then click Ruler.

Displaying the Guides

PowerPoint guides are used to align objects. The **guides** are two straight dotted lines, one horizontal and one vertical. When an object is close to a guide, its corner or its center (whichever is closer) *snaps*, or attaches itself, to the guide. You can move the guides to meet your alignment requirements. Because you are preparing the slide window to create the logo, perform this step to display the guides on the next page.

More *About*
Changing Tabs

The horizontal ruler displays tabs you set in your presentation or imported from a file created in another program, such as Microsoft Word. To change a tab stop, select the text that has the tab you want to move and drag the tab marker on the ruler to the new location.

Steps To Display the Guides

1 **Right-click anywhere on the blank slide, and then click Guides on the shortcut menu.**

The horizontal and vertical guides intersect in the middle of the slide window and align with the 0-inch tick marks on the horizontal and vertical rulers (Figure 4-10).

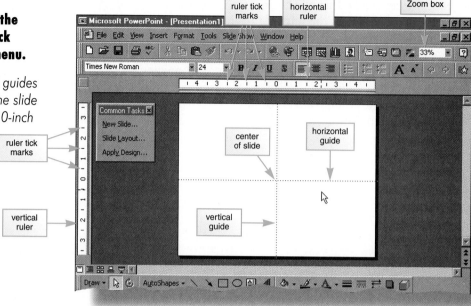

FIGURE 4-10

On the shortcut menu illustrated in Step 1, a check mark displays in front of the Ruler command because you activated it in the previous section. Recall that a check mark displays when a command is active, or turned on. In the same manner, when the Guides command is active, a check mark displays in front of the Guides command on both the shortcut menu and the View menu.

When you no longer want the guides to display on the screen or want to control the exact placement of objects, you can hide the guides. To hide the guides, right-click anywhere in the PowerPoint window except on an object, and click Guides.

Increasing the Zoom Percentage

Increasing the zoom percentage reduces the editing view of a slide in slide view, but it increases the editing view of individual objects. You increase the zoom percentage to make working with detailed objects or small objects easier. In this project, you increase the zoom percentage to 100 percent because it allows you to work more easily with the two objects. The following steps summarize how to increase the zoom percentage.

More About
Guides

You can display multiple vertical and horizontal guides on a screen. To display an additional guide, press and hold the CTRL key, and then drag one of the guides. When the new guide displays, drag it to the position where you want to place an object.

TO INCREASE THE ZOOM PERCENTAGE

1 Click the Zoom box arrow on the Standard toolbar.
2 Click 100%.

The zoom percentage changes to 100% (Figure 4-11). When you compare Figure 4-10 to Figure 4-11, you see that the ruler tick marks display 1/8-inch increments. You may need to drag the vertical or horizontal scroll boxes so the 0-inch tick marks on the horizontal and vertical rulers display in the center of the screen.

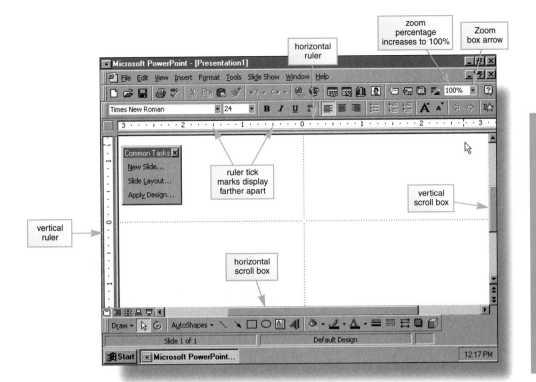

FIGURE 4-11

More *About*
Visual
Preferences

As you are creating your slides, you need to decide which visuals will be the most effective for your audience. While most viewers prefer colored visuals to black-and-white ones, the colors have no significant effect on the amount of information learned, according to researchers. Also, viewers prefer photographs, although line drawings may be more effective in communicating the message.

Drawing a Square

The next step in creating the Net-Train Corporation logo is drawing a square. A **square** is a plane with all sides at an equal distance from a given fixed point — the center. You draw a square using the **Rectangle button** on the Drawing toolbar. Because a Square button is not available, you constrain the shape of the object drawn using the Rectangle button. To draw a square, press and hold the CTRL+SHIFT keys, and then drag the mouse pointer as shown in the following steps.

 Steps **To Draw a Square**

1 **Click the Rectangle button on the Drawing toolbar. Press and hold the CTRL+SHIFT keys. Position the crosshair mouse pointer at the intersection of the horizontal and vertical guides.**

The Rectangle button displays recessed, which indicates it is selected (Figure 4-12).

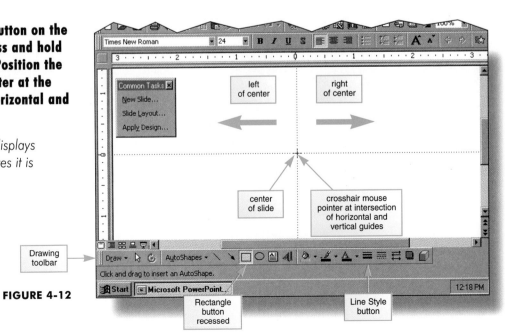

FIGURE 4-12

2 While holding the CTRL+SHIFT keys, drag the crosshair mouse pointer to the right of center until the pointer indicator on the horizontal ruler is on the 1¼ inch mark. Release the mouse button. Then release the CTRL+SHIFT keys.

A square displays the default attributes of the Default Design template: green fill color and black lines (Figure 4-13). Sizing handles around the square indicate it is selected. If necessary, drag the vertical or horizontal scroll boxes so the square displays in the center of the screen. The SHIFT key constrains the shape of the rectangle to draw a square. The CTRL key constrains the size of the square about center. When you release the CTRL+SHIFT keys, the Rectangle button is no longer recessed.

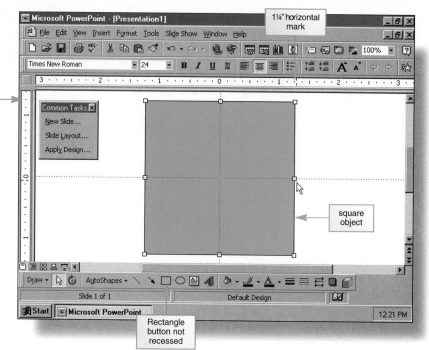

FIGURE 4-13

Changing the Logo Object Color

The next step in drawing the Net-Train Corporation logo is to change the logo object color from the default color green to the color pink. Perform the following steps to change the logo object color.

TO CHANGE THE LOGO OBJECT COLOR

1 Right-click the square object. Click Format AutoShape on the shortcut menu.

2 If necessary, click the Colors and Lines tab.

3 Click the Color box arrow in the Fill area.

4 Click the Pink box (row 5, column 1 under Automatic).

5 Click the OK button.

The new color pink displays in the square object (Figure 4-14).

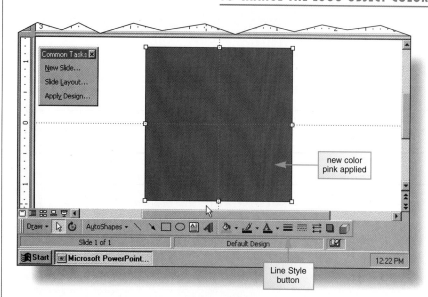

FIGURE 4-14

Changing a Logo Border

The next step in drawing the Net-Train Corporation logo is to add a border to the square object. Recall that a border is the visible line around the edge of an object and is composed of three attributes: line style, line color, and fill color. A border automatically displays around all objects you draw. The square shown in Figure 4-14 has a single-line border. Perform the following steps to add a two-line border.

TO CHANGE THE LOGO BORDER

1 If necessary, select the square object. Click the Line Style button on the Drawing toolbar.

2 Click the 3 pt two-line style from the Line Style list.

The new border displays around the square object (Figure 4-15).

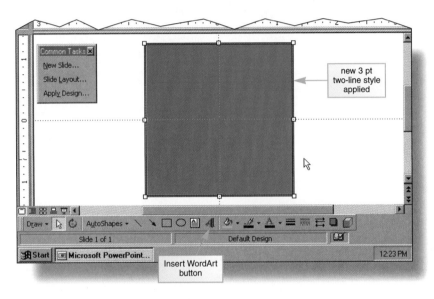

FIGURE 4-15

> **More** *About*
> **Borders**
>
> A border's line style and color affect the attention a viewer gives to a picture or object. A thick border draws more attention than a thin border, and *warm* colors, such as red and orange, draw more attention than *cool* colors, such as green or violet.

Adding Special Text Effects

The Net-Train Corporation logo contains letters that have been altered with special text effects. Using WordArt, you first will select a letter style for this text. Then, you will type the name of the corporation and shape these letters into a triangle, although many other predefined shapes could be used. Buttons on the WordArt toolbar also allow you to rotate, slant, curve, and alter the shape of letters. WordArt also can be used in the other Microsoft Office applications. The next several sections explain how to create the text object shown inside the square in Figure 4-8 on page PP 4.12.

Selecting a WordArt Style

PowerPoint supplies 30 predefined WordArt styles that vary in shape and color. Perform the steps on the next page to select a style for the Net-Train text.

> **More** *About*
> **Effective**
> **Preferences**
>
> If you are trying to persuade audiences with your PowerPoint slide show, some researchers believe Mondays, Tuesdays, and Sundays are the best days to deliver a presentation. Viewers typically are more relaxed and have time to consider your message on those days rather than at the end of the week.

Steps To Select a WordArt Style

1 **Click the Insert WordArt button on the Drawing toolbar. When the WordArt Gallery dialog box displays, click the WordArt style in row 2, column 5.**

The WordArt Gallery dialog box displays (Figure 4-16).

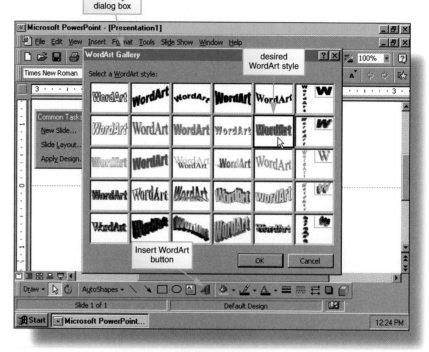

FIGURE 4-16

2 **Click the OK button.**

The Edit WordArt Text dialog box displays (Figure 4-17). The default text inside the dialog box is highlighted.

FIGURE 4-17

Entering the WordArt Text

To create a text object, you must enter text in the Edit WordArt Text dialog box. By default, the words, Your Text Here, in the Edit WordArt Text dialog box are highlighted. When you type the text for your logo, it replaces the selected text. When you want to start a new line, press the ENTER key. Perform the following steps to enter the text for the Net-Train Corporation logo.

 Steps **To Enter the WordArt Text**

1 **If necessary, select the text in the Edit WordArt Text dialog box. Type** Net-Train **and then press the ENTER key. Type** Corporation **but do not press the ENTER key.**

The two text lines display in the Text text box in the Edit WordArt Text dialog box (Figure 4-18). The default font is Impact, and the font size is 36.

FIGURE 4-18

2 **Click the OK button. If necessary, display the WordArt toolbar by right-clicking a toolbar and clicking WordArt.**

The Net-Train Corporation text displays in front of the square object (Figure 4-19). The WordArt toolbar displays in the same location and with the same shape as it displayed the last time it was used.

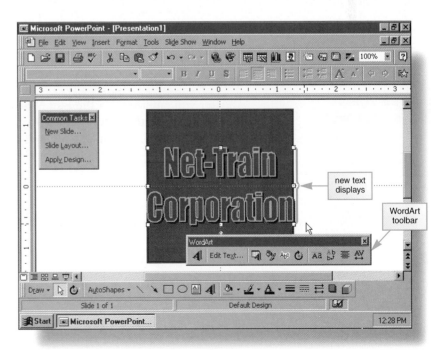

FIGURE 4-19

The WordArt toolbar contains the buttons that allow you to change an object's appearance. For example, you can rotate the letters, change the character spacing and alignment, scale the size, and add different fill and line colors. Table 4-2 explains the purpose of each button on the WordArt toolbar.

Table 4-2

BUTTON	BUTTON NAME	DESCRIPTION
	Insert WordArt	Creates a WordArt object
Edit Te_x_t...	WordArt Edit Text	Changes the text characters, font, and font size
	WordArt Gallery	Chooses a different WordArt style for the selected WordArt object
	Format WordArt	Formats the line, color, fill and pattern, size, position, and other properties of the selected object
Abc	WordArt Shape	Modifies the text shape
	Free Rotate	Turns an object around its axis
Aa	WordArt Same Letter Heights	Makes all letters the same height, regardless of case
Ab b	WordArt Vertical Text	Stacks the text in the selected WordArt object vertically — one letter on top of the other — for reading from top to bottom
	WordArt Alignment	Left-aligns, centers, right-aligns, word-aligns, letter-aligns, or stretch-aligns text
AV	WordArt Character Spacing	Displays options (Very Tight, Tight, Normal, Loose, Very Loose, Custom, Kern Character Pairs) for adjusting spacing between text

The next section explains how to shape the WordArt text.

Shaping the WordArt Text

After you enter text in the Edit WordArt Text dialog box, you want to choose the basic shape of the letters. The text in the Net-Train Corporation logo in Figure 4-8 on PP 4.12 displays pointed at the top and wide at the bottom. Perform the following steps to choose a shape for the logo text object.

More *About*
WordArt Text

To create a graphic object in WordArt using text created in another application, highlight the text in that application, copy the text by using the CTRL+C keys, and then paste it inside PowerPoint's Edit WordArt Text dialog box by pressing the CTRL+V keys.

To Shape the WordArt Text

1 **Click the WordArt Shape button on the WordArt toolbar. When the list displays, point to the Triangle Up shape (row 1, column 3).**

The WordArt shape list displays (Figure 4-20). By default, Plain Text is the selected shape.

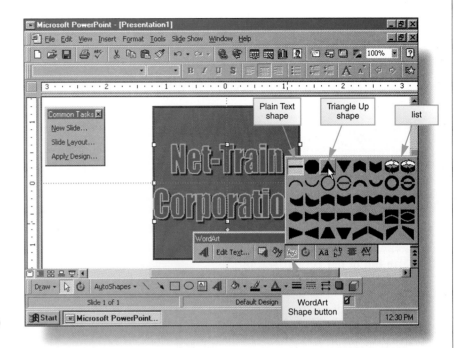

FIGURE 4-20

2 **Click Triangle Up.**

WordArt applies the Triangle Up shape to the text (Figure 4-21).

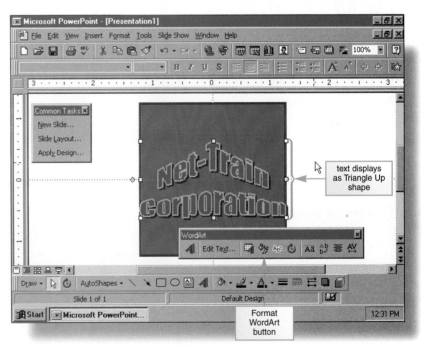

FIGURE 4-21

Changing the WordArt Height and Width

WordArt objects actually are drawing objects, not text. Consequently, they can be modified in various ways, including changing their height, width, line style, fill color, and shadows. Unlike text, however, they can neither display in outline view nor be spell checked. In this project, you will increase the height and decrease the width of the WordArt object. The Size tab in the Format WordArt dialog box contains two areas used to change an object's size. The first, the **Size and rotate area**, allows you to enlarge or reduce an object, and the rotate area allows you to turn an object around its axis. The second, the **Scale area**, allows you to change an object's size while maintaining its height-to-width ratio, or **aspect ratio**. If you want to retain the object's original settings, you click the Reset button in the **Original size area**. Perform the following steps to change the height of the WordArt object.

Steps To Change the WordArt Height and Width

1 **Click the Format WordArt button on the WordArt toolbar (see Figure 4-21 on the previous page). If necessary, click the Size tab in the Format WordArt dialog box.**

The Size sheet displays in the Format WordArt dialog box.

2 **In the Size and rotate area, triple-click the Height text box. Type 2.4 in the Height text box. Triple-click the Width text box. Type 2.4 in the Width text box. Point to the OK button.**

The Height and Width boxes display the new entries (Figure 4-22).

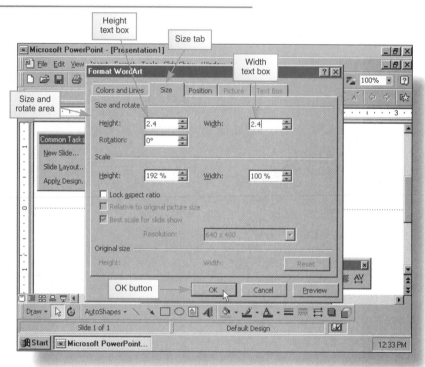

FIGURE 4-22

3 **Click the OK button.**

The WordArt text object displays in front of the square object (Figure 4-23).

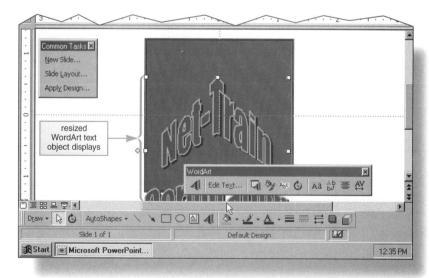

FIGURE 4-23

4 Drag the text object to the center of the square object. If necessary, you can make small adjustments in the position of the object by pressing the ARROW keys on the keyboard that correspond to the direction in which you want to move. Also, you can move the WordArt toolbar by dragging its title bar away from the text object.

The WordArt text object is centered in the square object (Figure 4-24).

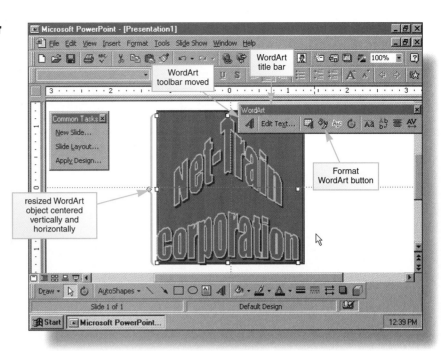

FIGURE 4-24

Changing the WordArt Fill Color

Now that the logo object is created, you want to change the font color to a dark blue. The Colors and Lines sheet in the Format WordArt dialog box contains an area to change the fill color. Perform the following steps to change the fill color.

Steps **To Change the WordArt Fill Color**

1 Click the Format WordArt button on the WordArt toolbar. If necessary, click the Colors and Lines tab in the Format WordArt dialog box.

The Colors and Lines sheet displays in the Format WordArt dialog box (Figure 4-25).

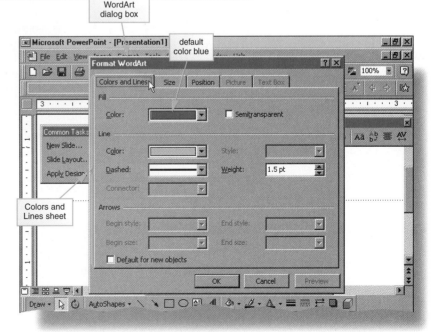

FIGURE 4-25

2 Click the Color box arrow in the Fill area. Click the color dark teal (row 2, column 5 under Automatic).

The color dark teal displays in the Fill area Color list box (Figure 4-26).

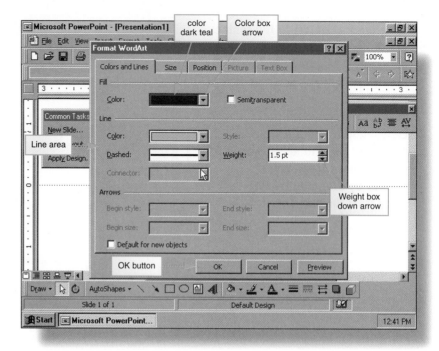

FIGURE 4-26

3 Click the Weight box down arrow in the Line area until 0.5 pt displays. Click the OK button.

The WordArt text object displays in front of the square object (Figure 4-27).

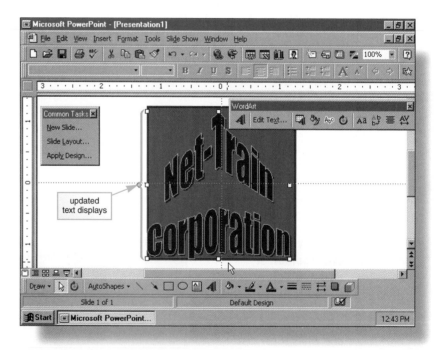

FIGURE 4-27

Grouping Objects

The final step in creating the Net-Train Corporation logo is to group the square object and the text object together to form one object. This action prevents one of the objects from being out of position when the logo is moved. Recall from Project 3 that you group objects together with the Group command on the short-cut menu. Perform the following steps to group the two objects.

TO GROUP OBJECTS

① Click Edit on the menu bar, and then click Select All.

② Right-click the selected objects, point to Grouping on the shortcut menu, and then click Group on the Grouping submenu.

③ Click the Save button on the Standard toolbar. If necessary, click the Look in box arrow, click 3½ Floppy (A:), and double-click the PowerPoint folder in the list. Type `Net-Train Logo` in the File name box. Press the ENTER key.

The two objects are grouped into one object (Figure 4-28). Sizing handles display around the grouped object. The logo is saved in the PowerPoint folder on the PowerPoint Project4 Data Disk in drive A.

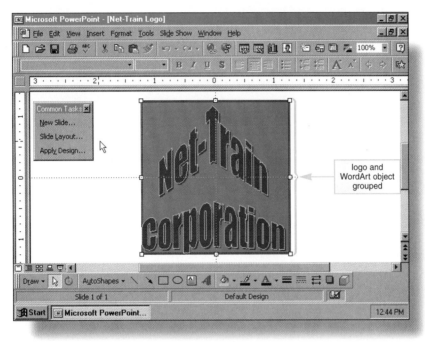

FIGURE 4-28

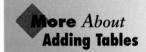

More *About*
Adding Tables

While PowerPoint does not have a Table feature, you can create a table on a slide in your presentation by using Microsoft Word's Table feature. To do so, click the Microsoft Word Table button on the Standard toolbar. Drag to indicate the number of rows and columns you want to insert. You can format the table by using Word tools and menus or by clicking Table on the menu bar and then clicking Table AutoFormat.

Grouping the text object with the square object converts the WordArt object into a PowerPoint object. If you need to modify the object, you must ungroup the logo, double-click the WordArt object, and then make the modifications.

Scaling an Object

The Net-Train logo object is too large to fit on the Internet Training San Fran seminar slides. To reduce the size of the object, you must scale it to 80 percent of its original size. Perform the steps on the next page to scale the logo object.

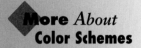

More *About*
Color Schemes

More than 15 percent of men have some form of red/green deficiency, which results in their seeing the color purple as blue and the color brown as green. This deficiency is more pronounced when they view these colors in small areas, such as the lines on charts. Thus, avoid using these colors in small areas of your slides, if possible.

Steps To Scale the Logo Object

1 **If necessary, click the logo object to select it. Right-click the logo object and then click Format Object on the shortcut menu.**

The Format Object dialog box displays.

2 **Click the Size tab. Click Lock aspect ratio in the Scale area, and then click the Height text box down arrow until 80% displays. Point to the OK button.**

The Height and Width text boxes both display 80% (Figure 4-29). When you change the percentage in the Height text box, the percentage in the Width text box also changes. In addition, the Height and Width text boxes in the Size and rotate area both change. The Lock aspect ratio check box is selected.

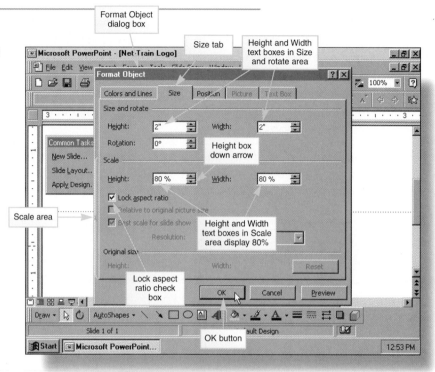

FIGURE 4-29

3 **Click the OK button.**

The logo object is reduced to 80 percent of its original size (Figure 4-30).

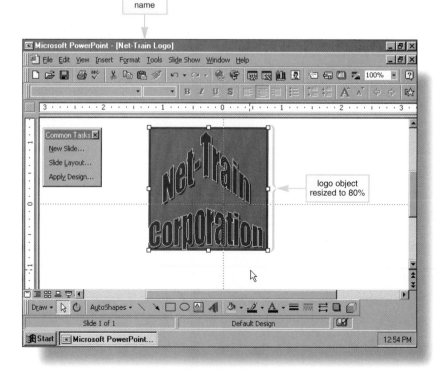

FIGURE 4-30

Adding an Object to the Slide Master

Your next step is to update the Internet Training San Fran presentation by adding your Net-Train logo object. You first must copy it from the Net-Train Logo presentation, and then paste it on the Internet Training San Fran presentation. If you want the logo to display on every slide, you must paste it on the slide master.

Perform the following steps to add the Net-Train Corporation logo to the slide master.

To Add an Object to the Slide Master

1 **Right-click the Net-Train Corporation logo, and then click Copy on the shortcut menu.**

A copy of the Net-Train Corporation logo is placed on the Clipboard.

2 **Click Window on the menu bar, and then point to 1 Internet Training San Fran (Figure 4-31).**

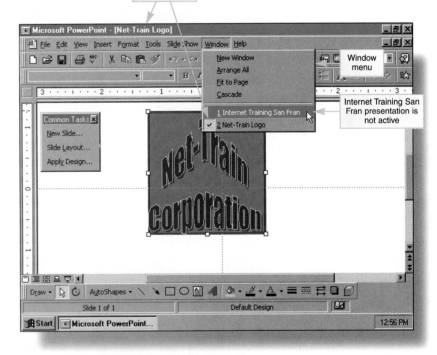

FIGURE 4-31

3 **Click 1 Internet Training San Fran.**

PowerPoint displays the Internet Training San Fran presentation (Figure 4-32). The Net-Train Logo presentation still is open but does not display.

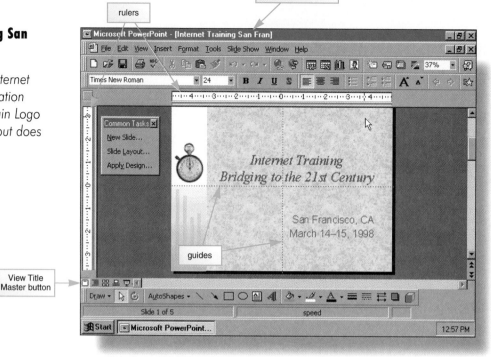

FIGURE 4-32

4 **Press and hold the SHIFT key, and then click the View Title Master button on the View button bar. Release the SHIFT key. Drag the vertical scroll box up to display the slide master.**

PowerPoint displays the slide master for the Internet Training San Fran presentation (Figure 4-33).

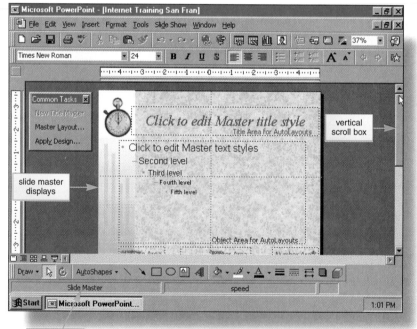

FIGURE 4-33

5 Right-click anywhere on the slide master, and then click Paste on the shortcut menu.

The logo object displays in the center of the slide master.

6 Drag the logo object to the upper left corner of the slide master so it covers the stopwatch object on the left side of the speed design template background.

The logo displays in the upper left corner of the slide master (Figure 4-34). If you want to make small adjustments in the position of the object, press the ARROW keys on the keyboard that correspond to the direction in which you want to move.

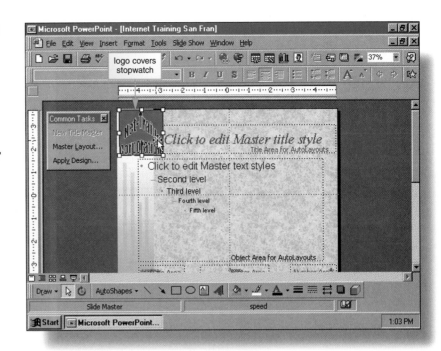

FIGURE 4-34

The rulers and guides stayed active when you changed presentation windows in Step 3. The Ruler command and the Guides command are PowerPoint settings, not slide attributes. Therefore, the rulers and guides display in the PowerPoint window whenever they are active, regardless of the presentation.

To inspect the logo and color scheme, click the Slide Show button. Notice the logo does not display on the title slide because the logo was pasted on the slide master, not the title master. Also notice the logo uses the color scheme of the slide. The next section explains how to paste the logo on the title slide.

Pasting an Object on a Title Slide

Because the San Francisco organizing team wants the Net-Train Corporation logo to display on every slide, you also must paste it on the title slide. Later in this project, you will animate the logo so it flies across the title slide from the right. Perform the steps on the next page to paste the logo on the title slide.

Steps To Paste an Object on a Title Slide

1 Click the Slide View button on the View button bar. Right-click the slide and then click Paste on the shortcut menu.

The logo displays in the center of Slide 1, the title slide (Figure 4-35).

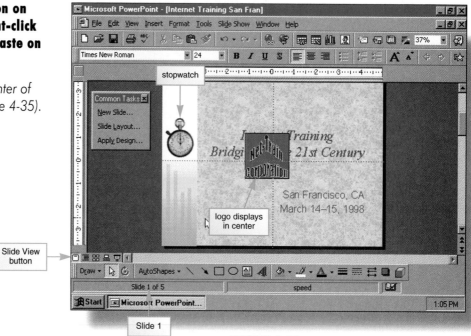

FIGURE 4-35

2 Drag the logo to cover the stopwatch on the background graphic of the title slide (Figure 4-36).

3 Click the Save button on the Standard toolbar.

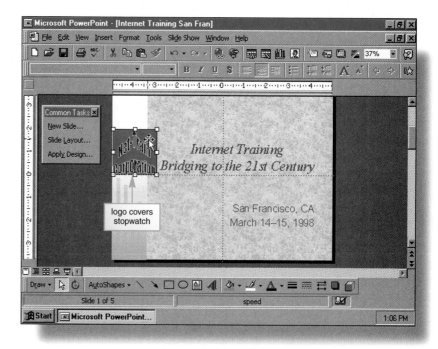

FIGURE 4-36

Because you do not need the rulers or guides when you modify the next slide, you want to hide them. Recall that a check mark displays in front of the Ruler and Guides commands on the shortcut menu and View menu when the commands are active. Perform the following steps to remove the check mark and deactivate, or hide, the rulers and guides.

TO HIDE THE RULERS AND GUIDES

1 Right-click Slide 1 anywhere except the slide title or object placeholders.

2 Click Ruler on the shortcut menu.

3 Right-click Slide 1 anywhere except the slide title or object placeholders.

4 Click Guides on the shortcut menu.

The rulers and guides no longer display.

Changing the Formatting of an Organization Chart

The black text and gold boxes and lines in the Microsoft Organization Chart on Slide 3 do not complement the new Bouquet texture. You therefore want to format the organization chart to change font color to white, the boxes color to pink, and the lines color to black. The shadow effects and border style selected in Project 3 can remain. Perform the following steps to change the organization chart formatting.

TO CHANGE THE ORGANIZATION CHART FORMATTING

1 Click the Next Slide button twice to display Slide 3.

2 Double-click an organization chart box to open the Microsoft Organization Chart application.

3 Click the Maximize button in the upper right corner of the Microsoft Organization Chart window.

4 Click Edit on the menu bar, point to Select, and then click All on the submenu.

5 Click Text on the menu bar, and then click Color.

6 Click the color White (row 1, column 2). Click the OK button.

7 With all the boxes in the organization chart still selected, click Lines on the menu bar, and then click Color.

8 Click the color Black (row 1, column 1). Click the OK button.

9 With all the boxes in the organization chart still selected, right-click one of the selected boxes. Click Color on the shortcut menu.

10 Click the color Pink (row 2, column 5). Click the OK button.

> ◆ **M**ore *About*
> **Handouts**
>
> Handouts distributed to audience members should include more material than you cover verbally during the presentation. Do not merely reproduce all the slides in your slide show. If you use a slide that is detailed and complex, such as an organization chart, include that visual in your handouts and leave room for viewers to take notes.

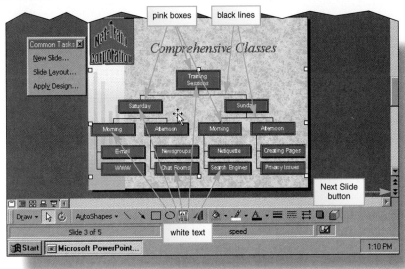

FIGURE 4-37

11 Click the Close button on the Microsoft Organization Chart – [Object in Internet Training San Fran] title bar. Click the Yes button in the Microsoft Organization Chart dialog box.

The Microsoft Organization Chart applies the new color white to the text, the color black to the lines, and the color pink to the boxes (Figure 4-37 on the previous page).

Creating an Interactive Document

The next step in customizing the Internet Training San Fran presentation is to add a slide to demonstrate two Internet Training sessions featured in the seminar. You add the new slide after Slide 3. Figure 4-38 illustrates the new Slide 4, which contains two action buttons to reference two sessions presented at the Internet Training San Fran seminar. An **action button** is a built-in 3-D button that can perform specific tasks such as display the next slide, provide help, give information, and play a sound. In addition, the action button can activate a **hyperlink**, which is a shortcut that allows you to jump to another program, in this case Microsoft Word, and load a specific document. A hyperlink also allows you to move to specific slides in a PowerPoint presentation or to an Internet address. In this slide, you will associate the hyperlink with an action button, but you also can use text or any object, including shapes, tables, or pictures. You specify which action you want PowerPoint to perform by using the **Action Settings** command on the Slide Show menu.

When you run the Internet Training San Fran presentation and click one of the action buttons on Slide 4, PowerPoint starts Microsoft Word and loads the designated file. For example, if you click the E-mail action button, PowerPoint opens the Microsoft Word application and loads the Word document, E-mail text. Once you have finished viewing the E-mail text document, you want to return to Slide 4. To do so, you will create another hyperlink in the E-mail text file and specify that you want to jump to Slide 4 in the Internet Training San Fran slide show.

Creating the slide shown in Figure 4-38 requires several steps. First, you add a new slide to your presentation. Next, you display the guides. Then you add two action buttons, scale them, and add color and shadows. Then you create hyperlinks to the two Microsoft Word files and back to Slide 4. The next several sections explain how to create Slide 4.

Adding a New Slide

The first step in creating Slide 4 in this project is to add a new slide. Perform the following steps to add a new slide.

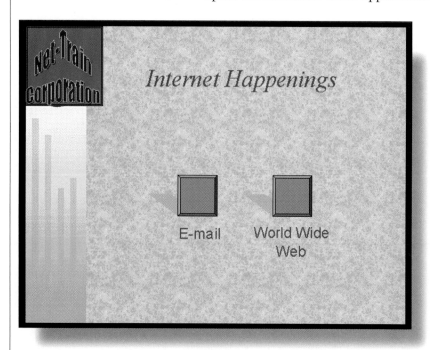

Internet Happenings

E-mail   World Wide Web

FIGURE 4-38

TO ADD A NEW SLIDE

① Click the New Slide button on the Common Tasks toolbar.
② When the New Slide dialog box displays, type 11 to select the Title Only AutoLayout.
③ Click the OK button.

The new Slide 4 displays the Title Only AutoLayout with the speed design template background graphics (Figure 4-39). PowerPoint automatically renumbers the original Slide 4 and Slide 5 as Slide 5 and Slide 6, respectively.

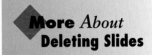

More *About* **Deleting Slides**

If you want to delete a slide in your presentation, display this slide, click Edit on the menu bar, and click Delete Slide. If you want to delete several slides simultaneously, click the Slide Sorter View or Outline View button, press the SHIFT key, click the slides you want to delete, and then press the DELETE key or click Edit on the menu bar and click Delete Slide.

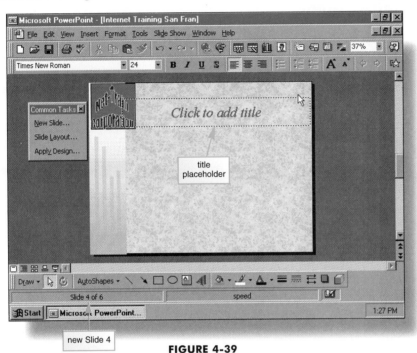

FIGURE 4-39

The title for Slide 4 is Internet Happenings. Perform the following step to add a slide title to Slide 4.

TO ADD A SLIDE TITLE

① Click the slide title placeholder and type Internet Happenings in that placeholder.
② Click anywhere on the slide except the slide title placeholder.

Internet Happenings displays in the title placeholder on Slide 4 (Figure 4-40).

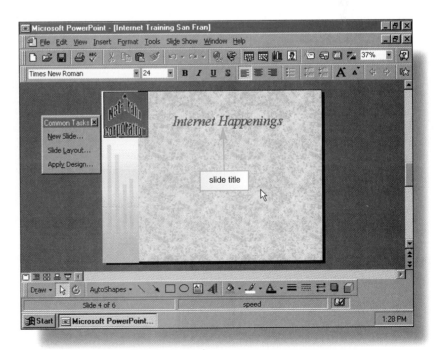

FIGURE 4-40

Adding Action Buttons and Action Settings

You want to feature two sessions that will be presented at the Internet Training seminar: E-mail and the World Wide Web. To obtain details on the E-mail session, you will click the left action button, and to obtain details on the World Wide Web session, you will click the right action button. When you click a button, a chime sound will play. The next section describes how to create the action buttons and place them on Slide 4.

Steps **To Add an Action Button and Action Settings**

① Click Slide Show on the menu bar, and then point to Action Buttons.

The Action Buttons submenu displays 12 built-in 3-D buttons (Figure 4-41).

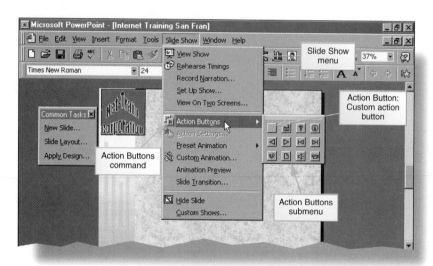

FIGURE 4-41

② Click the Action Button: Custom action button (row 1, column 1) in the list. Click anywhere on Slide 4 except the slide title placeholder.

The action button is placed on Slide 4, and the Action Settings dialog box displays (Figure 4-42). None is the default Action on click.

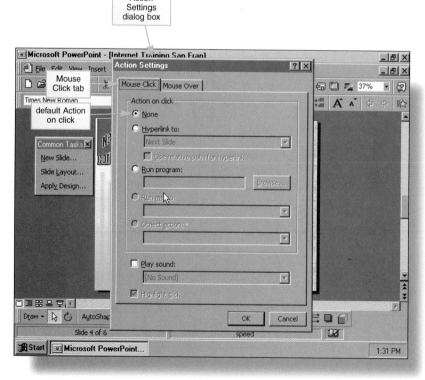

FIGURE 4-42

3 If necessary, click the Mouse Click tab. Click Hyperlink to in the Action on click area. Click the Hyperlink to box arrow. Point to Other File.

The list box displays the possible locations in the slide show or elsewhere where a hyperlink can be established (Figure 4-43).

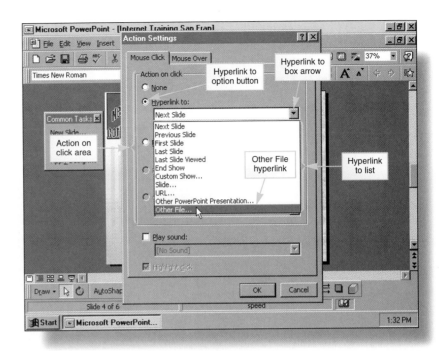

FIGURE 4-43

4 Click Other File. If necessary, click the Look in box arrow, click 3½ Floppy (A:), and then double-click the PowerPoint folder in the list. Click E-mail text in the list.

E-mail text is the Microsoft Word file you will link to the left action button (Figure 4-44).

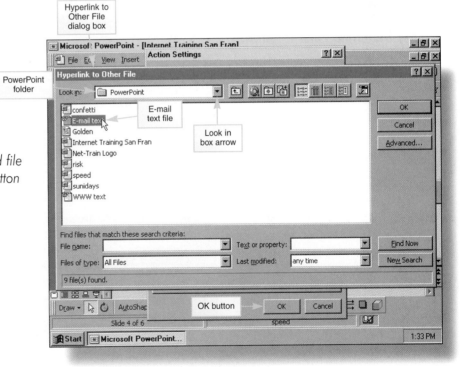

FIGURE 4-44

5 **Click the OK button in the Hyperlink to Other File dialog box. Click Use relative path for hyperlink. Point to Play sound.**

The Hyperlink to box displays E-mail text.doc (Figure 4-45).

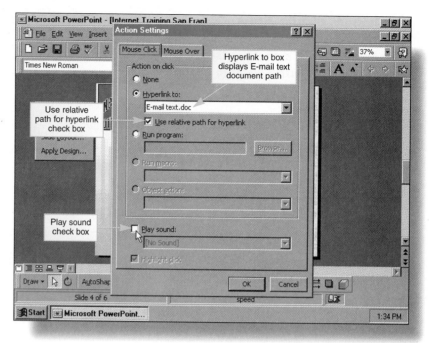

FIGURE 4-45

6 **Click Play sound. Click the Play sound box arrow. Point to Chime.**

The Play sound list displays sounds that can play when you click the action button (Figure 4-46).

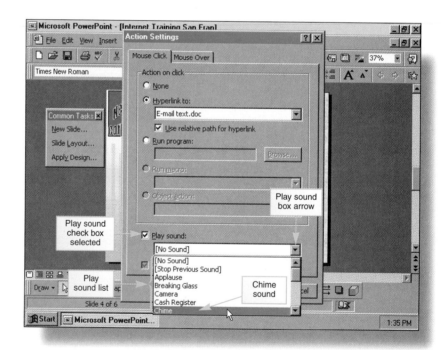

FIGURE 4-46

7 Click Chime. Click the OK button.

The action button is highlighted on Slide 4 (Figure 4-47).

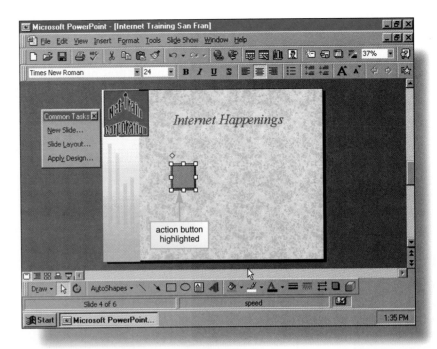

action button highlighted

FIGURE 4-47

Now that you have created an action button and linked the E-mail text document, you need to repeat the procedure for the WWW text document. Perform the following steps to create another action button and to hyperlink the second Microsoft Word document to your PowerPoint presentation.

TO CREATE A SECOND ACTION BUTTON AND HYPERLINK

1. Click Slide Show on the menu bar, point to Action Buttons, and click the Action Button: Custom action button (row 1, column 1) in the list.
2. Click anywhere on Slide 4 except the slide title placeholder or the first action button.
3. Click Hyperlink to in the Action on click area on the Mouse Click sheet.
4. Click the Hyperlink to box arrow. Click Other File.
5. Double-click WWW text in the list. Click Use relative path for hyperlink.
6. Click Play sound. Click the Play sound box arrow and click Chime.
7. Click the OK button.

Slide 4 displays with the second action button for the World Wide Web hyperlink (Figure 4-48 on the next page).

More *About*
Microsoft Graph

You can create or modify a graph by using Microsoft Graph, which is a program installed when PowerPoint was installed on your system. To build a graph, click the Insert Chart button on the Standard toolbar. Then, replace the sample data by clicking a cell on the datasheet and typing your data. You also can replace the sample row and column labels on the datasheet. To return to PowerPoint, click anywhere on the PowerPoint slide other than the chart.

When creating a presentation with interactive documents, you can set the path to the hyperlinks as absolute or relative links. When you use an **absolute link**, you assume you will keep your files in the same location, such as on a floppy disk, and you specify that precise location in the Hyperlink to text area. In this project, however, you use a **relative link** because you may need to move or copy these files to a different location, such as a hard drive.

Displaying Guides and Positioning Action Buttons

Recall that the guides assist you in placing objects at specific locations on the slide. When an object is close to a guide, it jumps to the guide. In this project, you use the vertical and horizontal guides to help position the action buttons and captions on Slide 4. The center of a slide is 0.00 on both the vertical and the horizontal guides. You position a guide by dragging it to a new location. When you point to a guide and then press and hold the mouse button, PowerPoint displays a box containing the exact position of the guide on the slide in inches. An arrow displays under the guide position to indicate the vertical guide is either left or right of center. An arrow displays to the right of the guide position to indicate the horizontal guide is either above or below center. Perform the following steps to display and position the guides.

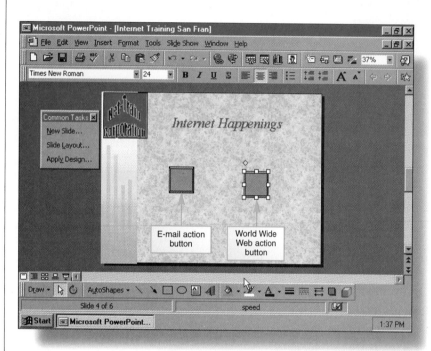

FIGURE 4-48

 To Display and Position the Guides

---

1 Right-click Slide 4 anywhere except on the title placeholder or the action buttons. Click Guides on the shortcut menu.

The horizontal and vertical guides display at the center of Slide 4.

2 Drag the vertical guide to 1.00 inch left of center (Figure 4-49).

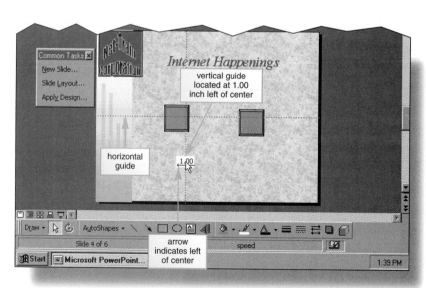

FIGURE 4-49

3 Click the horizontal guide to ensure it is displaying at the center (0.00) (Figure 4-50).

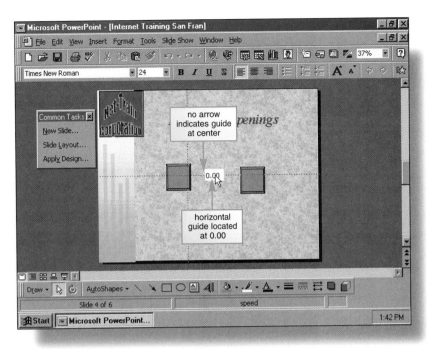

FIGURE 4-50

4 Drag the left action button for the E-mail text hyperlink until the top edge snaps to the horizontal guide and the left edge snaps to the vertical guide.

The top of the E-mail text action button aligns with the horizontal guide, and the left side of the button aligns with the vertical guide (Figure 4-51).

FIGURE 4-51

5 Drag the vertical guide to 1.50 inches right of center (Figure 4-52).

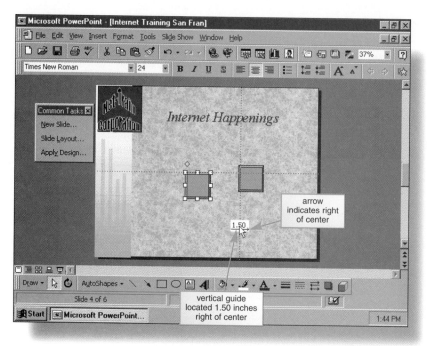

FIGURE 4-52

6 Drag the right action button for the WWW text hyperlink until the top edge snaps to the horizontal guide and the left edge snaps to the vertical guide.

The top of the World Wide Web action button aligns with the horizontal guide, and the left side of the button aligns with the vertical guide (Figure 4-53).

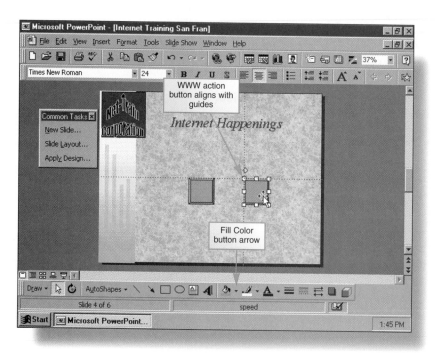

FIGURE 4-53

Scaling Objects

The action buttons on Slide 4 are too large in proportion to the screen. Perform the following steps to scale the two action buttons simultaneously.

TO SCALE ACTION BUTTONS

1. With the World Wide Web action button still selected, press and hold the SHIFT key. Click the E-mail action button. Release the SHIFT key.

2. Right-click either action button and then click Format AutoShape on the shortcut menu.

3. If necessary, click the Size tab. In the Scale area, click Lock aspect ratio, and then triple-click the Height text box. Type 90 in the Height text box.

4. Click the OK button.

Both action buttons are resized to 90 percent of their original size (Figure 4-54).

Adding Fill Color to the Action Buttons

To better identify the action buttons from the slide background, you must add fill color. Recall that fill color is the interior color of a selected object. Perform the following steps to add fill color to the action buttons on Slide 4.

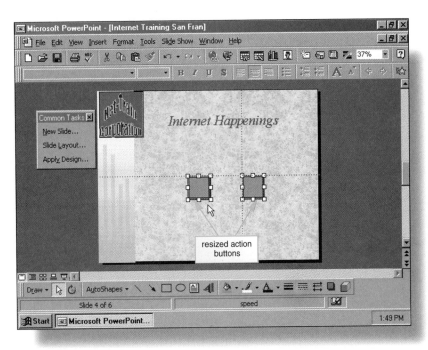

FIGURE 4-54

Steps To Add Fill Color to the Action Buttons

---

1. **With the two action buttons still selected, click the Fill Color button arrow on the Drawing toolbar.**

The Fill Color list displays (Figure 4-55). Automatic is highlighted, indicating that gray is the current default fill color.

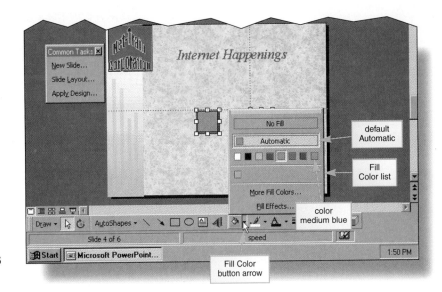

FIGURE 4-55

Click the color medium blue (row 1, column 8 under Automatic).

Both action buttons display filled with the color medium blue (Figure 4-56). Medium blue is the Follow Accent and Followed Hyperlink Scheme Color in the speed design template color scheme.

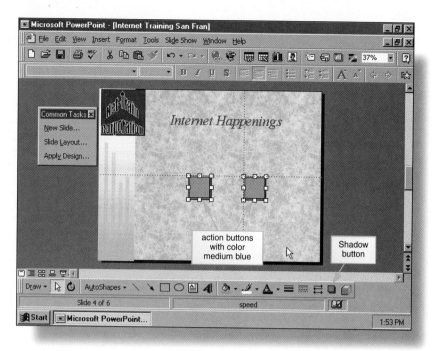

FIGURE 4-56

Adding Shadow Effects to the Action Buttons

To add depth to an object, you can **shadow** it by clicking the Shadow button on the Drawing toolbar. Perform the following steps to add shadows to the two action buttons on Slide 4.

TO ADD SHADOWS TO THE ACTION BUTTONS

1. Click the Shadow button on the Drawing toolbar.
2. Click Shadow Style 11 (row 3, column 3) in the style list.

PowerPoint adds the shadow to the two action buttons (Figure 4-57).

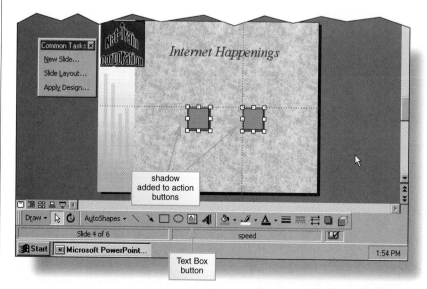

Adding Captions to the Action Buttons

The final components of Slide 4 that you need to add are the captions under the two action buttons. Perform the following steps to add captions to the action buttons on Slide 4.

FIGURE 4-57

TO ADD CAPTIONS TO THE ACTION BUTTONS

(1) Click the Text Box button on the Drawing toolbar.

(2) Click below the left action button. Type `E-mail` as the caption.

(3) Click the Text Box button on the Drawing toolbar.

(4) Click below the right action button, click the Center Alignment button on the Formatting toolbar, type `World Wide` as the first caption line, and then press the ENTER key. Type `Web` as the second caption line.

The captions for the two action buttons display (Figure 4-58).

Formatting Text

To add visual appeal to the captions, you want to change the font to Arial, increase the font size to 28, and change the color to the same color as the title text. Perform the following steps to format the captions for the action buttons on Slide 4.

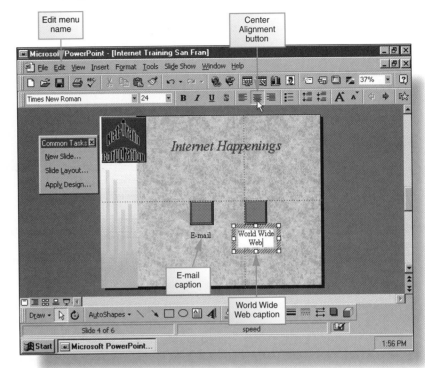

FIGURE 4-58

 To Format Text

1 **With the World Wide Web caption text highlighted, click Edit on the menu bar, and then click Select All.**

2 **Right-click the text and then click Font on the shortcut menu. When the Font list dialog box displays, click the Font box up arrow, and then scroll up and click Arial. Click the Size list box down arrow, and then click 28.**

Arial displays in the Font list box, and the font size 28 displays in the Size list box (Figure 4-59).

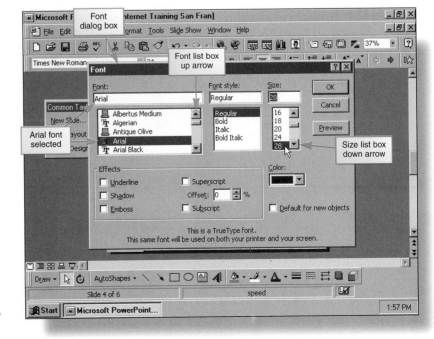

FIGURE 4-59

3 **Click the Color box arrow and then point to the color dark blue (row 1, column 4 under Automatic).**

The color dark blue is the Follow Title Text Scheme Color in the speed design template color scheme (Figure 4-60).

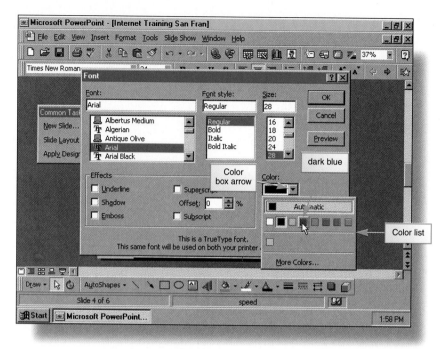

FIGURE 4-60

4 **Click the color dark blue.**

The color dark blue displays in the Color list box (Figure 4-61).

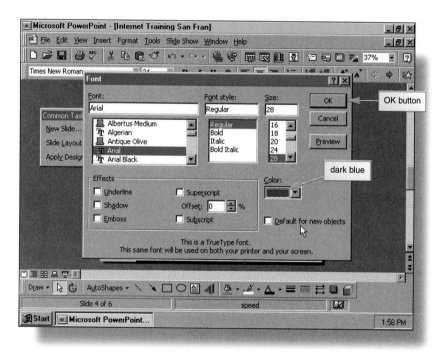

FIGURE 4-61

5 **Click the OK button and then click anywhere on a blank area of the slide.**

PowerPoint displays the World Wide Web caption with the 28-point Arial font and the color dark blue (Figure 4-62).

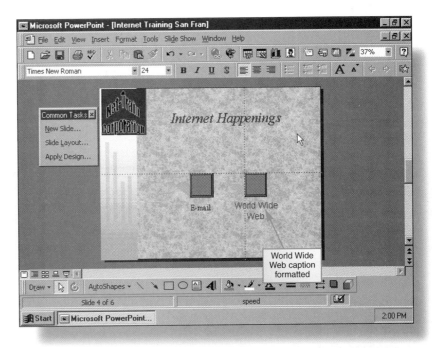

FIGURE 4-62

Now that you have formatted the World Wide Web caption text, you need to repeat the procedure to format the E-mail caption text. Perform the following steps to format the E-mail caption text.

TO FORMAT A SECOND CAPTION TEXT

1. Click the E-mail caption, click Edit on the menu bar, and then click Select All.
2. Right-click the text and click Font on the shortcut menu. When the Font dialog box displays, click the Font list box up arrow, and then scroll up and click Arial.
3. Click the Size list box down arrow, and then click 28.
4. Click the Color box arrow and then click the color dark blue (row 1, column 4 under Automatic).
5. Click the OK button and then click anywhere on a blank area of the slide.

Slide 4 is complete (Figure 4-63).

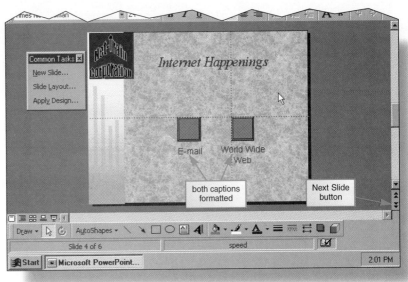

FIGURE 4-63

Now that the captions are added and formatted, you may need to make slight adjustments to their placement under the action buttons. If so, click the caption, click the border, and use the ARROW keys to position the text as shown in Figure 4-63.

Editing the Slide Title and Replacing a Picture

The Convenient Lodging slide, Slide 5, touts the features associated with staying at the housing in Park City, Utah. You want to change that slide to encourage prospective San Francisco workshop attendees to integrate educational activities with recreational activities in that city. Because this presentation is being customized for the San Francisco seminar, you will change the slide title and replace the picture of the lodge with the picture of the Golden Gate Bridge (Figure 4-72 on page PP 4.51). To replace a picture, first delete the existing picture and then insert the new picture, scale the picture, position and resize the picture to fit the slide, and then reapply the border. The next several sections explain how to replace the picture on Slide 5.

Editing the Slide Title

Because you want to emphasize the tourist activities available in San Francisco, you must change the title text on Slide 5. Recall that text objects that display on a slide can be edited in slide view or outline view and that you select text before editing it. Perform the following steps to display the title slide in slide view and then revise the title text.

TO EDIT TEXT

1. Click the Next Slide button to display Slide 5.
2. Double-click the word, Lodging, in the slide title.
3. Type Activities in place of the highlighted text.

Slide 5 displays the updated title text (Figure 4-64).

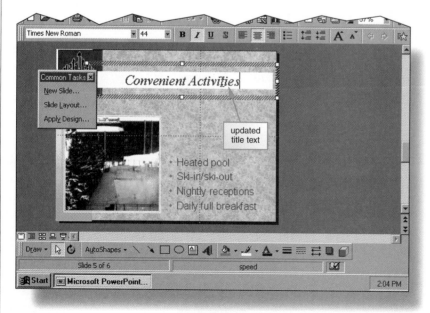

Editing a Bulleted List

You need to edit the bulleted list to change the text from housing features to tourist activities. Select the bulleted list on Slide 5 by dragging through all the text. Then type the replacement text. Perform the following steps to edit the bulleted list on Slide 5.

FIGURE 4-64

TO EDIT A BULLETED LIST

1 Drag through the text in the bulleted list to select it.

2 Type Golden Gate Bridge and then press the ENTER key. Type Fisherman's Wharf and then press the ENTER key. Type Chinatown and then press the ENTER key. Type Alcatraz but do not press the ENTER key.

Slide 5 displays the edited bulleted list (Figure 4-65).

Deleting an Object

A picture is an object. To delete any object in PowerPoint, you must select the object and then press the DELETE key. Perform the following steps to delete the Convenient Lodging picture on Slide 5.

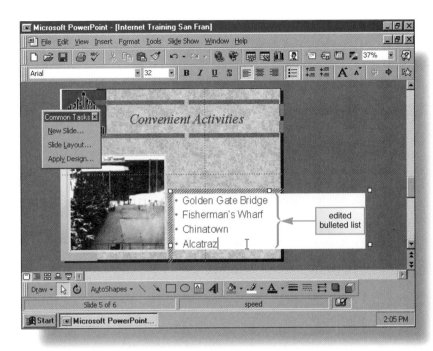

FIGURE 4-65

TO DELETE AN OBJECT

1 Click the picture of the lodge.

2 Press the DELETE key.

The picture is deleted (Figure 4-66).

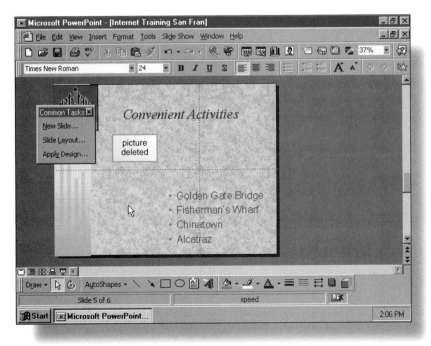

FIGURE 4-66

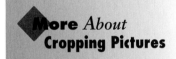

More *About*
Cropping Pictures

By cropping a picture, you can focus on a specific portion of the picture and trim the parts you do not want to see. To crop a picture, click the picture, click the Crop button on the Picture toolbar, place the cropping tool over a sizing handle, and drag to frame the portion of the picture you want to include on your slide.

Inserting a Picture

The Internet Training San Fran presentation displays a picture of the Golden Gate Bridge to enhance the Convenient Activities slide. Perform the following steps to insert a picture on Slide 5.

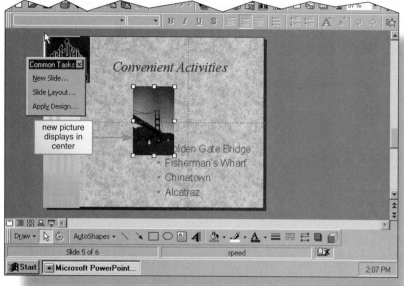

FIGURE 4-67

TO INSERT A PICTURE

1 Click Insert on the menu bar, point to Picture, and then click From File on the Picture submenu.

2 When the Insert Picture dialog box displays, if necessary, click the Look in box arrow, click 3½ Floppy (A:), and double-click the PowerPoint folder in the list. Double-click Golden.

The Golden Gate Bridge picture displays in the center of the slide (Figure 4-67).

Scaling an Object

To change the size of an object, you must scale it to retain the object's original proportions. Perform the following steps to scale the Golden Gate Bridge picture to 150 percent.

TO SCALE AN OBJECT

1 With the Golden picture selected, right-click the picture, and then click Format Picture on the shortcut menu.

2 Click the Size tab.

3 Triple-click the Height text box in the Scale area. Type 150 in the Height text box, and then click the OK button.

PowerPoint scales the picture to 150 percent of its original size (Figure 4-68).

Positioning and Resizing an Object

Recall that when an object is close to a guide, it jumps to the guide. Perform the following steps to position the Golden Gate Bridge picture using the vertical and horizontal guides.

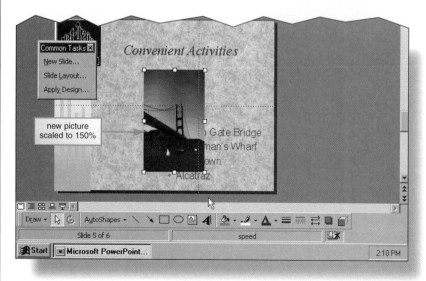

FIGURE 4-68

Steps **To Position and Resize an Object**

① **Drag the vertical guide to 0.75 inch left of center (Figure 4-69).**

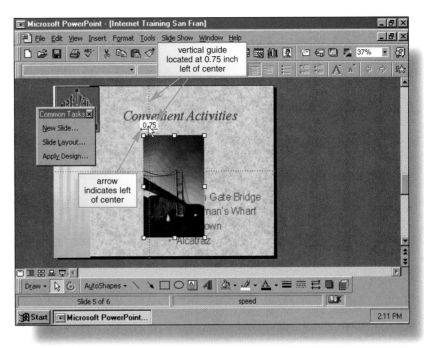

FIGURE 4-69

② **Drag the horizontal guide to 1.58 inches above center (Figure 4-70).**

FIGURE 4-70

3 **Drag the picture to the left until the top snaps to the horizontal guide and the right side snaps to the vertical guide.**

The top of the picture aligns with the horizontal guide, and the right side of the picture aligns with the vertical guide (Figure 4-71).

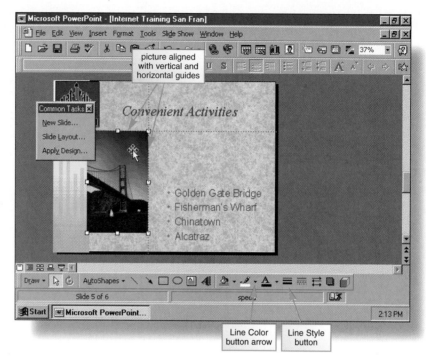

FIGURE 4-71

Now that the new picture is positioned correctly on Slide 5, the vertical and horizontal guides are not needed. Perform the following steps to hide the guides.

TO HIDE GUIDES

1 Right-click Slide 5 anywhere except on an object placeholder.
2 Click Guides on the shortcut menu.

The guides no longer display.

Adding a Border

The final step in replacing the picture on Slide 5, is to apply a two-line thin border. The Text and lines color in the speed design template color scheme is black. When you apply a line style, PowerPoint applies the text and lines color automatically. Perform the following steps to apply the 3 pt two-line border to the Golden Gate Bridge picture on Slide 5, and change the border color to dark blue.

TO ADD A BORDER

1 Click the picture.
2 Click the Line Style button on the Drawing toolbar.
3 Click the 3 pt two-line style on the list.
4 Click the Line Color button arrow on the Drawing toolbar. Click the color dark blue (row 1, column 4 under Automatic).

A dark blue, two-line border displays around the picture of the Golden Gate Bridge (Figure 4-72). The color dark blue is the Follow Title Text Scheme Color in the speed design template color scheme.

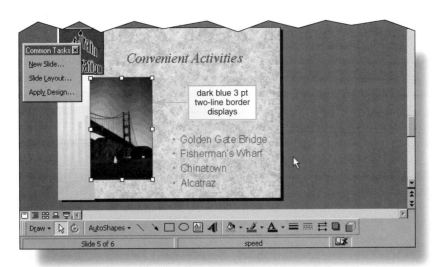

FIGURE 4-72

Ending a Presentation with a Black Slide

When you end a slide show, PowerPoint returns to the PowerPoint window. Recall that a closing slide allows you to end a slide show gracefully so the audience never sees the PowerPoint window. The Internet Training San Fran presentation currently uses Slide 6 for a closing slide.

The PowerPoint **End with black slide** option ends your presentation with a black slide. A black slide displays only when the slide show is running. A black slide ends all slide shows until the option setting is deactivated.

Ending with a Black Slide

To end with a black slide, complete the following steps.

 To End a Slide Show with a Black Slide

1 **Click Tools on the menu bar, and then click Options. If necessary, click the View tab. Click End with black slide.**

The Options dialog box displays (Figure 4-73). A check mark displays in the End with black slide check box.

2 **Click the OK button.**

The End with black slide option is activated.

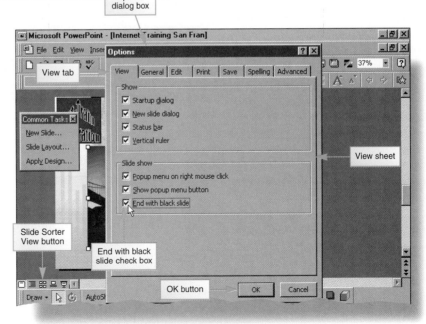

FIGURE 4-73

Applying Slide Transition Effects

Slide 4 was added to the presentation and therefore does not have slide transition effects applied. Recall from Project 3 that the Box In slide transition effect was applied to all slides except Slide 1. To keep Slide 4 consistent with the other slides in the presentation, apply the Dissolve slide transition effect as described in the following steps.

TO APPLY SLIDE TRANSITION EFFECTS

① Click the Slide Sorter View button on the View button bar.

② Click Slide 4.

③ Click the Slide Transition Effects box arrow. Click Box In.

PowerPoint applies the Box In slide transition effect to Slide 4. An icon displays below Slide 4 indicating a slide transition effect is applied (Figure 4-74).

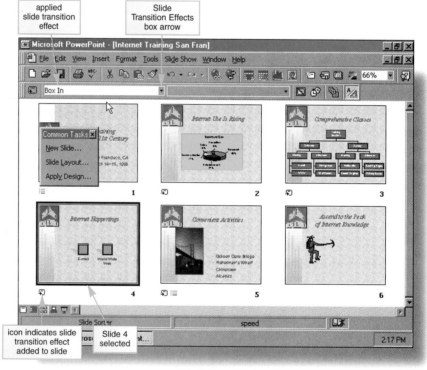

FIGURE 4-74

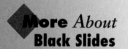

Hiding Slides

A **supporting slide** provides detailed information to supplement another slide in the presentation. For example, in a presentation to department chairpersons about the increase in student enrollment, one slide displays a graph representing the current year's enrollment and the previous three years' enrollment figures. The supporting slide for the slide with the graph displays a departmental student enrollment table for each year in the graph.

When running a slide show, you may not always want to display the supporting slide. You would display it when time permits and when you want to show the audience more detail about a topic. You should insert the supporting slide

*M*ore *About* **Black Slides**

Black slides can be useful within the presentation when you want to pause for discussion and have the audience focus on the speaker. To create a black slide, click New Slide on the Common Tasks toolbar, select the Blank slide layout, click Format on the menu bar, click Background, click the Background fill box arrow, and click the color black fill color.

after the slide you anticipate may warrant more detail. Then, you use the Hide Slide command to hide the supporting slide. The **Hide Slide command** hides the supporting slide from the audience during the normal running of a slide show. When you want to display the supporting hidden slide, press the H key. No visible indicator displays to show that a hidden slide exists. You must be aware of the content of the presentation to know where the supporting slide is located.

Hiding a Slide

Slide 4 is a slide that supports the session information displayed in Slide 3. If time permits, or if the audience requires more information, you can display Slide 4. As the presenter, you decide whether to show Slide 4. You hide a slide in slide sorter view so you can see the slashed square surrounding the slide number, which indicates the slide is hidden. Perform the following step to hide Slide 4.

 Steps **To Hide a Slide**

1 **Right-click Slide 4 and then click Hide Slide on the shortcut menu.**

A square with a slash surrounds the slide number to indicate Slide 4 is a hidden slide (Figure 4-75). The Hide Slide button is recessed on the Slide Sorter toolbar and on the shortcut menu.

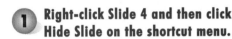

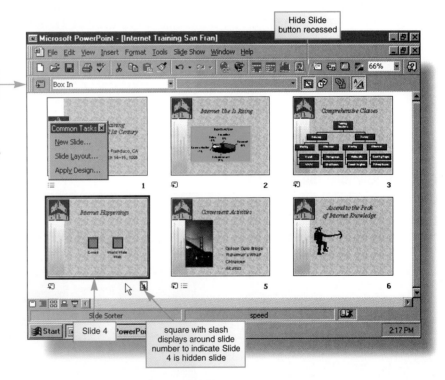

FIGURE 4-75

The Hide Slide button is a toggle — it either hides or displays a slide. It also applies or removes a square with a slash surrounding the slide number. When you no longer want to hide a slide, change views to slide sorter view, right-click the slide, and then click Hide Slide on the shortcut menu. This action removes the square with a slash surrounding the slide number.

An alternative to hiding a slide in slide sorter view is to hide a slide in slide view, outline view, or notes page view. In these views, however, no visible indication is given that a slide is hidden. To hide a slide in slide view or notes page view, display the slide you want to hide, click Slide Show on the menu bar, and

OtherWays

1. Click Hide Slide button on Slide Sorter toolbar
2. On Slide Show menu click Hide Slide
3. Press ALT+D, press H

More *About*
**Presentation
Conferencing**

PowerPoint's Conference Wizard helps you prepare your PowerPoint slide show to display over a Windows NT server and a Novell network, an intranet, and the Internet. You and your viewers all use the wizard to participate in the conference. You, as the presenter, can use Stage Manager tools such as the Slide Meter to time the presentation. All participants can write on the slides using the annotation pen. They will not be able to view embedded objects, however, such as the Excel chart on Slide 2 in this project.

then click Hide Slide. To hide a slide in outline view, select the slide icon of the slide you want to hide, click Slide Show on the menu bar, and then click Hide Slide. An icon displays in front of the Hide Slide command on the Slide Show menu, and it is recessed when the slide is hidden. You also can choose not to hide a slide in slide view, notes page view, and outline view by clicking Hide Slide on the Slide Show menu. The icon in front of the Hide Slide command no longer is recessed, and the slide then displays like all the other slides in the presentation.

When you run your presentation, the hidden slide does not display unless you press the H key when the slide preceding the hidden slide is displaying. For example, Slide 4 does not display unless you press the H key when Slide 3 displays in slide show view. You continue your presentation by clicking the mouse or pressing any of the keys associated with running a slide show. You skip the hidden slide by clicking the mouse and advancing to the next slide.

Animating Text and an Object

To seize the attention of the audience, the San Francisco Internet Training organizing committee wants the Net-Train Corporation logo to fly across the slide after the animated subtitle text automatically spirals onto the screen. The committee also wants you to make the mountain climber on Slide 6 move upward from the bottom of the slide. PowerPoint allows you to animate individual objects on a slide. The animation settings for objects are the same as those used for the text preset animation effects. Perform the following steps to animate the Net-Train Corporation logo object on Slide 1 and the mountain climber object on Slide 6.

Steps To Animate the Logo Object

1 **Double-click Slide 1 and then right-click the Net-Train logo object.**

Slide 1 displays in slide view. The logo object is selected and the shortcut menu displays (Figure 4-76).

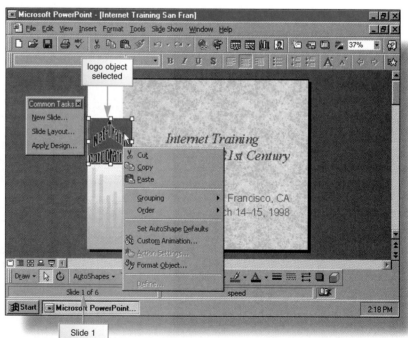

FIGURE 4-76

2 **Click Custom Animation on the shortcut menu. If necessary, click the Effects tab when the Custom Animation dialog box displays.**

The Custom Animation dialog box displays (Figure 4-77). No Effect is the default animation effect, as shown in the animation box. Text 2, the two lines of subtitle text, displays in the Animation order box because you applied the Spiral animation effect to it in Project 3.

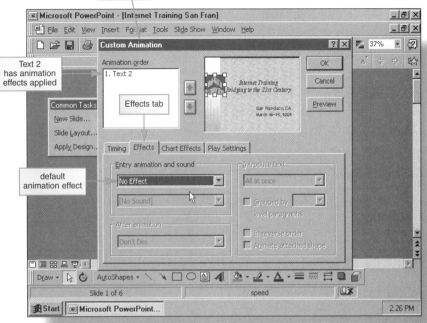

FIGURE 4-77

3 **Click the animation box arrow in the Entry animation and sound area. Click Fly From Right.**

Group 3, the Net-Train logo object, is added to the Animation order list box under Text 2 (Figure 4-78). When you run the presentation, each line of subtitle text will spiral onto the screen, and then the logo object will move across the screen from the right side.

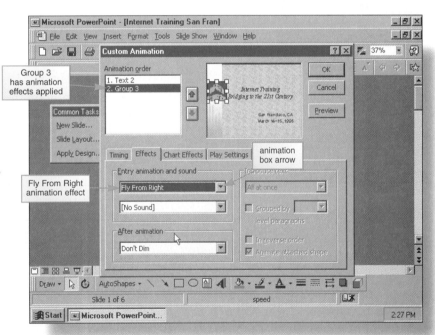

FIGURE 4-78

5 Click the Timing tab. Click Automatically in the Start animation area.

The logo object will move from the right edge of the screen automatically as soon as the subtitle text displays (Figure 4-79).

6 Click the Preview button.

The animation effects display in the preview area.

7 Click the OK button.

PowerPoint applies the animation settings and closes the dialog box.

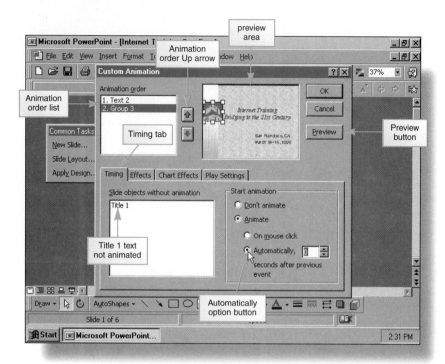

FIGURE 4-79

TO ANIMATE THE SUBTITLE TEXT AUTOMATICALLY

1 Right-click the subtitle text.

2 Click Custom Animation on the shortcut menu. If necessary, click the Timing tab when the Custom Animation dialog box displays.

3 Click Automatically in the Start animation area.

4 Click the Animation order Up arrow to move Text 2 as the first item in the Animation order list.

5 Click the Preview button.

6 Click the OK button.

PowerPoint applies the automatic animation settings and closes the custom animation dialog box.

Now that you have animated the logo object on Slide 1 and have set the subtitle text to display automatically, you want to animate the mountain climber on Slide 6 to have him move upward automatically from the bottom of the slide after the slide title displays. Perform the following steps to animate the mountain climber object on Slide 6.

Steps **To Animate the Mountain Climber Object**

1 **Click the Next Slide button five times to display Slide 6. Right-click the mountain climber object. Point to Custom Animation on the shortcut menu.**

The mountain climber object in Slide 6 is selected. The shortcut menu displays (Figure 4-80).

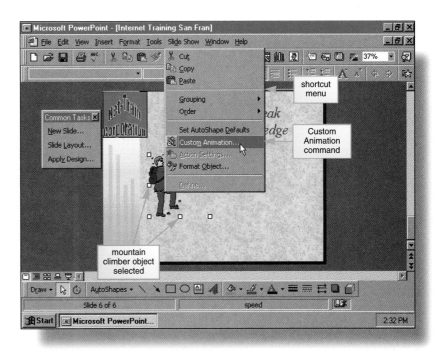

FIGURE 4-80

2 **Click Custom Animation. When the Custom Animation dialog box displays, click the animation box arrow. Scroll down through the list to select Crawl From Bottom. Click Crawl From Bottom.**

The Crawl From Bottom animation effect is selected (Figure 4-81). No Effects is the default animation effect.

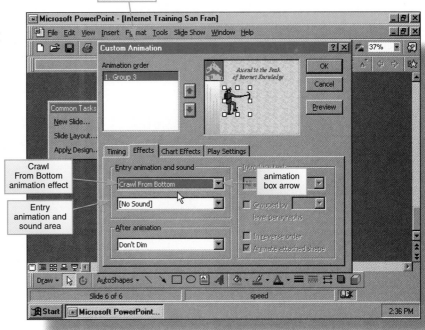

FIGURE 4-81

3 **Click the sound box arrow in the Entry animation and sound area. Point to Applause.**

The Applause sound effect is highlighted (Figure 4-82). No Sound is the default sound effect. The Applause sound effect will play when the mountain climber object moves upward from the bottom of the screen.

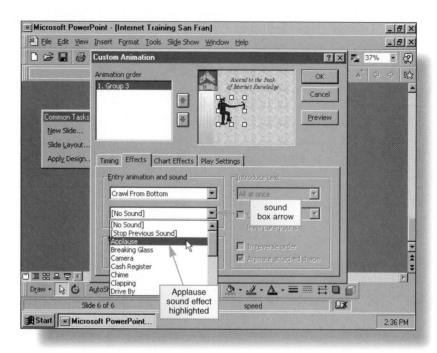

FIGURE 4-82

4 **Click Applause. Click the Timing tab. Click Automatically in the Start animation area.**

The mountain climber object will move upward from the bottom of the screen automatically as soon as the slide title displays (Figure 4-83). The slide title (Title 1) and small rocks object (Group 2) are not animated, as shown in the Slide objects without animation list box.

5 **Click the Preview button.**

The animation effect displays in the preview area, and the sound effect is applied.

6 **Click the OK button.**

PowerPoint applies the animation and sound effects and closes the custom animation dialog box.

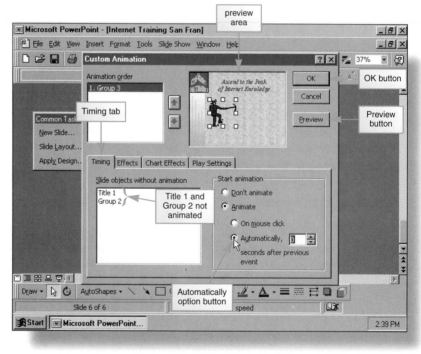

FIGURE 4-83

Spell Checking and Saving the Presentation

The presentation is complete. You now should spell check the presentation and save it again.

Running a Slide Show with a Hidden Slide and Interactive Documents

Running a slide show that contains hidden slides or interactive documents basically is the same as running any other slide show. You must, however, know where slides are hidden. When a slide contains interactive documents, you can activate them by clicking the action button that represents the document. In Figure 4-84, the E-mail text document displays in Microsoft Word. When you are finished displaying or editing the interactive document and want to return to the presentation, click the Back button on the Web toolbar of the interactive document. Perform the following steps to run the Internet Training San Fran presentation.

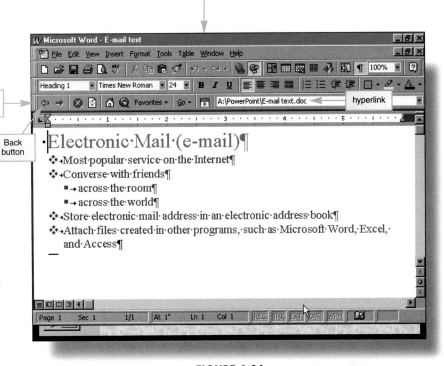

FIGURE 4-84

TO RUN A SLIDE SHOW WITH A HIDDEN SLIDE AND INTERACTIVE DOCUMENTS

1. Go to Slide 1. Click the Slide Show button on the View button bar.
2. After the subtitle text and logo display, click Slide 1 to display Slide 2. Click Slide 2 to display Slide 3.
3. Press the H key to display the hidden slide, Slide 4.
4. When Slide 4 displays, click the E-mail action button. If necessary, maximize the Microsoft Word window when the E-mail text document displays. Click the Back button on the Web toolbar.
5. Click the Word World Wide Web action button. If necessary, maximize the Microsoft Word window when the WWW text document displays. Click the Back button on the Web toolbar.
6. Click the background of Slide 4 to display Slide 5.
7. Click Slide 5 four times to display the bulleted list.
8. Click Slide 5 to display Slide 6.
9. Click Slide 6 to display the black slide that ends the slide show. Click the black slide to return to the PowerPoint window.
10. Click the Save button on the Standard toolbar.
11. Click the Close button on the title bar.

Slide 1 displays in slide view, PowerPoint quits, and then control returns to the desktop.

Project Summary

Project 4 customized the Internet Training seminar presentation created in Project 3. The first step was to save the presentation with a new file name to preserve the Project 3 presentation. You then changed design templates and selected and modified a new color scheme. Next, you used the drawing tools and added special text effects to create a company logo and pasted it on the slide master and on the title slide. Next, you created a slide containing hyperlinks to two Microsoft Word documents. Then, you replaced a picture and activated the option to end every presentation with a black slide. You added slide transition effects to the slide added to this project. Next, you hid the new slide because you will display it during the slide show only if time permits. Then, you added animation effects to objects on the slides. You ran the slide show to display the hidden slide and hyperlinked documents. Finally, you closed both presentations and quit PowerPoint.

What You Should Know

Having completed this project, you now should be able to perform the following tasks:

▶ Add a Border *(PP 4.50)*
▶ Add a New Slide *(PP 4.33)*
▶ Add a Slide Title *(PP 4.33)*
▶ Add an Action Button and Action Settings *(PP 4.34)*
▶ Add an Object to the Slide Master *(PP 4.27)*
▶ Add Captions to the Action Buttons *(PP 4.43)*
▶ Add Fill Color to the Action Buttons *(PP 4.41)*
▶ Add Shadows to the Action Buttons *(PP 4.42*
▶ Animate the Logo Object *(PP 4.54)*
▶ Animate the Mountain Climber Object *(PP 4.57)*
▶ Animate the Subtitle Text Automatically *(PP 4.56)*
▶ Apply Slide Transition Effects *(PP 4.52)*
▶ Change Text *(PP 4.8)*
▶ Change the Design Template *(PP 4.9)*
▶ Change the Font Color *(PP 4.10)*
▶ Change the Logo Border *(PP 4.17)*
▶ Change the Logo Object Color *(PP 4.16)*
▶ Change the Organization Chart Formatting *(PP 4.31)*
▶ Change the WordArt Fill Color *(PP 4.23)*
▶ Change the WordArt Height and Width *(PP 4.22)*
▶ Create a Custom Background *(PP 4.9)*
▶ Create a Second Action Button and Hyperlink *(PP 4.37)*
▶ Delete an Object *(PP 4.47)*

▶ Display and Position the Guides *(PP 4.38)*
▶ Display the Guides *(PP 4.14)*
▶ Display the Rulers *(PP 4.13)*
▶ Draw a Square *(PP 4.15)*
▶ Edit a Bulleted List *(PP 4.47)*
▶ Edit Text *(PP 4.46)*
▶ End a Slide Show with a Black Slide *(PP 4.51)*
▶ Enter the WordArt Text *(PP 4.19)*
▶ Format a Second Caption Text *(PP 4.45)*
▶ Format Text *(PP 4.43)*
▶ Group Objects *(PP 4.25)*
▶ Hide a Slide *(PP 4.53)*
▶ Hide Guides *(PP 4.50)*
▶ Hide the Rulers and Guides *(PP 4.31)*
▶ Increase the Zoom Percentage *(PP 4.14)*
▶ Insert a Picture *(PP 4.48)*
▶ Open a New Presentation *(PP 4.12)*
▶ Open a Presentation and Save It with a New File Name *(PP 4.7)*
▶ Paste an Object on a Title Slide *(PP 4.30)*
▶ Position and Resize an Object *(PP 4.49)*
▶ Run a Slide Show with a Hidden Slide and Interactive Documents *(PP 4.59)*
▶ Scale Action Buttons *(PP 4.41)*
▶ Scale an Object *(PP 4.48)*
▶ Scale the Logo Object *(PP 4.26)*
▶ Select a WordArt Style *(PP 4.18)*
▶ Shape the WordArt Text *(PP 4.21)*

1 True/False

Instructions: Circle T if the statement is true or F if the statement is false.

T F 1. When you create a custom slide background, the new background is displayed on all screens in the presentation if you click the Apply button in the Background dialog box.

T F 2. Buttons on the WordArt toolbar allow you to modify letters by rotating, slanting, and curving their shapes.

T F 3. Tick marks on the rulers display in one-quarter-inch segments.

T F 4. A slide can be hidden in any PowerPoint view except slide show view.

T F 5. Either the corner or the center of an object snaps to a guide.

T F 6. If you want a hidden slide to display, you should press the ENTER key when you are displaying the slide preceding the hidden slide.

T F 7. Increasing the zoom percentage reduces the editing view of a slide in slide view.

T F 8. A hyperlink is a shortcut that allows you to jump to another program, to another slide in the PowerPoint presentation, or to an Internet address.

T F 9. The text and lines color is the fundamental color of a PowerPoint slide.

T F 10. To make small adjustments to the placement of a selected object, press the ARROW keys on the keyboard that correspond to the direction in which you want to move.

2 Multiple Choice

Instructions: Circle the correct response.

1. A color scheme is a set of _____ colors assigned to a slide.
   a. five   b. eight   c. ten   d. twelve

2. A built-in 3-D button that can perform specific tasks, such as display the next slide in a presentation, display the first slide, or play a sound, is called a(n) _____ button.
   a. settings   b. jump   c. hyperlink   d. action

3. You can add a special effect to letters by using tools on the _____ toolbar.
   a. WordArt   c. Common Tasks
   b. Microsoft Organization Chart   d. Web

4. An action button can activate a hyperlink to a(n) _____ document.
   a. Microsoft Word   c. Microsoft PowerPoint
   b. Microsoft Excel   d. all of the above

5. To double the size of an action button, you _____ the object 200 percent.
   a. zoom   b. link   c. scale   d. embed

6. You can activate a hyperlink by clicking a(n) _____.
   a. action button   c. picture
   b. text object   d. all of the above

7. PowerPoint displays the exact position of a guide when you point to the guide and press the _____.
   a. left mouse button   c. SHIFT key
   b. right mouse button   d. CTRL key

(continued)

Test Your Knowledge

Multiple Choice *(continued)*

8. The two straight dotted lines, one horizontal and one vertical, used for aligning objects are
   _____.
   a. interactive objects   b. icons   c. rulers   d. guides
9. You can alter the appearance of an action button by changing its _____.
   a. fill color   b. shadow   c. size   d. all of the above
10. To add text to a slide, click the _____ button.
    a. Promote   b. Line Style   c. Text Box   d. New Slide

3 Understanding Guides in a PowerPoint Window

Instructions: Arrows in Figure 4-85 point to the major components of a window displaying guides. Identify the various parts of the window in the spaces provided.

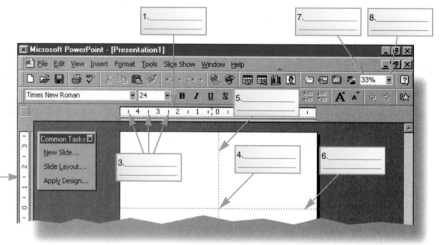

FIGURE 4-85

4 Understanding the WordArt Toolbar

Instructions: Answer the following questions using a separate piece of paper.

1. Which dialog box is used to enter text for an object?
2. How many predefined WordArt styles are available in the WordArt Gallery dialog box?
3. Which button on the WordArt toolbar allows you to display letters vertically?
4. How many shapes are available in the WordArt shape list?
5. Which WordArt shape resembles the shape of a stop sign?
6. Which button on the WordArt toolbar would you use to turn text 45 degrees?
7. How do you rotate text using the Format WordArt button?
8. What happens if you scale an object without selecting the Lock aspect ratio check box?
9. Which button on the WordArt toolbar allows you to make the spacing between letters very loose?
10. Which button on the WordArt toolbar makes all capital and lowercase letters the same height?

1 Learning More about Running a Slide Show and Adding ActiveX Controls

You want to present your Internet Training San Fran slide show at an unattended booth at your school. In addition, you want interested people to enter their names, addresses, and telephone numbers so you can contact them with details on the seminar. Microsoft Help can provide assistance.

Instructions: Perform the following tasks using a computer.

1. Start PowerPoint. When the PowerPoint dialog box displays, double-click Blank presentation and then type 12 to select the Blank AutoLayout. Click the OK button in the New Slide dialog box.
2. Click the Office Assistant button on the Standard toolbar. Type How do I run a slide show in the What would you like to do? text box and then click the Search button. Click Ways to run a slide show, and read the information. Right-click in the window and then click Print Topic on the shortcut menu. Click the OK button in the Print dialog box.
3. Click the link at the end of the Browsed at a kiosk (full screen) paragraph to find more information on the About self-running presentations topic. When the About self-running presentations topic displays, read and print the material.
4. Click the link at the end of the first item in the bulleted list, Automatic or manual timings, to obtain information about the Set timings for a slide show topic.
5. When the Set timings for a slide show topic displays, read and print the information. Click Set slide show timings manually, and print the material. Click the Show me link in item 2. Click the Close button on the Slide Transition dialog box title bar. Click the Back button.
6. Click the Set slide show timings automatically while rehearsing link, and then read and print the information. Click the Back button twice.
7. The fourth bulleted item at the bottom of the About self-running presentations topic discusses ActiveX controls. Click the ActiveX controls link and read and print the information.
8. Click the See a list of ActiveX controls link at the bottom of the Use ActiveX controls in a presentation topic. Read and print the information.
9. Click the Microsoft PowerPoint Help window Close button. When the Microsoft PowerPoint window displays, quit PowerPoint without saving the presentation.
10. Hand in the printouts to your instructor.

2 Expanding on the Basics

Instructions: Use PowerPoint Help to better understand the topics listed below. Begin each of the following by clicking the Office Assistant button on the Standard toolbar. If you cannot print the Help information, answer the question on a separate piece of paper.

1. How do you automatically record the time each slide displays when you rehearse your slide shows?
2. How do you set each slide to advance automatically after 30 seconds?
3. How do you set different timings for each slide, such as having the first slide display for 10 seconds, the second slide for 2 minutes, and the third for 45 seconds?
4. What is an action button and how do you add one to your presentation?
5. How do you assign the mouse-over method to an object to start an interactive action?

Apply Your Knowledge

1 Editing a Logo Object and Changing a Color Scheme

Instructions: Start PowerPoint. Open the Net-Train Corporation logo you created in Project 4 and saved with the file name, Net-Train Logo. If you did not create the Net-Train Corporation logo in Project 4, ask your instructor for a copy. Perform the following tasks to modify the logo to look like Figure 4-86.

1. Click File on the menu bar, and then click Save As. Save the presentation with the file name, Student Logo.
2. Right-click the logo object, point to Grouping on the shortcut menu, and then click Ungroup on the Grouping submenu. Click outside the logo object to deselect the ungrouped objects.
3. Click the border around the square. Click the Line Style button on the Drawing toolbar. Click the 4½ pt thick-thin line style, which is the second line style from the bottom of the list.
4. With the border still selected, click the Fill Color button arrow on the Drawing toolbar. Change the fill color to light purple (row 1, column 7).
5. Press the TAB key to select the WordArt object. Click the WordArt Edit Text button on the WordArt toolbar. If necessary, select the text in the Edit WordArt Text dialog box. Type your first name, press the ENTER key, and then type your last name.
6. Click the Font box arrow. Scroll up the list and click Century Schoolbook. Click the OK button in the Edit WordArt Text dialog box.
7. Click the WordArt Shape button arrow on the WordArt toolbar. Click the Button (Curve) shape (row 2, column 4) in the shape list.
8. Click the Format WordArt button on the WordArt toolbar. If necessary, click the Colors and Lines tab. In the Fill area, click the Color box arrow. Then, click the color Violet (row 4, column 7 under Automatic). In the Line area, click the Color box arrow. Click the color Indigo (row 2, column 7 under Automatic). Click the OK button in the Format WordArt dialog box. Close the WordArt toolbar by clicking the Close button on the WordArt title bar.
9. Click the Shadow button on the Drawing toolbar. Click No Shadow in the list.
10. If necessary, scale the WordArt object about center so your name fits inside the square. Click Edit on the menu bar, and then click Select All. Right-click the selected objects and then point to Grouping and click Regroup on the Grouping submenu.
11. Save the logo object again.
12. Print the logo slide using the Black & white and Scale to fit paper options.

FIGURE 4-86

In the Lab

1 Creating a Title Slide Containing a Logo

Problem: Fun 4-U Tours has hired you to design a slide show promoting the company's annual Spring Break trip to Florida. Company representatives want to approve the title slide of your presentation before you work on the entire project. The title slide contains the Fun 4-U Tours maroon logo centered in a magnifying glass clip art object. You will create the title slide shown in Figure 4-87.

1. Open a blank presentation, apply the Title Slide AutoLayout, and then apply the sunidays design template from the PowerPoint folder on the Data Disk that accompanies this book. The sunidays design template was retrieved from the Microsoft site on the Internet. Type the text for the title slide as shown in Figure 4-87.

2. Save the presentation with the file name, Spring Break.

3. Open a new presentation and apply the Blank AutoLayout. Insert the magnifying glass clip art picture that has the description, Focus Investigation Identify Small.

4. Create the logo text by clicking the Insert WordArt button on the Drawing toolbar. In the WordArt Gallery dialog box, select the WordArt style in row 1, column 1. Type Fun 4-U Tours on three lines. Choose the Button (Pour) shape (row 2, column 8). Change the WordArt text color to Plum (row 5, column 7 under Automatic). Then, change the border line color to Olive Green (row 2, column 3 under Automatic) with a weight of 0.5 pt. Scale the height of the WordArt object to 82 percent, and then center it on the magnifying glass. Group the WordArt text and the magnifying glass clip art object. Save the Fun 4-U Tours WordArt logo with the file name, Fun 4-U Logo.

5. Paste a copy of the Fun 4-U Logo on the Spring Break title slide. Scale the logo to 95 percent. Drag the logo to the upper-right corner of the slide.

6. Save the Spring Break presentation. Print the title slide using the Black & white and Scale to fit paper options. Close both presentations and quit PowerPoint.

FIGURE 4-87

In the Lab

2 Designing a Title Slide Using AutoShapes

Problem: Members of the astronomy club, the Stargazers, have asked you to create a title slide promoting the organization. You examine the available design templates and determine that you will need to modify one to create the vibrant astronomy theme. You will create the title slide shown in Figure 4-88.

1. Open a blank presentation, apply the Title Slide AutoLayout, and then apply the confetti design template from the PowerPoint folder on the Data Disk that accompanies this book. The confetti design template was retrieved from the Microsoft site on the Internet.

2. Right-click the slide anywhere other than the title or subtitle objects. Click Slide Color Scheme on the shortcut menu. In the Color Scheme dialog box, click the middle color scheme on the Standard sheet. Click the Apply button.

3. Type the text for the title slide as shown in Figure 4-88. Remove the shadow from the title text by selecting the text, clicking the Shadow button on the Drawing toolbar, and then clicking No Shadow. Format the subtitle text to a font size of 40 and the same font color blue as the title text, to follow the title text scheme color.

4. Display the guides and rulers. If necessary, align the guides and rulers with the 0-inch tick marks on the horizontal and vertical rulers.

5. Click the AutoShapes button on the Drawing toolbar, point to Basic Shapes, and click the Sun object in row 6, column 3. Click the slide to display the sun object. Right-click the sun object and then click Format AutoShape on the shortcut menu. If necessary, click the Size tab. Click Lock aspect ratio, scale the sun to 300 percent, and click the OK button.

6. Click the Fill Color button arrow on the Drawing toolbar, and then click More Fill Colors. Double-click the color Bright Yellow.

7. Drag the horizontal ruler to 0.75inch above center. Drag the sun to the upper right corner of the slide so the top and right rays touch the slide edges and the point of the bottom ray touches the horizontal ruler.

8. Click the AutoShapes button on the Drawing toolbar, point to Stars and Banners, and click the 5-Point Star (row 1, column 4).

9. Click the slide to display the star object. Click the Fill Colors button arrow on the Drawing toolbar, and click the Orange box (row 1, column 6 under Automatic). Click the Fill Colors button arrow again, and then click Fill Effects. If necessary, click the Gradient tab, and then click the upper-left variant sample in the Variants area. Click the OK button in the Fill Effects dialog box.

10. Right-click the 5-Point Star AutoShape, and then click Format AutoShape on the shortcut menu. If necessary, click the Size tab. Click Lock aspect ratio, scale the star to 200 percent, and then click the OK button.

11. Drag the horizontal ruler to 1.50 inches below center, and align the upper point of the star with the intersection of the horizontal and vertical rulers.

12. Click the AutoShapes button on the Drawing toolbar, point to Basic Shapes, and click the Moon object in row 6, column 4. Click the slide to display the moon. Right-click the moon object and then click Format AutoShape on the shortcut menu. If necessary, click the Size tab. Click Lock aspect ratio, scale the moon to 500 percent, and then click the OK button.

13. Drag the vertical ruler to 2.00 inches left of center and the horizontal ruler to 2.75 inches below center. Drag the moon so the bottom point aligns with the intersection of the guides.

14. Click the Insert WordArt button on the Drawing toolbar. Choose the WordArt style in row 1, column 1, and then click the OK button. Enter the club information shown in the lower-right corner of the slide, and substitute your name for the words, Student Name. Click the WordArt Shape button on the WordArt toolbar, apply the Cascade Up shape (row 5, column 7), and change the text to the color Blue (row 3, column 6 under Automatic). Apply a 0.25 pt color Dark Blue (row 2, column 6 under Automatic) border to the text. Scale the text to 60 percent.

FIGURE 4-88

15. Drag the vertical guide to 1.25 inches right of center and the horizontal guide to 1.00 inch below center. Align the WordArt object with these guides. You might need to make minor adjustments with the scaling to accommodate your name.

16. Save the presentation with the file name, Stars. Print the slide using the Black & white and Scale to fit paper options. Quit PowerPoint.

3 Linking PowerPoint Presentations

Problem: Las Vegas has become one of the top tourist destinations in the United States, so your school band and choir are planning a trip to that location at the end of the school year. You have offered to create a PowerPoint presentation promoting the city. You decide an interactive slide show would be the best vehicle to answer the students' questions. Develop the presentation shown in Figures 4-89 through 4-94 on pages PP 4.68 through 4.70.

Instructions Part 1: Perform the following tasks to create four presentations: one consisting of Figures 4-89 and 4-90, one of Figure 4-91, one of Figure 4-92, and one of Figure 4-93 on the next two pages.

1. Open a blank presentation and apply the Bulleted List AutoLayout. Display rulers and guides. If necessary, align them with the 0-inch tick marks on the horizontal and vertical rulers. Apply the risk design template from the PowerPoint folder on the Data Disk that accompanies this book.

(continued)

In the Lab

Linking PowerPoint Presentations *(continued)*

Type and center the slide title, and then type the bulleted list item shown in Figure 4-89. Insert the clip art picture with the description, Risk (as shown in Figure 4-89), and then scale it to 200 percent. Drag the vertical ruler to 2.17 inches left of center and the horizontal ruler to 3.33 inches below center. Align the top-left edge of the 10-of-diamonds card with the vertical ruler and the bottom-left edge of that card with the horizontal ruler.

2. Create the bulleted list slide shown in Figure 4-90. Apply the Checkerboard Across slide transition effect to both slides. Apply the Fly From Top entry animation effect to animate the cards automatically on Slide 1. Save the presentation with the file name, Vegas Shows. Print the presentation slides using the Black & white option. Close the presentation.

3. Open a new presentation, apply the Bulleted List AutoLayout, and then apply the risk design template. Create the slide shown in Figure 4-91. Increase line spacing to .5 lines after each paragraph. Apply the Blinds Horizontal slide transition effect. Save the presentation with the file name, Vegas Tours. Print the presentation slide using the Black & white option. Close the presentation.

FIGURE 4-89

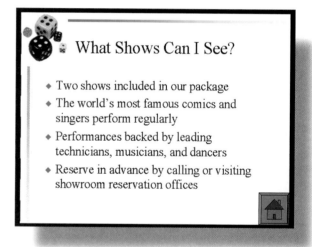

FIGURE 4-90

4. Open a new presentation, apply the 2 Column Text AutoLayout, and then apply the risk design template. Create the slide shown in Figure 4-92. Increase line spacing to .5 lines after each paragraph. Apply the Checkerboard Down slide transition effect. Save the presentation with the file name, Vegas Visit. Print the presentation slide using the Black & white option. Close the presentation.

5. Open a new presentation, apply the Bulleted List AutoLayout, and then apply the risk design template. Create the slide shown in Figure 4-93. Increase the line spacing for both paragraphs to .5 lines after each paragraph. Apply the Blinds Vertical slide transition effect. Save the presentation with the file name, Vegas Pack. Print the presentation slide using the Black & white option. Close the presentation.

In the Lab

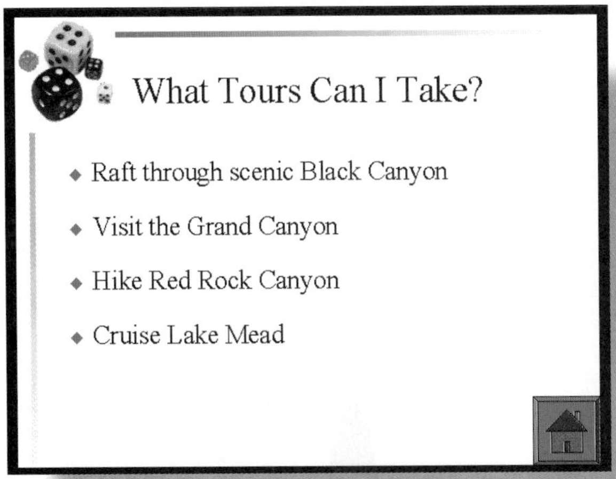

What Tours Can I Take?

- Raft through scenic Black Canyon
- Visit the Grand Canyon
- Hike Red Rock Canyon
- Cruise Lake Mead

FIGURE 4-91

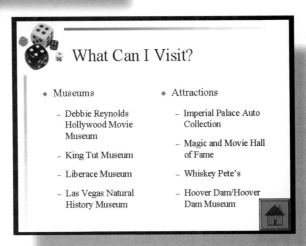

What Can I Visit?

- Museums
  - Debbie Reynolds Hollywood Movie Museum
  - King Tut Museum
  - Liberace Museum
  - Las Vegas Natural History Museum
- Attractions
  - Imperial Palace Auto Collection
  - Magic and Movie Hall of Fame
  - Whiskey Pete's
  - Hoover Dam/Hoover Dam Museum

FIGURE 4-92

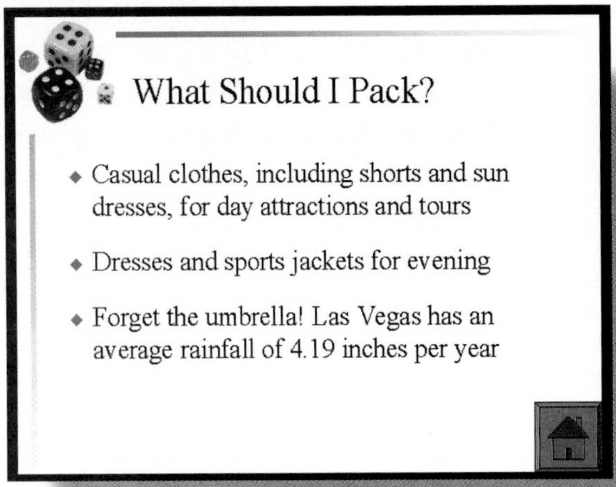

What Should I Pack?

- Casual clothes, including shorts and sun dresses, for day attractions and tours
- Dresses and sports jackets for evening
- Forget the umbrella! Las Vegas has an average rainfall of 4.19 inches per year

FIGURE 4-93

(continued)

In the Lab

Linking PowerPoint Presentations *(continued)*

Instructions Part 2: Perform the following tasks to create the presentation shown in Figure 4-94.

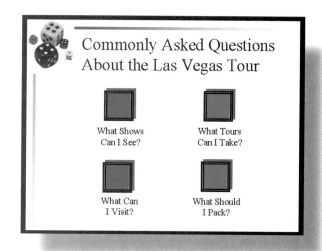

FIGURE 4-94

1. Open a new presentation, type 11 to apply the Title Only AutoLayout, and then apply the risk design template. Create the slide title shown in Figure 4-94.

2. Add the four action buttons, scale them to 90 percent, apply Shadow Style 2, change the border line style to 3 pt, and change the fill color to Red.

3. Type the caption What Shows Can I See? under the upper-left action button, What Can I Visit? under the lower-left action button, What Tours Can I Take? under the upper-right action button, and What Should I Pack? under the lower-right action button.

4. Create a hyperlink to the Vegas Shows presentation, created in Part 1, for the upper-left action button, the Vegas Visit presentation for the lower-left action button, the Vegas Tours presentation for the upper-right action button, and the Vegas Pack presentation for the lower-right action button.

5. Apply the Split Vertical Out slide transition effect. End the presentation with a black slide. Save the presentation with the file name, Vegas.

6. Add an action button to the lower-right corner of each of the four hyperlinked presentations, and hyperlink each button to the Vegas presentation. Change the buttons' fill color to Red. Save the four hyperlinked presentations.

7. Print the six presentation slides using the Black & white option.

8. Run the slide show. Click the What Shows Can I See? action button to display the hyperlinked presentation. Display both slides. Click the hyperlink at the bottom of the second slide to jump to the Vegas presentation. When the Commonly Asked Questions presentation returns, click the What Can I Visit? action button, read the new slide, and click the hyperlink at the bottom of the slide. Repeat this procedure for the What Tours Can I Take? and What Should I Pack? action buttons. Click to display the black closing slide. End the slide show and quit PowerPoint.

Cases and Places

The difficulty of these case studies varies: ❯ are the least difficult; ❯❯ are more difficult; and ❯❯❯ are the most difficult.

1 ❯ The latest dietary guidelines recommend eating two to four servings of fruit and three to five servings of vegetables daily. Although fruit and vegetables are less costly than snack foods, many adults and children buy junk food rather than the vitamin-laden fruit and vegetable alternatives. Vitamin A, found in oranges and dark green, leafy vegetables, helps repair and grow skin tissues and makes skin smooth and moist. Vitamin B is plentiful in bananas, sunflower seeds, lentils, and whole-grain cereals, and it helps prevent dry, cracking skin, especially at the corners of the mouth. The more active you are, the more you need vitamin B. Citrus juice and green and red peppers are rich in vitamin C. This vitamin helps your body manufacture the protein collagen, which keeps your skin firm. Your school cafeteria manager has asked you to prepare a PowerPoint presentation explaining the ABCs of fruits and vegetables to students. Using the techniques introduced in this chapter, create an interactive short slide show using three buttons that correspond to the three vitamins. Include your school logo, animated text, and slide transition effects. End with a black closing slide.

2 ❯ The marketing director of your local credit union has asked you to help with a membership campaign on campus. You decide to develop an interactive slide show to run in the bookstore during the start of the semester when students often stand in long lines to pay for their books and supplies. Prepare a short presentation aimed at encouraging students to join the credit union and begin a savings plan. One slide should show an Excel worksheet and 3-D Column chart explaining how saving even a small amount on a regular basis helps establish a nest egg. Other slides can feature additional credit union services, such as credit cards, vehicle loans, home equity loans, mortgages, and certificates of deposit. The final slide should give the address, telephone number, and hours of the office.

3 ❯❯ After completing the Internet Training San Fran presentation in Project 4, you are interested in attending the seminar. You inform your boss, who agrees that you and your company would benefit from the training. Funding is a problem, however, and the board of directors must approve the expenditure. Your boss believes you can persuade the board to release the money at the next board meeting if you develop a persuasive PowerPoint slide show. Prepare an Excel worksheet and Pie chart of your proposed expenses, and link them to the presentation as an interactive document. Include estimates of meals, housing, transportation, and incidental expenses, considering that two box lunches and one night's hotel room in central San Francisco are included in the $350 seminar fee. If you will be flying to the conference, visit a travel agent, search the Internet, or telephone several airlines to determine the least expensive airfare from your campus to San Francisco. Include other slides stating the components of the training sessions and how the company will benefit from your experience.

Cases and Places

4 ▶▶ Five of your friends have decided to form a jazz band, the Quintessential Quintet, and they want to perform at local events. They want you to help with their publicity, so you decide to create a slide show. You need to start by designing a logo that reflects the spirit of jazz music. Use PowerPoint and WordArt to create the logo. Then create a short slide show to present the logo to the Quintessential Quintet members. Explain your design and thoughts behind the logo component objects.

5 ▶▶ Many schools have an extracurricular or intramural athletic program to allow students to participate in a variety of sports in an informal, friendly atmosphere. Often the individual or team participants compete in tournaments at the end of the season. Research your school's athletic program by interviewing the athletic director or individual in charge of this student activity. Gather information about the sports, number of student participants, team standings, times and locations of games, and cost. Discuss how an interactive presentation might pique interest among students. Using this information, create the slide show. Enhance the presentation by including your school's logo, a modified design template background or color scheme, appropriate graphics, animated text, and slide transition effects. Deliver the presentation to the person with whom you spoke to collect your information.

6 ▶▶▶ Doctors and nutritionists recommend following a low-fat diet to help control body weight, prevent heart disease and diabetes, and reduce cholesterol. Many people, however, refuse to eliminate their favorite foods, such as potato chips and cookies. Fortunately, many food manufacturers have developed low- or no-fat alternatives to these high-fat foods, including salad dressings, ice cream, yogurt, desserts, candy bars, and pretzels. Visit a grocery store and compare labels of three dessert items, dairy products, and snack foods you normally eat that have both a regular and low- or no-fat version. Using this information and the techniques introduced in the project, prepare an interactive presentation that compares the serving sizes, calories, and fat grams of these foods. Enhance the presentation by adding graphics, using text preset animation effects, and applying slide transition effects. End the presentation with a black closing slide. Submit all files on a disk to your instructor.

7 ▶▶▶ Seventy-five percent of people older than 64 have an annual income of less than $10,000, including Social Security benefits. Fortunately, employees of public schools and certain not-for-profit organizations are eligible to participate in a 403(b) tax-deferred annuity (TDA) program. This special retirement benefit offers these employees the opportunity to reduce their tax liability while they are saving for retirement. Your school's business office has hired you to develop a PowerPoint presentation designed to encourage teachers to open a TDA. Call or visit life insurance companies to obtain information on this program. Research and then prepare an interactive slide show. Include an Excel worksheet demonstrating how much a teacher earning $30,000 annually would save on taxes after contributing $1,000 during the year. Prepare a second worksheet and a 3-D Column chart showing the power of tax-deferred growth during a 10- and 20-year period. Include slides answering questions of how the funds can be distributed and withdrawn and how much an employee can contribute during the year. Enhance the presentation by modifying a design template background or color scheme, adding appropriate graphics, animating text, and applying slide transition effects. Include a hidden slide. Run your presentation and perform a what-if scenario by increasing the contribution to $2,000 per year. Submit all files on a disk to your instructor.

Creating W eb Pages from a PowerPoint Presentation

Case Perspective

The Park City, Utah, Net-Train Corporation Internet Training Seminar has generated much interest. Net-Train employees have received many telephone calls from prospective attendees asking for specific details. Among their questions are health-related topics regarding high elevations. Many prospective attendees have heard and read about the effects of reduced oxygen on the body, and they have concerns about adjusting to the mountain elevations.

You have decided the easiest way to provide this information to Net-Train employees and prospective attendees is to prepare a PowerPoint presentation and then transfer the file on World Wide Web pages posted to the Internet and to Net-Train's intranet. That way, you can disseminate important information easily and accurately to many people. The presentation is saved on your Data Disk that accompanies this book. To do the transfer, you will need to save the presentation again as an HTML file (Web page). Then you will view the Web page by launching your default Web browser and opening the HTML document.

I ntroduction

The graphic design power of PowerPoint allows you to create vibrant presentations that convey information in a clear, interesting manner. Some of these presentations are created for small, specific audiences, such as a subcommittee planning a department office picnic. In this case, the presentation may be shown in an office conference room. Other presentations are designed for large, general audiences, such as workers at a corporation's various offices across the country learning about a variety of health insurance options. These employees can view the presentation on their company's **intranet**, which is an internal network that uses Internet technologies. On a grand scale, you can inform the entire world about the contents of your presentation by posting your slide show to the World Wide Web. To publish to the World Wide Web, you need an **FTP (File Transfer Protocol)** program to copy your presentation and related files to an **Internet service provider (ISP)** computer.

PowerPoint allows you to create Web pages in two ways. First, you can start a new presentation, as you did in Project 3 when you produced the Net-Train Internet Training Seminar presentation for Park City, Utah. PowerPoint provides Internet or information kiosk presentation templates in the

AutoContent wizard option when you start PowerPoint. The wizard helps you design an effective slide show for an intranet or for the Internet.

Second, by using a **Save as HTML wizard**, you quickly can convert an existing presentation to a format compatible with popular Web browsers, such as Microsoft Internet Explorer. The wizard allows you to control the content and format options of the presentation. This Integration Feature illustrates saving the PowerPoint High Altitude Health Hints presentation on your Data Disk as an HTML file. Once the presentation is saved as an HTML file, you can view the presentation using your default browser (Figure 1).

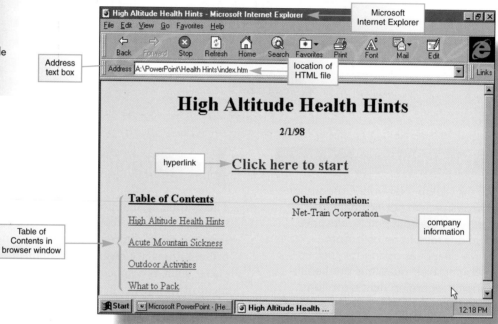

FIGURE 1

Saving the PowerPoint Presentation as Web Pages

Once your PowerPoint slide show is complete, you easily can save it as an HTML file by using the Save as HTML command on the file menu.

Because you are converting the High Altitude Health Hints presentation on your Data Disk to an HTML file, the first step in this project is to open the Health Hints file. Then you will start the Save as HTML wizard to turn the Health Hints presentation into a file for an intranet or for the Internet. Perform the following steps to convert the Health Hints presentation to Web pages.

Steps **To Save a PowerPoint Presentation as Web Pages**

1 **Start PowerPoint and then open the Health Hints file from the PowerPoint folder on your Data Disk that accompanies this book. Click File on the menu bar and then click Save as HTML.**

2 **Click the Next button. When the Layout selection panel displays, if necessary, click New layout and then point to the Next button.**

PowerPoint displays the Layout selection panel, requesting the type of layout (Figure 2). If you had designed and saved other HTML presentations previously, their file names would appear in the list box.

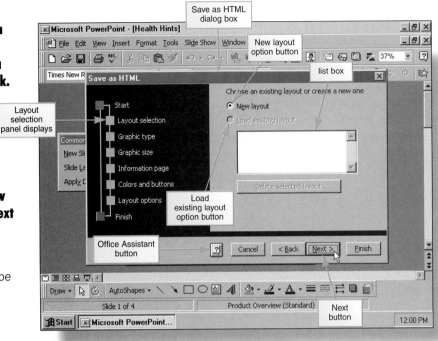

FIGURE 2

3 **Click the Next button. When the Select the page style area displays, if necessary, click Standard and then point to the Next button.**

PowerPoint displays the Select the page style area in the Save as HTML dialog box, asking for the layout style you want to use (Figure 3). A preview of each style displays beside its respective option button.

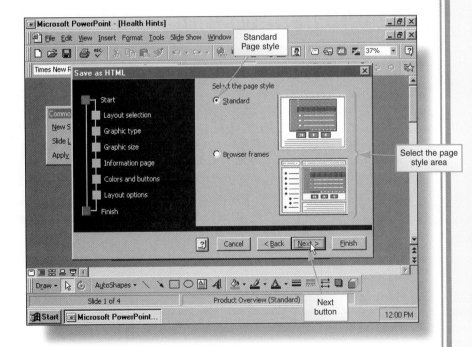

FIGURE 3

4 **Click the Next button. When the Graphic type panel displays, if necessary, click GIF – Graphics Interchange Format, and then point to the Next button.**

*PowerPoint displays the **Graphic type panel** in the Save as HTML dialog box (Figure 4). You would choose PowerPoint animation if you had graphics to animate. This animation option, however, requires a browser that supports the PowerPoint Animation Player, which is available on the Microsoft Web site.*

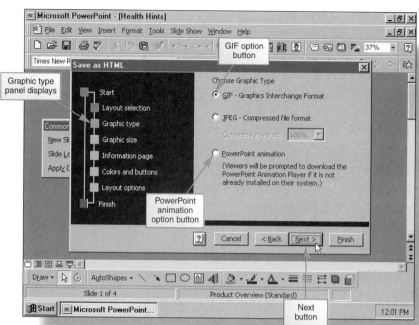

FIGURE 4

5 **Click the Next button. When the Graphic size panel displays, if necessary, click 640 by 480 and then point to the Next button.**

*PowerPoint displays the **Graphic size panel** in the Save as HTML dialog box, requesting the monitor resolution (Figure 5). All Web browsers can support the 640 by 480 monitor resolution; however, some graphics may look fuzzy on some monitors at this low resolution. If you are certain all users viewing the presentation have high-resolution monitors, you may choose one of the higher resolutions so sharper graphics display. Higher resolutions and width values create large bitmaps, which take a long time to load and may be too large to display on small monitors, such as on a notebook computer display.*

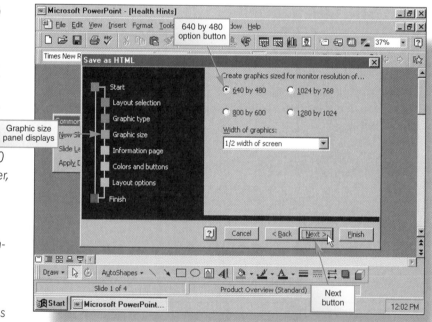

FIGURE 5

6 **Click the Next button. When the Information page panel displays, type** Net-Train Corporation **in the Other information text box. Point to the Next button.**

*PowerPoint displays the **Information page panel**, requesting information for the Table of Contents screen (Figure 6). The words, Net-Train Corporation, will display in the Other information area of the Table of Contents screen, which will be the first screen in your HTML pre-sentation when you view it with a browser (see Figure 1 on page PPI 2.2). You also can add your e-mail and home page addresses to this title slide.*

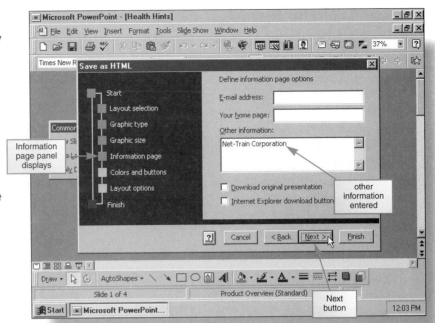

FIGURE 6

7 **Click the Next button. When the Colors and buttons panel displays, click Custom colors, and then click the Change Background button. Click the light blue basic color (row 1, column 5) in the Color dialog box, and then click the OK button in the Color dialog box. Click the Transparent buttons check box in the Save as HTML dialog box. Point to the Next button.**

*PowerPoint displays the **Colors and buttons panel**, asking for the colors you want to use on your Web page (Figure 7).*

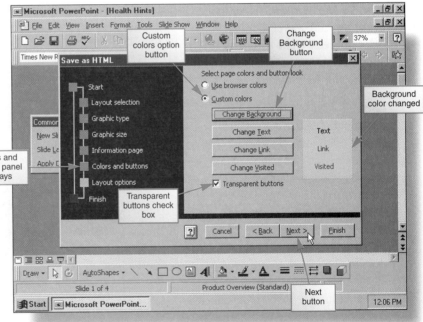

FIGURE 7

8 **Click the Next button. When the Select button style area displays, click the round button style, and then point to the Next button.**

PowerPoint displays the Select button style area, asking you to select the navigation button style you want to display on your Web page (Figure 8). You will click the navigation buttons to advance through the pages of the presentation or to review previous screens. You also can select text hyperlinks instead of buttons by clicking the Next slide option button.

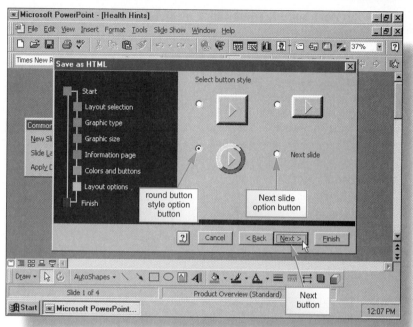

FIGURE 8

9 **Click the Next button. When the Layout options panel displays, click the lower right layout in the Place navigation buttons area. Point to the Next button.**

*PowerPoint displays the **Layout options panel**, requesting you to select a layout option that sets the position and orientation of the navigation buttons (Figure 9). Each option button includes a graphic representation of the layout. The lower right layout places the navigation buttons to the right of the Web page slide. Clicking the Include slide notes in pages check box will include your presentation notes from the PowerPoint notes pages in your HTML document.*

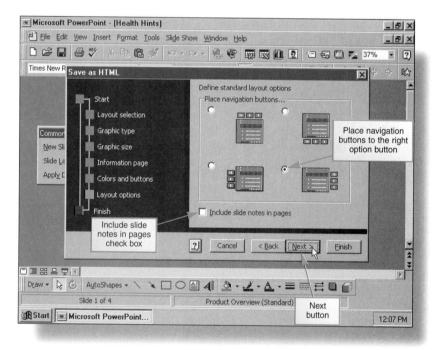

FIGURE 9

10 Click the Next button. Type
A:\PowerPoint\ in the Folder
text box. Point to the Next
button.

*PowerPoint will create an HTML
folder in the PowerPoint folder on
the Data Disk in drive A (Figure 10).*

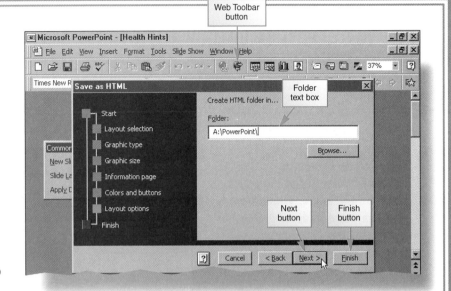

FIGURE 10

11 Click the Next button. When the
Finish panel displays, click the
Finish button. Click the Don't
Save button in the Save as HTML
dialog box (Figure 11). Click the
OK button in the Microsoft
PowerPoint dialog box.

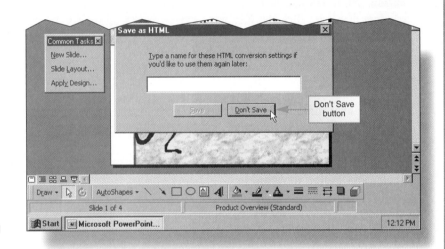

FIGURE 11

PowerPoint allows you to reuse HTML conversion settings, which is a
practical feature if you prepare many Web presentations with similar content and
format options, such as colors, button styles, and layout styles. Several HTML
export in progress messages display, indicating PowerPoint is creating Web pages
and exporting data as it is processing the four slides. PowerPoint creates a folder
with the file name Health Hints HTML, which contains the Web files needed for
the HTML pages.

Viewing a Web Page Document

Now that you have converted the PowerPoint presentation to HTML, you want
to view the Web pages in your default Web browser. These pages are located in
the Health Hints HTML folder created in the previous steps. You access these
pages by opening the index.htm file in this folder. Perform the following steps to
view your HTML pages.

More *About*
HTML

HTML may not support some
formatting in your PowerPoint
presentation. For example,
while you can bold, italicize,
and underline characters and
change their font size, you cannot apply shadows or set tabs.

Steps **To View an HTML File Using a Web Browser**

1 **If necessary, click the Web Toolbar button on the Standard toolbar to display the Web toolbar (Figure 12). Click the Go button on the Web toolbar, and then click Open on the menu. When the Open Internet Address dialog box displays, type**
`A:\PowerPoint\Health Hints\index.htm` **in the Address text box. Click the OK button. When the browser window displays, click the Maximize button in the upper-right corner of the browser window.**

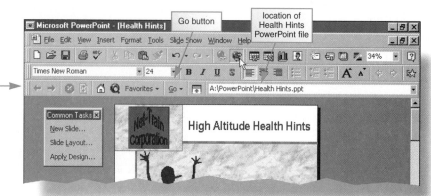

FIGURE 12

PowerPoint opens your Web browser in a separate window and displays the Table of Contents for the Health Hints HTML file in the browser window (see Figure 1 on page PPI 2.2).

2 **Click the hyperlink, Click here to start. Click the Next navigation button three times to advance through the pages. Click the First navigation button to return to the first page.**

The Next navigation button advances the presentation one slide forward, and the Previous navigation button reverses the presentation one slide (Figure 13). The First navigation button displays the first slide in the presentation, and the Last navigation button displays the final slide. The Index navigation button displays the Table of Contents slide (see Figure 1 on page PPI 2.2), and the Text navigation button launches a version of the Health Hints presentation with no graphics.

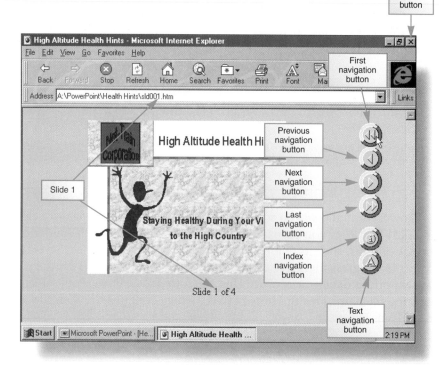

FIGURE 13

3 **Click the Close button in the Web browser window.**

PowerPoint closes the Health Hints HTML file, and the PowerPoint window redisplays.

The Web pages now are complete. The next step is to make your Web presentation available to others on your network, an intranet, or the World Wide Web. Ask your instructor how you can publish your presentation.

Summary

This Integration Feature introduced you to creating Web pages by saving an existing PowerPoint presentation as an HTML file. You can customize the pages by selecting page styles, choosing graphic style types, selecting monitor resolution, picking custom colors and buttons for the Web page, and choosing a layout style. Now that the Health Hints presentation is converted to HTML format, you can post the file to an intranet or to the World Wide Web.

What You Should Know

Having completed this Integration Feature, you now should be able to perform the following tasks:

▶ Save a PowerPoint Presentation as Web Pages (PPI 2.3)

▶ View an HTML File Using a Web Browser (PPI 2.8)

In the Lab

1 Use Help

Instructions: Start PowerPoint. If the Office Assistant is on your screen, click it to display its balloon. If the Office Assistant is not on your screen, click the Office Assistant button on the Standard toolbar. Type Save as HTML in the What would you like to do? text box. Click the Search button. Click the Save a presentation in HTML format hyperlink. In the second bulleted item in the Tips section, click the button to display information about the animation player. Read and print the information. Click the Help Topics button to display the Help Topics: Microsoft PowerPoint window. If necessary, click the Contents tab. Double-click the Working with Presentations on Intranets and the Internet book icon. Double-click the Working with Hyperlinks book icon. Double-click the Add, edit, and remove hyperlinks in a presentation topic. Read and print the topic. Close any open Help windows. Close the Office Assistant.

2 Creating Web Pages from a PowerPoint Presentation

Problem: Net-Train employees want to expand the visibility of their Park City, Utah, Internet Training Seminar you created in Project 3. They believe the World Wide Web would be an excellent vehicle to promote the seminar, and they have asked you to help transfer the presentation to the Internet.

Instructions:

1. Open the Internet Training presentation shown in Figures 3-1a through 3-1e on page PP 3.7 that you created in Project 3. (If you did not complete Project 3, see your instructor for a copy of the presentation.)
2. Use the Save as HTML wizard to convert the presentation. Change the page color background to yellow (row 2, column 2) and the text to dark blue (row 4, column 5). Do not make the buttons transparent. Select the square navigation button style (row 1, column 1), and place the navigation buttons on the top of the Web page slide (row 1, column 1 option button).
3. View the HTML file in a browser.
4. Ask your instructor for instructions on how to post your Web pages so others may have access to them.

3 Creating a PowerPoint Presentation and Creating Web Pages

Problem: The band and choir students promoting the Las Vegas tour have asked you to post the presentation you created in Project 4 to the school's intranet. You need to combine the five slides in Figures 4-89 through 4-93 on pages PP 4.68 through 4.69 into one PowerPoint presentation and then convert that presentation to an HTML file.

Instructions:

1. Open the Vegas Shows presentation shown in Figures 4-89 and 4-90 on page PP 4.68. (If you did not create this presentation, see your instructor for a copy of the files.)
2. Click the Next Slide button to display Slide 2. Click Insert on the menu bar. Click Slides from Files.
3. If necessary, click the Find Presentation tab in the Slide Finder dialog box. In the File text box, type the location of the Vegas Tours file displayed in Figure 4-91 on page PP 4.69, click the Display button, and click the Insert All button. Then type the location of the Vegas Visit file displayed in Figure 4-92 on page PP 4.69, click the Display button, and click the Insert All button. Finally, type the location of the Vegas Pack file displayed in Figure 4-93 on page PP 4.69, click the Display button in the Slide Finder dialog box, and then click the Insert All button. Click the Close button.
4. Delete each action button in the lower-right corner of slides 2, 3, 4, and 5 by clicking it and pressing the DELETE key. Save the presentation with the file name, Vegas Package. Then use the Save as HTML wizard to convert the presentation. In the Information page panel, type Support Your Band and Choir in the Other information text box. Change the page color background to red (row 2, column 1), the text color to dark green (row 5, column 3), the link color to dark blue (row 5, column 5), and the Visited color to dark purple (row 6, column 7). Do not make the buttons transparent. Select the rectangle navigation button style (row 1, column 2), and place the navigation buttons on the left side of the Web page slide (row 2, column 1 option button).
5. View the HTML file in a browser.
6. Ask your instructor for instructions on how to post your Web pages so others may have access to them.

Index

NOTE TO READER: This index contains references for Projects 1 through 4 and the Integration Features of the book, *Microsoft PowerPoint 97: Complete Concepts and Techniques*. The same references can be used for PowerPoint Projects 1 and 2 and Integration Feature 1 in the book, *Microsoft Office 97: Introductory Concepts and Techniques*, and PowerPoint Projects 3 and 4 and Integration Feature 2 in the book, *Microsoft Office 97: Advanced Concepts and Techniques*.

Microsoft **PowerPoint 97**